Parents and Families of Children with Disabilities

Effective School-Based Support Services

Craig R. Fiedler
University of Wisconsin–Oshkosh

Richard L. Simpson
University of Kansas

Denise M. Clark
University of Wisconsin–Oshkosh

PEARSON

Merrill
Prentice Hall

Upper Saddle River, New Jersey
Columbus, Ohio

Library of Congress Cataloging-in-Publication Data

Fiedler, Craig R.

  Parents and families of children with disabilities: effective school-based support services / Craig R. Fiedler, Richard L. Simpson, Denise M. Clark.

      p. cm.

Includes bibliographical references and index.

ISBN 0-13-019488-3 (pbk.)

1. Special education—Parent participation. 2. Parents of children with disabilities—Services for.
3. Children with disabilities—Family relationships. 4. School-linked human services. I. Simpson, Richard L.
II. Clark, Denise M. III. Title.

  LC4019.F54 2007

  371.9′04—dc22

  2005025042

#G14S3972

Vice President and Executive Publisher: Jeffery W. Johnston
Senior Acquisitions Editor: Allyson P. Sharp
Editorial Assistant: Kathleen S. Burk
Senior Production Editor: Linda Hillis Bayma
Production Coordination: Thistle Hill Publishing Services, LLC
Design Coordinator: Diane C. Lorenzo
Photo Coordinator: Monica Merkel
Cover Designer: Ali Mohrman
Cover Image: SuperStock
Production Manager: Laura Messerly
Director of Marketing: Ann Castel Davis
Marketing Manager: Autumn Purdy
Marketing Coordinator: Brian Mounts

This book was set in Novarese Book by Carlisle Publishing Services. It was printed and bound by R.R. Donnelley & Sons Company. The cover was printed by R.R. Donnelley & Sons Company.

Photo Credits: Steve Mason/Getty Images, Inc.–Photodisc, p. 1; Anne Vega/Merrill, pp. 31, 229, 255, 273, 299; Anthony Magnacca/Merrill, pp. 49, 191; Laima Druskis/PH College, p. 73; PH College, p. 93; Patrick White/Merrill, p. 129; George Dodson/PH College, p. 159.

Pearson Prentice Hall™ is a trademark of Pearson Education, Inc.
Pearson® is a registered trademark of Pearson plc
Prentice Hall® is a registered trademark of Pearson Education, Inc.
Merrill® is a registered trademark of Pearson Education, Inc.

Pearson Education Ltd.
Pearson Education Singapore Pte. Ltd.
Pearson Education Canada, Ltd.
Pearson Education—Japan

Pearson Education Australia Pty. Limited
Pearson Education North Asia Ltd.
Pearson Educación de Mexico, S.A. de C.V.
Pearson Education Malaysia Pte. Ltd.

10 9 8 7 6 5 4 3 2 1
ISBN: 0-13-019488-3

Preface

So much has been written and spoken about parents and families of individuals with disabilities. Indeed, over the past several decades, attention to this topic has been unprecedented. There is no question that these efforts have assisted, accentuated, and accelerated quality-of-life improvements and enhancements among individuals with disabilities, including increased positive attitudes and perceptions of the general public toward persons with special needs as well as improved opportunities for participation and inclusion. Social policy, legal and legislative supports, and mandates such as the Individuals with Disabilities Education Act (IDEA) and Americans with Disabilities Act (ADA) have also significantly contributed to improvements for individuals with disabilities and their families. More than ever before, parents and families of individuals with disabilities have opportunities and authority for involvement and decision making.

In spite of these trends and movements, it is equally apparent that parent and family needs are inadequately addressed and that the necessary basic supports for parents and families of children and youth with disabilities are routinely unavailable. Moreover, in spite of the backing of legislative and legal enactments and rulings, many parents and family members believe that they are not empowered to advocate for and assist in making decisions that directly affect the children and youth to whom they are connected. One need not work long in the disability arena to encounter the countless stories of parents and families that confirm the following:

- Needs that underpin and strengthen families of children and youth with disabilities are generally unrecognized and unsupported.
- Collaboration opportunities essential for their offspring's achievement of desired outcomes more often than not fail to bear productive fruit.
- A significant lack of service integration, coordination, and orchestration among the various agencies and entities that serve their children and families.
- Communication and information exchanges between these individuals and organizations are frequently faulty and inconsistent.
- Encouragement, counsel, and assistance that permit parents and families to advocate for members and assist others in their families to cope, adapt, achieve, and thrive are routinely unavailable.

These continuing deficiencies and inadequacies were the motivation, inspiration, and driving force for this book. At the same time, the authors are motivated by their optimistic belief that professionals desire to be more effective in assisting parents and families. It is our confident conviction that parents and families will experience the benefits of enhanced support when professionals possess the necessary knowledge, skills, motivation, and resources. In this regard, it is our hope that this book will help to achieve this goal.

Our philosophy is that school and community professionals must work in concert to assist and nurture families. Our premise is that schools are the logical and potentially most effective and cost-efficient organizations for coordinating and providing family support services. Yet, we fully recognize that schools cannot assume this Herculean task alone. School personnel must work in collaboration and concert with other professionals as well as parents and families. Together, these stakeholders will be most capable of achieving desired outcomes for students and their families. It is our firm belief that professionals and systems must focus their efforts on providing family-centered services that support the entire family, not just the family member with a disability.

ORGANIZATION OF THE TEXT

The book is divided into five major sections. Part I (chapters 1 and 2) establishes the context and rationale for school-based family support services. This section also provides the legislative, legal, and ethical rationale for serving diverse families via a school-based model. Part II (chapters 3, 4, and 5) of the book focuses on emotional and psychological supports for parents and families, including supports for siblings and coping and problem-solving strategies. Resources required for effective parent and family support, including those within school and community settings, is the topic of part III (chapters 6 and 7). Educational services are addressed in part IV (chapters 8, 9, 10, and 11), including supports required for effective advocacy and students' behavioral, academic, and transition management. Part V (chapter 12) of the book offers integrative stories of school-based supports for families.

ACKNOWLEDGMENTS

As is the case with virtually all textbooks, *Parents and Families of Children with Disabilities: Effective School-Based Support Services* reached fruition only through collaboration and collective effort. In this connection, we are especially grateful to Allyson Sharp and the editorial staff at Merrill/Prentice Hall. We also respectfully acknowledge the support, encouragement, and feedback we received from our families and colleagues. Indeed, we each owe a debt of gratitude to the many individuals who supported our individual efforts.

We would like to acknowledge the following reviewers for their insights and comments: Rebecca Bravo, Hunter College; Kimberly J. Callicott, Texas A&M University; Dennis J. Campbell, Arkansas State University; Mike Cass, SW Ross University; Greg Conderman, Northern Illinois University; Sandra Grider, University of Central Florida;

Melanie B. Jephson, Stephen F. Austin State University; Craig Miner, California State University–Fresno; Maria Nahmias, University of Arizona; Robert W. Ortiz, California State University, Fullerton; E. Michelle Pardew, Western Oregon University; Alec Peck, Boston College; Sharon Rosenkoetter, Oregon State University; and Karen Sealander, Northern Arizona University.

We are also particularly indebted to parents and families of individuals with disabilities. To be sure, the struggles and challenges that parents and families face daily were the rightful inspiration for this work. It is our hope that this resource will assist in improving the lives of families of children and youth with disabilities.

Craig Fiedler
Richard Simpson
Denise Clark

Discover the Merrill Resources for Special Education Website

● ● ● ● ● ● ● ● ● ● ● ● ● ● ● ● ● ○ ○ ○

Technology is a constantly growing and changing aspect of our field that is creating a need for new content and resources. To address this emerging need, Merrill Education has developed an online learning environment for students, teachers, and professors alike to complement our products—the *Merrill Resources for Special Education* Website. This content-rich website provides additional resources specific to this book's topic and will help you—professors, classroom teachers, and students—augment your teaching, learning, and professional development.

Our goal with this initiative is to build on and enhance what our products already offer. For this reason, the content for our user-friendly website is organized by topic and provides teachers, professors, and students with a variety of meaningful resources all in one location. With this website, we bring together the best of what Merrill has to offer: text resources, video clips, web links, tutorials, and a wide variety of information on topics of interest to general and special educators alike. Rich content, applications, and competencies further enhance the learning process.

The *Merrill Resources for Special Education* Website includes:

- Video clips specific to each topic, with questions to help you evaluate the content and make crucial theory-to-practice connections.
- Thought-provoking critical analysis questions that students can answer and turn in for evaluation or that can serve as basis for class discussions and lectures.
- Access to a wide variety of resources related to classroom strategies and methods, including lesson planning and classroom management.
- Information on all the most current relevant topics related to special and general education, including CEC and Praxis standards, IEPs, portfolios, and professional development.

- Extensive web resources and overviews on each topic addressed on the website.
- A search feature to help access specific information quickly.

To take advantage of these and other resources, please visit the *Merrill Resources for Special Education* Website at

http://www.prenhall.com/fiedler

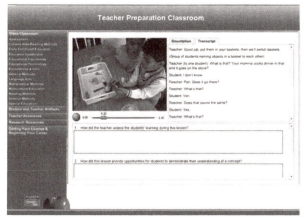

Brief Contents

Contents

CHAPTER 1
Understanding Family Support Services in the Schools   1

CHAPTER 6
Identifying and Accessing School Support Services for Parents and Families   129

CHAPTER 7
Partnering to Provide Community Support Services for Parents and Families   159

CHAPTER 8
Fostering Effective Parent and Family Educational Advocacy   191

CHAPTER 10
Educational Support Services to Assist Parents and Families in Designing and Implementing Academic Intervention Programs   255

CHAPTER 11
Educational Support Services to Assist Parents and Families in Transition Planning and Programming   273

CHAPTER 12
Family Stories Illustrating School-Based Support   299

Note: Every effort has been made to provide accurate and current Internet information in this book. However, the Internet and information posted on it are constantly changing, and it is inevitable that some of the Internet addresses listed in this textbook will change.

CHAPTER 1
Understanding Family Support Services in the Schools

In this chapter, you will understand:

- How children's development is influenced by parental involvement in education and the effect children with disabilities have on their families.
- Why schools are logical sources to provide a variety of family support services.
- Implications of Bronfenbrenner's social ecology model for the provision of school-based family support services.

- Legislative foundations for family support services.
- Key principles and characteristics of family-centered support services.
- Implications of school-based family support services on professional–family relationships.

Family Perspective: The Brewsters

"You feel so overwhelmed, lonely, and isolated at first," exclaimed Kathryn Brewster. She was describing the feelings she and her husband, Gordon, experienced when their youngest child, Peter, was diagnosed with autism. Yet, the Brewsters were fortunate to be living in a school district where the prevailing educational philosophy acknowledged the importance of providing comprehensive support services to the entire family, not just to the child with a disability. Peter was enrolled into a formal educational program provided by the local school district at age 3. "Working with supportive school staff has made all the difference for Peter and our entire family. Instead of feeling that we had to shoulder the whole burden of responding to Peter's needs, we quickly realized that we could count on a number of caring and competent educators," said Kathryn.

In the past 3 years, the school district has responded to the needs of the Brewster family in several respects. First, to combat the feelings of loneliness and isolation described by Kathryn and other parents, the early childhood special education teacher initiated a parent support group in the school district for families of children with autism. This group meets monthly, allowing the Brewsters an opportunity to share concerns, successes, and failures with other parents. The parent group provided much needed emotional and informational support to the Brewsters. In addition to organizing the parent support group, the early childhood special education teacher, along with a school psychologist, developed a directory of local, state, and national resources for children with disabilities and their families. Every month, in a school newsletter, several community resources are highlighted in one of the articles. The Brewsters used the school-developed directory to locate a sibling support group for their other two children and to receive assistance in accessing health care financing resources for Peter.

Kathryn and Gordon initially became concerned about Peter's development because he was not forming social relationships with other children and he was often aggressive toward his peers. School staff worked with the Brewsters in setting up a home behavioral management program that significantly reduced Peter's level of aggression. Further, the school counselor and special education teacher collaborated with Peter's first-grade teacher in establishing a Circle of Friends group. Peter's peers in the Circle of Friends group serve as "ambassadors" in facilitating his acceptance and involvement in the school environment. Also, in conjunction with after-school activities sponsored by the school district and the local YMCA, Peter now has numerous opportunities to interact with peers in a positive environment. In fact, Peter was just invited to another student's birthday party. "I just about cried when Peter got the birthday-party invitation. He had never been invited to another child's home before and we were wondering whether he ever would be," said Kathryn.

In addition to his behavioral and social issues, Peter's language skills are an area of concern for the Brewsters. The school district's speech and language pathologist developed a variety of language-stimulation activities for the home. "What I like about the home language program is that the activities can be easily incorporated into our daily routines. We do not need to set aside a distinct time for 'speech therapy,' which would be difficult given our hectic home life. Instead, the speech program makes us more sensitive in taking advantage of naturally occurring language-stimulation opportunities during the day," Kathryn responded. The benefits of school-based family support services are exemplified by the

Brewsters' experiences. Unfortunately, all too many families experience a different reality; a reality depicted in the following vignette about the Jacobson family.

Family Perspective: The Jacobsons

Paula Jacobson is a single parent of two children. Her oldest daughter, Rachel, has severe and multiple disabilities, including mental retardation, a seizure disorder, and vision and hearing impairments. Rachel, now 13 years old, needs considerable assistance in managing basic daily living activities such as feeding, dressing, and self-care. Rachel uses a wheelchair and has limited verbal skills. Paula describes her initial encounter with local school district personnel: "I moved to this area from another state in the middle of the summer. Realizing that Rachel has significant educational programming needs, I forwarded all of her educational and medical records to the new school district 3 months prior to our move. My first meeting with school staff during the summer was to develop Rachel's IEP for the upcoming school year. When I got to the meeting, I was handed a completed IEP the special education teacher had put together based on Rachel's prior educational records. The school's expectation was that I would simply agree to everything on the new IEP. I was stunned."

Paula left this first meeting frustrated and skeptical that the school was truly interested in developing a collaborative partnership. During the school year, Paula's suspicions and frustrations grew. Even though the school district had ample information on Rachel's needs, school staff made no attempt to link Paula with community resources that might assist her family. For example, Paula learned of the Katie Beckett Medical Assistance Program only from a chance encounter with another parent she met during parent–teacher conferences. Paula demanded that she be given input into Rachel's IEP. When she advocated for social-interaction goals on Rachel's IEP, the special education teacher expressed a concern that this would take away valuable school time for working on Rachel's self-feeding and other daily living activities. Although the special education teacher begrudgingly incorporated Paula's goals into the IEP, Paula did not feel that her ideas were respected or valued by the teacher.

During the school year, the main source of school–home communication was a notebook that went back and forth between Paula and the teacher. After a couple of months of reading the teacher's comments in the notebook, Paula lost motivation to write notes back to the teacher. Virtually all of the teacher's comments were related to problems or other negative information about Rachel at school. "It was so depressing and demoralizing to hear only about Rachel's deficiencies or her behavioral problems day after day. I wondered whether the school staff got any satisfaction out of working with Rachel. This caused me to mistrust the school. That's why I stopped communicating via the notebook," Paula stated.

During an IEP review meeting, several school staff asked Paula how much time she spent at home working on Rachel's self-feeding skills. Paula indicated that she attempted to do so at dinnertime but that there were many nights when she was either too busy or too tired to carry out this "training function." From comments of some of the school staff, Paula felt like she was being judged negatively as an uncaring and uninvolved parent for not devoting more time to Rachel's needs. After the meeting, Paula commented to a friend, "I wish school staff would be more sensitive to the daily demands faced by single parents trying to raise a severely disabled child. Most days, it is a substantial responsibility just being Rachel's mother, let alone her teacher and therapist. I am doing the best I can but the school makes me feel like I am shirking my parental obligations."

<u>Reflecting on the Family Perspectives</u>

1. What do you see as the key professional attitudinal differences between the first and second family perspectives?

2. How would you foster a sense of trust and collaboration during initial interactions with parents?

●   ●   ●

This chapter serves to establish the context and rationale for school-based family support services. We will discuss the importance of family participation in their children's education and consider the impact, both positive and negative, that children with disabilities have on their families. In addition, a rationale for schools to serve as key providers of family support services is established by reviewing the implications of Bronfenbrenner's social ecology model and the legislative foundations underlying the family support movement. Finally, we will identify key principles and characteristics of family-centered support services and consider the implications on professional–family relationships when schools and educators provide family-centered support services.

FAMILY PARTICIPATION IN EDUCATION

The stories of these two families obviously represent opposite ends on a continuum of providing school-based family support services. This book is about supporting and empowering families of children with disabilities to enable more positive school–family experiences as depicted by the experiences of the Brewster family. The first issue school professionals must consider is who constitutes a "family." The U.S. Census Bureau (1999) defined a family in a traditional and narrow manner as ". . . a group of two people or more related by birth, marriage, or adoption and residing together" (p. 3). This definition does not capture the reality of an increasing number of individuals who consider their living circumstances to represent "family life." Indeed, the stereotypical notion of a family represented by a working father, a stay-at-home mother, and two children describes only 3% of all families (Bauer & Shea, 2003). Given the alarming pronouncements of the demise of the family, it is comforting to note that the major changes impacting the family have revolved around its forms, not its functions (Dahlstrom, 1989). That is, a family can take on a multitude of structural forms and involve diverse living situations, but the function or purpose of a family remains constant—a group of individuals who care about each other and cooperate to meet both individual and mutual goals. Winton (1990) offered a more realistic perspective on families:

> Families are big, small, extended, nuclear, multi-generational, with one parent, two parents, and grandparents. We live under one roof or many. A family can be as temporary as a few weeks, as permanent as forever. We become part of a family by birth, adoption, marriage, or from a desire for mutual support. A family is a culture unto itself, with different values and unique ways of realizing its dreams. Together, our families become the source of our rich cultural heritage and spiritual diversity. Our families create neighborhoods, communities, states, and nations. (p. 4)

Demographic data clearly show that families of the 21st century are more diverse in terms of racial, cultural, structural, and economic factors (Simpson & Zurkowski, 2000). For example, one in three classroom students is Hispanic, African American, or Native American (Simpson & Zurkowski, 2000). Further, it is projected that 50% of all children will be living in a single-parent home at some point in their lives and nearly 25% of all children are living below poverty income levels (Weinberg, 1997).

However one defines family, it is clear that the family exerts a tremendous impact on the development of a child with a disability (Garwick & Millar, 1996; Lehman, 1997; Murphy, Lee, Turnbull, & Turbiville, 1995; Wade & Taylor, 1996). It is most appropriate to envision this impact as interactional; the family affects the development of the child, and the child impacts family functioning (Bronfenbrenner, 1979). Because families serve as the primary means of support for children with disabilities, there is a growing recognition that society, through its educational, health, and social welfare institutions, has a responsibility to support families in their caregiving responsibilities (Singer & Powers, 1993). This premise fueled the family support movement in the early 1980s. By supporting families and enhancing their coping skills, schools can foster children's development (Floyd & Gallagher, 1997).

Research establishes that children with disabilities benefit in multiple respects when their parents are actively involved in their education (Berry, 1995). Specifically, parental participation in their children's education has a positive effect on academic progress. Students whose parents are involved in school have higher achievement, better behavior, and more motivation than do other students whose parents are not actively involved (Keith, 1999). In a recent report to Congress on the implementation of the Individuals with Disabilities Education Act (IDEA), the U.S. Department of Education (2001) indicated that the most accurate predictor of a student's achievement and development is the family's ability to become actively involved in their child's education by creating a home environment that encourages learning and by expressing high expectations. The Department of Education found improved educational outcomes for children with disabilities when school support services are based on the premise that parents are the most important factors influencing their children's development.

In their literature review on school–family partnerships, Christenson and Cleary (1990) documented the following outcomes of active parent participation:

- Students' academic performance improved in terms of higher grades and test scores, more homework completed, and more classroom participation.
- Schools were rated as more effective by parents.
- Teachers expressed greater job satisfaction, and parents and administrators rated them as having high interpersonal and teaching skills.
- Parents provided more learning activities at home and the communication among the family, school, and child improved.

When considering family engagement in education, one caution is noteworthy. As stated by Simpson and Fiedler (1989), "It is a false and destructive dichotomy for educators to imply that 'good' parents are actively involved (*actively* as defined by school personnel's expectations for parents) in their child's education and that 'less than active' involvement is indicative of 'bad' parents. Expecting families to exhibit greater involvement than they are able may have detrimental effects on both the child and the parents" (p. 159). The key is to collaborate with families and learn about their daily demands, stressors, and resources. Through this collaborative perspective, educators can truly support families by fostering a level of educational participation that is realistic and comfortable for a given family.

What does research tell us about the level of family participation in their children's education? In general, parent participation in the education and care of their children with disabilities has increased substantially over the past 20 years (Fine & Nissenbaum, 2000). This trend can be explained by many factors. Two of the principal factors are the deinstitutionalization movement and special education legislation mandating parent participation rights (Simpson & Fiedler, 1989). Deinstitutionalization caused many families to resume primary caregiving responsibilities for their children who had been residing in state institutions. The 1997 amendments to IDEA strengthened parent participation in eligibility determination and IEP decisions, transition planning, consent for reevaluations, and due process rights (U.S. Department of Education, 2001). The 1997 amendments also required schools to provide parents with regular reports on their children's school performance.

As part of the U.S. Department of Education, Office of Special Education Programs' (OSEP) national assessment of the implementation of IDEA, the Special Education Elementary Longitudinal Study (SEELS) was launched. This is a 6-year longitudinal study of approximately 13,500 special education students, ages 6 to 12. There are several SEELS findings from the 1999–2000 school year that are informative on the issue of parental participation in special education:

- Over 85% of the parents surveyed attended school conferences or general school meetings on a regular basis.
- Approximately 75% of the parents attended school events or activities (e.g., school plays or concerts).
- Approximately 50% of the parents volunteered or assisted the school in some manner.
- Approximately 90% of the parents of elementary and middle school students with disabilities attended IEP meetings.
- Most of the parents (91%) agreed that the IEP goals for their child were appropriate, although about one third of the parents indicated that the IEP goals were developed primarily by school staff. The parents who revealed that the IEP goals were primarily developed by school staff clearly desired more involvement in the IEP decision-making process.
- Over 90% of the parents reported that their child's IEP services were either somewhat or very individualized.
- Approximately 25% of the parents participated in an informational or training meeting sponsored by the school, and the vast majority of such parents found those training meetings to be very helpful.
- Over 80% of the elementary schools surveyed provided parents of students with disabilities information on how to help their children with homework, how to develop study skills, and how to conduct learning activities at home.

The SEELS data reveal that the majority of families of children with disabilities are actively engaged in their children's education and that schools are quite responsive to addressing family needs.

CHILDREN WITH DISABILITIES AND FAMILY IMPACT

The family support movement has advocated that public policy must acknowledge and value the societal contributions made by families in raising their children with disabilities (Birenbaum & Cohen, 1993; Singer & Powers, 1993). A major step in advancing this public policy is taken when schools engage in family-centered practices that support the entire family, not just the child with a disability (Bailey, 2001; Simpson & Zurkowski, 2000; Taylor, 1999). The paradigm shift from a child-centered to a family-centered services focus fosters a more proactive educational system. Traditionally, schools and other family services agencies have been reactive by intervening only when a family has become overly stressed and at risk (Singer & Powers, 1993). Families should not have to be placed at risk before support services are provided. Mink (1993) noted that this shift in focus from a child-centered to a family-centered model should not decrease attention and services to the needs of children with disabilities. To the contrary, a family-centered approach simply recognizes the context in which a child lives and acknowledges the needs of other family members. A family-centered orientation understands that the final responsibility for children with disabilities resides with the family. Therefore, family services directly support the development of children with disabilities by fostering the long-term health and viability of families.

The conventional wisdom, which is well documented, is that most families experience significant stress from having a child with a disability (Agosta, 1995; Bauer & Shea, 2003; Carpenter, 2000; Doll & Bolger, 2000; Fine & Nissenbaum, 2000; Honig & Winger, 1995; McCubbin & Huang, 1989; Noh, Dumas, Wolf, & Fisman, 1989; Singer, G.H.S. & Irvin, L.K. 1989; Singer, L. & Farkas, K.J. 1989; Wade & Taylor, 1996). A variety of stressors involving a complex interaction of child, family, and community factors have been identified. Common family stressors include (a) financial strains, (b) societal stigma and rejection, (c) restrictions on family activities, (d) medical problems, (e) child-care time and energy demands, (f) changes in family routines and lifestyles, and (g) physical-care demands. The impact of these stressors can place families at greater risk for marital problems, parental anxiety and depression, employment problems due to increased usage of sick leave to meet the child's care needs, decreased leisure time, and strain on nondisabled siblings (Carpenter, 2000; Doll & Bolger, 2000). An example of a more complete list of family stressors and their impact is the Questionnaire on Resources and Stress (QRS) developed by Holroyd (1987). The QRS is a self-administered, 285-item true–false instrument that measures the level of stress in families who are caring for ill or disabled children. The QRS assesses 15 variables pertinent to family stress, including: (a) poor health mood, (b) excess time demands, (c) negative attitude, (d) overprotection/dependency, (e) lack of social support, (f) overcommitment, (g) pessimism, (h) lack of family integration, (i) limits on family opportunity, (j) financial problems, (k) physical incapacitation, (l) lack of activities, (m) occupational limitations, (n) social obtrusiveness, and (o) difficult personality.

Family and child characteristics can mediate or exacerbate the impact of stressors. For example, families with two parents, sufficient financial resources, an extended family and social support system, and effective coping skills typically are more successful in navigating through the stress and travails of raising a child with a disability (Fine & Nissenbaum, 2000). A number of studies have attempted to isolate child characteristics and impact on family stress levels. Honig and Winger (1995) found that the stress levels of mothers of young children with severe disabilities were significantly higher than those of mothers of young children with mild disabilities. Also, mothers of younger children with disabilities (less than 2 years old) reported significantly higher stress levels than mothers of older children with disabilities did. This finding reveals the increased coping skills and resilience that parents are able to develop as their children get older. Honig and Winger further investigated the impact of support services in ameliorating the stress experienced by families. In general, families with effective professional support services were more resistant to stress and more optimistic about the future than were families without those services. When a family does not have an intact social support network, it becomes even more critical that the school system provide family support services.

In another study on the differential effects on family stress of certain child characteristics, Noh et al., (1989) investigated parental stress among families of four types of children: children with conduct disorders, children with autism, children with Down syndrome, and children without disabilities. Their findings revealed that parents of children with conduct disorders experienced the most stress, closely followed by parents of children with autism. Interestingly, parents of children with Down syndrome mirror, and in some aspects, appear less stressed, than parents of children without disabilities. Further, the following child characteristics were associated with higher parental stress: (a) the child's inability to adjust to environmental changes; (b) the parent's perception of the child as less attractive, intelligent, or behaviorally appropriate; and (c) the child's frequency and severity of behavioral problems. In a study with some similar findings, Singer and Farkas (1989) found higher family stress associated with having children with intellectual disabilities and behavioral problems.

Educators learn that they can truly understand and effectively support the child only when they understand the child's family (Turnbull & Turnbull, 2001). Part of the responsibility of understanding families is to assess the impact of stress on the entire family unit and determine if a family is at risk. Once an assessment such as the QRS instrument is conducted, appropriate family support services can be provided. More on family stress and appropriate support services will be presented in chapter 5.

Counter to the long-held belief that families experience stress in raising a child with a disability and struggle to cope with the multitude of daily demands, a growing body of research offers an alternative perspective. This body of research demonstrates that most families of children with disabilities do not experience dysfunction and are able to cope very well with raising a child with a disability (Doll & Bolger, 2000; Fine & Nissenbaum, 2000; Floyd & Gallagher, 1997; Singer & Powers, 1993). In fact, families attribute many benefits to having a child with a disability.

Singer (1996) maintained that caring for a child with a disability can provide a family with a shared purpose and greater focus for cooperation. He argues that the need to address the day-to-day care demands of a child with a disability serves as a catalyst for more positive family interactions. The family is required to pull together and that collaborative spirit enhances family bonding and demonstrates responsibility. Doll and Bolger (2000) reviewed several studies and reported that families of children with disabilities have high levels of marital satisfaction characterized by strong feelings of respect, affection, and consensus between the parents. Finally, in an extensive review of existing research on the positive contributions children with disabilities make to their families, Summers, Behr, and Turnbull (1989) identified several examples. Examples of such positive contributions include (a) increased happiness, (b) greater love, (c) strengthened family ties, (d) strengthened religious faith, (e) expanded social network, (f) greater pride and accomplishment, (g) greater knowledge of disabilities, (h) learning not to take things for granted, (i) learning tolerance and sensitivity, (j) learning to be patient, (k) expanding career development, (l) increased personal growth, (m) assuming personal control, and (n) living life more slowly. Again, this topic will be discussed more extensively in chapter 5.

FAMILY-CENTERED PRACTICES: A SOCIAL ECOLOGY APPROACH

The classic and often referenced social ecology model developed by Bronfenbrenner (1979, 1986) is instructive in understanding and supporting families of children with disabilities. Berry (1995) stated, "Social ecology provides a framework for viewing difficult issues involving individual and family adjustment to societal change, including adjustments faced by individuals who have developmental disabilities and their families" (p. 379). Social ecology theory posits that the most important influence on a child is the family (Bronfenbrenner, 1979). Bronfenbrenner's social ecology model focuses on children and families as interactive members of a larger system of social institutions, including schools (Lehman, 1997). In the context of the family's interaction within this larger system of social institutions, those institutions (i.e., schools) have the influence to negatively or positively affect the family's capacity to enhance the development of their child with disabilities. In this sense, family-centered support services seek to empower families so they can play a pivotal role in their child's education, as opposed to the traditional professional–parent relationship, which revolved primarily around parental approval of professional recommendations (Carpenter, 2000).

Bronfenbrenner (1979) stated, "The ecological environment is conceived as a set of nested structures, each inside the next, like a set of Russian dolls" (p. 3). These nested structures consist of the microsystem, mesosystem, exosystem, and macrosystem. As a theoretical foundation for this book, school-based family support services can positively impact each of these social ecological structures and, therefore, enhance child and family functioning. Implications for school-based family support services at each structural level will be briefly discussed.

Microsystem

The microsystem involves interaction and relationships within the child's immediate family. This family-system focus acknowledges the central influence of the family on the child's development and life. School-based support services at this level can assist families by addressing their emotional needs such as parent–child bonding and nurturance issues. By providing parents with accurate information on the developmental needs of their children with disabilities, school professionals can cultivate more realistic parental expectations for their children. Realistic parental expectations are critical in maintaining a positive parent–child subsystem and serving as motivation for the parents to provide a nurturing home environment for their children.

Schools can enhance child and family functioning by providing information and training on positive parenting and behavioral supports for children with disabilities. Through supportive parental guidance, children learn socialization skills that are critical in all environmental settings. More information on providing parents with support services to aid them in designing and developing positive behavioral interventions is contained in chapter 9.

Mesosystem

The mesosystem entails the interrelationships between the family and other environments or settings in which the family interacts. Key relationships at this structural level involve the family and other social agencies and the family and the school. In terms of family-centered practices, schools can serve as a vital link to community-based support services for families. As the most pervasive social service institution in any community, schools may be the only contact point between families and the entire social services system. Therefore, it is critical that school professionals inform families of local, state, and federal resources that offer myriad support services for children with disabilities and their families. This topic will be discussed at length in chapter 7.

The second key relationship at the mesosystem level is between the family and the school. The quality of family-centered practices is largely dependent on the quality of interpersonal relationships between parents and school professionals. As Epstein (1995) observed, family–school relationships at the mesosystem level can be either institutional or individual. Institutional relationships engage a large number of families in school events (e.g., inviting families to a school concert) and can build a sense of identity with the school. However, true partnerships for educational planning purposes can be fostered only at the individual level. To accomplish these family–school partnerships, Epstein argues that interpersonal relationships must foster more "family-like schools." The importance of establishing this school atmosphere is captured by Bauer and Shea (2003): "Family-like schools welcome all families, not only those who are easy to reach. In partnership with the family-like school, the families become more 'school-like,' recognizing that their child is also a student" (p. 10). The theme of establishing family-like schools will be woven through the section of the book discussing emotional and psychological supports for families.

Exosystem

The exosystem does not directly involve the family but can affect or be affected by the family. Exosystem settings include the school, neighborhood, social-welfare system, health care system, and the community. According to Bronfenbrenner (1979), a critical issue at this level involves power dynamics and how decisions are made and resources allocated within an organization. Bronfenbrenner maintains that the developmental potential of children and their families can be enhanced to the extent that families have direct and indirect links to the organizational power sources. More active parental participation in educational decision making and larger school-based policy matters positively impacts the developmental potential of children with disabilities. This issue harkens to the old adage that "the squeaky wheel gets the grease." Educational support services to foster effective parent advocacy are the vehicle to provide families with legitimate access to school decisions at this environmental level. Educational advocacy and the skills needed by parents to function as effective advocates will be presented in chapter 8.

Macrosystem

Finally, the macrosystem involves the overarching system of ethnic and cultural values and economic and political policy. One implication of family-centered practices at the macrosystem level is that school professionals must cultivate cultural knowledge and sensitivity to families of differing racial, ethnic, socioeconomic, and sexual orientation backgrounds. Without this cultural sensitivity, diverse families will feel alienated from the school. This issue will be addressed at length in chapter 2. A second implication of understanding the macrosystem impact on families is that schools must inform parents of educational policies and funding resources. Parents have a right to be informed about the broader context in which decisions are made and resources allocated that directly impacts day-to-day educational services for their children. This relates to advocacy on a larger scale, so-called systems advocacy (Fiedler, 2000). Systems advocacy is the process of influencing policies, rules, laws, or practices of social and political institutions to bring about change for persons in a certain group or class. Systems advocacy will also be discussed in chapter 8. Figure 1.1 depicts Bronfenbrenner's social ecology model in terms of each structural system's impact on a child with disabilities and the child's family and implications for school-based support services.

THE NEED FOR SCHOOL-BASED FAMILY SUPPORT SERVICES

There is ample evidence that families often fail to receive the services they need in caring for their children with disabilities. In a survey conducted in 2000 by the Office of Special Education Programs (OSEP) of the U.S. Department of Education, the approximately 15,000 respondents, including parents of children with disabilities, indicated that families need greater access to information and support services in an effort to improve life opportunities for their children (U.S. Department of Education, 2001). Numerous studies document that many families constantly struggle to receive the support services they need to provide appropriate care for their children with disabilities (Yuan, Baker-McCue, & Witkin, 1996). It has been argued, "Child abuse, health, income support, and housing statistics suggest that families' access to support services for children is actually declining" (Sailor, Kleinhammer-Tramill, Skrtic, & Oas, 1996, p. 319). A sluggish economy at the beginning of the 21st century, coupled with threats

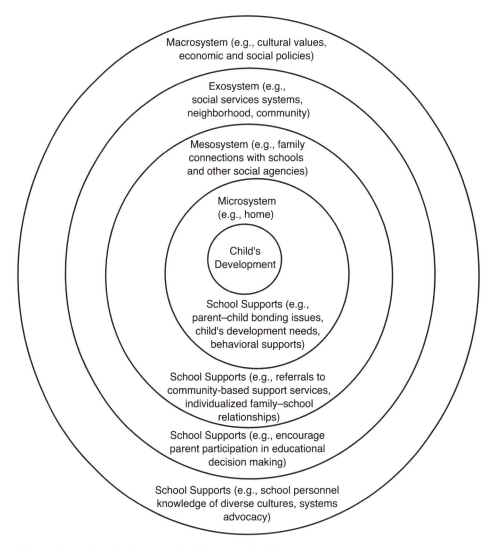

Figure 1.1 *Bronfenbrenner's Social Ecology Model*
Source: Based on *The ecology of human development* by U. Bronfenbrenner, 1979, Cambridge, MA: Harvard University Press.

of terrorism, has placed even more strain on already limited educational and social services budgets. As their children with disabilities transition from the school system to the community and adult services system, many families experience extreme frustration as they are left to their own devices without sufficient emotional support and necessary resources for their adult children (Clatterbuck & Turnbull, 1996). The problem of inadequate support services is exacerbated by funding patterns and service delivery systems based on categorical criteria that prevent many families from qualifying for needed services. In addition, families of children with disabilities confront an over-whelming and fragmented array of services throughout their children's life span.

Schools are the logical social institutions to provide family support services (Sailor et al., 1996; Wright & Stegelin, 2003). Schools are pervasive because they exist in almost every community. Further, schools are perceived as relatively neutral enti-ties without the stigma associated with some agencies (e.g., mental health agencies). Schools are easily accessible and families generally are comfortable entering local school buildings. Many schools are already serving as a natural support system for families of children with disabilities. Goetz, Anderson, and Laten (1989) identified three categories of school-based family support. The first type of family support is an adjunct to the direct provision of educational services to children. These adjunct sup-port services include parent-training groups, parent-support groups, and links to other community resources such as respite care and social services agencies. A sec-ond category of support comes in the form of emotional and moral support offered by school professionals. Professional empathy and emotional support serve as the fun-damental building blocks of family–professional partnerships. The final category of family support services consists of school assistance in enhancing parental participa-tion in IEP decision-making activities. This book will address examples of school-based family support services in all three of these categories. Families of children with disabilities indicate their greatest informational needs are about (a) future services, (b) present services, (c) how to teach their child, (d) the nature of their child's disabil-ity, (e) experiences of other families with a similarly disabled child, (f) handling the emotional and time demands of parenting, (g) community resources, and (h) legal rights (Gowen, Christy, & Sparling, 1993). Schools can address these informational needs of families by providing the school-based family support services listed in Com-munication and Collaboration Tips Box 1.1.

School reform has been a popular topic in the past 20 years. Most school-reform initiatives focused on the curriculum or student assessment or discipline (Simpson &

COMMUNICATION AND COLLABORATION TIPS   **BOX 1.1**

Examples of School-Based Family Support Services

- ❑ Health services
- ❑ Family resource centers—information and referral source
- ❑ Case management/service coordination
- ❑ Parental skills training—behavior management, academic instruction, coping, advocacy
- ❑ Family counseling
- ❑ Parent-to-parent support groups
- ❑ After-school recreation programs
- ❑ Sibling support groups
- ❑ Transitional planning services
- ❑ Independent ombudsperson

Zurkowski, 2000). More recent school-reform efforts have acknowledged the needs of families of children with disabilities. This acknowledgment has led to increased attention on school-based family support services or full-service schools. The promise of school-based family support services is in providing comprehensive educational, social, health, and employment services to families through a single point of contact (i.e., the school) where support services are either offered right in the school or coordinated by school professionals through linkages to community services. Instead of providing family support services in an independent and fragmented manner, schools and community agencies collaborate in team arrangements at the school. Further discussion of school–community agencies collaboration is reserved for chapter 7.

LEGISLATIVE FOUNDATIONS FOR FAMILY SUPPORT SERVICES

The concept of school-based family support services is found in education legislation. A family-centered services orientation has its origins in legislation mandating early intervention services. For example, Head Start programs were one of the first early intervention services to include a health provision (Hodapp & Zigler, 1993). In addition, family support efforts are rooted in the early-intervention provisions (children birth to age 3) of Part C of IDEA. Bailey (2001) observed that, "Part C of IDEA explicitly acknowledges that a primary goal of early intervention is to help families meet the special needs of their infant and toddler with disabilities" (p. 2). The principal family support provisions of Part C are the Individualized Family Service Plan (IFSP) and the service coordinator (Thompson et al., 1997). Families, along with their support network and service providers, engage in an assessment of family strengths and needs and use that information in developing an IFSP. The service coordinator works with the family to find and arrange necessary services.

Part B of IDEA addresses the educational needs of children from preschool through high school. Although Part B does not directly articulate family support goals, as does Part C, there are numerous legislative provisions detailing family participation rights and responsibilities. Bailey (2001) identified the parent participation and family support activities required under both Parts B and C of IDEA. This list is contained in Communication and Collaboration Tips Box 1.2. A more detailed discussion of parents' procedural and substantive protections under IDEA will occur in chapter 8.

IDEA also mandates that the school is responsible for providing related services to students with disabilities. Related services are defined as "services that may be required to assist the child with a disability to benefit from special education" (IDEA, 20 U.S.C. Sec. 1401 [a] [17]). If a child is (a) determined to be eligible for special education services and (b) a particular service is necessary to assist the child with a disability to benefit from special education, the school district is obligated to provide that particular related service. The list of related services in the IDEA Regulations contains several examples of what might fall into the category of family support services (IDEA Regulations, 34 C.F.R. Sec. 300.13). The most obvious example is *parent counseling and training*. This related service is defined as "assisting parents in understanding the special needs of their child and providing parents with information about child development" (IDEA Regulations, 34 C.F.R. Sec. 300.13). In

---

COMMUNICATION AND COLLABORATION TIPS   **BOX 1.2**

The school's responsibilities under Part B programs are as follows:

❏ Obtain informed parent consent before evaluating/reevaluating the child.
❏ Include parents as eligibility decision makers.
❏ Include parents as placement decision makers.
❏ Include parents as IEP team members.
❏ Obtain parental agreement on IEP goals and services.
❏ Use simple, understandable terminology in describing parents' rights in the family's native language.
❏ Provide parents with access to all educational records.
❏ Provide procedural protections such as due process and mediation.
❏ Provide written notice to parents prior to initiating or changing child's identification, placement, or services.

The school's responsibilities under Part C programs are as follows:

❏ Include families as members of the IFSP team.
❏ Use family-directed assessment of family resources, priorities, and concerns.
❏ Provide procedures in IFSP to address child and family needs.
❏ Provide explanation of IFSP in family's native language.
❏ Obtain informed parent consent prior to providing early intervention services.
❏ Inform parents of their right to accept or decline services.
❏ Provide procedural protections such as due process and mediation.
❏ Provide a service coordinator to implement IFSP and coordinate services with other agencies.
❏ Provide a review of the IFSP at least every 6 months.
❏ Provide written notice to parents prior to initiating or changing child's identification, placement, or services.

Source: Adapted from "Evaluating parent involvement and family support in early intervention and preschool programs," by D.B. Bailey, 2001, *Journal of Early Intervention, 24*(1), p.4.

addition, parent counseling and training are designed to assist parents in acquiring the necessary skills to allow them to support the implementation of their children's IEP or IFSP (IDEA Regulations, 34 C.F.R. Sec. 300.24). Certainly, this definition is broad enough to include a variety of typical family support services such as information and training on parenting skills, behavioral supports, academic interventions, transition planning, and advocacy.

Other legally mandated related services that could fall into the category of family support services are *counseling, psychological services, school health services,* and *social work services in the schools.* The definition of *counseling* is not particularly illuminating because it indicates only who may provide those services: "services provided by qualified social workers, psychologists, guidance counselors, or other qualified personnel" (IDEA Regulations, 34 C.F.R. Sec. 300.13). However, in the definition of *psychological services,* one of the identified functions is "planning and managing a program of psychological services, including psychological counseling for children and parents" (IDEA

Regulations, 34 C.F.R. Sec. 300.13). Related services under this definition could encompass a variety of emotional and psychological support services. Another related service, school health services, involves responsibilities performed by school nurses or other qualified personnel. Families often experience stress around health concerns of their children. Whether the family needs include monitoring of their child's health-related concerns, medication dispensing, information on health issues, or medical referrals, schools should provide these family supports as school health services. Finally, social work services in the school include "group and individual counseling with the child and family" and "mobilizing school and community resources to enable the child to learn as effectively as possible" (IDEA Regulations, 34 C.F.R. Sec. 300.13). Again, the school is mandated to address family emotional and psychological support needs. In addition, social work services involve linking families with relevant community resources to enhance child and family functioning.

Two additional federal statutes are prime examples of family support oriented legislation. The Goals 2000: Educate America Act of 1994 sought to enhance family participation in the governance of schools (Sailor et al., 1996). Section 2(8) of this statute identifies one of the legislative purposes as to provide assistance to ". . . every elementary and secondary school that receives funds under this Act to actively involve parents and families in supporting the academic work of their children at home and in providing parents with skills to advocate for their children at school." A second federal statute, the Families of Children with Disabilities Support Act of 1994, serves as a foundation for a variety of family-centered services for families who have children with disabilities. This law offers families the opportunity to identify their own needs and collaborate with community agencies in designing appropriate supports. The school could be involved in either providing or coordinating these family support services.

Finally, in an extensive study, Turnbull, Beegle, and Stowe (2001) identified 18 core concepts of public policy affecting families who have children with disabilities. Federal statutes were then reviewed to determine which of the 18 core concepts were reflected within statutory law (Turnbull, Wilcox, Stowe, & Umbarger, 2001). Several of the core concepts and corresponding federal statutes are indicative of a family support orientation. Examples of these family support–oriented core concepts and federal statutes will be discussed briefly in this section.

Capacity-Based Services

Capacity-based services regard the child with a disability and the child's family holistically, taking into account both limitations and strengths. Capacity-based service providers evaluate the unique strengths of the family, and the family is directly involved in assessing resources, priorities, and concerns. Statutes that reflect the core concept of capacity-based services include IDEA (20 U.S.C. Sec. 1400 et seq.), the Children's and Communities Mental Health Systems Improvement Act (29 U.S.C. Sec. 701 et seq.), and the Adoption and Safe Families Act (42 U.S.C. Sec. 629 et seq.). IDEA provides for an IFSP that builds on the strengths of the child's family. The Children's and Communities Mental Health Systems Improvement Act provides services that enhance family cohesiveness and requires consideration of family needs. Finally, the

Adoption and Safe Families Act assists states in developing and expanding family support and preservation service programs.

Empowerment/Participatory Decision Making

This core concept fosters family autonomy by service providers' sharing responsibility and decision making power with families. Empowerment/participatory decision making acknowledges the rights of families to be jointly involved with professionals in establishing outcome goals and determining necessary services. This is clearly evidenced in the parent-participation provisions of IDEA. Parents are entitled, under this law, to be equal educational decision makers at all stages of the special education process. Another example of a federal statute that fosters this core concept is the Developmental Disabilities Assistance and Bill of Rights Act (42 U.S.C. Sec. 15001 et seq.). This statute establishes a system of protection and advocacy (P&A) agencies in each state. These P&A agencies can assist families in prosecuting their complaints if they are dissatisfied with their child's special education services.

Family Integrity and Unity

The core concept of family integrity and unity seeks to keep the child's family intact. There is the recognition that the family is the fundamental unit of society and most children benefit from being raised within a family. This core concept attempts to preserve and strengthen the family and is respectful of the family's cultural, ethnic, and socioeconomic values. The Adoption and Child Welfare Act (42 U.S.C. Sec. 620 et seq.) provides adoption and foster care when the child's biological family is temporarily or permanently unable to care for a child. Title XIX of the Social Security Act (42 U.S.C. Sec. 1396n [b]) enables families to keep family members at home and, thus, avoid institutional placements by waiving some restrictions against the family being reimbursed for providing care to their child with a disability. Another federal statute, the Children's and Communities Mental Health Systems Improvement Act, establishes the legislative basis for wraparound services for children with serious emotional/behavioral disabilities and their families. Wraparound services are based on the philosophy of "whatever it takes" in meeting the support needs of families. Wraparound services are more fully discussed in chapter 7. Finally, IDEA fosters family integrity and unity by listing family counseling, home visits, and social work as early intervention services.

Family Centeredness: Services to the Whole Family

Family centeredness as a core concept recognizes that addressing the needs of the entire family serves the interests of the child with a disability as well. As stated earlier in this chapter, service providers view the family as the primary unit of service, not the child in isolation from the family unit. Several federal statutes reflect this core concept. First, as previously discussed, IDEA provides for related services that include services to a student's family. The aforementioned Title XIX of the Social Security Act is designed to provide services to the whole family. The Supplemental Security Income for the Aged, Blind, and Disabled of Title XVI of the Social Security Act (42 U.S.C. Sec. 1381 et seq.) provides cash benefits to families who meet federal poverty standards and whose children have severe disabilities. Title V of the Maternal and Child Health Services Block Grant (42 U.S.C. Sec. 701–709) attempts to promote family-centered, community-based care for children with special health-care needs. Finally, the Family and Medical Leave Act (29 U.S.C. Sec. 2601 et seq.) requires employers to grant leave to employees who must take leave to care for their child with health-related concerns.

PRINCIPLES AND CHARACTERISTICS OF FAMILY-CENTERED SUPPORT SERVICES

In a synthesis of several studies delineating the characteristics of family-oriented services, the Beach Center on Families and Disability defined family-centered support services as ". . . those practices that (a) include families in decision-making, planning, assessment, and service delivery at family, agency, and systems levels; (b) develop services for the whole family and not just the child; (c) are guided by families' priorities for goals and services; and (d) offer and respect families' choices regarding the level of their participation" (Murphy, Lee, Turnbull, & Turbiville, 1995, p. 25). Many researchers, commentators, and organizations have articulated key family-centered support principles and characteristics (Bergman & Singer, 1996; Karp, 1996; Mallory, 1996; Murphy et al., 1995; Shelton & Stepanek, 1994; Singer, 1996; Singer & Powers, 1993; Thompson et al., 1997; United Cerebral Palsy Association, 1993; Yuan et al., 1996). This section will briefly discuss these key family-centered support principles and characteristics.

Foster Collaborative Partnerships with Families

Traditionally, family–professional relationships have been characterized by a "power over" approach where the parental role was merely as the recipient of professionals' decisions (Turnbull & Turnbull, 2001). As the acknowledged experts, professionals portended a passive role for parents in educational decision making. Professional control over decision making keeps parents in a dependent role. In fact, parents who attempted to assert their wishes in regard to service decisions were viewed with skepticism at best or treated with disdain and derision. This "power over" perspective has slowly given way to a "power with" philosophy that promotes equality in the parent–professional relationship. In this partnership, professionals and parents collaborate to obtain mutually determined goals. Ultimately, with professional encouragement and support, the ideal collaborative relationship would empower parents to exercise "power within" in controlling their family's destiny. See Figure 1.2.

Address the Needs of the Entire Family

This support principle recognizes the prominent impact that families have on the developmental potential of their children with disabilities. Conversely, as discussed previously in this chapter, children with disabilities impact their families in a multitude

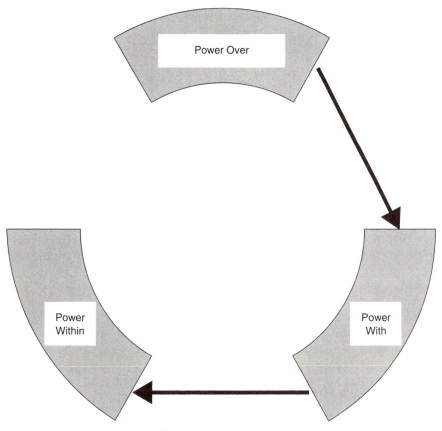

Figure 1.2   *Professional–Family Collaboration*

of ways. Any event that impacts one family member, ultimately impacts the entire family. This ripple effect demonstrates that disability is best viewed not as an individual phenomenon, but as a family phenomenon. Services that attempt to meet the needs of the entire family seek to promote family integrity and unity with the goal of maintaining the child at home in a caring, functional environment. Family-centered support services provide "whatever it takes" for families of children with disabilities to live as typically as possible (Karp, 1996).

Respect Family Diversity and Expertise

Professionals must be comfortable in working with diverse families from various ethnic, racial, and cultural backgrounds and values perspectives. The problem of stereotypes or judgmental thinking is captured by Fiedler (2000): "Judgmental professionals who possess stereotypical attitudes about certain families or are unable to suspend their judgment on family actions and lifestyles that conflict with their own prevent professionals from having empathy for a particular family's circumstance" (p. 43). Empathy allows you to gain respect for another person's situation that is beyond your experiential realm. Without this level of respect, it is unlikely that professionals will value the input of parents. Families deserve to be recognized as experts regarding their children. Families often have much more information about their children than do professionals; therefore, the family can better inform professionals about their children's skills, preferences for interactions, and general motivation.

Foster Family Networking and Utilization of Natural Supports

A tremendous source of stress for many families is feeling lonely and isolated, thinking that nobody knows what they are going through. A critical characteristic of family-centered services is the promotion of parent-to-parent support groups and family networking. When families are connected with other families, they learn from each other, and this experience can be empowering. Families can also feel more empowered when they are able to receive support from individuals in their natural support network (e.g., extended-family members, neighbors, coworkers, friends) as opposed to services provided by professionals or agencies. The utilization of natural supports lessens the family's dependence on professional support services. This fact is important in an era of shrinking social and educational budgets because some professional support services may be gone tomorrow, whereas every family hopes that its natural support network is stable and a constant in the family's life.

Acknowledge Family Strengths

Coinciding with the "power over" professional perspective, a medically oriented model has dominated professional attitudes toward families of children with disabilities until the past couple of decades. The medical-model approach tends to view families from a deficit or pathological perspective. In essence, many professionals blamed parents for their children's problems (Fiedler, 2000). Fortunately, this approach is receding in the face of family-centered principles that acknowledge and build on family strengths. According to Turnbull and Turnbull (2001), family strengths are whatever makes family members proud or happy about their family. Family strengths can include families' skills or activities that enhance their sense of well-being or balance individual needs with the needs of the entire family or foster open communication or assist families in obtaining needed supports and services. Sometimes families are not aware of their strengths as they struggle in responding to day-to-day demands in raising a child with a disability. Professionals enhance family functioning by acknowledging specific family strengths.

Provide Flexible, Accessible, Proactive, and Comprehensive Support Services

Children with disabilities and their families deserve individualized services, not a 'one-size-fits-all' approach. As bureaucratic institutions, schools tend to be inflexible and resistant to change (Cutler, 1993; Sailor & Skrtic, 1996). A common feature of bureaucratic institutions is that they tend to respond more to their own needs rather than to the needs of those they serve. Adherence to this key family-centered services principle will require each school to evolve into a "learning organization" (Senge, 1990). By fostering collaborative teams, learning organizations can be more flexible and responsive to client needs. Such organizations are able to be more proactive in serving their clients. More information on professional collaboration will be presented in chapter 7.

View Families as Benevolent

As a contrast to professionals blaming parents for their children's problems, this family-centered services principle maintains a belief that families attempt to act in their children's best interests. With this belief system, professionals are better positioned to respect family decisions that are in conflict with their own decisions or advice. Further, this principle should serve as a constant reminder to professionals that although all families have the same desire to act in their children's best interest, some families are presently unable to do so as a result of overwhelming stress, inadequate resources, or an inability to cope. This reminder should serve as sufficient motivation for professionals to address family needs in an effort to empower a family to have a more effective and positive impact on their own destiny.

Enhance Family Control over the Services They Receive

Families often express great vulnerability associated with uncertainty that they will receive the services necessary to effectively raise their children with disabilities (Fiedler, 1994). This is largely a control issue for families; will they have control over the support services needed to maintain family integrity and unity? Put into an empowerment framework, families need *perceived control*—the belief that they can apply their capabilities to affect what happens to them. When professionals acknowledge family expertise and engage families in collaborative partnerships, the resulting outcome should provide families with a greater sense of control over the services they receive. That is, families should lead the decision-making process concerning the types and amount of support they receive.

Acknowledge That Families Have the Responsibility to Help Themselves as Best They Can

Singer (1996) argued that family support services reflect a communitarian set of values that stresses the caregiving responsibility of families. But this principle cannot be reduced to a revised 21st-century notion of rugged individualism. Instead, this communitarian value recognizes the duty of the broader community to assist families in meeting their caregiving responsibilities. This communitarian principle of personal responsibility is compatible with Bronfenbrenner's social ecological model of families and the environments that impact them. As discussed earlier in this chapter,

Bronfenbrenner's model stresses the importance of interrelationships between families and larger social units or institutions (i.e., schools) in assisting families in maintaining vital functions such as caregiving for their children with disabilities.

FAMILY SUPPORT IMPLICATIONS FOR PROFESSIONAL–FAMILY RELATIONSHIPS

Adherence to the aforementioned family-centered support services principles and characteristics should lead to a fundamental change in professional–family relationships. As discussed earlier, traditional professional–family relationships are based on the view of parents as mere recipients of professionals' decisions. This perspective created an unequal power balance between professionals and families. Under this "partnership perspective," collaboration is impossible when families of children with disabilities are viewed as so traumatized that they are not seen as capable of making important contributions to their children's educational program (Doll & Bolger, 2000). The primary goal in these traditional professional–family relationships was for the parent to passively acquiesce to predetermined professional goals. This not only maintained families in an overly dependent state, but it also created very superficial professional–family relationships (Walker & Singer, 1993). In such relationships, parties are unlikely to question one another, state criticisms, or offer sentiments of support.

In the spirit of family-centered support services, as professionals and families establish more collaborative relationships, professionals must appreciate the developmental nature of professional–family relationships. That is, relationships should be viewed as dynamic and evolving rather than static and fixed. From this developmental perspective, some families may not be prepared for full collaboration with professionals (Fine & Nissenbaum, 2000). Doll and Bolger (2000) provided the following example of families not being ready for full collaboration with professionals. In their example, some families will clearly be overburdened by the demands of serving as their child's teacher, therapist, and advocate. In fact, these additional roles may decrease the enjoyment parents derive from simply interacting with their children. Professionals must ensure that families are not so stressed by the increased demands of collaboration that the family system becomes strained and problematic. With this caveat in mind, Walker and Singer (1993) identified the following beliefs contributing to professional–family collaboration.

1. Professionals achieve more constructive outcomes when they work as allies in helping families to accomplish their goals.
2. Professionals can offer a variety of constructive roles to family members.
3. Professionals can repeatedly seek informed consent for the actions they take in an effort to show respect for a family's autonomy and judgment.
4. Both families and professionals have unique knowledge and expertise to bring to collaborative relationships.

5. Both families and professionals are constrained by the systems in which they live and work. It is important to identify and clarify these constraints as part of their partnership and to either accept or overcome them.

6. Professionals increase their helpfulness to families when they value pluralism—a respect for differences in culture, beliefs, economic class, family structure, and personal styles.

Dunst, Trivette, and Snyder (2000) defined professional–family partnerships in this way: "Parents and other family members working together with professionals in pursuit of a common goal where the relationship between the family and professional is based on shared decision making, shared responsibility, mutual trust, and mutual respect" (p. 32). In an effort to understand how professional–family relationships can enhance family competence and have empowering consequences, Dunst and his colleagues conducted an extensive literature review of effective helpgiving practices of professionals working with families. This review generated a number of effective helpgiving practices:

- Demonstrating a sense of caring and warmth
- Displaying honesty
- Showing empathy
- Practicing active and reflective listening
- Maintaining confidentiality
- Expressing positive assumptions about family capabilities
- Emphasizing family strengths rather than weaknesses
- Focusing on solutions rather than causes of families' problems
- Involving families in the helpgiving process
- Focusing on needs/concerns identified by families
- Providing information to assist families in making informed decisions
- Enhancing family knowledge and skills needed to take actions in ways that are competency producing
- Providing suggestions/advice that are ecologically relevant to families
- Displaying acknowledgement, acceptance, and support of families' decisions
- Affirming the roles families played in achieving positive outcomes

The above-referenced examples of effective professional helpgiving practices were used in the development of the Helpgiving Practices Scale (Trivette & Dunst, 1994). This scale was administered to a sample of 220 parents of young children attending a number of different human services programs. A factor analysis yielded two general factors in effective helpgiving practices. The first factor was labeled as *participatory practices*. Helpgiving practices indicative of this factor actively involve families in collaborative partnerships with professionals where the relationship is characterized by reciprocity, shared decision making, and joint actions. The second factor was identified as *relational practices*. This helpgiving practice focused on interpersonal and attitudinal behaviors encompassing "good clinical practice" in building relationships (e.g., compassion, sense of caring, active listening, etc.).

In research conducted by Dunst and his colleagues to determine the relation between helpgiving practices and family empowerment, two consistent findings have emerged (Dunst, Trivette, Boyd, & Brookfield, 1994; Dunst, Trivette, Gordon, & Starnes, 1993; Trivette, Dunst, Boyd, & Hamby, 1996). First, professional helpgiving practices are the principal and most potent determinant in families' feeling empowered, more so than effects associated with child, parent, and family factors and professional personal characteristics or program characteristics. Second, the participatory practices are more significant than the relational practices of professional–family relationships in terms of fostering family empowerment. Unfortunately, as reported by Dunst (2002), education professionals are more effective at displaying relational as opposed to participatory practices. Further, families revealed they experienced fewer family-centered practices than professionals indicated they offered. The goal of this book is to close this apparent gap between family needs and school-based family support services.

SUMMARY STATEMENTS

- A family can take on a multitude of structural forms and involve diverse living situations, but the function of a family remains constant—a group of individuals who care about each other and cooperate to meet both individual and mutual goals.
- The family affects the development of the child and the child impacts family functioning. Since families serve as the primary means of support for children with disabilities, there is growing recognition that society, through its educational, health, and social-welfare institutions, has an obligation to support families in their caregiving responsibilities.
- Children with disabilities benefit in multiple respects when their parents are actively involved in their education.
- Schools should move from a child-centered to a family-centered services perspective in an effort to support the entire family, not just the child with a disability.
- A recent emerging realization is that most families of children with disabilities do not experience overwhelming stress, and they are able to successfully cope with raising a child with a disability.
- Bronfenbrenner's social ecology model focuses on children and families as interactive members of a larger system of social institutions, including schools. Those social institutions have the influence to negatively or positively affect the family's capacity to enhance the development of their child with disabilities.
- Schools are the logical social institutions to provide family support services.
- A foundation and rationale for school-based family support services can be found in education legislation, including IDEA.
- Family-centered support services include practices that involve families in decision making, develop services for the whole family, respect family priorities, and offer choices for family participation.
- Professional helpgiving practices can empower families.

QUESTIONS FOR DISCUSSION

1. Assume you are making a presentation to your local school board. You are advocating for increased school-based support services for families of children with disabilities. What would be the key arguments you would stress in your presentation?
2. What do you see as the critical features of family-centered support services?
3. How could the school best support Paula Jacobson and her family in the second family perspective described at the beginning of this chapter? What support services should the school provide?

RESOURCES FOR FAMILY SUPPORT SERVICES

- **Federal Resource Center for Special Education**
  (www.dssc.org/frc/index.htm).

  The Federal Resouce Center is a nationwide technical assistance network designed to respond to the needs of children with disabilities and their families.

- **National Dissemination Center for Children with Disabilities**
  (www.nichcy.org).

  This national information clearinghouse provides a wealth of information on children with disabilities, including programs and services and effective practices.

- **Beach Center on Disability**
  (www.beachcenter.org).

  The Beach Center is a research organization at the University of Kansas devoted to family support, family empowerment, and family quality-of-life issues.

- **Federation for Children with Special Needs**
  (www.fcsn.org).

  The federation provides information, support, and assistance to parents of children with disabilities. Emphasis is placed on family-centered policies, programs, and practices.

- **National Center to Improve Practice**
  (www.edc.org/FSC/NCIP).

  This information and dissemination center seeks to improve educational practices and outcomes for children with disabilities by encouraging the effective use of assistive and instructional technology.

REFLECTION ACTIVITIES

1. Review the most recent U.S. Department of Education annual report to Congress on the implementation of IDEA. This report is available by writing to ED Pubs, Education Publications Center, U.S. Department of Education, P.O. Box 1398, Jessup, MD 20794-1398. The annual report is also available on the U.S. Department

of Education's Web site at www.ed.gov/about/offices/list/osers/osep/ index.htm. As you review the most recent annual report to Congress, focus on findings that reveal family characteristics of students receiving special education services, family support needs, and family-centered services provided by schools.

2. Discuss with some parents the family impact (positive and negative) of raising a child with a disability. If you do not know any families of children with disabilities, you may be connected with some families by contacting local parent-support groups such as the ARC, Children and Adults with Attention Deficit/Hyperactivity Disorder (CHADD), Alliance for the Mentally Ill (AMI), and similar groups.

REFERENCES

Adoption and Child Welfare Act, 42 U.S.C. Sec. 620 et seq.

Adoption and Safe Families Act, 42 U.S.C. Sec. 629 et seq.

Agosta, J. (1995). *Family support policy brief.* Salem, OR: Human Services Research Institute.

Bailey, D. B. (2001). Evaluating parent involvement and family support in early intervention and preschool programs. *Journal of Early Intervention, 24*(1), 1–14.

Bauer, A. M., & Shea, T. M. (2003). *Parents and schools: Creating a successful partnership for students with special needs.* Upper Saddle River, NJ: Merrill/Prentice Hall.

Bergman, A. I., & Singer, G. H. S. (1996). The thinking behind new public policy. In G. H. S. Singer, L. E. Powers, & A. L. Olson (Eds.), *Redefining family support: Innovations in public–private partnerships* (pp. 435–464). Baltimore: Paul Brookes.

Berry, J. O. (1995). Families and deinstitutionalization: An application of Bronfenbrenner's social ecology model. *Journal of Counseling and Development, 73,* 379–383.

Birenbaum, A., & Cohen, H. J. (1993). On the importance of helping families: Policy implications from a national study. *Mental Retardation, 31*(2), 67–74.

Bronfenbrenner, U. (1979). *The ecology of human development.* Cambridge, MA: Harvard University Press.

Bronfenbrenner, U. (1986). Ecology of the family as a context for human development: Research perspectives. *Developmental Psychology, 22,* 723–742.

Carpenter, B. (2000). Sustaining the family: Meeting the needs of families of children with disabilities. *British Journal of Special Education, 27*(3), 135–144.

Children's and Communities Mental Health Systems Improvement Act, 29 U.S.C. Sec. 701 et seq.

Christenson, S. L., & Cleary, M. (1990). Consultation and the parent-education partnership: A perspective. *Journal of Educational and Psychological Consultation, 1,* 219–241.

Clatterbuck, C. C., & Turnbull, H. R. (1996). The role of education and community services in supporting families of children with complex health care needs. In G. H. S. Singer, L. E. Powers, & A. L. Olson (Eds.), *Redefining family support: Innovations in public–private partnerships* (pp. 389–412). Baltimore: Paul Brookes.

Cutler, B. C. (1993). *You, your child, and special education: A guide to making the system work.* Baltimore: Paul Brookes.

Dahlstrom, E. (1989). Theories and ideology of family function, gender relations and human reproduction. In K. Boh, M. Back, C. Clason, M. Pankratora, J. Ovortup, B. G. Sgritta, & K. Aerness (Eds.), *Changing patterns of European family life.* London: Routledge.

Developmental Disabilities Assistance and Bill of Rights Act, 42 U.S.C. Sec. 15001 et seq.

Doll, B., & Bolger, M. (2000). The family with a young child with disabilities. In M. J. Fine & R. L. Simpson (Eds.), *Collaboration with parents and families of children and youth with exceptionalities* (pp. 237–256). Austin, TX: Pro-Ed.

Dunst, C. J. (2002). Family-centered practices: Birth through high school. *The Journal of Special Education*, 36(3), 139–147.

Dunst, C. J., Trivette, C. M., Boyd, K., & Brookfield, J. (1994). Helpgiving practices and the self efficacy appraisals of parents. In C. J. Dunst, C. M. Trivette, & A. G. Deal (Eds.), *Supporting and strengthening families: Methods, strategies, and practices* (pp. 212–220). Cambridge, MA: Brookline Books.

Dunst, C. J., Trivette, C. M., Gordon, N., & Starnes, L. (1993). Family-centered case manager practices: Characteristics and consequences. In G. H. S. Singer & L. Powers (Eds.), *Families, disabilities, and empowerment: Active coping skills and strategies for family interventions* (pp. 89–118). Baltimore: Paul Brookes.

Dunst, C. J., Trivette, C. M., & Snyder, D. M. (2000). Family–professional partnerships: A behavioral science perspective. In M. J. Fine & R. L. Simpson (Eds.), *Collaboration with parents and families of children and youth with exceptionalities* (pp. 27–48). Austin, TX: Pro-Ed.

Epstein, J. L. (1995). School/family/community partnerships: Caring for the children we serve. *Phi Delta Kappan*, 76(2), 701–712.

Families of Children with Disabilities Support Act of 1994, 20 U.S.C. Sec. 1491 et seq.

Family and Medical Leave Act, 29 U.S.C. Sec. 2601 et seq.

Fiedler, C. R. (1994). Inclusion: Recognition of the giftedness of all children. *Network*, 4(2), 15–23.

Fiedler, C. R. (2000). *Making a difference: Advocacy competencies for special education professionals*. Boston: Allyn & Bacon.

Fine, M. J., & Nissenbaum, M. S. (2000). The child with disabilities and the family: Implications for professionals. In M. J. Fine & R. L. Simpson (Eds.), *Collaboration with parents and families of children and youth with exceptionalities* (pp. 3–26). Austin, TX: Pro-Ed.

Floyd, F. J., & Gallagher, E. M. (1997). Parental stress, care demands, and use of support services for school-age children with disabilities and behavior problems. *Family Relations*, 46(4), 359–385.

Garwick, A. E., & Millar, H. E. C. (1996). *Promoting resilience in youth with chronic conditions and their families*. Vienna, VA: National Maternal and Child Health Clearinghouse. (ERIC Document Reproduction Service No. ED398687)

Goals 2000: Educate America Act of 1994, 20 U.S.C. Sec. 5801 et seq.

Goetz, L., Anderson, J., & Laten, S. (1989). Facilitation of family support through public school programs. In G. H. S. Singer & L. K. Irvin (Eds.), *Support for caregiving families: Enabling positive adaptation to disability* (pp. 239–252). Baltimore: Paul Brookes.

Gowen, J. W., Christy, D. S., & Sparling, J. (1993). Informational needs of parents of young children with special needs. *Journal of Early Intervention*, 17(2), 194–210.

Hodapp, R. M., & Zigler, E. (1993). Comparison of families of children with mental retardation and families of children without mental retardation. *Mental Retardation*, 31(2), 75–77.

Holroyd, J. (1987). *Questionnaire on resources and stress*. Brandon, VT: Clinical Psychological Publishing.

Honig, A. S., & Winger, C. J. (1995, October). A *professional support program for families of handicapped preschoolers: Decrease in maternal stress*. Paper presented at the Annual Training Conference of the National Head Start Association, Washington, DC. (ERIC Document Reproduction Service No. EC303910)

Individuals with Disabilities Education Act (IDEA), 20 U.S.C. Sections 1400–1485.

Individuals with Disabilities Education Act (IDEA) Regulations, 34 C.F.R. Sec. 300.1–300.653.

Karp, N. (1996). Individualized wrap-around services for children with emotional, behavior, and mental disorders. In G. H. S. Singer, L. E. Powers, & A. L. Olson (Eds.), *Redefining family support: Innovations in public–private partnerships* (pp. 291–312). Baltimore: Paul Brookes.

Keith, N. Z. (1999). Whose community schools? New discourses, old patterns. *Theory into Practice*, 38(4), 225–336.

Lehman, C. M. (1997). *Qualitative investigation of effective service coordination for children and youth with emotional and behavioral disorders*. Monmouth, OR: Western Oregon State College. (ERIC Document Reproduction Service No. ED411640)

Mallory, B. L. (1996). Early intervention and family support. In G. H. S. Singer, L. E. Powers, & A. L. Olson (Eds.), *Redefining family support: Innovations in public–private partnerships* (pp. 135–150). Baltimore: Paul Brookes.

McCubbin, M. A., & Huang, S. T. T. (1989). Family strengths in the care of handicapped children: Targets for intervention. *Family Relations, 38,* 436–443.

Mink, I. T. (1993). In the best interests of the family: Some comments on Birenbaum and Cohen's recommendations. *Mental Retardation, 31*(2), 80–82.

Murphy, D. L., Lee, I. L., Turnbull, A. P., & Turbiville, V. (1995). The family-centered program rating scale: An instrument for program evaluation and change. *Journal of Early Intervention, 19*(1), 24–42.

Noh, S., Dumas, J. E., Wolf, L. C., & Fisman, S. N. (1989). Delineating sources of stress in parents of exceptional children. *Family Relations, 38,* 456–461.

Sailor, W., Kleinhammer-Tramill, J., Skrtic, T., & Oas, B. K. (1996). Family participation in new community schools. In G. H. S. Singer, L. E. Powers, & A. L. Olson (Eds.), *Redefining family support: Innovations in public–private partnerships* (pp. 313–332). Baltimore: Paul Brookes.

Sailor, W., & Skrtic, T. M. (1996). School/community partnerships and educational reform. *Remedial and Special Education, 17*(5), 267–270.

Senge, P. M. (1990). *The fifth discipline: The art and practice of the learning organization.* New York: Doubleday.

Shelton, T. L., & Stepanek, J. S. (1994). *Family-centered care for children needing specialized health and developmental services.* Bethesda, MD: Association for the Care of Children's Health.

Simpson, R. L., & Fiedler, C. R. (1989). Parent participation in individualized educational program (IEP) conferences: A case for individualization. In M. J. Fine (Ed.), *The second handbook on parent education* (pp. 145–171). San Diego: Academic Press.

Simpson, R. L., & Zurkowski, J. K. (2000). Parent and professional collaborative relationships in an era of change. In M. J. Fine & R. L. Simpson (Eds.), *Collaboration with parents and families of children and youth with exceptionalities* (pp. 89–102). Austin, TX: Pro-Ed.

Singer, G. H. S. (1996). Introduction: Trends affecting home and community care for people with chronic conditions in the United States. In G. H. S. Singer, L. E. Powers, & A. L. Olson (Eds.), *Redefining family support: Innovations in public–private partnerships* (pp. 3–38). Baltimore: Paul Brookes.

Singer, G. H. S., & Irvin, L. K. (1989). Family caregiving, stress, and support. In G. H. S. Singer & L. K. Irvin (Eds.), *Support for caregiving families: Enabling positive adaptation to disability* (pp. 3–25). Baltimore: Paul Brookes.

Singer, G. H. S., & Powers, L. E., (1993). Contributing to resilience in families: An overview. In G. H. S. Singer & L. E. Powers (Eds.), *Families, disability, and empowerment: Active coping skills and strategies for family interventions* (pp. 1–25). Baltimore: Paul Brookes.

Singer, G. H. S., Powers, L. E, & Olson, A.L. (1996) (Eds.), *Redefining family support: Innovations in public–private partnerships.* Baltimore: Paul Brookes.

Singer, L., & Farkas, K. J. (1989). The impact of infant disability on maternal perception of stress. *Family Relations, 38,* 444–449.

Summers, J. A., Behr, S. K., & Turnbull, A. P. (1989). Positive adaptation and coping strengths of families who have children with disabilities. In G. H. S. Singer & L. K. Irvin (Eds.), *Support for caregiving families: Enabling positive adaptation to disability* (pp. 27–40). Baltimore: Paul Brookes.

Supplemental Security Income for the Aged, Blind, and Disabled of Title XVI of the Social Security Act, 42 U.S.C. Sec. 1381 et seq.

Taylor, M. J. (1999). *Family support and resources in families having children with disabilities.* Logan, UT: Utah State University. (ERIC Document Reproduction Service No. ED434430)

Thompson, L., Lobb, C., Elling, R., Herman, S., Jurkiewicz, T., & Hulleza, C. (1997). Pathways to family empowerment: Effects of family-centered delivery of early intervention services. *Exceptional Children, 64*(1), 99–113.

Title V of the Maternal and Child Health Services Block Grant, 42 U.S.C. Sec. 701–709.

Title XIX of the Social Security Act, 42 U.S.C. Sec. 1396n (b).

Trivette, C. M., & Dunst, C. J. (1994). *Helpgiving practices scale.* Unpublished scale, Orelena Hawks Puckett Institute, Asheville, NC.

Trivette, C. M., Dunst, C. J., Boyd, K., & Hamby, D. W. (1996). Family-oriented program models, helpgiving practices, and parental control appraisals. *Exceptional Children, 62,* 237–248.

Turnbull, A. P., & Turnbull, H. R. (2001). *Families, professionals, and exceptionality: Collaborating for empowerment.* Upper Saddle River, NJ: Merrill/Prentice Hall.

Turnbull, H. R., Beegle, G., & Stowe, M. J. (2001). The core concepts of disability policy affecting families who have children with disabilities. *Journal of Disability Policy Studies, 12*(3),133–143.

Turnbull, H. R., Wilcox, B. L., Stowe, M. J., & Umbarger, G. T. (2001). Matrix of federal statutes and federal and state court decisions reflecting the core concepts of disability policy. *Journal of Disability Policy Studies, 12*(3), 144–176.

United Cerebral Palsy Association. (1993). *National family support legislation to become a reality in 1993.* Washington, DC: Author.

U.S. Census Bureau. (1999). *Current population survey (CPS)—Definitions and explanations.* Washington, DC: Author.

U.S. Department of Education (2001). *Twenty-third annual report to Congress on the implementation of the Individuals with Disabilities Education Act.* Washington, DC: Author.

Wade, S. L., & Taylor, H. G. (1996). Childhood traumatic brain injury: Initial impact on the family. *Journal of Learning Disabilties, 29*(6), 652–665.

Walker, B., & Singer, G. H. S. (1993). Improving collaborative communication between professionals and parents. In G. H. S. Singer & L. E. Powers (Eds.), *Families, disability, and empowerment: Active coping skills and strategies for family interventions* (pp. 285–316). Baltimore: Paul Brookes.

Weinberg, D. H. (1997). *Income and poverty.* Press briefing, Washington, DC.

Winton, D. (1990). *Report of the New Mexico home memorial 5 task force on young children and families* (Report 1). New Mexico: New Mexico Home Memorial 5 Task Force on Young Children and Families.

Wright, K., & Stegelin, D. A. (2003). *Building school and community partnerships through parent involvement.* Upper Saddle River, NJ: Merrill/Prentice Hall.

Yuan, S., Baker-McCue, T., & Witkin, K. (1996). Coalitions for family support and the creation of two flexible funding programs. In G. H. S. Singer, L. E. Powers, & A. L. Olson (Eds.), *Redefining family support: Innovations in public–private partnerships* (pp. 357–388). Baltimore: Paul Brookes.

CHAPTER 2
Providing Parental and Family Support in Diverse Schools

●●●●●●●●●●●●●●●●●●○○○○○○○

In this chapter, you will understand:

- Ways that identity affects worldview.
- Identity categories and their impact on interactions between family members and school personnel.
- Collaborative practices that demonstrate respect for diverse families and involve family members in their child's educational planning team.

Family Perspective: Susan's Conflict

Susan is a first-year special education teacher in her hometown. She is excited to work with children from her community and feels she will bond well with the families of her students because she knows their history and region intimately. Prior to the first day of school, she sent out an introductory letter describing herself, her teaching style, and upcoming school events. In her letter, Susan welcomed parents to stay awhile after they dropped off their children on the first day of school, to ease the transition to a new class. Susan believed this would help the families to feel comfortable that the children were safe and being well educated. On the first day, Susan was nervous and excited about meeting all the families and children. Of her 12 students, 9 parents walked their children to school and had brief conversations with Susan. The other children came with siblings or arrived by themselves. Only one parent decided to stay for the morning to help his child with the transition. Susan was shocked that Kyle's father had brought him to school. She knew that Gabriel and Roxanne, Kyle's parents, had gotten divorced when Gabriel had come out as a homosexual. Susan didn't know what to do. Having strong conservative values, she had negative feelings about Gabriel and was concerned that he was continuing to interact with a vulnerable young child. Susan had many mis-perceptions about gays and lesbians. She had a conflict between her values as a person and those related to her teaching philosophy. She wanted to welcome parents into the class, but Susan strongly believed that homosexuals could be harmful to the development of children and could prey on children. Certainly, at the very least, she believed they were horrible role models for living a clean and decent life. Susan was worried that Gabriel might get "too close" with one of the children in the class. Susan talked to Gabriel and thanked him for coming. He looked normal enough and was polite. However, she explained that his presence was upsetting to the classroom atmosphere, and she didn't think it was appropriate for him to stay in the class-room. She then asked him to leave and have Roxanne contact Susan at her next convenience, since Roxanne had primary custody of Kyle. In response, Gabriel explained that her remarks were homophobic, and it was her attitude that was upsetting to a healthy classroom environment. Before he walked out the door, Gabriel asked, "What example have you set for students in this class? Can't you leave your narrow-minded views at the door in order to reach all students? What if one of your students is gay?" Gabriel pro-ceeded to the principal's office and filed a formal complaint against Susan. In her mailbox at lunch, Susan found a note that directed her to come to the principal's office for a conference at the end of the school day.

Reflecting on the Family Perspective

1. How can Susan teach Kyle and work with his family?

2. If you were Susan's principal, how would you help mentor her so she can deal with this conflict?

3. On this exciting and stressful first day, the identity issues between Susan and Gabriel were too overwhelming for Susan to comprehend. What can you do when you are caught in a surprising situation relating to your core values?

We all carry worlds in our heads, and those worlds are decidedly different. We educators set out to teach, but how can we reach the worlds of others when we don't even know they exist? Indeed, many of us don't even realize that our own worlds exist only in our heads and in the cultural institutions we have built to support them. It is as if we are in the mid-dle of a great computer-generated virtual reality game, but the "realities" displayed in var-ious participants' minds are entirely different terrains. When one player moves right and up a hill, the other player perceives him as moving left and into a river. (Delpit, 1995, p. xiv)

IDENTITY CATEGORIES

When a school professional and a parent first meet, their reactions to each other will more likely be positive if they have similar worldviews and life perspectives. If their perspectives are different, it is more likely their first encounter will be neutral or negative. Life perspectives and worldviews emerge out of cultural identities and different life experiences. Therefore, differences between people in cultural identities and life experiences will lead to dissimilarity between them in perspectives as well. Examples of cultural identity categories include ethnic identification, race, socioeconomic status, gender (i.e., male or female), gender identity (i.e., masculine or feminine), sexual orientation, regionality, religious affiliation, alternative family structures, and disability status. Difficulties arise when two individuals' worldviews clash due to one person's limited understanding of the other's cultural identity. The people attempting to communicate may not recognize or accept each other's cultural identity. For example, disability may be seen as a gift or a punishment. The person who has embraced disability as a positive identity category discusses her disability as a gift. In contrast, the listener, immersed in the dominant view that disability is a punishment, believes only that the speaker feels she must put on a brave face in dealing with her disability. To increase your understanding of cultural identities, use the diagram in Figure 2.1 to define yourself in relation to each category.

Think about how each identity affects your perspective on life. Analyze how the perspectives intersect, overlap, or conflict. For example, does your ethnicity traditionally hold specific expectations of gender identification? Do women and men need to act in specific ways and be involved in certain roles in the family? Are your interests, hobbies, and manner of dress aligned with your gender expectations? These are a few examples of the different intersections of identities within individuals that complicate our collaborative efforts to work with family members whose identities differ from our own. Other alternative views impacted by identities are presented in Table 2.1.

In addition, what happens when the cultural conflict is between school personnel and a family? Based on both her traditional education as well as the combination of her ethnicity, gender identification, race, and religion, a teacher may have strong beliefs about raising children. What are your beliefs about discipline? What would you do if a parent spanked his or her child while in your classroom? What are your beliefs about popular Western medicine? What if a child's family refused to provide medication for behavioral issues or seizures?

In contrast to other writings on diverse populations, this chapter will not provide specific characteristics that have been historically demonstrated by members of a certain identity (e.g., African Americans interact with authority in this way, gay fathers interact with their children another way). Often, these descriptions of characteristics of specific identities become a checklist that can be used to reduce an individual to a stereotype. Thus, the descriptions minimize the team participation and advocacy actions of family members. Each individual is unique. The interactions of each identity and history create a unique perspective. It is important to understand how school personnel, who most frequently represent the currently dominant white culture, have interacted with family members who represent different diverse

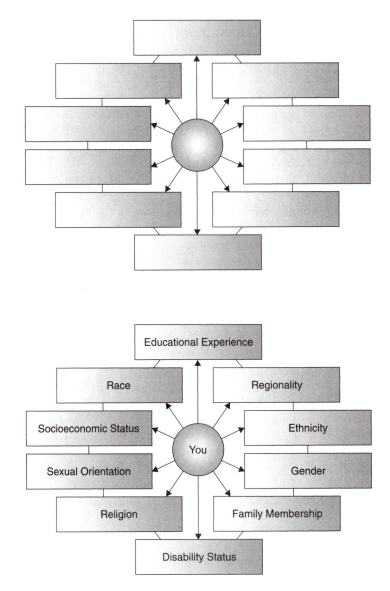

Figure 2.1 *Identity Web.*

Table 2.1   Contrasting Values.

Being	Doing
Family-group-community emphasis	Individual emphasis, privacy
Interdependence	Independence
Cooperation	Competition
Person-to-person orientation	Person-to-object orientation
Authoritarian orientation	Democratic orientation
Hierarchy, rank, status	Egalitarianism
Extended family	Nuclear/blended family
Rigid family-member roles	Flexible family-member roles
Favoritism to males	Increasing female roles
Formality	Informality
Indirectness	Directness/openness
Suppression of emotions	Expression of emotions
Fate	Mastery of one's own destiny
Balance and harmony, tradition	Change
Patience, modesty	Assertiveness
Personal interaction dominates	Time dominates
Spiritualism	Materialism

Source: Adapted from "The values Americans live by" by L. R. Kohls, 1984, Washington, DC: Meridian House International.

populations. This section of the chapter will describe categories of identities (e.g., gender, nationality, age) and the effects membership in specific identities can have on the interaction between school professionals and families.

Socioeconomic Status

The notion that everyone can be wealthy has supplanted the idea of the United States as a classless society. Indeed, the fantasy that cuts across class is the dream of a world where everyone can be wanton and wasteful as they consume the world's riches. Endless indulgence of a fantasy life used to be solely the cultural terrain of rich white men. More than any other group they had the power to realize dreams and fantasies. Advertising changed all that. Through the manipulation of images, it constructs a fictive United States where everyone has access to everything. And no one, no matter their politics or values, can easily remain untouched by these insistent narratives of unlimited plenty posthypnotically telling us we are what we possess. (hooks, 2000, p. 80)

Class matters. Race and gender can be used as screens to deflect attention away from the harsh realities class politics exposes. Clearly, just when we should be paying attention to class, using race and gender to explain its new dimensions, society, even our government, says let's talk about race and racial injustice. It is impossible to talk meaningfully about ending racism without talking about class. Let us not be duped. (hooks, 2000, p. 7)

Socioeconomic status (SES) has a significant impact on the amount of energy teams (and researchers) expend to involve families of children with behavioral disorders in behavioral and educational planning (Harris, 1996). Significant research has been conducted with high and middle SES families of children with behavioral disorders, but little research has occurred with families from low SES. This is an especially problematic relationship considering that the number of students with behavioral issues who come from low SES is much larger than that coming from middle or high SES. At the same time that more children from low SES are being labeled with behavioral disorders, fewer low SES families are being invited to be involved in their children's education and the development of methods to assist in positive behavioral programming (Harris, 1996). Similarly, students with severe disabilities who come from families of low SES have a poor education; they are less likely to be integrated or included in general education classes than are children with severe disabilities who come from higher SES families. An inequity in special education has been created as it is often the parents who have the monetary ability to advocate for longer periods of time whose children receive appropriate supports and education.

Race/Ethnicity

There are five federally accepted categories of race: White/Caucasian, Black/African American, American Indian/Alaskan Native, Asian, and Native Hawaiian or other Pacific Islander. Latino/Hispanic is no longer considered a race, but a cultural status. People who identify as Latino/Hispanic can also identify as any of the five race categories. A sixth category of "Some other race" is also included. The U.S. Census inquires about these five race categories, and Table 2.2 is demonstrative of the increasing diversity of the American population. Figure 2.2 provides commonly accepted definitions of the categories of race.

Table 2.2 Population (in Millions) by Race and Hispanic/Latino Status.*

Race	White/Caucasian	Black/African American	American Indian/ Alaskan Native
1990**	199	30	2
2000**	216	36	4

Source: From *National population briefing, national population estimates for July 2000*
*A person who identified as Latino/Hispanic status can be of any race.

**There have been changes in the reporting that contribute to some of the changes in

---

American Indian and Alaskan Native: A person having origins in any of the original peoples of North America. The individual maintains cultural identification through tribal affiliation or community recognition.

Asian: A person having origins in any of the original peoples of the Far East, Southeast Asia, and the Indian subcontinent.

Black or African American: A person having origins in any of the Black racial groups of Africa.

White or Caucasian: A person having origins in any of the original peoples of Europe, North Africa, or the Middle East.

Some other race: A person who identifies as having origins with a race not listed.

Figure 2.2 *Definitions of Race.*
(U.S. *Census Bureau*, 2000)

The Council of Economic Advisors (1998) estimated that by the year 2050, one half of the U.S. population will be of Hispanic, African American, Native American, or Asian/Pacific descent. School professionals have historically viewed families of color through a deficit model. In other words, the differences between school professionals and the students and families they serve are perceived as negatives rather than alternatives or positive differences. For example, the classroom climate in traditional American classrooms has valued students who are task oriented, logical, scheduled, objective, and factual. In contrast, the learning styles of non-White children are often outside of these Euro-Western expectations. Their learning style is often process oriented, creative, subjective, humanistic, flexible, and group oriented. The negative effects of this deficit model are noticeable in all areas of American education, from informal classroom expectations to standardized test scores and overidentification of children of color in special education.

Similar to the lack of adaptation of the school system to allow for diverse learners, the interaction of school professionals with diverse family members has also

Asian	Native Hawaiian/ Other Pacific Islander	Latino/Hispanic	Some other race
7	>1	22	9
12	1	35	18

by U.S. Census Bureau, 2000, http://www.census.gov/statab/www.part1a.html

population per race category (numbers have been rounded to whole millions).

been negative. The racism inherent in the educational system devalues any alternative to the expectation of interactions with a traditional white family. This devaluing of students' family culture reinforces the continual exclusion of the family members from collaborative planning. The students' life beyond school is not valued. Without consideration of the child's larger world, educational plans are futile.

There are ways to make your interactions with families whose race is different from your own more positive and productive for all team members. Teacher Tips Box 2.1 describes ways school personnel can become educated about diverse families.

TEACHER TIPS   BOX 2.1

- ❏ Talk to your students and their families about their experiences.
- ❏ Learn about your students' home and community.
- ❏ Read books, articles, and magazines created by authors of different races.
- ❏ Use the Internet to obtain general information about various races.
- ❏ Learn from a variety of knowledgeable community members from different races who are comfortable helping educators.
- ❏ Participate in ethnically oriented community events.
- ❏ Join professional organizations designed to advocate for diverse people.

Sexual Orientation

Similar in outcome to the effect of SES, the sexual orientation of family members has a significant negative impact on the willingness of school personnel to invite families into the collaborative team process. In fact, the taboo that still surrounds family members who identify as gay, lesbian, bisexual, or transgender (GLBT) is so strong that school personnel have been reported to actively harass, ignore, and exclude families from participating in school activities (Dispenza, 1999; Kozik-Rosabel, 2000; Lamme & Lamme, 2001/2002). In some cases, school personnel who have been willing to address issues related to sexual orientation have been viewed as inappropriate and incompetent, to the point of dismissal from teaching (Zirkel, 2002). Although this may seem archaic or unreasonable to those readers with more accepting mind-sets, if these homophobic incidents are still common enough to maintain a significant discussion in professional literature, the daily effects of more subtle bias and maltreatment are evident.

Homophobic reactions to family members who identify as GLBT are becoming more prominent in special education as three trends continue. First, larger numbers of GLBT people are "coming out" and approaching all facets of life, including involvement in their children's schools, with an openness in regard to their sexuality (Wisenkale & Heckart, 1993; Wolfson, 1996). Many GLBT individuals who would have previously hidden their sexual identity from school personnel are now bringing this issue into view. Second, larger numbers of GLBT individuals and couples are having children (Patterson, 1994). As the number of families headed by GLBT parents increases, it is to be expected that if the proportion of children with disabilities born to GLBT families is the same as within the general population, there will be an increase in the number of families who have not only children, but children with disabilities. Third, there is a growth in the number of GLBT individuals who are becoming foster parents to children with disabilities (Guggenheim, Lowe & Curtis, 1996). This trend will even more directly affect the number of GLBT parents supporting children in the special education system.

Religion

Membership in a religious community has been both a documented strength and a stressor for families with children with disabilities (Dollahite, Marks, & Olson, 1997; Zhang & Bennett, 2001). Some families have found comfort and acceptance of their child in the religious community, whereas others have been disowned, shamed, or blamed as the cause of their child's disability (Weinberg & Sebian, 1980). When spiritual beliefs of the family differ from those of school personnel, there can be negative educational ramifications. For instance, there has been a common history of dismissal of the family's values or a view that families disregard the needs and possible achievements of their child due to their spiritual beliefs (Brown & Shepard, 2000; Dollahite et al., 1997; Williams, 1991; Zhang & Bennett, 2001). This dismissal of the family's desires for their child's education can put a quick halt to the collaborative relationship between family members and school personnel. In some cases, when the school personnel continue to disregard family concerns, it has been more difficult for families to advocate at the team level, and an increase in legal advocacy has occurred (Harris, 1996).

Disability Status

Parents with disabilities have faced more direct criticism of their parenting skills by school personnel and service providers than possibly any other group of parents. Frequently seen as inherently less capable than parents who do not experience disabilities, parents with disabilities have had to fight to be viewed as whole sexual beings, individuals capable of having children, and adults able to demonstrate appropriate parenting skills. The parenting abilities of individuals with disabilities range the full spectrum of competence, as do those of any other group. Beyond the deficits that have been historically attributed to parents with disabilities, there are also strengths this group possesses to a greater degree than do other parents of children with disabilities. These parents have been involved with the special education system as individuals. They have an understanding of the experience of being a person with a disability and may be more likely than nondisabled parents to have an early acceptance of their child's disability. Parents with disabilities have knowledge of how the special education system works. This can lend itself to a better capacity for empathy and understanding of their child's experiences. Disabled parents of children with disabilities can be role models of successful living for their children. Another demonstrated strength of parents with disabilities is their awareness of supports and assistive technology. For example, Harris (2001) found that deaf mothers of deaf children were more successful in presenting signed utterances spontaneously and within natural contexts. This resulted in the deaf mothers' deaf infants having greater language comprehension at 18 months than the deaf children whose mothers were hearing.

Family Membership

> We define families in an inclusive sense to be composed of not only persons related by blood, marriage, or adoption, but also sets of interdependent but independent persons who share some common goals, resources, and a commitment to each other over time. (Bubolz & Sontag, 1993, p. 435)

Our cultural identities greatly affect how we define family. It is necessary to examine personal bias about family construction, then allow students' families to dictate who the members of the family are. Across different groups, different family members will be key decision makers, regardless of blood or marriage ties. Examples of this include families headed by a grandparent, aunt, sibling, partner of the parent, or whoever most supports the child. If the supporters of the family and student aren't welcome in the school environment, then it is less likely that any family member will step forth to collaborate. Asking the initial main contact parent who will be involved in educational decision making is critical. Some families may define themselves in multiple ways. For example, a child may consider the people he or she lives with as his or her family, and these individuals may include siblings, foster siblings, a parent, and a parent's partner. This type of understanding is often referred to as the functional family (Hildebrand, Phenice, Gray, & Hines, 2000). On the other hand, there may be a set of people related by legally recognized structures, including marriage and adoption, who do not live with a child but still may be legally considered to be family members.

For example, children who come from one-parent households do not necessarily have only one parent involved in their life. Divorce proceedings often end with a joint custody agreement for the couple's children. Joint custody includes two elements: legal custody and physical custody. Joint legal custody requires collaboration in all decisions regarding a child's health, education, and welfare unless otherwise specified by the court. Courts most often place the child in the main physical custody of one parent with visitation by the other parent. But this does not mean that other rights are similarly divided. Educational personnel must remember that physical custody given to one parent does not mean that the other parent is unfit or uninterested in the welfare of the child (Tarriff & Levine, 1993). School professionals should make every effort to involve both parents in routine correspondence, intermittent progress reports, yearly events, and special occasions. When beginning a relationship with a family, it is best to find out which family members are involved and should be included in collaborative activities with the school team. Double mailings of newsletters, lunch menus, invitations to IEP meetings, and photocopies of report cards should be provided to parents who have joint legal custody (Tariff & Levine, 1993).

Fathers or paternal figures are family members often forgotten on the educational teams of their children (League & Ford, 1996). This is unfortunate because they have a unique relationship with their child and may have insights that differ from those of female family members, who often dominate educational teams. When fathers are involved in the education of their children with disabilities, academic motivation and achievement increase. To increase the involvement of fathers on educational teams, special effort should be exerted to include fathers in the addressing of documents and informal notes sent home. Fathers' support groups have assisted men in adjusting to the identity of their child with a disability (League & Ford, 1996). These fathers' support groups often differ in structure from those designed for mothers in that they begin with an unrelated group activity, then later move to issues related to their relationship with their child with disabilities.

It is important for school professionals to investigate the membership and educational decision-making partners of each family and child who is served. The extra effort of notifying multiple households or family members is far outweighed by the strength of a true collaborative team.

Collaborating with families is so complex because it is rare that all school personnel and family members claim similar identities in all categories. Subsequent sections will describe ways to assist in collaborating with families whose identities differ from those of school personnel.

COMMUNICATION WITH FAMILIES WHOSE BACKGROUNDS DIFFER FROM YOUR OWN

> One of the most difficult tasks we face as human beings is trying to communicate across our individual differences, trying to make sure that what we say to someone is interpreted the way we intend. This becomes even more difficult when we attempt to communicate across social differences, genders, race, or class lines, or any situation of unequal power. (Delpit, 1995, p. 135)

Interactions between families and school personnel have been measured using a family-friendliness scale. According to Singh and Curtis (1997), "Family friendly is [defined] . . . as services that are aligned with the needs of the families and developed in a manner that shows professionals value and respect family involvement, empowerment, and cultural differences" (p. 83).

Considering all of the ways the school system as well as individual professionals have hindered previous collaboration with families who represent diverse identities, it should be understood that it will require a different approach to bring back these disillusioned families to the collaborative meeting table. Family-friendliness may require school professionals to go beyond the comfort of traditional structures and locations. Family members may be uncomfortable with the school environment, not have the time to attend meetings during school hours, or have a fear of criticism by school personnel (Simpson, Whelan, & Zabel, 1993). For low SES families and families from a variety of nondominant cultures, there are several ways to increase the likelihood of their involvement and make their involvement on the educational team more comfortable

---

❑ Use audio and video both to educate parents and to enhance family involvement in the special education process (e.g., conference calls, distance technology for family involvement in meetings). This can decrease the stress of scheduling, loss of instructional time for teachers, lost work hours and wages for family members, and travel issues for both families and teachers (Santelli, Turnbull, Sergeant, Lerner, & Marquis, 1996).

(Harris, 1996). For some families, lack of transportation to meetings at school may be prohibitive. Be aware of the student's home address and arrange meetings nearby. If there is a local community center, church, or other gathering place, have all the meetings from that neighborhood in the alternate location. This eases the scheduling concerns when having meetings off-campus and prevents any given family from feeling singled out. An alternate location will also even the playing field and enable families who may be uncomfortable with the level of formality at the school building to feel more at ease. Another strategy for increasing school collaboration with families is presented in Communication and Collaboration Tips Box 2.2.

Beyond location, it is important to be aware of the norms and values of the culture. Working to establish a relationship based on respect and trust can be encumbered or enhanced by the differences between the family's and the school personnel's culture, depending on each individual's willingness to acknowledge and understand the value differences based on identity.

To encourage the involvement of families who speak a non-English primary language, it is important to have individuals from each cultural group represented within the school and student's team. If an interpreter is needed, a professional interpreter or consultant with specific expertise should be hired (Harris, 1996). Often schools will use an individual from the educational setting who is not trained as an interpreter. This can be problematic. It is critical that the individual understand his or her role as translator and interpret without altering the intent of the language.

Another important factor in determining the quality of the relationship and interaction between school professionals and families is religious differences. Religious differences between school personnel and family members have caused significant philosophical differences in the cause, acceptance, treatment, and future goals of students with disabilities. A useful communication strategy to initiate positive interactions with families at the outset is described in Communication and Collaboration Tips Box 2.3.

❑ When starting the school year, teachers should interact with family members and describe an achievement their child reached. This interaction will establish your relationship as child focused, nonbiased, and positive.

CONSTRUCTING A CLASSROOM THAT REFLECTS OUR DIVERSE SOCIETY

Schools that do not actively address intolerance and prejudice toward diverse groups are more likely to be the setting for violence (Simpson, Kline, Barnhill, & Griswold, 2000). There are a variety of curricula available to educate school professionals and students in prosocial attitudes regarding diverse people. The implementation of such programs creates a safe climate for all learners and all families to be active in the educational community (Simpson et al., 1993).

School professionals can increase the modeling and demonstration of prosocial behavior by inviting moral mentors into the classroom (Honig & Wittmer, 1996). These individuals may be students' relatives or community members who demonstrate caring, support, volunteerism, inspiration, and generosity toward others. Using bias-free curricula supplemented with well-chosen class materials promotes prosocial behavior between children from diverse backgrounds. Emphasis on these curricula also demonstrates an appreciation of difference and acceptance of students and families from diverse backgrounds (Honig & Wittmer, 1996). Movies or other forms of media used in the classroom should represent positive social and behavioral models as well as a diverse cast (Honig & Wittmer, 1996).

PREPARING TEACHERS TO EMBRACE DIVERSE FAMILIES

> We say we believe that all children can learn, but few of us really believe it. Teacher education usually focuses on research that links failure and socioeconomic status, failure and cultural difference, and failure and single-parent households. It is hard to believe that these children can possibly be successful after their teachers have been so thoroughly exposed to so much negative indoctrination. When teachers receive that kind of education, there is a tendency to assume deficits in students rather than to locate and teach to strengths. To counter this tendency, educators must have knowledge of children's lives outside of school so as to recognize their strengths. (Delpit, 1995, p. 172)

Children from diverse groups are failing in school, not because of their characteristics, but because school personnel fail to recognize and value their cultural, social, behavioral, and linguistic differences (Cartledge, Kea, & Ida, 2000). Recommendations for teacher preparation include the ability to work with linguistically diverse families, knowledge of the effects of ESL issues on student success, and awareness of at-risk populations and overrepresentation of students from minority groups in special education (Cartledge et al., 2000). Beyond knowledge and ability to be culturally sensitive, teachers must have strong collaborative skills and must work to empower children and families to increase the probability of success.

This preparation of special education professionals must not be considered the responsibility of teacher preparation programs, but a joint effort among colleges, school districts, and teachers who continue to seek out ongoing training and information regarding their collaborative skills and knowledge of the community in which they teach. The ongoing training and information may be partially delivered in in-service staff development but must also include peer mentoring, technical assistance, and observation and evaluation of teachers while they work with diverse children and families.

There is a critical shortage of special education teachers and related service providers in rural and urban areas. The shortage is even worse when looking at special professionals from underrepresented groups. Considering that the population of students in special education programs is becoming increasingly diverse (Hosp & Reschly, 2003), the lack of professionals from diverse backgrounds is an even more significant concern. There are few special education professionals who come from these communities and areas of diversity and can act as role models for the students and families being served. Teachers who represent diverse groups not only act as role models for families and individuals with disabilities but also enhance the cultural sensitivity, experience, and diversity-related skills for all other educators and students with which they interact.

KYLE AND SUSAN REVISITED

Susan was so surprised that her first day of teaching brought such challenges. Her principal, who at first was angry with Susan's response and fearful of a public scandal, developed a plan to address the situation. The plan had two parts, one to help Susan, Kyle, and his family; the other to make a change in the larger school community. Based on his conversation with the school principal, Gabriel agreed to stay away from school for 1 month except for transportation and formal school events. During this time, he was promised that the school would work to make the environment more open toward diverse identities.

The school principal started by talking openly at the first faculty meeting about his concerns and described the incident (without mentioning names). He also explained his goals for the school climate. Then, he opened the conversation for the entire school faculty to interact and brainstorm about their ideas of the current climate and what should happen in the future. The principal was pleasantly surprised when many of his ideas about increasing acceptance levels in the school were brought out. During one faculty meeting, a group from Parents and Friends of Lesbians and Gays (PFLAG) made a presentation at the school. During another meeting, issues of SES and bullying were discussed. Several other groups came and had meetings with a task force on diversity that included teachers from each grade level and the principal. By the end of the school year, the school had added sexual orientation, gender, and gender identity to its nondiscriminatory policies and had added valuing diversity to its mission statement. These actions were more than words added to documents; rather, they were the result of many conversations and learning experiences. That year was full of growth for Susan, Kyle, Gabriel, and the school community. Susan worked through her feelings of anger and guilt to begin to see this as a learning opportunity. She maintained her beliefs, but wanted to be certain she could teach all children and reach all families. Like Susan, her students would need to learn to live in a diverse society; whether they left their hometown or not, there would be people whose values and identities conflicted with their own. From that perspective, Susan began to talk to her students about differences and how to deal with conflict.

Gabriel, still enraged at the teacher's behavior, was trusting of the principal and wanted his son to have a positive school experience. After briefly considering removing Kyle from Susan's class, he decided that he, too, would need to learn to face the negative reactions of society toward his family. At least this school situation would be a controlled opportunity for Kyle to learn about how to hold on to self-identity and the ones he loved. After the first month, Gabriel attended all functions, visited the classroom, worked hard to maintain a connection to Susan, and collaborated at Kyle's IEP meetings.

Although it wasn't an ideal situation, the team slowly came closer together and were able to work together with Kyle's best interests at heart.

SUMMARY STATEMENTS

- Individual values are based on complex individual combinations of identities that affect worldview.
- Membership in multiple identity categories impacts each person's behavior and has an impact on interactions between family members and school professionals.
- Although identity categories are neither positive nor negative, membership in the different categories has had both positive and negative impact on family members of children with disabilities.
- When family members' identities differ from those of school professionals, there is a greater likelihood of conflict or disagreement about outcomes for the student.
- It is critical for school professionals to examine their identities, the beliefs formed from those identities, and the ways these impact school professionals' relationships with families whose identities differ from their own.

QUESTIONS FOR DISCUSSION

1. What are regional assumptions, expectations, and values in your community? How do different subgroups acknowledge, value, or become excluded due to these values based on regional identity?
2. How do the identities of a school's professionals affect its students and family-member involvement? Are the identities of school professionals less of an issue if the identities are generally homogenous or heterogeneous?
3. What can school professionals do proactively to offset the initial effect of identity differences between families and school personnel?

RESOURCES FOR PROVIDING PARENTAL AND FAMILY SUPPORTS IN DIVERSE SCHOOLS

- Hale, J. E. (2001). *Learning while black: Creating educational excellence for African Americans*. Baltimore: Johns Hopkins University Press.
- Kunjufu, J. (2002). *Black students, middle class teachers*. Chicago: African American Images.
- Delpit, L. (1995). *Other people's children: Cultural conflict in the classroom*. New York: New Press.
- *Matters of Race*. PBS video #MRAC700. This video describes the significance of race in the classroom, ways to develop a positive classroom environment for all children, and collaborative strategies when working cross-culturally.

- Tatum, B. D. (2003). *Why are all the black kids sitting together in the cafeteria? And other conversations about race: A psychologist explains the development of racial identity* (5th ed.). Philadelphia: Basic Books.
- *Understanding hate crimes: A service for Jeremy Wong.* VHS #JCE10752. Princeton, NJ: Films for the Humanities & Sciences.
- Wise, T. http://academic.udayton.edu/race/04needs/educate01.htm

  This Web site provides extensive information about creating a classroom that respects and honors diversity, including collaboration with cross-cultural students and school personnel.
- www.ed.gov/about/offices/list/ocr/edlite-raceneutralreport2.html

  This Web site provides information regarding family involvement in racially diverse programs and a plethora of links to similar sites.

REFLECTION ACTIVITIES

1. Construct and explain your definition of family.
2. Make an exhaustive list of groups to which you belong. Brainstorm how your membership in each group affects your interpretation of daily events and inter-actions with others.
3. Talk to three people whom you recognize as being different from yourself. Ask their views about current events, family issues, and education. Reflect on this experience and your interpretation based on your cultural lenses.
4. Be aware of the messages around you. Watch 1 hour of television and list all of the stereotype images you view.
5. Write down ways stereotypes have affected you and your interactions with others. Discuss these with a classmate and determine the origination of and alternatives to these interactions.

REFERENCES

Brown, R. D., & Shepard, T. L. (2000, June 3). *Examining the beliefs of involved adults concerning the moral and religious development of individuals with mental retardation.* Paper presented at the Annual Meeting of American Association on Mental Retardation (124th Washington, DC). (ERIC Document Reproduction Service No. ED444290)

Bubolz, M. M., & Sontag, M. S. (1993). Human ecology theory. In P. G. Boss, W. J. Doherty, R. LaRossa, W. R. Schumm, & S. K. Steinmetz (Eds.), *Sourcebook of family theories and methods: A contextual approach* (pp. 419–448). New York: Plenum Press.

Cartledge, G., Kea, C. D., & Ida, D. J. (2000). Anticipating differences—Celebrating strengths: Providing culturally competent services for students with serious emotional disturbance. *Teaching Exceptional Children, 32*(3), 30–37.

Council of Economic Advisors for the President's Initiative on Race. (1998). *Changing America: Indicators of social and economic well-being by race and Hispanic origin.* Washington, DC: U.S. Government Printing Office. (ERIC Document Reproduction Service No. ED424344)

Delpit, L. (1995). *Other people's children: Cultural conflict in the classroom.* New York: New Press.

Dispenza, M. (1999). *Our families, our children: The lesbian and gay child care task force report on quality child care*. Seattle, WA: Lesbian and Gay Child Care Task Force. (ERIC Document Reproduction Service No. ED437174)

Dollahite, D. C., Marks, L. D., & Olson, M. M. (1997). *Faithful fathering in trying times: Religious beliefs and practices of latter-day saint fathers of children with special needs*. (ERIC Document Reproduction Service No. ED416034)

Guggenheim, M., Lowe, A. D., & Curtis, D. (1996). *The rights of families*. Carbondale: Southern Illinois University Press.

Harris, K. C. (1996). Collaboration within a multicultural society: Issues for consideration. *Remedial and Special Education*, 17, 355–362.

Harris, M. (2001). It's all a matter of timing: Sign visibility and sign reference in deaf and hearing mothers of 18-month-old children. *Journal of Deaf Studies and Deaf Education*, 6(3), 177–185.

Hildebrand, V., Phenice, L. A., Gray, M. M., & Hines, R. P. (2000). *Knowing and serving diverse families* (2nd ed.). Upper Saddle River, NJ: Merrill.

Honig, A. S., & Wittmer, D. S. (1996). Helping children become more prosocial: Ideas for classrooms, families, schools, and communities (Part 2). *Young Children*, 51(2), 62–70.

hooks, b. (2000). *Where we stand: Class matters*. New York: Routledge.

Hosp, J. L., & Reschly, D. J. (2003). Referral rates for intervention or assessment: A meta-analysis of racial differences. *The Journal of Special Education*, 37(2), 67–80.

Kohls, L. R. (1984). *The values Americans live by*. Washington, DC: Meridian House International.

Kozik-Rosabel, G. (2000). "Well we haven't noticed anything bad going on," said the principal: Parents speak about their gay families and school. *Education and Urban Society*, 32, 368–389.

Lamme, L. L., & Lamme, L. A. (2001/2002). Welcoming children from gay families into our schools. *Educational Leadership*, 59(4), 65–69.

League, S. E., & Ford, L. (1996, March). *Fathers' involvement in their children's special education program*. Paper presented at the Annual Meeting of the National Association of School Psychologists, Atlanta, GA.

Patterson, C. J. (1994). Children of a lesbian baby boom. In N. B. Green & G. M. Herek (Eds.), *Lesbian and gay psychology: Theory, research, and clinical applications* (pp. 156–175). Thousand Oaks, CA: Sage.

Santelli, B., Turnbull, A., Sergeant, J., Lerner, E.P., & Marquis. J.G. (1996). Parent to parent programs: Parent preferences for support. *Infants and Young Children*, 9(1), 53–62.

Simpson, R., Kline, S. A., Barnhill, G., & Griswold, D. (2000). Three building blocks of safe and effective schools. *Today's Youth: The Community Circle of Caring Journal*, 4(2), 40–42.

Simpson, R. L., Whelan, R. J., & Zabel, R. H. (1993). Special education personnel preparation in the 21st century: Issues and strategies. *Remedial and Special Education*, 14(2), 7–22.

Singh, N. N., & Curtis, W. J. (1997). Family friendliness of community-based services for children and adolescents with emotional and behavioral disorders and their families: An observational study. *Journal of Emotional & Behavioral Disorders*, 5(2), 82–93.

Tarriff, H. M., & Levine, V. (1993). Involving divorced parents. *Principal*, 73(1), 37–38, 40.

U.S. Census Bureau. (2000). National population briefing, National Population estimates for July 2000. Retrieved June 2002, from http://www.census.gov/statab/www.partla.html.

Weinberg, N., & Sebian, C. (1980). The Bible and disability. *Rehabilitation Counseling Bulletin*, 23(4), 273–281.

Williams, C. B. (1991). Teaching Hispanic deaf students: Lessons from Luis. *Perspectives in Education and Deafness*, 10(2), 2–5.

Wisenkale, S. K., & Heckart, K. E. (1993). Domestic partnerships. *Family relations*, 42, 199–204.

Wolfson, E. (1996). Why should we fight for the freedom to marry? *Journal of Gay, Lesbian, and Bisexual Identity*, 79, 8–12.

Zhang, C., & Bennett, T. (2001). Multicultural views of disability: Implications for early intervention professionals. *Infant-Toddler Intervention: The Transdisciplinary Journal*, 11(2), 143–154.

Zirkel, R. (2002). Are you gay? *Phi Delta Kappan*, 81, 332–333.

CHAPTER 3
Emotional Supports for Parents and Families

●●●●●●●●●●●●●●●●●●●●●○○○○○

In this chapter, you will understand:

- The rationale and need for identifying and serving a range of parent and family emotional and psychological support needs using school and community programs and resources.
- Strategies and options for responding to parent and family emotional and psychological support needs using school programs and resources.
- The importance of community resources for parents and families with emotional and psychological support needs.

Family Perspective: The Hewitts

Kristen and Leonard Hewitt are the biological parents of 13-year-old Kenneth. At an early age Kenneth was diagnosed as having moderate to severe mental retardation and significant delays in cognitive, language, and social development. He also has a history of aggressive behavior toward himself and others, a problem that has worsened as he has approached puberty. Medical treatment of Kenneth's aggression has resulted in some improvement, primarily related to the use of the drug Risperdal. However, the medication has a side effect of repressing feelings of appetite cessation. As a result, Kenneth has become a voracious eater, and his weight has increased to well over 200 pounds. Failure to immediately respond to Kenneth's food requests, especially on the part of his mother, results in aggression. His mother in particular has been the subject of a number of attacks that have resulted in cuts and bruises, including several incidents that have required emergency room treatment. Kenneth also attacked his mother while they were driving in her car, provoked by her unwillingness to stop at a favorite fast-food restaurant in their neighborhood.

Both parents have grown children from previous marriages. Kristen's unmarried and unemployed daughter and her two young children have periodically lived with the Hewitts over the past 3 years, usually for periods of time ranging from 4 weeks to 6 months. These times are stressful for Mr. and Mrs. Hewitt, often related to Mrs. Hewitt's efforts to persuade her daughter to "be more responsible" and to adopt life habits that her daughter characterizes as "contrary to my prairie wind ways." Kenneth also becomes more agitated when Mrs. Hewitt's daughter and grandchildren are in the house and when his normal routines are disrupted. Moreover, Kenneth has on several occasions attempted to attack the two toddlers, and as a result, Mrs. Hewitt's daughter has vowed to never again come to the Hewitts' home. For the past month, the family has been comprised of Mr. and Mrs. Hewitt and Kenneth. However, both parents anticipate that Mrs. Hewitt's daughter will show up anytime without prior notice and request to live in their house.

Approximately a year ago, Kristen Hewitt was diagnosed with lymphoma cancer. Following diagnosis, she began an aggressive treatment program that her doctors tell her seems to be working. However, the weakness and nausea associated with her treatment has made it difficult for her to care for Kenneth. Her treatment-related difficulties have been particularly upsetting to Kenneth, and he has increasingly become aggressive toward his mother. His aggressive responses are significant, taking the form of hitting and kicking his mother when she fails to immediately respond to his wants and needs. That Kenneth has limited expressive language has made it difficult for persons other than his mother to understand what he is requesting. Even though Mr. Hewitt had taken virtually no responsibility for Kenneth's care prior to his wife's illness, he has responded to the family crisis by assuming more and more of the duties involved in Kenneth's care. He has assumed responsibility for getting Kenneth up and ready for school in the morning, and he prepares him for bed in the evening. This division-of-household-labor modification has been beneficial to Mrs. Hewitt; however, Kenneth has not been pleased that his mother is not as involved in his care and support as she was prior to her illness. While the overall level of Kenneth's aggression is less than what was occurring prior to his medication treatment, he nevertheless displays chronic self-directed aggression as well as regularly occurring attempts to hit and kick his parents. This situation has significantly added to the already exceptionally high level of stress experienced by the family.

Mr. and Mrs. Hewitt have investigated foster-home care and residential placement for their son. However, after considerable research and discussion, they have decided that it is their duty to care for their son as long as they are physically able. This decision in no small way was connected to their perception that their son has an extremely talented and dedicated school team. Accordingly, they have decided to keep their son in their home for as long as possible. However, they are also candid in sharing that they are both under considerable emotional and psychological stress and that they require support.

Reflecting on the Family Perspective

1. Identify the primary stressors and psychological and emotional support needs of the Hewitt family.

2. Identify those supports and related services for which school personnel should be responsible, and those supports and services that should be the responsibility of community agency personnel, and others.

◉   ◉   ◉

This chapter discusses the role of schools in addressing the emotional and psychological support needs of parents and families of children and youth with disabilities. We discuss emotional and psychological support needs of parents and families, along with the role of schools in meeting these needs. We also discuss strategies for assisting families and parents to cope with the stress and related issues that often accompany living with a family member with a disability. The chapter also discusses community resources and their role in augmenting the efforts of school resources and personnel in responding to parent and family emotional and related needs.

PARENT AND FAMILY EMOTIONAL AND PSYCHOLOGICAL NEEDS

This chapter is based on the notion that it is imperative that schools acknowledge that parents and families of persons with disabilities are vulnerable to problems associated with emotional and psychological stress, and that they should be willing to assist parents and families in identifying and fully using those supports and coping resources available to them. It is clear that school personnel and school systems cannot assume this responsibility on their own. Accordingly, communities, states, and related entities and organizations must work with school personnel to ensure that parents and families have available suitable options for addressing their emotional support needs. At the same time, however, it is equally clear that school organizations must not renounce their responsibility in this essential related service area. Further discussion on family stress and coping issues can be found in chapter 5.

The existence of higher levels of parental stress among parents and families of children with disabilities when compared to nondisabled groups has been well confirmed for decades (Doll & Bolger, 2000; Floyd & Gallagher, 1997; Friedrich & Friedrich, 1981; Innocenti, Huh, & Boyce, 1992; Kazak & Marvin, 1984). Moreover, the historical assumption that a child with a disability will always cause a negative and pathological reaction within families has prevailed, even in the face of contrary evidence. Indeed, most families learn to cope with the challenges of having a member with special needs or disabilities, sometimes without assistance from outside their family. Moreover, a number of positive family experiences and perceptions are directly associated with children with disabilities. Stainton and Besser (1998), for instance, reported that among parents of children with intellectual disabilities, their children are often a source of happiness; that parents and family members had an increased sense of purpose and priorities; and that parents reported expanded personal and social networks, increased spirituality, and increased tolerance, understanding, and interpersonal strength.

It is clear that not every parent and family of children with a disability will require emotional and psychological support services (Estrada & Pinsof, 1995). Yet, although often neglected, and in spite of the capacity of many parents and families to independently deal with emotional and psychological issues connected to having a family member with a disability, these needs are nevertheless common (Carpenter, 2000). Accordingly, many families of children with disabilities will periodically require or will benefit from emotional and coping support, psychological counseling, and related programs (Reeve & Cobb, 2000; Schalock & Alonso, 2002). That many parents and families of children and adolescents with disabilities periodically experience crisis, conflicts, and related problems makes the need for support services even more apparent (Schalock & Alonso, 2002).

The extent to which psychological and emotional support needs are addressed will have a significant impact on the quality of life and overall functioning of a child and family (Blaska, 1998; Schalock & Alonso, 2002). Some of these needs, such as self-determination assistance, advocacy aid, accessibility problems, and identification of resources to meet assistive technology requirements, will be directly connected to assisting a family member with a disability, albeit without specifically focusing on family emotional and psychological support matters. Other needs for family support, such as employment assistance, social security application interpretation, health care support, housing, legal aid, and program options for persons experiencing abuse and neglect, may be indirectly related to a child with a disability. Of course, the aforementioned examples of needs have traditionally not been the responsibility of most school personnel. These needs will nevertheless impact a family, including members' emotional and psychological resolve and ability to cope. Thus, when ignored or inadequately dealt with, these unmet needs will often increase family stress and other difficulties; for example, exacerbating school problems experienced by a student with a disability (Fine & Nissenbaum, 2000; Sharpley & Bitsika, 1997; Sivberg, 2002).

The impact of a child's disability on a family's emotional and psychological functioning and coping capacity is a topic on which much has been written (Fine & Nissenbaum, 2000; Foster, 1988; Seligman & Darling, 1997; Simpson, 1996; Turnbull & Turnbull, 2001). Yet, relatively little is specifically and scientifically known about this important topic, including effective practices and related strategies that may be used by school personnel to assist parents and families in addressing their emotional and psychological needs. That many schools have chosen to ignore these needs or have assumed that community organizations are fully responsible for addressing these issues has further contributed to problems of identifying and implementing cost-effective and efficacious parent and family support programs.

We are in agreement with Buscaglia's (1975) time-honored and sage observation that "a disability is not a desirable thing and there is no reason to believe otherwise. It will, in most cases, cause pain, discomfort, embarrassment, tears, confusion and the expenditure of a great deal of time and money" (p. 11). A child with a disability will almost always create conditions leading to additional stress and unique challenges for his or her family. Frustration related to unfulfilled expectations, increased medical and other expenses associated with a disability, and increased time requirements related to caring for a family member with special needs are only a few of the hurdles that families face. While some families may choose to deal with these matters using internal resources and other intrafamily options, it is nevertheless clear that families generally benefit from knowing that there are knowledgeable and skilled support professionals who are available to help them understand and cope with the emotional and stress-related challenges that accompany a disability (Bauer & Shea, 2003; Fine & Nissenbaum, 2000; Koegel et al., 1992).

As previously noted, it is our experience and assumption that parents and families of individuals with disabilities periodically require emotional and psychological support to assist them in coping with and accommodating the special needs of family members with disabilities. Even though this premise has not been subjected to extensive scientific scrutiny, it is widely accepted. However, the specific emotional and psychological support needs of families are often poorly understood and vary significantly in accordance with individual family and community variables (Bailey, 2001). Furthermore, even when parent and family support programs are available, they often have been designed by school and clinical professionals based on outdated and nonempirical assumptions and literature (Buck, 1950; Gorham, 1975; Love, 1973). Accordingly, programs based on outdated and inaccurate principles and assumptions have unfortunately failed to fully address and support the needs of parents and families. For example, some family support programs have been designed on the premise that there are common and predictable family and parent reactions to children with disabilities, and that those family members will generally have similar emotional reactions and experiences relative to a family member with a disability. In this regard, we are in agreement with professionals who have observed that individual person and family differences more commonly characterize parent and family members' responses to children with disabilities than do common and predictable reactions (Blacher, 1984; Carpenter, 2000; Wright & Stegelin, 2003). Increasingly, practitioners and researchers are recognizing that parent and family reactions and experiences associated with children with disabilities vary in accordance with a number of factors, including (a) parent gender, age, health, and the nature of a child's disability (Sharpley & Bitsika, 1997; Weiss, 2002); (b) informational and emotional and psychological resources and availability of accommodation supports (Fine & Simpson, 2000); (c) parent and family structures such as members' role assignments and expectations (Fine & Nissenbaum, 2000); (d) family strength and level of functioning, including cohesion, communication, trust, and flexibility (Bauer & Shea, 2003; Kazak & Marvin, 1984); (e) family composition, including the number, ages, involvement, and health of its members (Schilling, Kirkham, Snow, & Schinke, 1996); (f) economic variables, including resources available to assist in the support of family members with special needs (Blacher, 1984; Fine & Nissenbaum, 2000); and (g) numerous other variables that are linked to family characteristics (Barnett & Boyce, 1995; Fewell & Gelb, 1983; Karp, 1996). In accordance with this reality, it is essential that school and community professionals address parent and family needs using models and strategies that emphasize individual assessment of family emotional, psychological, and coping needs;

that parents and families be placed in prominent positions of authority relative to identifying their support and coping needs; and that a variety of practical options for addressing these needs be available to meet individual family needs.

THE ROLE OF SCHOOLS AND SCHOOL PERSONNEL IN SUPPORTING PARENT AND FAMILY EMOTIONAL, PSYCHOLOGICAL, AND COPING NEEDS

The heterogeneous and ever-changing emotional and psychological circumstances of families of children and adolescents with disabilities defy conventional, rigid, and simplistic need-assumption and service models. Effectively serving the coping and related support needs of parents and families requires flexible and dynamic programming by school personnel along with support from community and clinical organizations. Moreover, parent and family emotional and psychological assistance programs are most effective when based on a foundation of generic support elements in conjunction with availability of flexibly designed specific systems that address unique needs. Consistent with this orientation, we discuss in the following sections generic and foundational supports along with specialized school-based programs that have promise for assisting parents and families with their emotional, psychological, and coping needs. Elements of these discussions can also be found in other chapters of this book (see chapter 5).

Effective Educational Programs for Students with Disabilities

Ensuring that students with disabilities are provided an effective educational program is not uniquely a matter of parent and family member emotional and psychological support. That is, school programs may be crafted to address students' campus-based needs, with little or no consideration of parent and family support. It is nevertheless quite clear that failure to provide parent and family support will increase emotional and psychological stress, anger, agitation, and anxiety among parents and families.

As a baseline and foundation condition, it is important that parents and families of students receive information about student progress and outcomes from educational personnel. That is, not only must students receive an effective education, but parents and family members must receive information and assurances that the individualized needs of their family member are being met, they must be provided with evidence that students are making appropriate progress, and they must be made aware of day-to-day occurrences at school. Moreover, we consider it mandatory that parents and other family members be partners in the program selection, implementation, and evaluation process. Accordingly, an effective educational program is clearly a foundational element of a supportive parent and family program. Indeed, schools must provide assurances to parents and family members that students are in physically and emotionally secure environments that are staffed by qualified and committed individuals and that the teachers and staff members who are responsible for their children's education are using effective methods and curricula. This process includes dissemination of objective information and data that demonstrate that children and youth are making acceptable rates of progress on salient and pivotal educational objectives, and that parents and family members are partners whose voices are heard relative to their involvement in making important educational decisions.

Parent and family emotional, psychological, and coping needs cannot be satisfactorily addressed merely by offering students with disabilities an effective educational program. Yet, it is evident that high-quality educational programming is a baseline condition on which other emotional, psychological, and coping support elements are based.

Formation and Maintenance of Trust-Oriented Relationships with Parents and Families

Relative to parent/family and professional relationships, trust is the foundation on which emotional and psychological support programs are based. Indeed, little is accomplished in the absence of trust, and emotional and psychological assistance, collaboration, and partnerships will be dependent on trust-based relationships and interactions (Adelman, 1994; Friend & Cook, 2004; Rogers, 1969; Schalock & Alonso, 2002).

Dependability is a salient element of trust, which is the belief that an individual will conscientiously and reliably perform in accordance with agreed-on rules and expectations. Persons who are trusted can be counted on to reliably behave in accordance with specified agreements and prescribed standards. To understand, explore, and adapt to the often stressful circumstances with which they are confronted, and to ultimately experience emotional and psychological comfort and growth, parents and family members of persons with disabilities need to know that the individuals who are educating their children and with whom they are working will faithfully make decisions that have students' and family members' interests in the forefront, and that these professionals will maintain family confidence and otherwise demonstrate their trustworthiness.

That psychological growth and enhanced coping skills require that individuals be willing to take interpersonal risks and reveal sensitive and confidential elements of themselves and their families when necessary and appropriate underscores the importance of trust. Thus, the risk-taking and change elements that often underpin new coping strategies require that parents and family members be open to new ways of perceiving situations and to considering novel strategies for dealing with problems and challenges. Such willingness occurs best when parents and family members have confidence and trust in the school personnel with whom they and their child are involved.

Trusting relationships, and the conditions for effective collaboration with which they are connected, rarely occur without significant effort and time. Indeed, to facilitate robust and enduring trusting relationships, professionals must first create an atmosphere of safety, and then must maintain this atmosphere over an extended period of time. That is, parents and family members must be confident that professionals will do what they say they will do, that the best interests and preferences of children and families will be primary considerations in the decisions they make, and that professionals will maintain the confidence of the student and family members in a variety

---

COMMUNICATION AND COLLABORATION TIPS   BOX 3.1

Trust-Enhancement Suggestions for Use with Parents and Families

Maintain a positive and sincere demeanor with parents and family members.

Strive to be sensitive and accepting of the emotional and psychological needs of parents and families.

Demonstrate respect and professionalism related to personal and sensitive information that individuals share.

Be willing to acknowledge your limitations and the limitations of your school district or organization in meeting the emotional and psychological needs of parents and family members, and recognize that community organizations are available to assist in meeting parent and family members' emotional and coping needs.

Don't make hasty judgments about parents and family members.

Avoid making promises that you may not be able to keep.

Include parents and family members in decisions related to students.

Engage in activities that will allow an understanding of students' home lives and circumstances.

Follow through with what you say you will do.

Demonstrate warmth and genuine regard when interacting with parents and family members.

Encourage parents and family members to take risks related to considering novel coping strategies.

Remember that trust is a process that takes time to develop.

---

of situations over time. Communication and Collaboration Tips Box 3.1 provides trust-enhancement suggestions for use with parents and family members.

A long-held trust-based notion that has withstood the test of time is that an authentic display of regard and warmth for parents and family members can be used to promote a safe, trusting, supportive, and collaborative atmosphere needed for family–professional partnerships (Friend & Cook, 2004; Kroth, 1985). Decades ago, Rogers (1962) termed this positive demeanor and attitude "positive regard," and argued that only in the presence of therapeutic and humanistic warmth and genuine regard can collaborative and supportive relationships develop and thrive. Even though most educators are not trained counselors and therapists, they nevertheless can significantly promote parent and family members' interpersonal growth and emotional security via a positive and caring demeanor. Such an attitude of positive regard and related behaviors also promotes greater willingness on the part of parents and family members to collaborate with professionals, including jointly taking responsibility for seeking solutions to problems and differences of opinion.

Relationships between families and professionals that are grounded in trust are those wherein both parties acknowledge they are advocates for children, albeit based on different roles, perspectives, experiences, knowledge, and skills. That is, based on their respective roles, parents, family members, and educators are trusted to independently analyze and respond to situations in a fashion that has children's interests as the guiding beacon. Such an attitude supports the notion that collaboratively achieved solutions will, in the majority of cases, best meet students' and families' needs. Such a process necessitates that professionals and family members be sensitive to the perceptions and perspectives of others, and that they be willing to attempt to understand and be sensitive to their frame of reference. Such a process promotes a collaborative, solution-oriented problem-solving process that is characterized by openness to a number of possible solutions to problems that inevitably arise in the course of children's education. Moreover, it tends to steer both professionals and family members away from such behaviors as blaming, criticizing, and so forth. Finally, according to a variety of authorities (Hoover-Dempsey, Bassler, & Brissie, 1992; Wright & Stegelin, 2003), such problem-solving efforts promote parent and family empowerment, confidence, and feelings of efficacy, which are essential components of emotional and interpersonal support.

Honesty and integrity are clearly essential ingredients of trust and collaboration. Thus, independent of other factors, professionals and family members must be honest and consistently demonstrate in their day-to-day actions the characteristics of rectitude, respectability, loyalty, and faithfulness. Rogers (1969) termed this interpersonal skill authenticity, noting that "when the facilitator is a real person, being what he is, entering into a relationship with the learner without a front or facade, he is more likely to be effective" (p. 106). As with honesty, awareness of and sensitivity to value issues are central to establishing and maintaining a trust-based and emotionally supportive relationship with students and their families (Bailey, 2001; Bauer & Shea, 2003; Sontag & Schacht, 1994; Turnbull, Turnbull, Erwin, & Soodak, 2005). As thoroughly discussed in chapter 2, the ever-changing, divergent, and contradictory values of our world make understanding myriad values and beliefs a challenging task for every educator. An awareness of one's personal values and an openness and sensitivity to others' beliefs and values thus bodes well for promoting supportive and trusting relationships with parents and families.

The Trust Assessment Questionnaire shown in Communication and Collaboration Tips Box 3.2 is a self-assessment measure designed to evaluate an individual's capacity for creating trusting and collaborative relationships with parents and family members. Evaluations of an individual's willingness, tolerance, or comfort in taking certain actions or allowing certain things to occur is measured by noting the degree of security and comfort using the continuum of "very secure and comfortable" to "very insecure and uncomfortable." Although informal and without standardized norms, this measure can be used to gauge an individual's trust position and to informally assess changes on this variable over time. The questionnaire can also be used to compare personal perceptions with those held by colleagues and families.

Effective Communication as an Emotional and Psychological Support Foundation

Not surprisingly, the importance of effective communication in furthering parent and family emotional and psychological support has been prominently noted for decades. For instance, Dewey (1938) suggested that listening is a key element of effective communication and a significant vehicle for facilitating feelings of acceptance and value in others. Dale Carnegie (1936) similarly noted that effective communication involves,

---

COMMUNICATION AND COLLABORATION TIPS   BOX 3.2

Trust Assessment Questionnaire

	1 Very Secure/ Comfortable	2	3 Neutral	4	5 Very Insecure/ Uncomfortable

1. Telling parents/families you made a mistake related to their child.
2. Telling parents/families that another teacher or professional made a mistake related to their child.
3. Telling parents/families that you don't know.
4. Telling parents/families that you recommend that they or their child seek therapy.
5. Confronting parents and family members.
6. Displaying your emotions in front of parents and families, e.g., anger, sorrow, and so forth.
7. Having parents and families observe you teaching.
8. Defending and explaining your curriculum, teaching methods, and so forth.
9. Making parents "equal partners" in school meetings.
10. Making available records and materials for parents and family members to review.

---

by its very nature, demonstrating interest in another person, and thus is a basic means of establishing rapport. Accordingly, although often overlooked because of its ubiquitous nature and perceived simplicity, use of effective communication methods with parents and family members of students with disabilities is an essential and foundational emotional and psychological support tool.

Accordingly, while the content of interactions between professionals and families cannot be discounted, neither can the listening and communication process itself. Commenting on this importance, a variety of authorities (Bauer & Shea, 2003; Wright & Stegelin, 2003) have observed that the technical information provided by professionals may be secondary to the listening and communication process itself. Capturing this theme in an often quoted historically significant remark, Rogers (1962) commented that "the quality of my encounter is more important in the long run than is my scholarly knowledge, my professional training, my counseling orientation, the techniques I use in the interview" (p. 416). Thus, educators and other professionals are advised to recognize the communication process as not only an opportunity to attend to and learn from parents and family members, but also a key means of showing interest and conveying emotional and psychological support. Furthermore, effective listening also sets the stage for stress-reduction strategies and introducing coping-skill plans and recommendations.

In spite of general agreement on the importance of listening, professionals lack agreement on the salient elements of the process. Nevertheless, basic styles of listening are recognized, including active and passive types (Goldenberg & Goldenberg, 2002; Kroth, 1985). The demeanor and behavior of passive listeners is generally considered to be a style that facilitates others' talking. Accordingly, this type of listener may encourage parents and family members to share information about their attitudes, feelings, goals, aspirations, and frustrations and to generally support and promote their talking. In contrast to passive listeners, active listeners are thought to be more directly and openly interactive. That is, active listening involves significant verbal and nonverbal reactivity when compared to passive responding. However, both active and passive listening styles are useful in creating an emotionally and psychologically supportive environment for parents and family members. Individuals tend to use a particular listening style because of a natural preference for interacting with others, and to gear their interactions to match a philosophical approach or to accomplish a particular goal. Both listening styles involve a willingness to listen to parents and family members and their points of view, and thus both can serve to create an emotionally and psychologically supportive environment. Regardless of professionals' listening style, a willingness to create an appropriate interpersonal environment and to otherwise use effective communication skills is an essential foundation element for making parents and family members active participants and collaborators and creating supportive and growth-enhancing relationships (Turnbull et al., 2005). That parents and family members are able to share important information about their children that professionals often have no way of otherwise obtaining or knowing, and because parents and family members have a legal and ethical right to program involvement, further adds to the importance of creating a suitable listening environment.

Communication-based emotional and psychological supports for parents and family members also include an awareness and sensitivity to their affective needs and emotional messages. In this connection, we encourage professionals to be sensitive to the feelings of parents and family members as well as to the manifest content of their messages. This important process involves individuals' listening for the emotional and unstated elements of interactions as well as overt content. This process of empathy, derived from a Greek term that means "suffering in," involves extending an understanding attitude wherein professionals attempt to experience, understand, and accept the world and situation of parents and family members, frequently without challenge. The climate created by such a process not only facilitates acceptance of parent and family situations, but the process of attempting to understand their internal world advances the process of information sharing, collaboration, and emotional and psychological support as well. The affective listening process is based on various strategies, including professionals' reflecting back to parents and family members the feelings that were sensed or heard, offering clarifying statements when comments or information are unclear, restating or paraphrasing content, and using silence to facilitate an interactive process (Cobb & Reeve, 1991; Ekman, 1964; Friend & Cook, 2004; Simpson, 1996).

The ability of educators and other professionals to accurately listen and to communicate with parents and family members is a primary skill needed for obtaining and disseminating information. Just as important, the creation of an appropriate listening and communication environment is a primary first step in supporting the emotional and psychological needs of parents and family members. Hence, this baseline process serves as the foundation for introducing and recommending coping, stress reduction, intervention, and other emotional and psychological support programs. In this connection, Communication and Collaboration Tips Box 3.3 identifies several tips related to listening and communication.

Educators' Emotional and Psychological Support Referral Role

School and community professionals have a shared responsibility to assist parents and families in addressing their need for emotional and psychological support and identification of coping strategies (Lawson & Sailor, 2000). As noted previously, school personnel and school organizations play a primary and ongoing role in creating the foundation for emotional supports. That is, through development of collabo-

---

COMMUNICATION AND COLLABORATION TIPS   **BOX 3.3**

Communication and Listening Enhancement Suggestions Related to Parents and Family

Be willing to include parents and family members in discussions related to relevant information that is received about students.

Don't patronize parents and family members.

Be sensitive to the body language and verbal and nonverbal messages of parents and family members.

Strive to create an environment wherein others will be comfortable in speaking.

Allow parents opportunities to talk and share information.

Don't ignore the emotional and stress-related messages and remarks of parents and family members.

Remember that you can likely learn as much from parents and family members as they can learn from you.

Demonstrate a genuine interest in what others are saying, rather than looking at notes or materials, planning what you will say next, and so forth.

Allow time in every meeting for parents and family members to share their agenda and perspectives.

Avoid becoming angry, defensive, argumentative, or critical, even if provoked by others.

rative and partner-oriented relationships, trust, and effective communication and information-exchange programs, parents and family members are afforded basic supports needed to deal with child and family disability-related issues and challenges. Yet, because school personnel and school organizations do not typically have the resources and expertise to address the entire spectrum of parent and family emotional and psychological needs, community efforts and school-based community programs are required (Foster, 1988; Seligman & Darling, 1997; Weiss, 2002; Wright & Stegelin, 2003). Of course, not all parents and families of children with disabilities will require emotional, psychological, and coping support and assistance. Yet, these needs will periodically surface in many families and some family members can be expected to have a significant and ongoing need for support (Reeve & Cobb, 2000; Schalock & Alonso, 2002; Sharpley & Bitsika, 1997). Thus, these needs warrant attention, even though they have historically been neglected and underserved, and even though current school financial problems, policy reforms, and foci of education leaders make an emphasis on or allocation of significant new resources to support parent and family emotional needs unlikely.

Accordingly, administrators, teachers, and related service personnel, particularly school counselors, school social workers, and school psychologists, are encouraged to become more adept at referring parents and family members to appropriate community programs, personnel, agencies, and organizations for psychological counseling and other forms of clinical and social assistance (Bauer & Shea, 2003; Fine & Nissenbaum, 2000).

Obviously, educators and other school professionals need to have a good working knowledge of school and community programs and resources to effectively fulfill their role of serving the array of emotional and psychological needs of the parents and family members that they can be expected to encounter. Such knowledge includes the referral processes for obtaining services, financial information for program use, types of services available, criteria for program participation, and other details that parents and family members will require.

Finally, it is important that school personnel be made aware that when they are able to assist parents and others in actually contacting key individuals connected to recommended services, and when they are able to assist in circumventing the bureaucratic and often cumbersome steps that are associated with social service and mental health programs, access to and use of programs and services are significantly increased.

Ideally, the mental health and emotional needs of parents and families are served through collaborative community school partnership programs (Dunst, Trivette, & Snyder, 2000; Franklin & Streeter, 1998; Sailor & Skrtic, 1996). As we discuss in chapters 6 and 7, the organization of community agency partnerships permits clinical, social, agency, and other community organizations to offer counseling, home-based intervention training, crisis-intervention, problem-solving, stress-reduction, and coping programs, and related emotional and psychological supports on a school campus. Similarly, medical and social agency services may also be included as part of community–school partnerships (Wright & Stegelin, 2003).

Individual and Group Emotional and Psychological Counseling and Other Psychological Supports for Parents and Families

Addressing parent and family emotional and psychological needs includes providing options for individuals needing group and individual support, information, counseling, and therapeutic intervention (Bauer & Shea, 2003; Patterson, 1986). These programs and strategies range from prevention and promotion of social and emotional health to those that focus on mental health problems and mental disorders of students and families. While such services can be provided by both school personnel and community professionals, mental health professionals and clinical professionals more commonly undertake mental health problem treatment, especially in regard to more severe problems (Rones & Hoagwood, 2000). In contrast, school personnel tend to concentrate more on information dissemination, prevention, and short-term emotional support and coping strategies (Policy Leadership Cadre for Mental Health in School, 2001).

According to Reeve and Cobb (2000), counseling "may be thought of primarily as educative, facilitative or remedial" (p. 178). The *educative* element relates to information sharing, including making available to parents and family members resources that discuss the nature, prevalence, characteristics, etiology, and progression of specific disabilities. School personnel, including teachers and related service professionals, are well positioned and typically well qualified to provide this type of counseling. Depending on the nature of the educational needs of parents and family members, and the nature of the organization, community agency, and community service, nonschool professionals are also typically competent in addressing this need. Parents and family members of individuals with disabilities may also be involved in educative counseling programs, either as members of a counseling team or through programs that independently have parents and family members serve as support-group coordinators.

Clarence Walters is a special education teacher in an elementary school. His students are identified as having mild disabilities, and all of the children spend significant numbers of hours in general education settings. One of Clarence's students, Sally, is a child with a learning disability. Sally's mother and father are actively involved in their daughter's life and education, and sought information about the causes of learning disabilities. Partially because Sally's father indicated he thought he had an undiagnosed learning disability and partially to satisfy their curiosity about learning more about their child's school-related difficulties, they asked Mr. Walters for reading recommendations on the topic of learning characteristics and learning problems. Mr. Walters not only provided a list of books, articles, and Web sites, but he extended an invitation to meet with them to discuss any questions they had over the materials. He also connected the parents to a parent group that regularly met to discuss issues related to children with learning disabilities.

Facilitative counseling involves attempting to support emotional and stress-related needs of individuals while at the same time providing utilitarian information related to particular issues. In this connection, Reeve and Cobb (2000) observed that "The facilitative component involves assisting the family in identifying its strengths and developing new ways of coping with the inevitable stresses of having a member with a disability" (p. 179). As with educative counseling, facilitative counseling can be undertaken by both school personnel and community agencies and community professionals, depending on the nature of the issues and needs of parents and family members. Parents and family members may also assist in facilitative counseling programs and activities.

Kay Lackey, a school social worker for a large urban school district, met with Arnold and his mother biweekly during his last semester of public school enrollment. Arnold was a 19-year-old youth who had been identified with a severe psychiatric disorder in elementary school, and who attended a public-school alternative program during high school. Arnold's mother was particularly concerned about Arnold's postschool job and support options as well as opportunities for him to live on his own at some future point. Lackey's facilitative counseling largely took the form of connecting Arnold and his mother with social agency resources they could use after he left public school (vocational rehabilitation, social security). She also worked with Arnold's mother on management options that were based on natural consequences and making Arnold more responsible for his decisions and choices.

Remedial counseling involves use of more therapeutic interventions than are used in educative and facilitative counseling. Reeve and Cobb (2000) described remedial counseling as "targeting dysfunctional patterns and developing strategies for helping parents to correct a problem" (p. 179). They also observed that this form of counseling may involve professionals "assessing the interactions among family members and perhaps teaching entirely new patterns of relating to each other" (p. 179). Remedial and other forms of therapeutic counseling are more often done by mental health professionals, although school personnel may also have the skill and training to provide such services. Thus, depending on the organizational structure and resource allocation for parent and family support, school professionals may also be involved in providing therapeutic services.

Terri Jenkins is a licensed psychologist who works for a large suburban school district. Her position as a school psychologist is unique in that she spends approximately half her time doing parent training and therapeutic counseling. In this role, she became acquainted with Dan Rawlings, a preschooler enrolled in the district's early intervention program. Terri worked intensively with Dan's parents, including at her school district office and in their home. Her work initially focused on teaching Dan's parents management skills and strategies they could use in their home and community. Subsequent to bringing Dan under better control at home and school, their meetings shifted to discussions of Dan's mother and father disagreeing over their child-rearing roles and responsibilities. Dan's father worked full time, and because his wife was a stay-at-home mom, he believed that child-related duties were primarily her responsibility. In contrast, Dan's mother was overwhelmed with the responsibility of dealing with her son alone. Her stress and the couple's disagreements were viewed by Terri as significant impediments to their creating a maximally supportive family environment. Subsequent to several weeks of counseling, Terri referred the parents to a marriage counselor for additional therapy.

Counseling and other emotional and psychological supports for parents and families can often be delivered within group settings. Groups allow for greater cost and time efficiency as well as the benefits connected to the informational and therapeutic interactions that occur among participants (Dryfoos & Maguire, 2002; Miller & Hudson, 1994; Simpson, 1996). That is, parents and family members may learn from other participants about issues and points of view that are directly relevant to them and their family. Groups of individuals who are members of families with children with disabilities are uniquely related to their members' experiences, and thus they offer an exceptional forum for individuals to share and discuss their perceptions, attitudes, and feelings related to the challenges of living with and raising a child with a disability (Blank, Melaville, & Shah, 2003; Rutherford & Edgar, 1979). Group forums provide support for parents and families as well as respite from the social isolation that these individuals often experience.

School-run groups that provide emotional and other supports for parents and family members can be structured to address a variety of informational needs, including information about particular disabilities, descriptions of educational programs, and evaluation methods for assessing student and program outcomes. Group formats can also be used to help parents and family members become more effective consumers of educational services and advocates for their member with a disability, including their rights and responsibilities relative to their special-needs child and strategies for more effectively participating in educational conferences. Similarly, groups can be used to train parents and family members to use effective-practice behavior management methods (see chapters 6 and 9) and to function as tutors for their child in home settings (see chapters 6 and 10). As previously discussed, a group format can be used for parent and family support groups, stress management groups, venues for discussing coping strategies, and for presenting strategies for facilitating communication and enhancing family relationships (Dinkmeyer & Mckay, 1976; Goldenberg & Goldenberg, 2002; Gordon, 2000).

Conflict Resolution Programs and Strategies

Conflicts between educators and other professionals and parents and family members are not only inevitable but also beneficial, when conflict is defined as normally occurring differences of opinion regarding perceptions, goals, expectations, and so forth. That is, related to their unique experiences and roles and connected to their knowledge, skills, attitudes, and expectations and myriad other variables, families and professionals can be expected to have differences of opinion regarding the needs and preferred strategies for students with disabilities. It is these differences that offer great potential for collaborative problem solving and creative partnerships. In no way does such a conceptualization of conflict detract from the need for rapport, trust, effective communication, and parent–professional partnerships. Indeed, when parents, family members, and professionals are able to discuss their unique opinions and otherwise interact in a constructive and open fashion regarding their differences, collaborative partnerships and creative problem solving, along with enhanced communication, can be expected (Covey, 1989; Goldenberg & Goldenberg, 2002). It is equally clear that when professionals and parents fail to recognize these dissimilarities and when these differences are not openly discussed and dealt with, that unhealthy and unproductive conflicts may occur. Hence, professional–parent differences of opinion can power collaborative partnerships and facilitate problem solving, or they can contribute to communication and trust difficulties along with other emotional and psychological problems, depending on how they are responded to and accommodated (Fiedler & Swanger, 2000).

Without a means of voicing differences of opinion with regard to positions, policies, and decisions of educators and other professionals, parents and family members will fail to have a real say in making decisions that affect their children. Under such conditions, it is far more likely that parents and family members will display unhealthy forms of conflict, such as anger, increased frustration and stress, and so forth. When parents and family members are forced to express their differences of opinion and other conflicts via such means, professional–parent communication, trust, and rapport will be negatively affected. Moreover, parent and family stress and children's progress may also be affected (Simpson, 1996; Wright & Stegelin, 2003). Accordingly, strategies and programs for managing parent and family-member conflict are significant emotional and psychological support elements.

As suggested above, preventive management of opinion differences is a far more productive and effective strategy than attempting to remediate unhealthy conflict after it arises. Thus, school professionals' preventive measures are essential. Such measures include (a) creating forums and opportunities for parents and family members to voice their opinions and to participate in collaborative activities with school personnel; (b) maintaining an open and ongoing exchange of information between school professionals and parents and family members such that both groups are kept abreast of events and matters that affect children; (c) offering to train and otherwise inform parents and family members about policies, procedures, and protocol that are followed in developing, implementing, and evaluating programs for children and youth with disabilities; and (d) striving to develop and maintain positive levels of trust between educators and families. These elements are not independently applied as parent and family member emotional and psychological support strategies. Rather, these variables, when used in an ongoing fashion as part of an integrated parent and family interaction program, have the effect of serving as emotional and psychological support mechanisms.

Effective conflict management and prevention of conflict-related problems may be facilitated by use of four basic strategies: (a) a functional and accurate use of factual information; (b) a willingness on the part of professionals to collaboratively make decisions and to take action and create change that best serves the needs of students; (c) an ability to gain administrative and other institutional supports for collaborative decisions; and (d) use of effective communication and problem-solving skills (conflict resolution skills are more fully discussed in chapter 8). Related to conflict management, the *functional and accurate use of factual information* is a reference to the need for accurate and current background and protocol information, policies and guidelines, mandated procedures, records related to differences of opinion, and so forth. Although factual information rarely serves by itself to quell differences of opinion and otherwise resolve conflicts, it does serve as a foundation for understanding and responding to these differences. For example, members of a family who wanted to alter the categories of information on their child's IEP, relative to a desire to make IEP meetings more time efficient, were permitted to offer their opinion of what they considered to be salient individualized planning recommendations. However, school-district personnel indicated that they were required to follow guidelines prescribed by district and state policy.

Replete in this book is the notion that *collaborative decision making and a willingness to take action and create change that best serves the need of students* is a sine qua non of an effective parent/family and professional partnership. Relative to conflict management, this factor refers to professionals using their decision-making authority and power to create change in a prudent and supportive fashion. That is, professionals are encouraged to demonstrate a conscientious and reliable willingness to take action when it is needed, and to make their actions based on input from various stakeholders. Although it is clear that professionals must ultimately make many decisions, and that these decisions may not always be based on consensus, participants must nevertheless be given opportunities to have their voices heard and to otherwise offer input relative to decisions that affect their children and families.

Conflict management and prevention of unhealthy conflicts also involves professionals' and other stakeholders' *obtaining support from administrative and other institutional bodies for their decisions*. Thus, policy makers, board members, senior administrators, and others must be included in the decision-making and collaborative process. This basic rule is even more significant when collaboratively based decisions and recommendations may appear to be inconsistent with stated policies, albeit in the best interests of students and families. For example, the principal of an elementary school, on behalf of the IEP team of a student with autism, advocated to the director of special education and superintendent of schools to permit the student's mother to be paid a mileage allowance to transport the boy to and from school. While the request was not in compliance with the school district's transportation policy, the parents and student's teacher presented compelling information to the IEP team that the sensory problems of the boy were heightened by the noise and smells associated with the bus experience. The principal subsequently successfully argued to the superintendent and special education administrator that deviating from the set transportation policy served the best interests of the student and his family

Finally, *the use of effective communication and problem-solving skills* is both basic and essential to managing differences of opinion and preventing unhealthy professional–family conflicts. Included in this all-important recommendation is that school and community professionals be sensitive to the psychological, emotional, and other needs of parents and family members; that they acknowledge and attempt to understand the issues and challenges that families of students with disabilities confront; and that they willingly permit them to serve as collaborative partners on behalf of their children.

The Hewitts Revisited

Kristen and Leonard Hewitt continue to struggle to provide a safe and supportive home for Kenneth. In spite of Kenneth's difficulties, including continuing occasional acts of aggression toward members of his family and others, progress has occurred. Accordingly, Mr. and Mrs. Hewitt perceive themselves to be less stressed and more in control of their son and their own lives, and, therefore, better able to manage their home and family responsibilities.

Mr. Hewitt has become more resolute and practiced in managing his son. Moreover, he is more comfortable in interacting with Kenneth and enjoys the time he and his son spend together. Mr. Hewitt credits this positive change to two primary factors. First, observing and interacting with Kenneth's teacher relative to working with and managing his son has made him more confident that he has the skills to successfully direct and interact with Kenneth. The second factor that Mr. Hewitt attributes this improvement to is time. He notes that as he and Kenneth have been spending more time together, they have bonded and have become more comfortable with the relationship.

Mr. and Mrs. Hewitt have also sought out the support of a therapist and appear to have benefited from her guidance and suggestions. In particular, their time in therapy has led them to structure their daughter's visits to their home by establishing conditions and contingencies prior to her moving in with them. The psychotherapist has also worked with Mr. and Mrs. Hewitt regarding Kristen Hewitt's medical condition, their changing family responsibilities connected to Mrs. Hewitt's illness and treatment, and long-term planning for Kenneth. That the referral for the therapist was made by Kenneth's school team has made Kristen and Leonard Hewitt even more appreciative and aware of their role in supporting their family. This support role has also strengthened the home–school communication link and led to more effective information sharing and collaboration.

SUMMARY STATEMENTS

- Parents and family members connected to children with disabilities can be expected to have a range of emotional and psychological support needs.
- School and community programs and resources are responsible for and needed to accommodate the emotional, psychological, and coping needs of parents and families of students with disabilities.
- A variety of school- and community–professional-applied strategies are available for supporting parent and family emotional and psychological needs.
- Parent and family emotional and psychological needs are most effectively and efficiently addressed when school and community professionals are involved in service planning and delivery.

QUESTIONS FOR DISCUSSION

1. Identify the emotional, psychological, and coping strengths and needs of the parents and family members of a child with a disability.
2. Identify strategies that will most effectively satisfy the needs you perceive the family you identified in question 1 to have. Include in your analysis the individuals or organizations, including school and community professionals, who are best suited to address these needs.

RESOURCES FOR FAMILY SUPPORT

- **National Mental Health Consumers' Self-Help Clearinghouse**
  (www.mhselfhelp.org)
  A Web site with multiple sources of information, including consumer information and referrals, consultation, a consumer library, a newsletter, and a consumer-supported nationwide database.

- **National Respite Locator Service**
  (www.respitelocator.org/)
  This Web site provides a state respite-care provider database.

- **Pacer Center: Parent Advocacy Coalition for Educational Rights**
  (www.pacer.org)

  A variety of user-friendly materials and resources, including resource links and publications, are available on this site.

- **Frontier Mental Health Services Resource Network**
  (www.wiche.edu/mentalhealth/frontier)

  This Web site provides information and technical assistance regarding mental health programs and resources, particularly in rural areas.

- **Parents Helping Parents: The Parent-Directed Family Resource Center for Children with Special Needs**
  (www.php.com)

  This Web site provides a variety of resource ideas and options for families of children with special needs.

- **National Institute of Mental Health**
  (www.nimh.nih.gov)

  This Web site provides information on a variety of mental disorders that impact children, adolescents, and adults.

- **National Technical Assistance Center for Children's Mental Health**
  (http://gucdc.georgetown.edu/)

  This site provides information and monographs, consultation, and agency and organization collaboration recommendations.

- **National Technical Assistance Center (NTAC) for State Mental Health Planning**
  (www.nasmhpd.org/ntac.cfm)

  This site provides state, regional, and national consultation; conference information; and technical assistance.

- **Technical Assistance Partnership for Child and Family Mental Health**
  (www.tapartnership.org/)

  This site focuses on technical assistance and related resources.

REFLECTION ACTIVITIES

1. Based on your experiences and the information presented in this chapter, identify emotional and psychological support needs experienced by parents and families of children with disabilities.
2. Request that a parent(s) or family critique and otherwise evaluate the emotional and psychological support needs you identified in Reflection Activity 1.
3. Recommend school and community resources and programs that would address the emotional and psychological support needs you identify for a family of a child or youth with a disability.

4. Request that a parent(s) or family critique and otherwise evaluate the school and community resources and programs that you recommended for addressing the emotional and psychological support needs you identified in Reflection Activity 3.

REFERENCES

Adelman, H. (1994). Intervening to enhance home involvement in schooling. *Intervention in School and Clinic, 29*(5), 276–287.

Bailey, D. B. (2001). Evaluating parent involvement and family support in early intervention and preschool programs. *Journal of Early Intervention, 24*(1), 1–14.

Barnett, W., & Boyce, G. (1995). Effects of children with Down syndrome on parents' activities. *American Journal on Mental Retardation, 100*, 115–127.

Bauer, A. M., & Shea, T. M. (2003). *Parents and schools: Creating a successful partnership for students with special needs.* Upper Saddle River, NJ: Merrill/Prentice Hall.

Blacher, J. (Ed.). (1984). *Severely handicapped young children and their families.* Orlando, FL: Academic Press.

Blank, M. J., Melaville, A., & Shah, B. P. (2003). *Making the difference: Research and practice in community schools.* Washington, DC: Coalition for Community Schools, Institute for Educational Leadership.

Blaska, J. (1998). *Cyclical grieving: Reoccurring emotions experienced by parents who have children with disabilities.* St. Cloud, MN: Department of Child and Family Studies, St. Cloud University. (ERIC Document Reproduction Service No. ED419349)

Buck, P. (1950). *The child who never grew.* New York: Day.

Buscaglia, L. (1975). *The disabled and their parents: A counseling challenge.* Thorofare, NJ: Slack.

Carnegie, D. (1936). *How to win friends and influence people.* New York: Simon & Schuster.

Carpenter, B. (2000). Sustaining the family: Meeting the needs of families of children with disabilities. *British Journal of Special Education, 27*(3), 135–144.

Cobb, H., & Reeve, R. E. (1991). Counseling approaches with parents and families. In M. J. Fine (Ed.), *Collaboration with parents of exceptional children* (pp. 129–143). Brandon, VT: Clinical Psychology Publishing.

Covey, S. (1989). *The 7 habits of highly effective people.* New York: Simon & Schuster.

Dewey, J. (1938). *Experience and education.* New York: Collier.

Dinkmeyer, D., & Mckay, G. (1976). STEP: *Systematic training in effective parenting.* Circle Pines, MN: American Guidance Service.

Doll, B., & Bolger, M. (2000). The family with a young child with disabilities. In M. J. Fine & R. L. Simpson (Eds.), *Collaboration with parents and families of children and youth with exceptionalities* (pp. 237–256). Austin, TX: Pro-Ed.

Dryfoos, J., & Maguire, S. (2002). *Inside full-service community schools.* Thousand Oaks, CA: Corwin Press.

Dunst, C. J., Trivette, C. M., & Snyder, D. M. (2000). Family–professional partnerships: A behavioral science perspective. In M. J. Fine & R. L. Simpson (Eds.), *Collaboration with parents and families of children and youth with exceptionalities* (pp. 27–48). Austin, TX: Pro-Ed.

Ekman, P. (1964). Body position, facial expression, and verbal behavior during interviews. *Journal of Abnormal and Social Psychology, 68*, 295–301.

Estrada, A. U., & Pinsof, W. M. (1995). The effectiveness of family therapies for selected behavioral disorders of childhood. *The Journal of Marital and Family Therapy, 21*(4), 403–438.

Fewell, R., & Gelb, S. (1983). Parenting moderately handicapped persons. In M. Seligman (Ed.), *The family with a handicapped child: Understanding and treatment* (pp. 175–202). Orlando, FL: Grune & Stratton.

Fiedler, C. R., & Swanger, W. H. (2000). Empowering parents to participate: Advocacy and education. In M. J. Fine & R. L. Simpson (Eds.), *Collaboration with parents and families of children with disabilities* (pp. 437–464). Austin, TX: Pro-Ed.

Fine, M. J., & Nissenbaum, M. S. (2000). The child with disabilities and the family: Implications for professionals. In M. J. Fine & R. L. Simpson (Eds.), *Collaboration with parents and families of children with disabilities* (pp. 3–26). Austin, TX: Pro-Ed.

Fine, M. J., & Simpson, R. L. (Eds.). (2000). *Collaboration with parents and families of children with disabilities.* Austin, TX: Pro-Ed.

Floyd, F. J., & Gallagher, E. M. (1997). Parental stress, care demands, and use of support services for school-age children with disabilities and behavior problems. *Family Relations, 46*(4), 359–385.

Foster, M. (1988). A systems perspective and families of handicapped children. *Journal of Family Psychology, 2,* 54–56.

Franklin, C., & Streeter, C. (1998). School-linked services as interprofessional collaboration in student education. *Social Work, 43*(1), 67–69.

Friedrich, W., & Friedrich, W. (1981). Stress and coping among parents of handicapped children: A multidimensional approach. *American Journal of Mental Deficiency, 85,* 551–553.

Friend, M., & Cook, L. (2004). *Interactions: Collaboration skills for school professionals.* White Plains, NY: Longman.

Goldenberg, H., & Goldenberg, I. (2002). *Counseling today's families.* Pacific Grove, CA: Brooks/Cole.

Gordon, T. (2000). *Parent effectiveness training.* New York: Wyden.

Gorham, K. A. (1975). A lost generation of parents. *Exceptional Children, 41*(8), 521–525.

Hoover-Dempsey, K., Bassler, O., & Brissie, J. (1992). Exploration in parent–school relations. *Journal of Educational Research, 85,* 287–294.

Innocenti, M., Huh, K., & Boyce, G. (1992). Families of children with disabilities: Normative data and other considerations on parenting stress. *Topics in Early Childhood Special Education, 12,* 403–427.

Karp, N. (1996). Individualized wrap-around services for children with emotional, behavior, and mental disorders. In G.H. S. Singer, L. E. Powers, & A. L. Olson (Eds.), *Redefining family support: Innovations in public–private partnerships* (pp. 291–312). Baltimore: Paul Brookes.

Kazak, A., & Marvin, R. (1984). Differences, difficulties, and adaptation: Stress and social networks in families with a handicapped child. *Family Relations, 33,* 67–77.

Koegel, R., Schriebman, L., Loos, L., Dirlich-Wilhelm, H., Dunlap, G., Robbins, F., et al. (1992). Consistent stress profiles in mothers of children with autism. *Journal of Autism and Developmental Disorders, 22,* 205–216.

Kroth, R. (1985). *Communicating with parents of exceptional children.* Denver: Love.

Lawson, H. A., & Sailor, W. (2000). Integrating services, collaborating, and developing connections with schools. *Focus on Exceptional Children, 33*(2), 1–22.

Love, H. D. (1973). *The mentally retarded child and his family.* Springfield, IL: Thomas.

Miller, S., & Hudson, P. (1994). Using structured parent groups to provide parental support. *Intervention in School and Clinic, 29*(3), 151–155.

Patterson, C. (1986). *Theories of counseling and psychotherapy* (4th ed.). New York: Harper & Row.

Policy Leadership Cadre for Mental Health in School. (2001). *Mental health in schools: Guidelines, models, resources and policy considerations.* Retrieved October 16, 2004 from http://smhp.psych.ucla.edu/pdfdocs/policymakers/cadreguidelines.pdf.

Reeve, R. E., & Cobb, H. C. (2000). Counseling approaches with parents and families. In M. J. Fine & R. L. Simpson (Eds.), *Collaboration with parents and families of children with disabilities* (pp. 177–193). Austin, TX: Pro-Ed.

Rogers, C. (1962). The interpersonal relationship: The core of guidance. *Harvard Educational Review, 32*(4), 416–429.

Rogers, C. (1969). *Freedom to learn.* Columbus, OH: Merrill.

Rones, M., & Hoagwood, K. (2000). School-based mental health services: A research review. *Clinical Child and Family Psychology Review, 3,* 223–241.

Rutherford, R., & Edgar, E. (1979). *Teachers and parents: A guide to interaction and cooperation.* Boston: Allyn & Bacon.

Sailor, W., & Skrtic, T. (1996). School–community partnerships and educational reform: Introduction to the special issue. *Remedial and Special Education, 17*(5), 267–283.

Schalock, R. L., & Alonso, M. A. V. (2002). *Handbook on quality of life for human service practitioners*. Washington, DC: American Association on Mental Retardation.

Schilling, R., Kirkham, M., Snow, W., & Schinke, S. (1996). Single mothers with handicapped children: Different from their married counterparts? *Family Relations, 35*, 69–77.

Seligman, M., & Darling, R. B. (1997). *Ordinary families, special children: A systems approach to childhood disability*. New York: Guilford Press.

Sharpley, C., & Bitsika, V. (1997). Influence of gender, parental health, and perceived expertise of assistance upon stress, anxiety, and depression among parents of children with autism. *Journal of Intellectual and Developmental Disabilities, 22*, 19–29.

Simpson, R. L. (1996). *Working with parents and families of exceptional children and youth*. Austin, TX: Pro-Ed.

Sivberg, B. (2002). Family system and coping behaviors: A comparison between parents of children with autistic spectrum disorders and parents with non-autistic children. *Autism: The International Journal of Research and Practice, 6*(4), 397–409.

Sontag, J., & Schacht, R. (1994). An ethnic comparison of parent participation and information needs in early intervention. *Exceptional Children, 60*(5), 422–433.

Stainton, T., & Besser, H. (1998). The positive impact of children with an intellectual disability on the family. *Journal of Intellectual and Developmental Disability, 23*, 56–70.

Turnbull, A. P., & Turnbull, H. R. (2001). *Families, professionals, and exceptionality: Collaborating for empowerment*. Upper Saddle River, NJ: Merrill/Prentice Hall.

Turnbull, A. P., Turnbull, H. R., Erwin, E., & Soodak, L. (2005). *Families, professionals, and exceptionality: Positive outcomes through partnerships and trust*. Upper Saddle River, NJ: Merrill/Prentice Hall.

Weiss, M. J. (2002). Hardiness and social support as predictors of stress in mothers of typical children, children with autism, and children with mental retardation. *Autism: The International Journal of Research and Practice, 6*(1), 115–130.

Wright, K., & Stegelin, D. A. (2003). *Building school and community partnerships through parent involvement*. Upper Saddle River, NJ: Merrill/Prentice Hall.

CHAPTER 4
Providing Supports
for Siblings

● ● ● ● ● ● ● ● ● ● ● ● ● ● ● ● ● ● ○ ○ ○

In this chapter, you will understand:

- Commonly occurring needs of siblings of learners with disabilities.
- Programs and related interventions that may assist siblings of students with disabilities in understanding and effectively responding to their needs.
- The role of schools and community agencies in supporting the needs of siblings of students with disabilities.

Family Perspective: The Kilmers

Charles and Judith Kilmer began dating as high school students and were married shortly after graduating. Their oldest child, Rebecca, who is 12, was born when her parents were both 19. Rebecca's parents began observing her behavioral and learning difficulties from an early age. She was diagnosed in the third grade with learning disabilities, ADHD, and behavior problems. Although Rebecca is "much loved" by her parents and family, she is described as "high maintenance," related to persistent impulsive and sometimes aggressive actions, "extreme immaturity," poor capacity to responsibly fulfill home and school assignments, and difficulty in interacting with peers.

Rebecca has twin brothers, Tom and Tim, who are 3 years younger than she is. Charles and Judith divorced when Rebecca was 10 and the twins were 7. The dissolution of the marriage was attributed to Charles and Judith's marrying at a young age and to the stress related to caring for Rebecca. Mr. Kilmer remarried approximately a year following the divorce. Ms. Kilmer has not remarried, and is the custodial parent for the couple's three children, although Mr. Kilmer regularly sees his children on weekends and is involved in their school and community activities. Ms. Kilmer works full time. However, the family has only a modest annual income and they constantly seem to be faced with difficult decisions regarding allocation of dollars to support various family needs. As a result of this economic reality, Ms. Kilmer and the children each occasionally perceives that he or she fails to receive the support he or she deserves.

Tom and Tim Kilmer attend the same school as their older sister, Rebecca. They are considered to be average students and have a number of friends at school and in the neighborhood. They ride the same school bus as their sister and they regularly see Rebecca at school, including in the cafeteria and in the hallways. Tom and Tim have shared with their parents on several occasions that they are often embarrassed and confused by Rebecca's behavior. Thus they often will act as if they don't know Rebecca, especially if she is observed entering the special education resource room or when she is engaged in a problem behavior. They are aware that their sister has a disability and that she "can't help herself." Nevertheless, they find their sister to be someone about whom they are constantly offering excuses to their friends.

Ms. Kilmer makes few requests of her sons related to care and supervision of Rebecca. Because Ms. Kilmer has limited dollars to support a sitter, Rebecca takes the school bus to Ms. Kilmer's mother's home after school. Rebecca's grandmother indicates that she is "stressed" by the responsibility of caring for Rebecca. However, she begrudgingly accepts this role because she acknowledges that there are no other options. Ms. Kilmer picks up Rebecca at her grandmother's home on her return from work. Tom and Tim take the bus from school to their home at the end of the day and care for themselves until their mother arrives home after work. Ms. Kilmer cares for her three children on weekends, except when they are with their father. Unlike her brothers, who are involved in numerous out-of-home weekend and evening activities, Rebecca spends her weekends and evenings with one of her parents.

Reflecting on the Family Perspective

1. What strategies can school personnel use to identify the needs of Tom and Tim Kilmer?

2. Related to their sister, what responsibility and role do school personnel play in helping Tom and Tim Kilmer respond to their needs for information and emotional support?

3. How can school personnel help Tom and Tim Kilmer better understand the needs of their sister, and what can they do to support the boys relative to having a sister with a disability?

⊙   ⊙   ⊙

There is strong agreement that children and youth with disabilities are significantly influenced by their parents and families (see chapter 1). This point has been much discussed, and there is overwhelming evidence that home influences are salient determinants of children's school, home, and community development and progress (Bauer & Shea, 2003; Brinker, 1992; Jackson, Sifers, Warren & Velasquez, 2003; Simpson, 1996). Less often discussed but no less evident is that normally developing and achieving children who are members of families with a child with a disability are also significantly influenced by family experiences, including those connected to a sibling with special needs (Dyson, 1996; Mason, Kruse, Farabaugh, Gershberg, & Kohler, 2000; Powell & Gallagher, 1993; Roos, 2002). In this regard, it is clear that a reciprocal pattern of influence exists in families of children with disabilities. That is, not only do parents and families influence children with disabilities, but children with disabilities also have a significant influence on their parents and siblings (Damiani, 1999; Muscott, 2002). Relative to children with disabilities, this chapter focuses on the impact of individuals with exceptionalities on their brothers and sisters. We also discuss strategies and programs that family members, schools, and communities can use to understand and support siblings of students with special needs.

UNDERSTANDING SIBLINGS OF CHILDREN WITH DISABILITIES WITHIN THE CONTEXT OF A FAMILY

In spite of their heterogeneity, including characteristics, needs, interests, and capacity to be involved in supporting family members with special needs, members of a family unit are interrelated in myriad ways. In this connection, events that affect one member of a family also impact others in the family (Carter & McGoldrich, 1980; Fine & Nissenbaum, 2000). Accordingly, we consider it essential that needs of nondisabled children in a family with a special-need individual not be overlooked, and that schools and communities offer sibling support opportunities. Thus, when homes and schools are perceived to be interconnected systems, parents and families and school and community professionals are better positioned to consider and collaboratively develop support systems for siblings whose brothers and sisters have disabilities.

Research literature on the impact of a child with a disability on his or her siblings is anything but clear. In fact, researchers have for decades reported variable findings related to this issue (Cuskelly, Chant, & Hayes, 1998; Farber, 1959; Mason et al., 2000). That is, while there is general consensus that the presence of a person with a disability in a family will impact its members (Fine & Carlson, 1992; Turnbull & Turnbull, 2001), the exact nature of this influence is unclear (Brody & Stoneman, 1986; Fussell, Macias, & Saylor, 2002; Lobato, 1990; Phillips, 1999; Rivers & Stoneman, 2003).

The notion that a child with a disability will have a deleterious effect on his or her siblings and parents has consistently been assumed for decades. For example, Klein (1972), Love (1973), and Telford and Sawrey (1977) each reported that siblings of children with disabilities frequently have negative experiences and outcomes associated with living in a family with a sibling with a disability. This association was noted to be particularly evident when siblings were required to assume major child-care responsibilities and when their normal childhood and adolescent experiences and opportunities were disrupted. Tew and Lawrence (1973) also suggested that siblings of children with disabilities may feel neglected and resentful if their parents fail to give them appropriate amounts of attention and otherwise fail to address their needs because of an exceptional brother or sister. In more recent studies, Hollidge (2001) reported that siblings of children with diabetes frequently experienced emotional distress, sadness, and guilt related to their sibling's disability, and Hastings (2003) reported that siblings of children with autism were rated as having more problems with peers, more adjustment problems, and lower rates of prosocial behavior when compared to a group of peers who did not have exceptional siblings. Similarly, Fishman et al. (1996) reported that siblings of children with pervasive developmental disorders had more behavioral difficulties than did brothers and sisters of children with Down syndrome or a control group. Finally, there have been a number of suggestions that parents can follow to mitigate the impact of children's exceptionalities on their siblings (Phillips, 1999; Stavros, 1989).

It is significant to note, however, that others have reported and suggested that brothers and sisters of children with disabilities may not suffer negative outcomes that can be attributed to a sibling's disability (Dyson, 2003; Dyson, Edgar, & Crnic, 1989; Simeonsson & Simeonsson, 1993). In a historically significant study, Graliker, Fishler, and Koch (1962) reported that teenage siblings of children with mental retardation generally led typical lives, including opportunities for peer relationships and social experiences. Moreover, the researchers reported that the siblings generally were satisfied with their home lives and that they understood and accepted the disabilities and special needs of their brothers and sisters.

The aforementioned conflicting literature provides some insight regarding the influences of a child with a disability on siblings. That is, there appears to be considerable variability on assumed sibling impact related to a disabled family member (Fishman et al., 1996; Mason et al., 2000). Interpretation of this variability can at least in part be attributed to factors such as culture, family size, family beliefs and values, economic status, family interaction patterns, age and health of parents and other family members, age and gender of siblings, type and severity of disability of affected children, and a host of related variables. For example, a family of high SES with financial resources to secure out-of-home after-school caretakers for a child with a severe disability might logically be expected to experience less stress than a family of lesser means, which must assume total support for a child with a disability, using only family members as caretakers. There is also evidence that sisters of children with disabilities, especially older sisters, are apt to have more caregiving responsibilities than other children in a family, and thus may be more likely than other family members to experience stress and resentment related to a child with a disability (Brody, Stoneman,

Davis, & Crapps, 1991; Cleveland & Miller, 1977; Mason et al., 2000; Stoneman, Brody, Davis, Crapps, & Malone, 1991). At the same time, there is some evidence that sisters generally have more factual information and a better understanding of a sibling's disability than their brothers do (Damiani, 1999), and that they have more positive contact and attitudes when compared to brothers of siblings with disabilities (Orsmond & Seltzer, 2000). There is also evidence that younger brothers of children with disabilities, especially males who are close in age to siblings with severe disabilities, are especially vulnerable to mental health problems related to their exceptional sibling (Breslau, 1982; Hannah & Midlarsky, 1999).

While the type of disability may not strongly correlate with siblings' acceptance of and adjustment to having a disabled brother or sister (Breslau, Weitzman, & Messenger, 1981; Lobato, 1983b), the severity of a disability does appear to be a significant factor (Grossman, 1972; Mason et al., 2000). Particularly when the severity of a child's disability necessitates assistance in such basic life activities as dressing, eating, toileting, and related supports and when a disability interferes with family activities and functions, siblings tend to be most affected and to more often have negative perceptions. This tends to be especially the case when siblings are required to assist their brother or sister in the aforementioned activities. Ironically, children with mild disabilities also tend to be viewed negatively by their siblings, possibly because the cause of many mild learning and behavioral disabilities is not immediately and clearly evident. Moreover, this pattern may be a function of siblings' perceptions that children with mild disabilities and related challenges may be assumed to be able to independently overcome their disability, and because the disability may require parental attention that siblings without disabilities may not understand or accept (Dyson, 1996; Lardieri & Swanson, 2000).

Not surprisingly, there is evidence that well-adjusted and supportive families are best able to adjust to and accommodate the needs of an exceptional family member, particularly if high-quality school and community resources are available to assist them (Dyson et al., 1989; Simpson & Zurkowski, 2000). Yet, regardless of the strengths of families and individual family members, it appears that having a brother or sister with a disability will have an impact on families. Moreover, stress among siblings and other family members of a person with a disability will be higher than among those in families who do not have a member with a disability (Beal & Chertkov, 1992; Roos, 2002). Commenting on this presumed impact, Crnic and Leconte (1986) observed the following:

> Although it seems clear from both research and clinical reports that the effects of having a handicapped sibling vary greatly from individual to individual, and we cannot automatically assume that the effects will be deleterious, normal siblings are at risk for any number of social, behavioral, or emotional difficulties. This at-risk status is a function of the ongoing stress associated with the presence of a handicapped sibling, and it is likely that the nature of these risks and stress vary across the sibling's life-span. (p. 93)

In light of the impact of exceptional children on their siblings, it is important that appropriate consideration be given to the needs of brothers and sisters of special-needs children. We offer suggestions for meeting sibling needs and reducing potential problems related to living in a family with a child with a disability.

RESPONDING TO THE NEEDS OF SIBLINGS
OF CHILDREN WITH DISABILITIES

The uniqueness of families makes it difficult to make accurate general inferences about the needs and supports that might be most beneficial to siblings of children with disabilities. Yet, as previously noted, there is strong evidence that many brothers and sisters of children and youth with special needs are at risk for various problems. Thus, a number of these individuals will benefit from appropriate resources and services. That such service has not routinely been provided by schools and communities in no way diminishes this need.

Resources for Siblings of Special-Needs Students

We recommend the following resources for siblings of special-needs students: (a) opportunities to receive information about exceptionalities, including the disability that affects their brother or sister; (b) opportunities to observe and discuss with school personnel the educational program of siblings with a disability, including methods, procedures, curricula, and supports; (c) communication, discussion, and support opportunities with school and community professionals and other siblings of students with disabilities; and (d) individualized opportunities and decision-making roles related to participating in the educational and home-life support of siblings with disabilities.

Opportunities to Receive Information About Exceptionalities   Children and youth whose brothers and sisters have disabilities will often benefit from information about exceptionalities, including books, magazine and journal articles, video- and audio-tapes, CDs, and computer-based information (Crnic & LeConte, 1986; Glasberg, 2000). Of particular interest to brothers and sisters of pupils with special needs is information about the characteristics of special education programs and disabilities in general and specific disorders associated with unique interests. Relative to specific exceptionalities, facts and discussions about the nature, prevalence, etiology, prognosis, and so forth may be of particular interest. It is important that information that professionals recommend for consumption by children and youth be not only accurate in its content but also age appropriate. For instance, not only do young children need developmentally suitable materials, but these materials are most effective when parents, teachers, or other adults assist these children in fully and accurately comprehending their meaning and provide opportunities to discuss their content. Even when considering the needs of bright and educationally sophisticated adolescents, it is apparent that many textbooks are intended for adult readers and fail to address the needs of many youth, even if factually correct. It is also recommended that information about disabilities focus not only on the clinical deficits and challenges associated with disabilities but also on the individual differences that are an element of each person and that are an underpinning of human disability. The positive outcomes that frequently occur when students with special needs are exposed to effective educational, home, and community coordinated efforts, including when families are supportive of students' educational programs and efforts, are also important to share with siblings. Finally, it is recommended that siblings of individuals with disabilities receive information regarding their own vulnerability related to a disability that affects a sibling. That is, it is not uncommon for many brothers and sisters of students with disabilities to question the extent to which they and their future offspring are at risk for problems. Accordingly, materials that address this and related questions in a straightforward and developmentally appropriate manner are most suitable and most utilitarian for siblings.

Although many siblings of students with disabilities may be reluctant to independently seek out information about disabilities and to request adult assistance in obtaining and understanding such information, it is evident that many young people will be interested in and will benefit from these resources (Damiani, 1999; Mason et al., 2000; Powell & Gallagher, 1993). For that reason, school and community professionals should initiate contacts with parents and siblings regarding the availability and potential benefit of such materials, as opposed to assuming that interested individuals will take the initiative to seek out these resources.

Along with reading and reviewing disability-related materials, siblings of students with disabilities need to have opportunities to discuss the information. Moreover, providing opportunities for siblings to discuss the content with reference to specific characteristics and needs of affected brothers and sisters is imperative. Although confidentiality protocol will dictate specific content and activities, it is clear that siblings will require opportunities to discuss the content with a trusted adult. Professionals have long known that many parents of children with disabilities require opportunities to discuss the nature, diagnosis, and implications of a disability. It is logical that this same need, albeit in a different form, will exist for siblings of children with disabilities. Simply receiving information and discussing it with an adult will likely not answer all questions or quell all the concerns of siblings about the condition of a brother or sister. However, it is also clear that this process will typically help them understand and deal with their exceptional family member. This process will also serve as a springboard for better understanding of future expectations for themselves and their family, and the implications the disability has for them and their family.

Examples of information designed to educate elementary-age students about disabilities is provided in Communication and Collaboration Tips Box 4.1. Provided as a general outline, this information provides a general curriculum for teachers, presenting information about exceptionalities and individual differences to typically developing children, including siblings of students with disabilities. This information was found to be most useful when combined with opportunities for discussion with a knowledgeable and concerned adult. Additional resources that can be used to educate siblings about disabilities are provided in the "Resources for Sibling Support" section at the end of this chapter.

Opportunities for Siblings of Students with a Disability to Learn About Their Sibling's Educational Program and Discuss It with School Personnel and Other Professionals   As an extension of providing opportunities for siblings to receive information about disabilities, it is recommended that interested students be permitted to learn more about

---

Examples of Information on Disabilities Designed for Elementary-Age Siblings of Persons with Disabilities

Differences and Similarities

Similarities and differences among people are discussed, including how people with disabilities are much like everyone else, how differences affect the way a person is viewed, and how learning more about a person and his or her individual differences can change our perceptions.

Students with Disabilities: School-Related Implications

Siblings of students with disabilities are provided information and discussion opportunities related to the impact of certain disabilities on a person's ability to do school-related tasks. While the focus is not on specific categories of disabilities, students are exposed to how the impact might relate to cognitive, language, academic, physical, and emotional disabilities. The content also provides insight into how accommodations and strategies can facilitate school success.

Students with Disabilities: Implications for Home and Community Living

This element of the information and discussion process focuses on how disabilities may affect home and community living. Independent living and community and home expectations are also dealt with in this section.

Friendships and Family Living

Siblings consider the characteristics of persons whom they choose as friends and compare these characteristics with attributes of siblings and other family members with whom they must regularly interact. As part of this discussion, siblings are led through a discussion of their friends' perception of their brother/sister with a disability, and their role in promoting an understanding and acceptance of their sibling. Brothers and sisters of students with disabilities are also exposed to information on how they might facilitate and support their sibling with a disability at home and school.

---

their sibling's specific educational program, including curricula, teachers and other personnel, classroom strategies, activities, and so forth. The outcomes of such opportunities are numerous, including siblings' gaining a more accurate picture of a child's strengths and challenges. Such opportunities also assist children and youth who are unfamiliar with special education by demystifying their sibling's education programs and the anxiety that may accompany them; by providing opportunities to connect their own classroom activities and programs with those of their brother or sister with special needs; and by empowering a brother or sister to be more understanding and involved in a sibling's education. This element of gaining experiences that may lead to a more accurate perception of a family member and a better understanding of his or her program may involve both formal and structured activities as well as informal methods. That is, special education teachers may invite groups of brothers and sisters of students enrolled in their programs to view the classroom and its curricula and hear from the teachers about the program. In contrast, informal activities may involve issuing invitations to siblings individually or in groups to view the special education program and visit with the teachers and staff at designated times. Permitting brothers and sisters of special education students to become more aware of and familiar with their sibling's program through formally or informally observing and interacting with their sibling's teachers and other knowledgeable adults regarding classroom activities and curricula will often result in significant benefits.

Opportunities for Communication, Discussion, and Support   A child with a disability will almost certainly have a significant impact on his or her family, including brothers and sisters (Bateman, 1992; Rivers & Stoneman, 2003; Roos, 2002). Considered a less-than-perfect reflection of the family or individual family members, a brother or sister with a disability may generate a variety of emotional reactions among siblings, including guilt, resentment, anxiety, stress, and other emotions (Hannah & Midlarsky, 1999). The presence of a family member with a disability may also make others in the family more vulnerable to everyday stress, pressures, and frustrations (Lardieri & Swanson, 2000).

In response to these challenges, professionals may assist siblings who require emotional support by creating opportunities for them to talk to professionals and interact with other siblings regarding issues related to having a brother or sister with a disability. In either individual meetings or group sessions, these opportunities for siblings to discuss their perceptions, ideas, feelings, and concerns with knowledgeable and nonjudgmental listeners can benefit both the children and other members of the family. Moreover, the increased understanding and empathy toward a brother or sister with a disability that hopefully are outcomes of these sessions may increase family cohesion and family members' willingness and ability to support a member with special needs. Finally, supportive and professionally valid strategies for dealing with family issues related to a sibling with a disability will hopefully alleviate stress and increase family members' capacity to be involved in the education and life of a member with special needs.

It should be clear that not every sibling of a child with a disability will have an interest or a need to participate in a sibling support group or individual counseling program. Accordingly, siblings and their parents and families should make decisions regarding whether a child should participate in a support program. Yet, although such decisions should, without question, be made by parents and families, it is important that school and community professionals make it known that such opportunities exist and that siblings often benefit from participating in these programs. It should be noted that these benefits occur even if siblings are experiencing no overt symptoms or other related problems. In accordance with meeting this need for sibling support, and because so many brothers and sisters of students with disabilities will experience, to some degree, a need for emotional support (Hastings, 2003; Hollidge, 2001; Lardieri & Swanson, 2000), it is apparent that professionals must be willing to make available trained staff and individual and group support session resources. For that

Table 4.1   Sibling Support Group Problem Solving and Learning Facilitation and Learning Strategies for Students with Special Needs.

Equation	Answer
1. 3 F = Y*	3 feet equal 1 yard
2. 60 M = H*	60 minutes equal 1 hour
3. 12 I = F*	12 inches equal 1 foot
4. 1 T = 2000 P*	1 ton equals 2000 pounds
5. 3 S = O**	3 strikes and you are out
6. 1 FG = 2 P**	1 field goal equals 2 points

*During cueing period, the group leader indicates item relates to measurement.

**During cueing period, the group leader indicates item relates to a common game rule.

smaller percentage of siblings who require more intensive counseling and therapy, school personnel are advised to form cooperative partnerships with mental health organizations and other partners or otherwise identify additional resources for supporting these individuals and their families.

An example of an activity that may be used within a sibling support group meeting is shown in Table 4.1. The objective of this exhibit is to help peers understand that learning is difficult when individuals don't have guidelines and an understanding of problem-solving rules. The group leader distributes the problem-solving equations shown in Table 4.1, with the only instructions being that the students have 3 minutes to solve the problems. No questions are permitted during this time, even though the participants will likely be unable to independently solve the problems. After 3 minutes, the group leader shares that each letter in the equation stands for a word, and that the equations represent common measurements or game rules. If students require additional assistance, the group leader indicates that the answer to the equation "3 F = Y" is "three feet equals one yard." Following independent work on the remaining puzzle items, the group leader discusses with the participants that children and youth with disabilities require additional accommodations, structure, support, and learning strategies to facilitate learning and school participation, and that with these additional supports, they are capable of much learning. Examples of such items are shown and discussed with the siblings.

Individualized Opportunities and Decision-Making Roles Related to Support of Siblings with Disabilities   Related to the need for family members to be involved in the support and education of children and youth with disabilities, along with the at-risk and vulnerable nature of siblings of special needs persons, we consider it essential that all members of a family, including siblings, be given appropriate involvement opportunities. This involvement includes a voice in those activities and responsibilities that siblings have a connection with or interest in, including those at home, at school, and in the community. Thus, it is essential that brothers and sisters of students with disabilities be given a voice in choosing and otherwise negotiating those activities in which they participate. For example, child care and related responsibilities as well as requests to be involved in a home-based tutoring program for a sibling would follow discussions among parents and children regarding the nature and degree of involvement. We strongly suggest that professionals recommend that parents be open to such discussions; that those professionals be permitted to lead or participate in these discussions, including outlining areas for potential sibling involvement; or both. Furthermore, we think it is important that professionals initiate discussions with parents regarding potential problems that may arise when siblings fail to be actively involved in decisions related to their role and involvement with brothers and sisters with disabilities. As noted, we recommend that educators and other professionals offer to assist in facilitating these discussions regarding sibling involvement relative to special-needs children. Of course, some parents may view decisions regarding their children's involvement with brothers and sisters, including in support roles and school-related activities, to be their exclusive domain and therefore not open to school-personnel involvement. Nevertheless, a leadership role by professionals in this area bodes well for effective sibling participation in children's support and care and for long-term family health, cohesion, and collaboration.

Sibling participation in children's education and care is clearly an element and extension of a family-school-community partnership. In this regard, siblings of children with disabilities are most effective as support participants, advocates, and so forth when permitted to participate in decision making and related activities. Accordingly, within the parameters of siblings' ages, interests, skills, motivation, time and other resources, and so forth, brothers and sisters of children with disabilities may be encouraged to participate in such activities as information sharing, IEP program development and implementation, tutoring, social skill and social interaction and management program development and implementation, advocacy and community support, as well as to be a resource for child care and related family assistance.

Examples of possible areas of involvement for siblings of children with disabilities to participate in the home and school life of a special-needs brother or sister are provided in Communication and Collaboration Tips Box 4.2.

STRATEGIES FOR SIBLING SUPPORT AND INVOLVEMENT: A CASE EXAMPLE

Presented in the following section is an illustration of strategies cooperatively and collaboratively used by professionals and parents to respond to the needs of siblings of a child with a disability. The example is designed to illustrate representative sibling issues associated with having a special-needs family member, as well as strategies for responding to the presented challenges.

A Younger Brother with a Severe Developmental Disability

Paula Williams is an exceptionally mature and responsible 16-year-old. She is consistently listed on her school's scholastic honor role and aspires to attend college to

---

COMMUNICATION AND COLLABORATION TIPS   **BOX 4.2**

Examples of Home and School Involvement Options for Siblings of Children with Disabilities

Peer tutor

Homework assistant

Socialization and game partner

Assistant in self-help activities (e.g., dressing, toileting, grooming) and mobility (e.g., home, school and neighborhood orientation, safety, and bus riding)

Participant in IEP and other school-related meetings among families and school and community professionals

Presenter on the topic of disabilities for general education classes that are studying individuals with disabilities

Community volunteer for organizations that support persons with disabilities, such as Special Olympics and so forth.

---

become a teacher or social worker. She has a number of friends at school and in her neighborhood, although none with whom she consistently spends time. Paula is described by her peers as a thoughtful and nurturing person, albeit somewhat reserved. Paula infrequently participates in school social activities, except occasionally attending after-school academic clubs. She was nominated to be secretary of the school's French Club; however, Paula declined to have her name on the ballot because she had competing obligations that restricted the time she could devote to the club.

Paula is the oldest of three children. She and her two younger brothers, Tim, age 14, and Larry, age 11, live with their parents in a working-class neighborhood that includes several relatives, including both sets of grandparents. Tim is described as a "lively, typical boy" who enjoys sports. He is an average student, although his parents and teachers describe him as having the potential to do better in school. Unlike his sister, Tim is not particularly responsible and often neglects his home duties. Larry, the youngest boy, has a significant developmental disability. Although officially identified by school personnel as having severe mental retardation, several professionals have also noted that he also has a number of characteristics of autism, including self-stimulatory behavior, an insistence on environmental sameness, a lack of interest in others, and an absence of verbal language. Larry attends a self-contained special education classroom for students with severe and multiple disabilities. The parents and family members consider the program to be very good and are pleased with Larry's progress. They also have an excellent relationship with Larry's teacher and the classroom staff and consider themselves fortunate to have such a good teacher and supportive program. The parents attend school IEP conferences and special-occasion events, and they exchange notes with the teacher several times a week. In spite of their absence from many school functions, they consider themselves to be strong advocates for their children and their school programs.

The extended family and neighbors are closely connected and often socialize during holidays. Paula's parents both work at full-time jobs. Paula's father is a foreman at a meat-packing company and often spends long hours at his demanding job. Thus, except for weekends, he has minimal time that he is able to spend with his family. To arrive at his job for a 6:00 a.m. shift change, he needs to leave home by 5:20 a.m. Thus, he often goes to bed by 9 p.m., thereby even further restricting the time he is able to spend with his family. Paula's mother works for a catering company and has a more flexible schedule than her husband does, but she often is required to work evenings and weekends.

Paula is expected to care for Larry after school and on weekends. She is also expected to "keep an eye on Tim," although Tim rebels at his sister's attempts to monitor or control his behavior. Tim does not have any responsibilities in caring for Larry, primarily because his parents agree that "he couldn't do it" and because Paula is excellent at caring for her brother with a disability. Tim also ignores his brother whenever possible and has indicated that he is embarrassed by his brother's disability. More recently, Tim has begun to not recognize Larry as a member of the family. For example, on a recent school document that called for a listing of family members, Larry listed only his mother, father, and sister.

Paula generally indicates she enjoys and receives satisfaction from interacting with and assisting in the care of her younger brother. However, she also shares with friends that her family-care responsibilities have interfered with her ability to spend time with others, participate in hobbies, and otherwise pursue areas of interest. Because care of Larry is such a demanding task, Paula is unable to do other activities while caring for her brother. She has also found that Larry becomes so upset when she attempts to take him places that she generally keeps him at home after school, except for an occasional walk to visit one of the grandparents.

Paula appears to enjoy her time with her brother, including the respect and compliments she receives from her parents and relatives regarding her willingness and skill in caring for her brother. However, she is unhappy that these responsibilities so interfere with her opportunities to pursue her own interests. She feels guilty for having these feelings, but at the same time she resents that she may not be able to leave home to attend college because there would be no one to take her place to care for Larry. Finally, she is resentful toward her brother Tim for his unwillingness to assume any responsibility for Larry or to assist with other household tasks. However, she has not talked with her parents regarding this matter, because she knows that her parents are struggling to support the family in the best way they know, and because she understands that there are no other alternatives available to support Larry's care after school and on weekends.

Strategies for Assisting the Siblings

The case of Larry Williams and his family is a clear illustration of the overlapping home, school, and community elements that comprise the primary systems of which the Williamses are a part. Moreover, this case illustrates that the events, structures, and circumstances that are connected to a family member with a disability also have an impact on others in the family, including brothers and sisters. Accordingly, an appropriate and comprehensive plan of support, care, and education for Larry should also consider each of the members of the family, including Paula and Tim. Suitable and effective strategies for Larry and his family should involve collaborative planning among school, home, and community agencies and professionals. Collaboration has as a desired outcome a comprehensive plan that considers and appropriately builds on the needs, resources, and preferences of each family member.

In accordance with this need for a comprehensive intervention schema, Larry's teacher took a leadership role in discussing with the parents the need for a plan to address Larry's siblings' needs. That she had an excellent relationship with the parents was a significant advantage in facilitating such a process. Included in the plan was an invitation to Paula and Tim to receive information about their brother's disability. When offered reading materials related to disabilities, Paula enthusiastically chose several books and magazine articles, particularly those that were recommended by Larry's teacher. These items included a novel about a sibling of a boy with a severe disability who served as her brother's surrogate parent following the death of the parents, along with several magazine articles about individuals with disabilities. Tim initially declined offers by the teacher to direct him to materials about disabilities. However, several weeks following the initial offer, he contacted Larry's teacher about getting a book that he subsequently reviewed as a means of fulfilling a course requirement. Subsequent to reviewing the book, Tim checked out a video from the public library about a deaf student who played college football and later became a successful high school coach. Larry's teacher also indicated to both Paula and Tim that she was willing to discuss any matters that pertained to the readings or related matters. She also identified individuals within the siblings' respective schools who could answer questions or discuss issues about Larry, and she identified individuals within the school system who were willing to discuss with them the materials they read about disabilities.

Both Paula and Tim were also invited to observe Larry in his classroom. Paula was quick to accept the invitation and indicated she learned a number of strategies that she could use with her brother based on these sessions. Interestingly, Paula was also able to suggest several prompting and redirecting techniques, which the staff incorporated into Larry's management and instructional programs. Subsequent to the third observation, Paula began asking staff questions about Larry and his program, as well as discussing whether she herself might be at risk for giving birth to a child with a disability. Paula subsequently volunteered to be a peer tutor in a special education classroom at her high school. In contrast, Tim was reluctant to participate in the opportunity to observe his brother at school. However, Larry's teacher and Tim's health class teacher agreed to collaborate on a program wherein Tim was permitted to complete a class project by observing and reporting on the curricula and methodology used in his brother's classroom. That this alternative permitted Tim to leave his school during regular class times to travel to his brother's school several blocks away made the option particularly appealing.

Neither the school system that the Williams children attended nor the community mental health system had a formal sibling support program. Nevertheless, Paula and Tim, as well as other members of the family, were invited to join a generic family support group that was run by their church pastor and a volunteer mental health practitioner. This invitation was unanimously declined by the parents and children. The siblings were also referred to a school counselor in their building who could discuss matters related to their brother. These counselors were contacted by Larry's teacher regarding the situation and their possible involvement, and both individuals initiated contact with Paula and Tim. Neither youth contacted their school counselors for an appointment subsequent to hearing from them. However, Paula maintained informal contact with Larry's teacher, and this individual served as a support and information resource.

Following the classroom observations by Paula and Tim, the parents were contacted by Larry's teacher regarding allowing the siblings to participate in future IEP and selective other meetings with school personnel. Paula subsequently attended IEP and progress-report conferences with her parents, and she and Larry's teacher collaborated on a home-based self-help and augmentative communication project for Larry. Paula also began participating in the home–school communication-exchange program that had previously been developed with the parents. Tim declined participation in these meetings, and his decision to not be involved was challenged by neither the parents nor school personnel.

The most difficult challenge in negotiating the sibling involvement plan related to Paula's and Tim's support of their brother after school and on weekends. The parents affirmed that they were unable to afford private after-school care for Larry, and they also indicated that they were reluctant to request that the grandparents or other relatives assume this responsibility. However, they were open to using a county-funded family support and respite-care program several days a month. The program permitted Larry to attend recreational programs for individuals with disabilities after school and on weekends as well as allowing Paula additional time to pursue other interests. The parents and teacher, in collaboration with Larry's siblings, also agreed to require that Tim be involved in a series of household chores that heretofore had been assigned to Paula. The teacher, parents, and Tim also worked to design a program that rewarded Tim for interacting with his brother. Based on Tim's suggestion, he received special privileges for having his brother attend his baseball practice sessions and games. Tim acknowledged his brother at these activities and because he independently provided Larry with a team cap to wear on these occasions, his parents judged that the program was a success.

The Kilmers Revisited

Tom and Tim Kilmer continue to attend the same school as their older sister Rebecca. While they admit that they continue to be perplexed and occasionally embarrassed by their sister's unpredictable behavior, they have been exposed to several experiences and have been provided with resources that have assisted them in better understanding and accepting their sister and her disability. Of particular benefit have been opportunities for Tom and Tim to talk with their sister's special education teacher. Ms. Russell, Rebecca's resource room teacher, not only provided the brothers with an explanation of their sister's curriculum and program but also discussed with them how her program is generally the same as that of other students. Tom and Tim have also benefited from this teacher's discussions of social and behavioral challenges that sometimes accompany learning disabilities and ADHD. Her specific suggestions on how the boys might use this information to assist their friends and classmates in better understanding disabilities have been frequently used.

Recently, the three children have successfully been involved in family outings with their mother and independently with their father. These experiences have led Rebecca and her brothers to comment that they feel more connected as a family. These comments are in sharp contrast to previous behaviors and remarks that seemed to suggest the boys and their sister preferred to lead parallel and relatively autonomous and uninvolved lives.

Tom and Tim were encouraged by their parents to attend a church-supported weekend retreat designed for siblings of children with disabilities. The boys were reluctant to participate; however, they consented to attend when both their mother and father agreed that the program was required. Subsequent to attending the program, Tom and Tim have spoken only briefly about the experience, noting only that it was "OK," "kind of interesting," and so forth. However, Ms. and Mr. Kilmer and Ms. Kilmer's mother have noted positive changes that they attribute to the experience. Ms. Kilmer summarized the changes by observing that she has the sense that her sons are now more comfortable with their sister and consider her more a "regular part of their family."

SUMMARY STATEMENTS

- Siblings of students with disabilities have variable needs related to this role and are at risk for a number of possible problems.
- School and community professionals, in collaboration with parents and families, have a responsibility to identify and assist in addressing the needs of siblings of students with disabilities.
- Individualization is essential to meet the variable needs of siblings of students with disabilities. For general planning purposes, however, providing them information about exceptionalities; creating opportunities to observe and discuss with school personnel the educational programs of special-needs siblings; allowing communication, discussion, and support opportunities with school and community professionals and other siblings of students with disabilities; and providing decision-making opportunities for participating in the educational and home-life support of siblings with disabilities will be useful.

QUESTIONS FOR DISCUSSION

1. Identify the perceived needs of a sibling of a student with a disability, including the need for information about disabilities; opportunities to observe and discuss with school personnel the educational programs of a brother or sister with a disability; communication, discussion, and support opportunities; and opportunities to participate in the educational and home-life support of a sibling with a disability.
2. Relative to the above needs, describe possible activities that would be most appropriate and suitable for the sibling and family.
3. How can schools collaboratively work with community organizations and professionals to help siblings of students with disabilities better understand and adjust to their brother or sister with special needs?

RESOURCES FOR SIBLING SUPPORT

- **National Mental Health Consumers' Self-Help Clearinghouse**
  (www.mhselfhelp.org)
  This Web site provides multiple sources of information, including a library and a database that identifies materials for siblings and peers of students with disabilities.

- **Pacer Center: Parent Advocacy Coalition for Educational Rights**
  (www.pacer.org)
  The Pacer Center's Web site has a variety of user-friendly materials and resources, including some items appropriate for siblings of children and youth with disabilities.

- **Parents Helping Parents: The Parent-Directed Family Resource Center for Children with Special Needs**
  (www.php.com)
  This Web site provides a variety of resource ideas and options for families with children with special needs, including siblings.

- ***Exceptional Parent* magazine**
  (www.eparent.com)
  This publication and site offer information and resources for parents and families of persons with disabilities, including brothers and sisters.

- Harris, S. (1994). *Siblings of children with autism*: A *guide for families*. Bethesda, MD: Woodbine.
  Written for families, this book identifies helpful information, especially as needed by brothers and sisters of individuals with autism.

- Lobato, D. (1990). *Brothers, sisters and special needs: Information and activities for helping young siblings of children with chronic illness and developmental disabilities*. Baltimore: Paul H. Brookes.
  This helpful resource is designed to assist parents and other adults in disseminating information about children with disabilities to brothers and sisters. Activities are included in this book.

- McCaffrey, F., & Fish, T. (1989). *Profiles of the other child: A sibling guide for parents*. Columbus, OH: Ohio State University.
  This guide for parents serves as a resource for communicating about disabilities to siblings.

- Meyer, D. (Ed.). (1997). *Views from our shoes: Growing up with a brother or sister with special needs*. Bethesda, MD: Woodbine.
  This book includes personal stories and reflections of persons who grew up in homes with a sibling with a disability.

- Stoneman, Z., & Berman, P. W. (Eds.). (1993). *The effects of mental retardation, disability, and illness on sibling relationships: Research issues and challenges*. Baltimore: Paul H. Brookes.
This edited book focuses on a number of issues germane to siblings of individuals with disabilities.

REFLECTION ACTIVITIES

1. Request that a sibling of a student with a disability discuss his or her perspectives on and experiences of living with a brother or sister with a disability.
2. As part of the discussion, request that he or she offer recommendations about how school and community professionals might best help him or her and his or her family support and adjust to living with the special-needs family member.

REFERENCES

Bateman, V. (1992). A new beginning. *The Exceptional Parent*, 22, 44–47.

Bauer, A. M., & Shea, T. M. (2003). *Parents and schools: Creating a successful partnership for students with special needs*. Upper Saddle River, NJ: Merrill/Prentice Hall.

Beal, E., & Chertkov, L. (1992). Family–school intervention: A family systems perspective. In M. Fine & C. Carlson (Eds.), *The handbook of family–school intervention: A systems perspective* (pp. 288–301). Boston: Allyn & Bacon.

Breslau, N. (1982). Siblings of disabled children: Birth order and age spacing effects. *Journal of Abnormal Child Psychology*, 10, 85–96.

Breslau, N., Weitzman, M., & Messenger, K. (1981). Psychological functioning of siblings of disabled children. *Pediatrics*, 61, 344–353.

Brinker, R. P. (1992). Family involvement in early intervention: Accepting the unchangeable, changing the changeable, and knowing the difference. *Topics in Early Childhood Special Education*, 12 (3), 307–332.

Brody, G., & Stoneman, Z. (1986). Contextual issues in the study of sibling socialization. In J. J. Gallagher & P. M. Vietze (Eds.), *Families of handicapped persons* (pp. 197–218). Baltimore: Brookes.

Brody, G., Stoneman, Z., Davis, C., & Crapps, J. (1991). Observations of the role relations between older children with mental retardation and their younger siblings. *American Journal of Mental Retardation*, 95, 527–536.

Carter, E., & McGoldrich, M. (1980). The family life cycle and family therapy: An overview. In E. Carter & M. McGoldrich (Eds.), *The family life cycle: A framework for family therapy* (pp. 3–19). New York: Gardner Press.

Cleveland, D., & Miller, N. (1977). Attitude and life commitments of older siblings of mentally retarded adults. *Mental Retardation*, 15, 38–41.

Crnic, K., & Leconte, J. (1986). Understanding sibling needs and influences. In R. Fewell & P. Vadasy (Eds.), *Families of handicapped children: Needs and supports across the life span* (pp. 75–98). Austin, TX: Pro-Ed.

Cuskelly, M., Chant, D., & Hayes, A. (1998). Behavior problems in siblings of children with Down syndrome: Associated with family responsibilities and parental stress. *International Journal of Disability, Development, and Education*, 45, 295–311.

Damiani, V. B. (1999). Responsibility and adjustment in siblings of children with disabilities: Update and review. *Families in Society*, 80, 34–40.

Dyson, L. L. (1996). The experiences of families of children with learning disabilities: Parental stress, family functioning and siblings' self-concept. *Journal of Learning Disabilities*, 29, 280–286.

Dyson, L. L. (2003). Children with learning disabilities within the family context:

Comparisons with siblings in global self-concept, academic self-perception, and social competence. *Learning Disabilities Research and Practice, 18*, 1–9.

Dyson, L. L., Edgar, E., & Crnic, K. (1989). Psychological predictors of adjustment by siblings of developmentally delayed children. *American Journal of Mental Retardation, 94* (3), 292–302.

Farber, B. (1959). *Mental retardation: Its social context and social consequences*. Boston: Houghton Mifflin.

Fine, M. J., & Carlson, C. (1992). *The handbook of family–school intervention: A systems perspective*. Boston: Allyn & Bacon.

Fine, M. J., & Nissenbaum, M. S. (Eds.). (2000). The child with disabilities and the family: Implications for professionals. In M. J. Fine & R. L. Simpson (Eds.), *Collaboration with parents and families of children with disabilities* (pp. 3–26). Austin, TX: Pro-Ed.

Fishman, S., Wolf, L., Ellison, D., Gillis, B., Freeman, T., & Szatmari, P. (1996). Risk and protective factors affecting the adjustment of siblings of children with chronic disabilities. *Journal of the American Academy of Child and Adolescent Psychiatry, 35*, 1532–1542.

Fussell, J. J., Macias, M., & Saylor, C. (2002). Social skills and behavior problems of children with disabilities, with and without siblings. *Journal of Developmental and Behavioral Pediatrics, 23*, 397.

Glasberg, B. A. (2000). The development of siblings' understanding of autism spectrum disorders. *Journal of Autism and Developmental Disorders, 30*, 143–156.

Graliker, E., Fishler, K., & Koch, R. (1962). Teenage reaction to a mentally retarded sibling. *American Journal of Mental Deficiency, 66*, 838–843.

Grossman, F. (1972). *Brothers and sisters of retarded children: An exploratory study*. Syracuse, NY: Syracuse University Press.

Hannah, M. E., & Midlarsky, E. (1999). Competence and adjustment of siblings of children with mental retardation. *American Journal of Mental Retardation, 104*, 22–37.

Hastings, R. (2003). Brief report: Behavioral adjustment of siblings of children with autism. *Journal of Autism and Developmental Disorders, 33*, 99–104.

Hollidge, C. (2001). Psychological adjustment of siblings to a child with diabetes. *Health and Social Work, 26*, 15–25.

Jackson, Y., Sifers, S., Warren, J. S., & Velasquez, D. (2003). Family protective factors and behavioral outcome: The role of appraisal in family life events. *Journal of Emotional and Behavioral Disorders, 11*(2), 103–121.

Klein, S. (1972). Brother to sister: Sister to brother. *Exceptional Parent, 2*, 10–15.

Lardieri, J. B., & Swanson, H. L. (2000). Sibling relationships and parent stress in families of children with and without learning disabilities. *Learning Disability Quarterly, 23*, 105–116.

Lobato, D. (1983a). Siblings of chronically ill or developmentally disabled often develop altruistic qualities. *The Brown University Child and Adolescent Behavior Letter, 7*, 1–3.

Lobato, D. (1983b). Siblings of handicapped children: A review. *Journal of Autism and Developmental Disorders, 13*, 347–364.

Lobato, D. (1990). *Brothers, sisters, and special needs*. Baltimore: Brookes.

Love, H. (1973). *The mentally retarded child and his family*. Springfield, IL: Thomas.

Mason, E. J., Kruse, L. A., Farabaugh, A., Gershberg, R., & Kohler, M. S. (2000). Children with exceptionalities and their siblings: Opportunities for collaboration between family and school. In M. J. Fine & R. L. Simpson (Eds.), *Collaboration with parents and families of children with disabilities* (pp. 69–88). Austin, TX: Pro-Ed.

Muscott, H. (2002). Exceptional partnerships: Listening to the voices of parents of children with disabilities. *Preventing School Failure, 46*(2), 66–69.

Orsmond, G. I., & Seltzer, M. M. (2000). Brothers and sisters of adults with mental retardation: Gendered nature of the sibling relationship. *American Journal of Mental Retardation, 105*, 486–508.

Phillips, R. S. (1999). Intervention with siblings of children with developmental disabilities from economically disadvantaged families. *Families in Society, 80*, 569–577.

Powell, T. H., & Gallagher, P. (1993). *Brothers and sisters: A special part of exceptional families* (2nd ed.). Baltimore: Brookes.

Rivers, J. W., & Stoneman, Z. (2003). Sibling relationships when a child has autism: Marital stress and support coping. *Journal of Autism and Developmental Disorders, 33,* 383–394.

Roos, S. (2002). Chronic sorrow: Siblings of children with disabilities have needs too. *The Brown University Child and Adolescent Letter, 18,* 1–3.

Simeonsson, R., & Simeonsson, J. (1993). Children, families and disability: Psychological dimensions. In J. Paul & S. Simeonsson (Eds.), *Children with special needs* (pp. 25–50). Fort Worth, TX: Harcourt Brace Jovanovich.

Simpson, R. L. (1996). *Working with parents and families of exceptional children and youth.* Austin, TX: Pro-Ed.

Simpson, R., & Zurkowski, J. (2000). Parent and professional collaborative relationships in an era of change. In M. J. Fine & R. L. Simpson (Eds.), *Collaboration with parents and families of children with disabilities* (pp. 89–102). Austin, TX: Pro-Ed.

Stavros, H. (1989). But not enough to tell the truth: Developmental needs of siblings. *The Exceptional Parent, 19,* 38–41.

Stoneman, Z., Brody, G., Davis, C., Crapps, J., & Malone, D. M. (1991). Ascribed role relations between children with mental retardation and their siblings. *American Journal of Mental Retardation, 95,* 537–550.

Telford, C., & Sawrey, J. (1977). *The exceptional individual.* Englewood Cliffs, NJ: Prentice Hall.

Tew, B., & Lawrence, K. (1973). Mothers, brothers, and sisters of patients with spina bifida. *Developmental Medicine and Child Neurology, 15,* 69–76.

Turnbull, A. P., & Turnbull, H. R. (2001). *Families, professionals and exceptionality: Collaborating for empowerment* (4th ed.). Upper Saddle River, NJ: Merrill/Prentice Hall.

CHAPTER 5
Providing Coping and Stress Supports for Parents and Families

In this chapter, you will understand:

- Implications of several theoretical models of stress and coping.
- How specific stressors typically impact families of children with disabilities.
- What key demographic factors are associated with either increased or decreased levels of family stress.
- How parents of children with disabilities experience positive effects and transformations.

- What key characteristics are common in strong, resilient families.
- How family coping strategies such as stress reduction techniques, cognitive coping, and support services reduce stress and empower families.

Family Perspective: Zachary's Family

For 2 years we navigated unfamiliar terrain—we met with numerous doctors, and Zachary endured endless tests. Finally we found our answer—autism. Although this was a diagnosis we knew little about, I was relieved that day because at least we knew something.

My initial relief gave way to other feelings. I found myself waking up in the middle of the night, jolted awake by feelings of panic and terror. How were we going to manage? What kind of life could we create for Zachary? Will he have friends? What kind of adult will he be? Will someone always be there for him? I was so frustrated that this had happened to Zachary and to us. I had done all of the right things during my pregnancy. Was there something I missed? I was angry at the pediatricians who had ignored and dismissed my concerns about Zachary. I was angry at the pediatric neurologist who gave my son a life sentence at age 3, telling us that Zachary would need to be placed in a residential setting. Why wasn't there more information to help us do the best we could for Zachary? Guilt joined my feelings of frustration. (Santelli, Poyadue, & Young, 2001, p. 13)

Reflecting on the Family Perspective

1. How could school professionals best support Zachary's parents during the time described above?
2. Do you believe there is a "typical path" parents go through in dealing with the emotional states they experience in learning of their child's disabilities?

◉   ◉   ◉

Although the family depicted in the above perspective survived and actually thrived in their parenting of a child with a disability, the fears, uncertainties, and self-doubts expressed by Zachary's mother are real for many families. The journey of discovery, hope, and revitalization experienced by families of children with disabilities will be the focus of this chapter. The substantial body of research investigating the family impact of raising a child with a disability has yielded conflicting results. Traditionally, it was assumed by most professionals and supported by prevailing research in the 1950s through the early 1990s that the overall impact on the entire family of a child with a disability was primarily negative. This gloomy forecast has been mediated by more recent research revealing positive benefits in parenting a child with a disability. Even considering these equivocal research findings, it is still widely accepted that the discovery that a child has a disability produces stress for the family. How the family handles and responds to that stress largely determines whether the impact of this traumatic event will be primarily negative or positive on family functioning. Professionals engaged in providing effective school-based family support services must understand the nature of stress experienced by families of children with disabilities as well as how families successfully cope and, indeed, become strengthened through such experiences. This chapter focuses on reviewing the theoretical and empirical literature on family stress, characteristics of resilient families, and how school professionals can help families develop effective coping strategies.

THEORETICAL MODELS OF STRESS AND COPING

A commonly accepted definition of stress is offered by Holroyd and Lazarus (1982) as existing when "environmental and/or internal demands tax or exceed the individual's resources for managing them" (p. 22). Walsh (2003) indicated that stress may be manifested *biologically* (e.g., leading to bodily or physical effects such as fatigue, exhaustion, cardiovascular strain, reduced immune response, headaches, gastrointestinal upset, decreased appetite, and vulnerability to illness), *psychologically* (e.g., cognitive and emotional effects such as shock, terror, irritability, anger, guilt, grief, helplessness, impaired concentration, confusion, decreased self-esteem, and decreased self-efficacy, among others), and *socially* (e.g., the disruption of a social unit such as a family). Families of children with disabilities experience psychological stress first. A family's ability to adapt and adjust to the stressor (i.e., having a child with a disability) will determine the extent of biological and social stress experienced by individual family members and the family as a whole.

Coping involves the process by which a family adjusts and adapts to stress. Coping is what one does using resources from inside oneself, inside the family, and throughout the community. It is the actions the family takes to remove or reduce the stressor, live with the hardships caused by the stressor, or develop new resources in response to a crisis. Lazarus and Folkman (1984) defined coping as "constantly changing cognitive and behavioral efforts to manage specific external and/or internal demands that are appraised as taxing or exceeding the resources of the person" (p. 141).

The importance of families effectively coping with the stress they experience in having a child with a disability cannot be overstated. How well a family copes with stress influences family functions, satisfaction, feelings of efficacy, and children's life outcomes (Zeitlin & Rosenblatt, 1985). Indeed, effective coping fosters family quality of life. Family quality of life has been defined by Park, Turnbull, and Turnbull (2002) as "family members (a) having their needs met, (b) enjoying their life together as a family, and (c) having opportunities to pursue and achieve goals that are meaningful to them" (p. 153). As family stress increases and continues unabated, behavior problems of children increase (Jackson, Sifers, Warren, & Velasquez, 2003). On the positive side, as noted by Jackson et al., a positive family environment created by effective coping skills assists children in developing adaptive coping resources of their own. In addition, improved parental coping is correlated with increased parent involvement in the educational programming of their child (Peterson, 1982).

Ineffective coping with family-related stress impairs parenting skills. For example, Singer (1993) argued that parental depressive symptoms as a result of inability to cope with stress are associated with decreased parental responsiveness in raising their children. Active parent–child engagement fosters children's cognitive development and serves as a solid foundation for school. Along the same lines, it has been found that parents whose coping strategies are less adaptive appear to provide lower quality parenting, negatively impacting their children's social development (Bradley, Rock, Whiteside, Caldwell, & Brisby, 1991). Longitudinal research reveals that the climate of the home affects the social development of children (Floyd & Gallagher, 1997).

Hill's ABCX Model

To put a human touch on theoretical models of stress and coping, Patty Gerdel (1985), a mother of a child with cerebral palsy, provided the following "statistics" about her family's stress and coping issues: "Eighty-five percent of the time I feel pleased with my child. Seventeen percent of the time I question my world and wonder why I've been put in this position. Twenty-two percent of the time I wish society could be a little more understanding of my child's needs. Eight percent of the time I get tired of continually assisting my child in doing things he could do for himself. Ninety-one percent of the time I feel I could burst with pride over my family and the love we share. One hundred percent of the time I take one day at a time" (p. 5). What is remarkable about these "family statistics" is that they are truly unremarkable. That is, these same issues, joys, and frustrations could apply to most families—whether or not they have a child with a disability.

The family crisis model, ABCX, was originally developed by Hill (1949, 1958) as a framework for examining factors associated with the family's recovery from the disruptive effects of stress. In Hill's model, A (characteristics of the stressor event) interacting with B (the family's crisis-meeting resources) interacting with C (the definition the family makes of the event) produces X (the crisis). Berry and Hardman (1998) provided an example of how the ABCX model may predict family concerns and stress:

> . . . the birth of a child with a cleft palate would be A, the stressor event, which would include both normative stress (the family transition involved in the birth of a child) and nonnormative stress (the medical and specialized care needs of this infant). Family resources (B) would include availability of medical care and health insurance. The definition or appraisal by the family (C) might be that this situation is terrible because funds are not available to provide the complete medical and cosmetic interventions the child needs. This would produce X, the crisis. (pp. 73–74)

A visual depiction of the ABCX model follows:

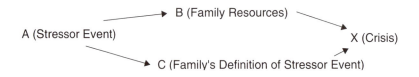

The focus of the ABCX model is on the interactions among the precrisis or buffer factors (B and C) and their influence on X. Factors B and C account for the differences in how families cope with the aftermath of stressor or transition events. Factor B refers to the resources the family possesses to address the crisis. Included in this factor is the family's structure and values. The second precrisis factor (C) represents the family's subjective definition of the stressor event. Variations in the family's definition of the stressor event are dependent on the perceived seriousness of the event and the amount of difficulty the family predicts in the changes caused by the event. The precrisis factors determine if a crisis will result and, if so, what the extent of the crisis will be. A stressor event (A) produces crisis in the family. Hill distinguished normative and nonnormative stressors. Normative stressors are events and transitions generally expected to occur over a family's life cycle (e.g., graduation, children leaving home, etc.). Nonnormative stressors are sudden and unexpected events (e.g., birth of a child with a disability) that produce disruption in the family.

McCubbin and Patterson's Double ABCX Model

McCubbin and Patterson (1982) expanded on Hill's original framework by incorporating the results of longitudinal studies of American families with a father or husband held prisoner or missing in action during the Vietnam War. The focus in this model is family adaptation, which refers to the family's efforts to reach a new level of balance after a crisis occurs. This model acknowledges the impact of an accumulation of demands that may already exist in the family system prior to a particular stressor event. The new demands resulting from a stressful event (e.g., having a child with a disability), combined with the accumulated demands already in existence, may overwhelm the family's ability to adapt.

   In the Double ABCX model, each of the four factors is expanded. Factor aA refers to family stress and change and highlights the cumulative nature of stress. There are three stressors that can accumulate in the family system during a crisis. They are the initial stressor event, stressors that are the result of family changes, and stressors that result from the family's efforts to respond to the crisis (Behr, 1989). Factor bB, family resources, represents resources that decrease the stressor's impact and coping resources developed in response to the stressor event. Factor cC is defined as "the family's perception of the original stressor event, plus the pile-up of other stressors and strains ('aA' factor), plus its perception of its resources ('bB' factor)" (Patterson, 1993, p. 224). Finally, factor xX, the family crisis, involves adaptation as the family struggles with postcrisis adjustment. Family adaptation represents a successful outcome to a stressor event because family unity is maintained, the well-being of individual members is facilitated, and the family system is enhanced. Continuing the example of the family with a child born with a cleft palate, Berry and Hardman (1998) showed how the Double ABCX model operates. Their example proceeds with the assumption that

> the family may already be under stress because the parents are unemployed (aA). They may, however, be able to appraise (cC) not just their own limited financial resources, but their capacity for problem solving (bB). The mother might remember that a social worker came to speak to her parenting preparation class and told of community resources available to children and families." (p. 74)

The operation of this model clearly demonstrates the importance of family adaptation in the stress and coping process and can be depicted in this manner:

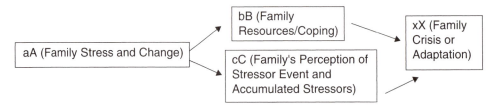

Patterson's Family Adjustment and Adaptation (FAAR) Model

The final model of stress and coping discussed in this chapter is Patterson's FAAR model (Patterson, 1988, 1989, 1993). This model emphasizes the processes families use to restore balance between stressor demands and resources in an effort to minimize stress. Like the Double ABCX model, the FAAR model focuses on cognitive appraisals, or the meanings families use in adjusting and adapting to stressor events. Patterson (1993) indicated there were two meaning levels used by families in their adaptation to having a child with a disability. There are *situational* and *global* meanings. Situational meanings refer to how a family defines the demands of a specific situation and how they assess their capability to address the demands. For example, a family may face the situation that their son with emotional/behavioral disabilities is constantly being suspended from school for his behavioral outbursts. One situational meaning the family could assign to this stressor event is that their son is out of control and they must just accept the school's punitive approach to dealing with his misbehavior. An alternative and better coping approach would be to define this situation as a call to become more informed about their son's special education legal rights. The family could assess their capability to become better informed advocates for their son by recognizing the need to contact a local parent information center. This support organization could assist the family in learning about the school's legal obligation to conduct a functional behavioral assessment (see chapter 9) and develop a positive behavior intervention plan for their son.

Global meanings extend beyond a specific situational crisis and involve cognitive beliefs about relationships within the family and between the family and the community. Patterson (1993) referred to these cognitive beliefs as "family schema" and identified five dimensions of an adaptive family schema:

- **Shared purpose**—the family develops a deeper commitment to life where often family priorities are reordered and there is a greater appreciation of "little things" and individuals
- **Collectivity**—the family realizes it must work closely together
- **Frameability**—the family gains a more optimistic outlook on life
- **Eelativism**—the family becomes more tolerant and flexible
- **Shared control**—the family understands they have less control over their life and they develop more assertiveness in working with professionals

The FAAR model also includes two phases: adjustment and adaptation. During the adjustment phase, the family makes only minor changes to achieve balance between demands and resources. The family either makes minor changes to reduce demands or they increase their ability to meet the demands. As noted by Berry and Hardman (1998), these minor changes may be either real and objective or very subjective, involving the appraisal of a situation differently. For a family with a child with attention deficit hyperactivity disorder (ADHD), a real and objective change would be hiring a babysitter one night a week so the parents can have a night to relax by themselves. A subjective change would entail a redefinition of this child with ADHD by the parents, noting that their child's behavior reflects high energy and enthusiasm—two traits admired by employers.

If the stress continues and there remains an imbalance between family demands and resources, greater changes are in order. This involves the adaptation phase. During adaptation, families restructure their boundaries, roles, and rules. For the family with the ADHD child, that persistent behavior may wear thin over time and lead to emotional and physical exhaustion of the parents. The parents may adapt by making some role changes in the family, asking extended family members to take responsibility for childcare a couple of nights a week. The parents may also request assistance from the school staff in setting up family rules that require the hyperactive child to play independently in his own room for at least 1 hour after dinner. Families who are able to effectively adjust to short-term stressful situations and adapt to long-term stressors will possess more positive perceptions of their circumstances and become more empowered.

STRESSORS IMPACTING FAMILIES OF CHILDREN WITH DISABILITIES

The issues and concerns confronted by families of children with disabilities are likely stressors for those families (Crnic, Friedrich, & Greenberg, 1983; Friedrich, Wilturner, & Cohen, 1985). Research into whether raising a child with a disability generates greater family stress than that experienced by families without a child with a disability has yielded conflicting results (Baxter, Cummins, & Polak, 1995; Dyson, 1993). Some studies have concluded that families of children with disabilities experience increased stress compared to families without a child with disabilities (Dyson & Fewell, 1986; Wilton & Renault, 1986); other investigations report no differences in family stress levels (Gowen, Johnson-Martin, Goldman, & Appelbaum, 1989; Harris & McHale, 1989; Salisbury, 1987). Without attempting to reach an unequivocal conclusion on the earlier-stated research question, educators must acknowledge that stress has become an inevitable phenomenon and fact of everyday life for all kinds of families. Indeed, as stated by Selye (1980), "complete freedom from stress is death" (p. 128). In their efforts to support families of children with disabilities, school professionals must possess a thorough understanding and sensitivity to the typical stressors impacting those families. This section will briefly review typical stressors impacting families of children with disabilities, categorized into the following five areas: (a) transitional stress, (b) family functioning stress, (c) emotional stress, (d) caregiving stress, and (e) stress from negative professional/societal attitudes and assumptions.

Transitional Stress

As a component of the family systems model, family life cycle theory attempts to explain how a family changes over time. It is important to recognize that family life cycle transitions usually create heightened stress for families due to changes in family dynamics and roles (Turnbull & Turnbull, 2001). These changes may create confusion and conflict for families wrestling with new transitional issues. Among the numerous life-cycle transitions impacting families, three key transition periods are (a) after the child's diagnosis, (b) when the child enters school, and (c) when the child leaves school (Baxter et al., 1995).

The diagnosis of a child's disability is a stressful event for parents. Initial parental reactions to the diagnosis typically include shock, disbelief, denial, and anger (Eakes, 1995; Tanner, Dechert, & Friedan, 1998). While a diagnosis provides confirmation of parental concerns about their child's development, the diagnosis does not answer their questions about what they need to know about a particular disability and what steps they need to take next in raising their child (Cohen, 1993). These uncertainties and the prospect of entering a totally different world of medical and special education professionals is a daunting new reality for parents. Parents have been thrust into new roles and responsibilities in raising a child with a disability. As parents contemplate these new realities, they may struggle with their confidence in being able to meet their new responsibilities. At this transitional stage, professionals must be first and foremost empathetic in their interactions with families. Professionals can support families by displaying sensitivity to their emotional needs and feelings of vulnerability. The next step for professionals is to address the parents' needs for information so they can begin to construct how to respond to their new roles and responsibilities. At the very least, parents should be provided with information on the educational implications of their child's disability, available services within the school and broader community, and parental rights and responsibilities in educational decision making. Communication and Collaboration Tips Box 5.1 provides some suggestions on how school professionals can demonstrate empathy and sensitivity to families.

COMMUNICATION AND COLLABORATION TIPS   **BOX 5.1**

School professionals can demonstrate empathy and sensitivity to families by:

- ❑ Listening to parents' concerns before offering recommendations
- ❑ Using reinforcing statements to encourage parents to continue talking about family concerns and issues
- ❑ Using positive and responsive facial expressions while listening to parents
- ❑ Identifying areas of common experience and agreement with parents
- ❑ Displaying a keen interest in forming a collaborative partnership with parents
- ❑ Encouraging parents to attend to their needs as well as the needs of their child with a disability

As the child with a disability enters the school system, this transition causes the parents to interact with school professionals. Although parents often feel a sense of relief that their child is experiencing a normal transition in attending school, parents also begin to become acutely aware of how their child may be lagging socially and academically compared to age peers (Melnyk, Feinstein, Moldenhouer, & Small, 2001). The developmental gap between children with disabilities and their nondisabled peers typically grows with each passing school year, causing increased stress for the parents. Parents worry about how well their child will adjust to the demands of a new environment as the child gets acclimated to school routines. It is important at this transition stage that school professionals allay parental concerns by demonstrating confidence that the educational program will address the child's needs and that the school is eager to establish a collaborative relationship with the parents.

A final critical transition stage in a family's life cycle is when the child is preparing to leave the school. The primary stressor for families at this stage is uncertainty of the future (Baxter et al., 1995). Depending on their child's support needs, parents often face a number of unanswered questions related to vocational and residential services. How independently can my child live? What job possibilities exist in the community? What decision-making assistance will my child require as an adult? What social and recreational opportunities exist for my child? Parents may be confronting the reality that their child will never be totally self-supporting. Parents are cast into the responsibility to be continuous life planners for their child (Hughes, 1999). This can be an overwhelming responsibility for some families. The stress associated with responding to the uncertainty of the future should be minimized if the school has actively involved the parents in comprehensive transitional planning in the last several years of the student's school career. More specific information on how schools can support families during the transition from school to postschool life will be provided in chapters 7 and 11.

Family Functioning Stress

The presence of a child with a disability impacts the entire family. This impact may be positive, negative, or neutral (Turnbull & Turnbull, 2001). When there is a negative impact, the family experiences stress because the family system has been disrupted and its ability to adequately address family functions (e.g., affection, self-esteem, spirituality, economics, daily care, socialization, recreation, and education) has been impaired. A family's inability to meet their needs in any of the eight family functions listed above causes stress. For example, family affection needs may be negatively impacted due to strain in the marital relationship (Blacher, 1984; McDonald, Kysela, & Reddon, 1987) or sibling resentment over the amount of parental attention given the child with the disability (Hughes, 1999; Latson, 1995). Marital strain is often due to disagreements between the father and mother over the existence or implications of the disability or how to deal with behavioral problems (Latson, 1995).

Socialization and recreational needs of the family may be impaired as some parents report feelings of isolation and lack of social acceptance of their child with a disability (Hughes, 1999). It can be a source of stress for families as they struggle to meet the socialization and recreation needs of their child with a disability.

The parental concern is that their child will be rejected by peers and not develop friend-ships (Turnbull & Ruef, 1997). Economic functions of the family are typically strained because of increased costs of raising a child with a disability (Birenbaum & Cohen, 1993; Fujiura, Roccoforte, & Braddock, 1994). Extraordinary costs for families of chil-dren with disabilities often include adapted clothing, architectural modifications, en-vironmental modifications, consumer electronics, dental or related needs, exercise equipment, furniture, vehicle modifications, wheelchairs or other prosthetic devices, medical costs, and specialized diets (Fujiura et al., 1994). Two issues exacerbate the potential financial strain on families. First, along with the increased costs of raising a child with a disability, families also may experience reduced employment opportuni-ties. Some families forego new and better paying job offers because they would need to relocate away from current service providers (Barnett & Boyce, 1995; Birenbaum & Cohen, 1993). Second, a major study investigating state financing trends for family support found that families caring for children with disabilities received a dispropor-tionately small share of the public spending allocated for developmental disabilities services (Parish, Pomeranz-Essley, & Braddock, 2003).

Emotional Stress

The stage model of grief developed by Kubler-Ross (1969) in her work with termi-nally ill people has been applied to families of children with disabilities to explain typical emotional reactions of those families. According to Kubler-Ross's model, families could be expected to meet the news of their child's disability with initial shock followed by feelings of denial, guilt, depression, anger, and anxiety. It is an-ticipated that these negative feelings will eventually give way to acceptance of their situation and family reorganization. Many professionals have criticized the appli-cation of Kubler-Ross's model to families of children with disabilities as too sim-plistic, rigid, and negative (Berry & Hardman, 1998). However, there is research evidence concluding that families of children with disabilities are at risk for stress associated with grief reactions (Beckman, 1991; Berry & Jones, 1995; Brannan & Heflinger, 1997; Roach & Orsmond, 1999). Further, there are a number of books written by parents of children with various disabilities acknowledging their grief feelings (Featherstone, 1980; Kupfer, 1982; Spiegle & van den Pol, 1993; Turnbull & Turnbull, 1985).

Moses (1987) argued that the emotions associated with the grief process are a natural and adaptive response by parents as they learn to respond to their child's diag-nosis of disability. As envisioned by Moses, parents experience their child's disability as a loss because their dreams and hopes for their child have been altered or, as some par-ents feel, shattered. Parents must be allowed to experience each of the aforementioned emotions to "separate from the lost dream and generate new, more attainable dreams" (Moses, 1987, p. 8). Indeed, a more appropriate and supportive professional perspective on these grief emotional states is to view them as necessary adaptive responses to trou-bling new information, instead of indications of parental pathology or maladjustment. Table 5.1 summarizes the adaptive functions served by grief feelings and how profes-sionals can be supportive to families experiencing these feeling states.

Table 5.1   Grief Feeling States.

Feeling state	Adaptive function	Supportive professional responses
Denial	■ Buys time to deal with difficult news ■ Helps locate resources and develop a support system	■ Do not pressure parents; let them come to their understanding at their own pace ■ Connect parents with other parents of children with similar disabilities
Guilt	■ Assesses the reality of what you are and are not responsible for ■ Develops a sense of control and may serve to explain the unexplainable	■ Be a good listener ■ Do not argue with a guilt-ridden person ■ Show empathy
Depression	■ Develops new definition of strength or competency ■ Common reaction to a loss	■ Show empathy ■ Help parents develop supportive relationships with other families (to avoid isolation tendencies) ■ Foster renewed sense of strength or competence in parents
Anger	■ Redefines internal sense of fairness or justice	■ Do not respond in kind to parental anger ■ Follow suggestions listed in Box 5.2
Anxiety	■ Redefines or prioritizes parental responsibilities ■ Provides energy to seek out necessary information	■ Make interactions with parents comfortable and welcoming ■ Encourage parents to strike a balance in family responsibilities and needs ■ Provide parents with information they are seeking

Caregiving Stress

Families must address the daily care needs of their members (Turnbull & Turnbull, 2001). The needs of children with disabilities vary tremendously. Some children have extensive physical care needs in feeding, dressing, toileting, and navigating their environment. Other children have significant medical needs and require specialized

COMMUNICATION AND COLLABORATION TIPS   Box 5.2

Suggestions for Interacting with Angry or Upset Individuals

(Summarized from Simpson, 1996 and Turnbull & Turnbull, 2001)

❏ Allow the angry/upset individual to express her feelings and concerns without interruption.
❏ Record the concerns of the angry/upset individual and show him the list to ensure that it is complete.
❏ To ensure that the communication focuses on the most critical issues or concerns, assist the angry/upset individual in prioritizing her concerns.
❏ Once the angry/upset individual calms down, ask for his suggestions on how to solve any of the issues or concerns expressed, and write down those suggestions.
❏ Concentrate on keeping a low voice tone and a relaxed posture, and avoid defensive or intimidating gestures. As the angry/upset individual speaks more loudly, speak more softly in response.
❏ Avoid arguing with an angry/upset individual. Similarly, do not become defensive or discount the person's feelings or concerns.
❏ Request clarification on any statements that are not understood.
❏ Avoid attempts to engage the angry/upset individual in collaborative problem solving. Let the person vent her feelings and calm down prior to engaging in rational problem solving.
❏ Avoid responding to generalized accusations (e.g., "You are incompetent") or threats (e.g., "I'm going to call my lawyer").
❏ Avoid promising the angry/upset individual something that may not be possible to produce or accomplish.
❏ Recognize that most anger can be translated into energy to motivate collaborative problem-solving efforts.

Sources: Adapted from *Working with parents and families of exceptional children and youth: Techniques for successful conferencing and collaboration,* by R.L. Simpson, 1996, Austin, TX: Pro-Ed; *Families, professionals, and exceptionality: Collaborating for empowerment,* by A.P. Turnbull and H.R. Turnbull, 2001, Upper Saddle River, NJ: Merrill/Prentice Hall.

diet, medication administration, or therapies. Some children require 24-hour-a-day monitoring. Other children need parental assistance with school work on a continuous basis. These daily care needs are unrelenting, with associated time and energy drains on the parents. Simply stated, children with disabilities typically require more time and attention than children without disabilities do (Hughes, 1999; McDonald, Kysela, & Reddon, 1987; Roach & Orsmond, 1999). The drain on parents' time and energy causes fatigue and makes parents more vulnerable to stress. The excessive daily care needs emphasize the child's dependence on the parents (Bauer & Shea, 2003). Because of the child's disability, the parents may not be able to reasonably expect, as parents of nondisabled children do, that their child's dependence will substantially lessen over time. This realization can cause considerable stress and anxiety for parents. Managing the needs of children with behavioral problems exacerbates the time and energy drains on parents (Berry & Hardman, 1998; Simpson, 1996). Dealing with the time and energy demands of raising a child with a disability can be stressful enough, but stress levels are aggravated when parents experience less leisure time and parental reinforcement (Koegel et al., 1992).

Stress from Negative Professional and Societal Attitudes/Assumptions

Fiedler (2000) noted that historically the relations between professionals and families of children with disabilities have often been the source of stress for many families. The origin of much of the stress experienced by parents in interacting with professionals can be traced to negative attitudes and assumptions maintained by some professionals. Some of these negative attitudes and assumptions are remnants of negative societal reactions toward individuals with disabilities. Vohs (1993) maintained that there is still a significant amount of stigma directed at individuals with disabilities. She argued that societal stigma about disabilities is the most potent stressor impacting families. Fiedler (2000) identified the following examples of negative professional attitudes and assumptions.

- Professionals assume that they know what is best for a child with a disability, that parents should gratefully and unquestionably follow the advice of the expert.
- Judgmental professionals who possess stereotypical attitudes about certain families or are unable to suspend their judgment on family actions and lifestyles that conflict with their own.
- Professionals assume that caring, loving parents will be actively involved in their child's education; thus, those parents not actively involved must not care about their child.
- Professionals with negative attitudes and animosity toward parents who assert their children's educational rights by functioning as an advocate.
- Professionals blame parents for their child's problems.
- Professionals tend to emphasize only the child's problems, disabilities, and other negatives when communicating with parents.
- Professionals take a minimalist perspective, asking "What do I have to do?" as opposed to asking "What can be done to appropriately serve the child and family?"

When professionals bring any of these negative attitudes or assumptions to their interactions with families, relationship strain is the usual outcome. At a time when families are hoping to rely on professional support, they may instead feel criticized, devalued, and alienated. In addition to unfulfilled expectations for support due to negative professional attitudes and assumptions, parents may experience increased isolation or rejection from extended family members and friends (i.e., their social support network; Turnbull et al., 1993). Some extended family members or friends do not feel comfortable around individuals with disabilities, or they do not know what to say to console the parents during their difficult times.

In addition to understanding the typical stressors impacting families of children with disabilities, it is instructive to professionals to comprehend demographic factors that are associated with greater or lesser stress levels among families of children with disabilities. In addressing family factors, several studies have concluded that stress levels are higher in single-parent families (Beckman, 1991; Duis & Summers, 1997; Floyd & Gallagher, 1997; Schilling, Kirkham, Snow, & Schinke, 1986). These stress-level differences can be explained by the greater time and energy demands when there is only one parent. Single mothers have less leisure time and missed more work than married mothers do (Duis & Summers, 1997). Higher stress levels are also found in families whose nondisabled siblings demonstrate strong feelings of embarrassment about their sibling with a disability (Duis & Summers, 1997). An interesting finding is that more educated parents often experience greater stress as they struggle with accepting their child's disability, which they tend to view as a tragedy (Palfrey, Walker, Butler, & Singer, 1989; Winkler, 1988).

There are several parent/family factors associated with decreased stress levels. Families with more financial resources typically are able to respond more positively to the demands of raising a child with a disability (Bradley et al., 1991; Duis & Summers, 1997; Murphy, Behr, & Summers, 1990). Further, families with strong marital relationships and close, cohesive unity are better equipped to respond more positively to their situation (Behr, 1989; Duis & Summers, 1997; Jackson et al., 2003). Families who have developed a religious perspective and frequently attend church have been associated with less stress (Behr, 1989; Winkler, 1988). Finally, Scorgie, Wilgosh, and McDonald (1996) conducted a qualitative study with 15 parents of children with disabilities. Their research identified several themes or characteristics of families who effectively manage the stress experienced in raising a child with a disability. Among the significant personal character traits of the parents with less stress were patience, humor, and a commitment to serve as their child's advocate.

In addition to family factors, certain professional interaction characteristics or issues have been identified as relevant factors in determining family stress levels. In general, parents often express that their interactions with professionals are inherently stressful (Scorgie et al., 1996). However, professionals who effectively provide support to families or refer parents to community organizations alleviate parental stress to a large degree (Duis & Summers, 1997). Parents have further indicated that their stress levels increase when they believe professionals fail to consult with them about important issues concerning their child with a disability (Baxter et al., 1995). This issue elevates the importance of establishing open communication and a collaborative partnership between parents and professionals. Another important issue in parent–professional interactions is communication barriers. In a review of research conducted by the Office of Special Education Programs (OSEP) of the U.S. Department of Education, Singer (1993) stated, "Families for whom English is not spoken as the first language often face increased stress" (p. 5). In research conducted by Singer and his associates, Latino families with children in neonatal intensive care units (NICUs) experienced added stress due to communication and cultural barriers with professionals. These barriers caused misunderstandings, distrust, and a perceived inaccessibility of professionals (OSEP, 2001).

POSITIVE EFFECTS AND TRANSFORMATIONS IN PARENTING A CHILD WITH A DISABILITY

More recent research on the family impact of raising a child with a disability has concluded that successful families who are able to move on from initial feelings of devastation are far more than simply engaged in effective coping; they are experiencing personal transformations (Scorgie & Sobsey, 2000; Taunt & Hastings, 2002). Several studies have revealed that families who have adapted successfully to the demands of raising a child with a disability display positive perspectives and report positive experiences. The most commonly mentioned positive impacts of children with disabilities on their families were: (a) pleasure/satisfaction in providing care for the child; (b) the child as a source of joy/happiness; (c) the child providing a challenge or opportunity to learn and develop; (d) strengthened family and/or marriage; (e) a new or increased sense of purpose in life; (f) development of new skills, abilities, or career opportunities; (g) family members' experiencing personal growth (e.g., becoming more compassionate, less selfish, more tolerant, more confident); (h) expanded social and community networks; (i) increased spirituality; and (j) a changed perspective on life (e.g., determining what is important in life, relishing every day, living at a slower pace) (Behr, Murphy, & Summers, 1992; Scorgie & Sobsey, 2000; Scorgie, Wilgosh, & McDonald, 1999).

Taunt and Hastings (2002) conducted interviews of 14 parents of children with developmental disabilities, and an additional 33 parents responded to similar questions in an Internet-distributed survey. Parents were asked what they believe are the positive aspects of caring for their child with disabilities and whether they believe the presence of the child with a disability has had any positive effects on their other children or extended family members. Finally, parents were asked about the future for their child with a disability and their family, including their hopes and fears. Similar to previous research findings, a number of positive impacts on parents were identified: (a) positive aspects of the child (e.g., happy disposition of the child, child's achievements), (b) changed perspective on life (e.g., don't take things for granted; have new goals; value other people more; experience changed life expectations, career expectations, or both), (c) increased sensitivity (e.g., increased tolerance, awareness of others, more patience), (d) support from other families (e.g., receiving and sharing information with other parents), (e) opportunities to learn (e.g., learning about disabilities, psychology, special education), (f) improved family dynamics (e.g., brought family closer together, spend more time together as a family), (g) opportunities to expand social network or make a difference (e.g., meeting and sharing with others, chance to influence policy makers), (h) increased confidence or assertiveness (e.g., increased confidence in dealing with others, involvement in advocacy), and (i) strengthened religious faith.

In Taunt and Hastings's (2002) study, parents noted a number of positive impacts on siblings and extended family members:

- Increased sensitivity (e.g., better understanding of disability, more tolerant and patient, more caring and willing to help others)

- Positive effect on siblings (e.g., increased maturity, pride in the sibling with a disability)
- Changed perspective on life (e.g., learned not to take life for granted and to be content with what one has)
- Improved extended family dynamics (e.g., brought extended family closer together, demonstrated that family was willing to help)
- Opportunities to learn (e.g., opportunity to learn about disabilities and other difficulties in life)
- Positive attitude toward others (e.g., demonstration of caring, compassion, tenderness, warmth, thoughtfulness, sensitivity)
- Greater sense of responsibility (e.g., more maturity, willingness to stand up for people with disabilities)

In terms of the parents' hopes and fears for the future, a very small percentage reported negative feelings or concerns. Twenty percent of the interviewed parents were generally fearful or anxious about the future, whereas only 6% of the Internet respondents held similar views. More parents in both groups were hopeful about the future or they were ". . . able to see positive things amongst the expected difficulties or were focused on life in the present and gaining most from this" (Taunt & Hastings, 2002, p. 414).

In addition to the aforementioned positive effects that children with disabilities may have on their families, some parents experience personal transformations. Palus (1993) defined a transformative experience as "a life event and its outcome, such that the event is given a central role within a self narrative in causing, catalyzing, or symbolizing substantial, lasting psychological change" (p. 40). Personal transformations typically evolve out of traumatic events that disrupt an individual's psychological equilibrium (Janoff-Bulman, 1992). Developmental growth during adulthood occurs during periods of disequilibrium and ultimate reorganization (Hague, 1995; Palus, 1993). Transformative experiences are distinguished from coping, which involves finding techniques to continue one's life as it was before. Personal transformation, on the other hand, "involves the disintegration or abandonment of one's previous life in favor of a new and clearly better way of living" (Scorgie & Sobsey, 2000, pp. 197–198). The diagnosis of a child's disability is a traumatic experience that shakes the foundation of most parents' assumptions about life. This event, if handled correctly, can set in motion the process of transformative change for the parents.

In a two-part qualitative study, Scorgie and Sobsey (2000) interviewed 15 parents of children with disabilities. Specifically, parents were asked (a) "How have you personally been changed through parenting (name of the child with a disability)? and (b) What has (name of the child with a disability) taught you through his/her life?" (p. 199). In the second part of the study, themes identified from the initial parent interviews were used to survey 80 parents of children with disabilities to ascertain their agreement with the themes from the first stage of the study. The survey respondents indicated they had received positive benefits in parenting a child with a disability. The parent respondents agreed with most of the survey statements on transformational outcomes. Scorgie and Sobsey (2000) classified the transformational outcomes under three main themes: (a) personal transformations, (b) relational transformations, and (c) perspectival transformations.

Personal transformations reflect positive changes parents have noted in themselves. The positive personal changes more frequently mentioned by parents cluster into two themes: acquired roles and acquired traits. Through their parenting of a child with a disability, parents have acquired new roles such as advocate, leader, conference speaker, teacher, or organization member. Some parents even experienced vocational changes as a result of having a child with a disability. As one parent remarked, "My child helped me discover a side of myself I never knew existed. I might have never broadened my horizons without this experience" (Scorgie & Sobsey, 2000, p. 201). These new roles assumed by many parents fostered their development of new traits or characteristics. Parents learned to speak out to ensure the rights of their children with disabilities. Many parents' self-esteem was enhanced as they expressed more confidence, felt stronger, and believed they could accomplish more. In addition, parents observed they were more compassionate and laughed more since the diagnosis of their child's disability. Maintaining a sense of humor in difficult times restores a sense of balance to one's life. As one parent put it, "For every funny story you probably have about 10 or 20 difficult stories—stories of challenges and trials. But it's the funny stories that keep you going" (p. 201).

Relational transformations impact how parents relate to other people. Parents identified relational transformations in four categories: family relationships, advocacy relationships, friendship networks, and attitudes toward people in general. Although not a universal response, many parents felt their marriage was stronger due to the demands of raising a child with a disability. Even if some parents did not describe their marriage as stronger, there was a general consensus that their families were more open in their communication with each other and more effective as problem solvers. Through their advocacy relationships, many parents reported discovering a new passion that revitalized them. They believed their advocacy could "make a difference" in another person's life. Most of the surveyed parents indicated that their friendship network had been expanded as a result of having a child with a disability. They met other parents of children with disabilities, agency personnel, and caring professionals. These new relationships were often described as containing more depth than typical friendships. On the negative side, parents commented that they lost some friendships or experienced difficulties in interacting with professionals. Finally, in terms of transformed attitudes toward other people, parents generally reported a newly gained appreciation of the value of life. They developed more meaning in their lives through a refined sense of social justice. As one parent noted, "Another important change for me is the growing affinity I feel for the most powerless and most vulnerable in society; {my} sense of social justice is heightened" (Scorgie & Sobsey, 2000, p. 203).

Perspectival transformations involve changes in how a person views life. These changes cause individuals to reorder their priorities based on a new life perspective. The significant perspectival transformations identified by parents included (a) making the most of each day, (b) celebrating life more, (c) having a more authentic view of success, and (d) learning what is important in life. These life-affirming declarations are tempered by most parents' realism that during the ebb and flow of the demands of real life, sometimes they just survive day to day.

Parents who have been successful in focusing on the positives in raising their child with a disability and have experienced personal transformations strengthen their family structure and functioning. Indeed, Floyd and Gallagher (1997) referred to "resilient disruption" to illustrate the fact that raising a child with a disability disrupts family life, but for many families, the quality of family relationships and well-being remain intact or even enhanced.

A number of studies have identified specific strengths of families that include a member with a disability (Bailey & Smith, 2000; Curan, 1983; Dyson, 1997; Krauss, 1991; Schwab, 1989; Stinnett & DeFrain, 1989; Thames & Thomason, 1998; Trute & Hauch, 1988). Key characteristics of strong, resilient families are identified in Table 5.2.

McCubbin and his associates have been leaders in studying the concept of family resilience over the past decade. Family resilience is defined as

> 1. The property of the family system that enables it to maintain its established patterns of functioning after being challenged by risk factors (elasticity) and 2. The family's ability to recover quickly from a misfortune, trauma, or transitional event causing or calling for changes in the family's patterns of functioning (buoyancy). (McCubbin, Thompson, & McCubbin, 1996, p. 1)

Within the family resiliency framework (McCubbin & McCubbin, 1993, 1996), resilience involves two family processes: adjustment (elasticity) and adaptation (buoyancy). Adjustment involves the influence of **family protective factors** in enhancing the family's ability and efforts to maintain their integrity, functioning, and developmental tasks in the face of risk factors. Adaptation involves **family recovery factors** in promoting the family's ability to bounce back and adapt to crisis situations.

In two national surveys of family stressors over the family life cycle conducted by McCubbin and his associates (1996), several family protective and recovery factors were identified. The most prominent family protective factors over all stages of the family life cycle are (a) *family celebrations* (e.g., acknowledging birthdays, religious occasions, and other special events), (b) *family hardiness* (e.g., family members' sense of control over their lives, commitment to the family, and confidence that the family will

Table 5.2   Characteristics of Strong, Resilient Families.

- Open and honest communication
- Commitment to each other and contentment with their life
- Sense of family history
- Sense of humor
- Optimism
- Spiritual wellness
- An active social support system
- Sufficient time spent together as a family
- Appreciation shown to each other

COMMUNICATION AND COLLABORATION TIPS   **BOX 5.3**

(Based on the research of Stinnett & DeFrain, 1989)
School professionals can increase family resilience by encouraging these communication behaviors:

- ❏ Family members realize that good communication requires a great deal of time
- ❏ Family members know how to listen and they avoid sermonizing
- ❏ Family members check things out with each other by asking questions seeking out each other's feelings
- ❏ Family members avoid trying to read each other's minds
- ❏ Family members get inside the other person's world through good listening and empathy
- ❏ Family members create a caring climate where it is safe to express fears, insecurities, and failings
- ❏ Family members avoid criticism, evaluating, psychoanalysis, and acting superior, which are all barriers to positive communication
- ❏ Family members avoid brutal honesty
- ❏ Family members allow negative feelings to dissipate before trying to rationally discuss an issue
- ❏ Family members handle one problem at a time
- ❏ Family members are specific and define terms
- ❏ Family members become allies, attacking the problem rather than each other
- ❏ Family members "ban the bombs," which are those most destructive, hurtful comments that people sometimes use in arguments
- ❏ Family members look at disagreement as an opportunity for growth and enrichment

survive no matter what), (c) *family time and resources* (e.g., family meals, chores, togetherness, and other ordinary routines contributing to continuity and stability in family life), and (d) *family traditions* (e.g., honoring holidays and important family experiences carried across generations). The critical family recovery factors are (a) *family integration* (e.g., the parents' efforts to keep the family together and maintain an optimistic outlook); (b) *family support and esteem building* (e.g., the parents' efforts to receive support from the community and friends and to develop their self-esteem and confidence); (c) *family recreation orientation, control, and organization* (e.g., the family actively seeks out recreational activities and emphasizes control and family organization, rules, and procedures); and (4) *family optimism and mastery* (e.g., the family maintains hope and optimism about the future and seeks out relevant information to become informed consumers of services). Finally, school professionals can enhance resilience by encouraging family members to actively practice the communication behaviors listed in Communication and Collaboration Tips Box 5.3.

FAMILY COPING STRATEGIES

As stated earlier in this chapter, coping involves the process by which a family adjusts and adapts to stress. This section will discuss specific coping strategies designed to assist families in their adjustment and adaptation to the impact of raising a child with a disability. Families learn to cope with stress in their lives either by systematically reducing stressors or by learning new coping skills. This section will discuss coping in the following three areas: (a) stress-reduction techniques, (b) cognitive coping strategies, and (c) support strategies. The role of professionals in supporting families in their coping endeavors will be emphasized.

Stress-Reduction Techniques

The first order of business for parents in learning to systematically reduce the stressors in their lives is to acknowledge that taking care of themselves and their family relationships is just as important as taking care of their child with a disability. Parents must remember that they are a family first. Parents must learn relaxation techniques and how to take a temporary break from daily problems and responsibilities. This, however, is a constant challenge for parents of children with disabilities. In investigating the amount of leisure and recreation time spent by parents of children with Down syndrome, Barnett and Boyce (1995) discovered that they spent more time on child care and less time on social and recreational activities than did parents of children without disabilities. Further, daily challenges to engaging in recreational activities are noted by this parent:

> I know that Jason needs to get out and do things—go to the zoo, go to the park, see other children. I try to take him out as much as I can. But it's such a hassle. Getting in and out of the car. Getting the wheelchair in and out of the car. Making sure the other kids have what they need, plus diapers for the baby. Getting everyone organized to go. And then you get there and you find out the place isn't accessible. Or people stare at the wheelchair and the other kids get uncomfortable. . . . I know it's wrong—but it's a lot easier to just stay home. (Simons, 1987, pp. 19–20)

The danger is increased isolation for the entire family.

Professionals can assist families in their coping efforts by encouraging the use of passive appraisal techniques. Passive appraisal involves ignoring a problem or acting as if it does not exist (Muscott, 2002). Passive appraisal may take several forms such as denial, refusal to think about the future, and relaxation. Previously in this chapter, the adaptive function of denial as one of the typical grieving states was discussed. Professionals provide support for parents who are in a state of denial by not pressuring them to "move on" before they are ready to assimilate this new information and reality. In addition, professionals can encourage parents to develop specific relaxation techniques. For example, one of the authors of this book has employed relaxation exercises in workshops he has conducted for parents of children with disabilities. Examples of relaxation exercises include simple breathing activities and guided imagery.

Professionals can teach systematic stress management techniques to parents. For example, Hawkins and Singer (1989) provided instruction in (a) self-monitoring of stressful events and their reactions to them, (b) muscle relaxation skills, and (c) modification of cognitions associated with distress. For the self-monitoring skills, parents were taught to identify their particular symptoms of stress and to identify environmental events associated with those symptoms. Writing in journals, parents evaluated their tension levels three times per day and noted any event that triggered increased tension. The second component of the training program involved learning progressive muscle relaxation techniques. Parents were taught to systematically tense and release large muscle groups. To assist in their learning, the trainers provided parents with taped messages to guide their practice at home. In the final stage of this training program, parents learned to identify their thoughts at times during the day when they felt tense. Parents learned to recognize when they were engaged in distorted thinking, and how to think in more realistic ways.

A final example of how professionals can help parents to systematically reduce the stressors in their lives is another workshop activity used by one of this book's authors when working with parents of children with disabilities. This activity is based on the premise that individuals under considerable stress are typically not clear thinkers and expend a lot of wasted time and energy fretting about their circumstances. In an effort to help parents focus on their situation and prioritize a plan of action, try the following exercise with parents.

1. Parents list as many stressors as they can that are currently impacting them.
2. Parents cross out those stressors on their list that are beyond their control.
3. Parents cross out those stressors on their list that they deem not to be worth the time and energy to address right now.
4. Parents place an asterisk next to those stressors on their list that they impose on themselves.
5. Parents circle those stressors on their list that they can positively address. This final list becomes their prioritized plan of action.

Cognitive Coping Strategies

As indicated in the section reviewing theoretical models of stress and coping, a common component of those models involves how the family appraises what they are experiencing. That is, stress can be reduced when stressors are appraised as challenges or viewed in a positive light. Indeed, changing how one perceives a given situation may help an individual feel better about an event. This section will briefly discuss a variety of cognitive coping strategies.

Cognitive Adaptation   Taylor (1983) proposed a theory of cognitive adaptation to explain how individuals adjusted to crisis events in their lives. This theory included three cognitive themes: (a) a search for meaning in the crisis event, (b) an attempt to achieve control over the crisis event, and (c) an attempt to enhance one's self-esteem. As noted by Berry and Hardman (1998), ". . . families who cope well look for ways to accept aspects of their lives that cannot be changed, gain as much control over their complicated lives as possible, and assign positive meanings to the reality of their daily lives" (p. 79). In the search-for-meaning cognitive theme, individuals are able to move beyond the "why me?" stage, which research has found leads to more effective coping (Shapp, Thurman, & Ducette, 1992), to a more philosophical position on the meaning of their lives after the crisis experience. Simply stated, when positive meaning is developed from a negative event, better adjustments result.

The second cognitive theme of gaining mastery or control over a crisis event involves recognizing what you can control and what you cannot control in your life. High-functioning families channel their time and energy into issues over which they can assert either direct control (e.g., establishing a family routine to divide household chores so that those responsibilities do not fall disproportionately on the mother) or indirect control (e.g., ensuring that the school district meets its legal obligation to provide their child with a disability an appropriate speech and language program). Although it is often difficult, once they are able to acknowledge the issues in their lives that they cannot exert control over, a burden is lifted from parents. For example, one family reported that long-endured emotional frustration had been lifted from their minds when they finally admitted that they could not change negative attitudes of some of their extended family members toward their child with severe mental retardation. They had done all of the educational efforts over the years that they could; some people are just uncomfortable around individuals with disabilities.

Parents of children with disabilities often judge themselves very harshly. This form of self-criticism is demoralizing and destroys parental confidence. By enhancing their self-esteem, parents become more effective in their coping skills. This cognitive theme can take several forms (Behr & Murphy, 1993). First, parents may engage in *downward social comparisons*. This cognitive strategy involves a comparison between your situation and the circumstances of someone perceived to be less fortunate. For example, a parent of a student with a learning disability indicated he coped with his son's disability by repeatedly reminding himself that there are many children who do not have the cognitive or physical ability to feed or toilet themselves. A second cognitive strategy is the use of *upward social comparisons*, whereby a parent compares his or her situation with that of another parent, who is handling life events more successfully. In doing this social comparison, parents can become encouraged by what they see other parents accomplishing. The notion here is "If they can do it, so can I." Finally, parents can employ the cognitive strategy of *positive contributions*. This causes parents to focus on the positive contributions their children with disabilities have contributed to their family.

Reframing   Another cognitive coping strategy, reframing, is defined as "the family's ability to redefine a demanding situation in a more rational and acceptable way in order to make the situation more manageable" (Olson et al., 1983, p. 143). This strategy involves two steps: (a) distinguishing situations that can be changed from those that are beyond one's control and (b) taking action on alternative situations that can be changed. Professionals can aid families in redefining stressful situations by encouraging them to use reframing.

As an example of reframing, Fiedler (2000) described a situation that he faced as a parent of a daughter with severe and multiple disabilities. For several years, his daughter's school district had been sending her to a regional special education program in a nearby school district. The parents were not satisfied with this educational arrangement and repeatedly complained to school officials requesting that their daughter be educated in their home school district so that she could begin developing relationships with other students in the community. As a former lawyer, Fiedler first framed the "problem" as a matter of legal rights. His legal research, however, revealed that courts had generally allowed school officials considerable discretion in determining educational placements for children with disabilities. Although there is a clear legal preference for educating children with disabilities in their home schools, there have been no court decisions obligating school districts to educate every student with a disability in his or her neighborhood school. Therefore, the parents did not feel they would be successful in a legal challenge to their daughter's educational placement. Finally, the parents reframed the situation as a "political problem."

> My wife and I asked these questions: Are there any other families in our community who have children with severe disabilities and are their children receiving special education services via out of district placements? If so, are those families similarly dissatisfied with their children's out of district special education placements? With this simple reframing of the problem, we were able to develop an alternative advocacy strategy. (p. 207)

This revised problem-solving approach proved successful as several parents of children with severe disabilities joined forces to persuade the school district to bring their children back to their home schools for the next school year.

Support Strategies

As discussed previously in this chapter, families of children with disabilities who access various support services—personal and professional—are able to cope more successfully with stress. In this section, several examples of support strategies will be reviewed, including parent social support, professional formal support, respite care, and spiritual support.

Parent Social Support   Social support for parents includes receiving emotional, informational, and material support from friends, relatives, neighbors, coworkers, or others that an individual can turn to during stressful times (Hughes, 1999; Muscott, 2002). Parent social support can take several forms. Opportunities for parent social support can be provided by professionals or by parents themselves. In addition, support can be provided in a group setting or through a one-to-one connection. Many parent support groups are organized and facilitated by professionals. Typically, parent support group meetings have an informational component where a guest speaker shares information on a relevant topic (e.g., early intervention services, estate planning, managing challenging behaviors, sibling issues). In addition, there is an emotional component to parent support meetings. The chance to share feelings about being a parent of a child with a disability with other parents is reassuring and comforting for many parents. Some parent support groups develop lasting friendships among the members. The importance of parent support groups has been confirmed by studies that reveal that these social networks enhance parent and family well-being, positive caregiving, positive parental attitudes, positive parent–child interactions, and improved child behavior (Dunst, Trivette, Gordon, & Pletcher, 1989).

Professionals provide one-to-one support whenever parents seek their assistance in individual meetings. This support can also serve both informational and emotional needs. As noted by Berry and Hardman (1998), "There is an enormous potential for professionals to be strong sources of support for parents" (p. 88). The extent that professionals can serve this one-to-one support function is largely dependent on the quality of their collaborative relationship with the parent involved. If the relationship is based on mutual trust and respect, the ultimate goal of professional support should be to instill greater confidence, independence, and feelings of empowerment in parents. Perhaps, as noted by Fiedler (2000), the greatest support professionals can offer parents is to advocate for their children at the schools where they work, in their home communities, and in their volunteer activities.

Social support can also be provided by parents themselves. In fact, the first choice of many parents is to be connected with other parents who have had or are having experiences similar to their own. Numerous parent support groups have been started by parents with the desire to share their feelings and experiences with other parents of children with disabilities. Parent support groups often have a single disability focus (e.g., children with ADHD, autism, mental retardation), but groups are also formed on the basis of specific issues (e.g., children with challenging behaviors) or on the child's attendance in a particular program (e.g., parents whose children attend the same early intervention program). Parent groups that are led by parents foster a greater sense of ownership in the parent members than do groups directed by professionals. This sense of ownership and commitment contributes to the long-term viability of the group.

Finally, parent social support also comes in the form of one-to-one support provided by parents. Parent to Parent programs began in Nebraska in 1975 and provide a unique form of individualized support to families who have a child with a disability (Santelli, Poyadue, & Young, 2001). The Beach Center on Families and Disability at the University of Kansas (www.beachcenter.org) maintains a listing of Parent to Parent programs in the United States. Parent to Parent programs offer the opportunity for parents of newly diagnosed children to be matched with parents who know firsthand about the trials, tribulations, and joys of raising a child with a disability. These matches may be short term, to deal with a specific crisis or issue, or long term, with many such matches turning into lifelong friendships. Some parents shared the impact that this type of social support had made in their lives in a book on how to start a Parent to Parent program by Santelli et al., (2001). For instance, one parent stated,

> When Daniel was 4 months old, his pediatric neurosurgeon told me about Parent to Parent of Georgia. I called right away and a supporting parent called me back the next day. We talked for nearly 2 hours. It was a relief to be able to express my feelings openly and honestly—even the ones I was ashamed of. I was afraid, exhausted, lonely, and angry. None of this came as a surprise to the woman on the telephone, and her understanding and support enabled me to begin to deal with my emotions and to start looking outside of myself. I began to learn about disabilities and to explore the services available in our community. (p. 8)

Parent to Parent programs are based on a simple principle: when parents are nurtured and supported, they will be better at nurturing and supporting their children. Parent to Parent programs educate and match parents to parents of children with disabilities that are referred to the program. The content of the parent education typically includes the history of Parent to Parent, the grieving process, active listening and communication skills, problem-solving skills, and the role of the support parent. A number of factors enter into the parent matching process, including the following: child's disability; age of children; concerns or problems at issue; ability of the supporting parent to respond in 24 hours; proximity of the two families' homes; family structure, culture, or ethnic background; parents' age; and parents' education and income. In a 3-year national study investigating the impact of Parent to Parent programs, an overwhelming majority of parents indicated that the social support they received was very helpful to their families, and they expressed the belief that such assistance could not have come from any other source (Santelli et al., 2001). Effective social support was characterized by the following:

- Nurtures and promotes an ordered worldview
- Promotes hope
- Promotes timely withdrawal and initiative
- Provides guidance
- Provides a communication channel with the social world
- Affirms one's personal identity
- Provides material help
- Contains distress through reassurance and affirmation
- Ensures adequate rest
- Mobilizes other personal supports

Professional Formal Support   Families of children with disabilities must be able to access formal support services provided by a variety of community agencies and professionals. How to access such services and the skills required to work effectively with professionals will be the focus of chapter 7. In this section, we will address a specific professional support for parents: problem-solving-skills training. Professional assistance in helping parents acquire problem-solving skills has resulted in better coping outcomes for families of children with disabilities (Melnyk et al., 2001). Problem-solving-skills training involves teaching parents how to systematically apply the following steps:

1.   *Identify and define the conflict.* Ensure that you have both parties' perspectives. For example, a conflict has arisen between a teacher of a student with emotional–behavioral disorders and the student's mother. In an effort to motivate the student to complete his homework assignments, the teacher has begun withholding this 9-year-old's recess privileges. He is required to stay in during recess to catch up on his homework. The mother is concerned that this intervention is restricting her son's access to nondisabled peers. Further, because of the implementation of this intervention, her son has become very moody and more disruptive at home. A definition of this "problem" must include both the teacher's and the mother's concerns. That is, the problem is how to increase the student's completion of homework assignments while fostering maximum interaction opportunities with more appropriate behavioral role-model peers.

2.   *Generate possible solutions.* Be creative. At this point, the parties to the conflict should not impose any constraints on the idea generation process. A number of possible solutions quickly emerge: tutorial assistance provided by another student, hire a tutor to provide after-school homework assistance, more use of cooperative learning activities, parental assistance with homework at home, token economy system for completed homework assignments, after-school homework club where the student will receive extra assistance on his homework, and after-school detention during days his homework is not done.

3.   *Evaluate the alternative solutions.* At this step of the problem-solving process, both parties must weigh the possible risks, gains, and likelihood of success, and costs of each possible solution identified in the brainstorming session. Here is where the parties must evaluate the real-world constraints such as time, money, energy, and support and determine which possible solutions are feasible. In reviewing possible solutions identified in Step 2 above, the mother indicated that as a single parent, she does not have ample time right now to provide much homework assistance in the evenings for her son. Further, the mother is adamant that the teacher not impose a punishment (e.g., after-school detention to complete homework) as a solution to this problem. The teacher indicates that the school principal, given tight budgetary constraints, will not approve the hiring of an after-school tutor for her son.

4.   *Decide on the best solution.* The mother and the teacher agree to assign another student to provide tutorial assistance for her son. This is an especially attractive solution to the mother because this will also foster interaction with a nondisabled student.

5.   *Implement the decision.* Establish objective evaluation criteria. Determine in advance when you will meet again to review the data on this intervention. Before the mother and teacher end their problem-solving meeting, it is critical to agree on how long they will try the agreed-on solution and how they will evaluate whether the solution is effective. They agree to provide the student tutorial assistance for 4 weeks. At that time, they will meet again to review objective information and decide if they need to continue with that intervention or develop a new approach.

6.   *Follow-up evaluation.* The mother and teacher agree that the intervention will be evaluated based on the following objective criteria: percent of assignments the student is turning in on time, percent of correct responses on those assignments, and the number of positive interactions the student is having with peers during the morning recess time.

Respite Care   Another source of valuable social support for families is respite care. Respite care services provide families with temporary relief from the demands of caring for a child with a disability. These respite periods can be for only a few hours, for a weekend, or for several days. This break from caregiving responsibilities provides parents with an opportunity to relax and rejuvenate. One mother of a child with a chronic illness described how important respite care was for her family:

The week that our family stayed at the beach was the most wonderful gift. . . . It gave us the opportunity to stand outside the situation and view it from a distance. It enabled us to review what had gone on before, to put things into perspective, think, and plan. We were also physically restored, and were able to go on with much strength . . . caring for our daughter. (Ambler, 1996, p. 2)

To provide parents with peace of mind that their children are being well cared for, respite care providers need specialized training in caring for children with disabilities. This training should include managing challenging behaviors, feeding and positioning skills for children with physical care needs, emergency procedures, and developmentally appropriate activities for children of varying functional abilities (Neef & Parrish, 1989). Parents typically identify respite care as the most valuable support service, and such programs have been found to reduce family stress levels (Sherman, 1995).

Spiritual Support   Families who use spiritual support as a coping mechanism rely on their own personal, philosophical, or religious perspectives in assigning meaning to having a child with a disability (Muscott, 2002). Through their spiritual or religious beliefs, families are enabled (a) to make meaning of their experience in having a child with a disability and (b) to develop a religious community that can provide emotional support (Turnbull & Turnbull, 2001). Indeed, many families report that having a child with a disability has increased their spirituality (Behr & Murphy, 1993). Wolfensberger (1994) advocated a return to the "Greco-Judaic-Christian" perspective in an attempt to value individuals with disabilities. In a five-factor model on crisis theory for families of children with disabilities, Cook (1990) included two components not found in traditional stress and coping models: the family's faith and the family's definition of God.

There are research findings to support the coping function of spiritual support. Winkler (1988) found that families who attended church regularly and maintained intense personal spiritual beliefs experienced less stress than families without a sense of spirituality. Weisner, Beizer, and Stolze (1991) studied 102 parents of 3- to 5-year-old children with developmental disabilities. These researchers concluded that religion provided meaning to many of these parents. Finally, Maton (1989) also found that religion was a major part of the coping process for parents.

Zachary's Family Revisited

Zachary's family expressed very typical feelings after discovering that their son had a disability. Many parents encounter uncertainty about the impact of their child's disability and what the future holds. School professionals can be supportive and effective by meeting the parents' informational needs. Based on the fears expressed by Zachary's parents, school professionals could start by addressing peer relationships and how to foster friendships between Zachary and nondisabled youngsters. Zachary's IEP should contain goals to enhance his social skills and provide him with plenty of interaction opportunities with nondisabled peers.

In addition to specific informational needs, Zachary's parents appear to have significant emotional support needs. Most communities have parent support groups where parents can meet other parents with similarly disabled children. The school could function as a referral agent to link Zachary's parents to a parent support group. The fear of the future can be lessened when parents can see into the future by interacting with a family who has an older child with a similar disability. Parents can learn how other families have coped with issues that they currently may be seeing only as insurmountable obstacles. Parents can be empowered when they learn that other families have successfully encountered and overcome similar obstacles.

SUMMARY STATEMENTS

- It is still widely accepted that the discovery that a child has a disability produces stress for the family. How the family handles and responds to that stress largely determines whether the impact of this traumatic event will be primarily negative or positive on family functioning.
- Coping is what one does with resources both from inside the family and throughout the community. It is the actions the family takes to remove or reduce the stressor, live with the hardships caused by the stressor, or develop new resources in response to a crisis.
- There are several theoretical models that explain how families attempt to cope with stress. Most of these models look at family adjustment and adaptation to stress as being a function of A (characteristics of the stressor event) interacting with B (the family's crisis-meeting resources) interacting with C (the definition the family makes of the event), producing X (the crisis).
- Typical stressors impacting families of children with disabilities revolve around issues associated with transitional times (e.g., entering or leaving school), family functioning, emotional reactions to learning that your child has a disability, caregiving demands, and problematic interactions with various professionals.
- Several demographic factors are associated with increased family stress, including single-parent families, nondisabled children's resentment toward or embarrassment of their sibling with a disability, children with behavioral problems, children with more severe caregiving needs, families with younger children with disabilities, more highly educated parents, and interactions with professionals where there are language barriers or the professionals fail to establish collaborative relationships with the parents.
- Decreased family stress levels are associated with greater family financial resources, strong family relationships, maintaining a religious or spiritual perspective, and professional support and referrals to community organizations.
- Many families report numerous benefits associated with parenting a child with a disability. Indeed, some families said they experienced a personal transformation as a result of parenting a child with a disability. Transformative experiences are distinguished from coping, which involves finding techniques to continue one's life as it was before. Personal transformations, however, involve the disintegration or abandonment of one's previous life in favor of a new and clearly better way of living.
- Strong, resilient families share the following characteristics: open and honest communication, commitment to each other and contentment with their life, sense of family history, sense of humor, optimism, spiritual wellness, social support system, time together, and appreciation for each other.

- Cognitive coping strategies involve thinking about stressful situations in a different or more positive light. Examples include cognitive adaptation, whereby individuals employ the following three adjustment themes: (a) search for meaning in the crisis event, (b) an attempt to achieve control over the crisis event, and (c) an attempt to enhance one's self-esteem. Reframing is another example of a cognitive coping strategy that involves redefining a demanding situation to make it more manageable.

QUESTIONS FOR DISCUSSION

1. Which of the theoretical models explaining family stress and coping do you find most useful in understanding family support issues?
2. Why has traditional research focused on the negative aspects of raising a child with a disability? How would you assist families in realizing the potentially positive aspects of parenting a child with a disability?
3. Can school professionals foster resilient characteristics in families of children with disabilities? How?

RESOURCES FOR FAMILY STRESS AND COPING

- **National Respite Locator Service**
  (www.respitelocator.org)
  This Web site maintains a database of respite care providers in all of the states.

- **Counseling Center at the New Jersey Institute of Technology**
  (http://counseling.njit.edu/stressprevention.html)
  This Web site provides specific examples of relaxation techniques.

- **Parents Helping Parents: The Parent-Directed Family Resource Center for Children with Special Needs**
  (www.php.com)
  Parents Helping Parents is a family resource center serving children with special needs, their families, and the professionals who serve them. Numerous family support groups are listed on this Web site.

- **Exceptional Parent Magazine**
  (www.eparent.com)
  This magazine Web site for parents of children with disabilities provides a variety of support information, including resources, education, health care, life planning, technology, mobility, sports, and other family concerns and issues.

- **National Institute of Mental Health**
  (www.nimh.nih.gov)
  This Web site provides information on a variety of mental disorders that impact children, adolescents, and adults.

- **Pavnet Online**
  (www.pavnet.org)
  This is the Web site of the Partnerships Against Violence Network, which provides information from seven federal agencies about effective violence prevention initiatives.

- ***Special Child* magazine**
  (www.specialchild.com)
  An online magazine for parents of children with disabilities.

- Santelli, B., Poyadue, F. S., & Young, J. L. (2001). *The parent to parent handbook: Connecting families of children with special needs.* Baltimore: Brookes. This book provides specific information on how to establish a Parent to Parent program.

REFLECTION ACTIVITIES

1. Identify your specific coping strategies during particularly stressful periods in your life. What worked for you? How could other people have best supported you during these stressful periods?

2. Work with a local special education teacher to obtain permission to survey families of children with disabilities. Ask those parents to identify the positive contributions their children with disabilities have provided to their families. How could this information be used in developing more supportive and collaborative IEP meetings with parents?

REFERENCES

Ambler, L. (1996). *Respite care.* Washington, DC: National Information Center for Children and Youth with Disabilities.

Bailey, A. B., & Smith, S. W. (2000). Providing effective coping strategies and supports for families with children with disabilities. *Intervention in School and Clinic, 35*(5), 294–296.

Barnett, W. S., & Boyce, G. C. (1995). Effects of children with Down syndrome on parents' activities. *American Journal on Mental Retardation, 100*(2), 115–127.

Bauer, A. M., & Shea, T. M. (2003). *Parents and schools: Creating a successful partnership for students with special needs.* Upper Saddle River, NJ: Merrill/Prentice Hall.

Baxter, C., Cummins, R. A., & Polak, S. (1995). A longitudinal study of parental stress and support: From diagnosis of disability to leaving school.

International Journal of Disability, Development and Education, 42(2), 125–136.

Beckman, P. J. (1991). Comparison of mothers' and fathers' perception of the effect of young children with and without disabilities. *American Journal on Mental Retardation, 95,* 585–595.

Behr, S. K. (1989). *Underlying dimensions of the construct of positive contributions that individuals with disabilities make to their families: A factor analytic study.* Unpublished doctoral dissertation, University of Kansas, Lawrence.

Behr, S. K., & Murphy, D. L. (1993). Research progress and promise: The role of perceptions in cognitive adaptation to disability. In A. P. Turnbull, J. M. Patterson, S. K. Behr, D. L., Murphy, J. G. Marquis, & M. J. Blue-Banning (Eds.), *Cognitive coping, families, and disability* (pp. 151–164). Baltimore: Brookes.

Behr, S. K., Murphy, D. L., Summers, J. A. (1992). *User's manual: Kansas Inventory of Parental Perceptions* (KIPP). Lawrence, KS: Beach Center on Families and Disability.

Berry, J. O., & Hardman, M. L. (1998). *Lifespan perspectives on the family and disability*. Boston: Allyn & Bacon.

Berry, J. O., & Jones, W. H. (1995). The Parental Stress Scale: Initial psychometric findings. *Journal of Personal and Social Relationships, 12*, 463–472.

Birenbaum, A., & Cohen, H. J. (1993). On the importance of helping families: Policy implications from a national study. *Mental Retardation, 31*(2), 67–74.

Blacher, J. (Ed.). (1984). *Severely handicapped young children and their families: Research in review*. Toronto: Academic Press.

Bradley, R. H., Rock, S. L., Whiteside, L., Caldwell, B. M., & Brisby, J. (1991). Dimensions of parenting in families having children with disabilities. *Exceptionality, 2*(1), 41–61.

Brannan, A. M., & Heflinger, C. A. (1997). The Caregiver Strain Questionnaire: Measuring the impact on the family of living with a child with serious emotional disturbance. *Journal of Emotional and Behavioral Disorders, 5*(4), 212–223.

Cohen, M. H. (1993). The unknown and the unknowable: Managing sustained uncertainty. *Western Journal of Nursing Research, 15*, 77–96.

Cook, R. S. (1990). *Counseling families of children with disabilities*. Dallas: Word.

Cooley, W. C. (1994). The ecology of support for caregiving families. *Developmental and Behavioral Pediatrics, 15*, 117–119.

Crnic, K. A., Friedrich, W. N., & Greenberg, M. T. (1983). Adaptation of families with mentally retarded children: A model of stress, coping, and family ecology. *American Journal of Mental Deficiency, 88*, 125–138.

Curan, D. (1983). *Traits of a healthy family*. New York: Ballantine Books.

Deal, A. G., Trivette, C. M., & Dunst, C. J. (1988). *Family Functioning Style Scale: An instrument for measuring family strengths and resources*. Asheville, NC: Winterberry Press.

Duis, S. S., & Summers, M. (1997). Parent versus child stress in diverse family types: An ecological approach. *Topics in Early Childhood Special Education, 17*(1), 53–74.

Dunst, C. J., Trivette, C. M., Gordon, N. J., & Pletcher, L. L. (1989). Building and mobilizing informal family support networks. In G.H.S. Singer & L. K. Irvin (Eds.), *Support for caregiving families: Enabling positive adaptation to disability* (pp. 121–141). Baltimore: Brookes.

Dyson, L. L. (1993). Response to the presence of a child with disabilities: Parental stress and family functioning over time. *American Journal on Mental Retardation, 98*(2), 207–218.

Dyson, L. L. (1997). Fathers and mothers of school-age children with developmental disabilities: Parental stress, family functioning, and social support. *American Journal on Mental Retardation, 102*(3), 267–279.

Dyson, L. L., & Fewell, R. F. (1986). Stress and adaptation in parents of young handicapped and nondisabled children: A comparative study. *Journal of the Division for Early Childhood, 10*, 25–35.

Eakes, G. (1995). Chronic sorrow: The lived experience of parents of chronically mentally ill children. *Archives of Psychiatric Nursing, 9*, 77–84.

Featherstone, H. (1980). *A difference in the family*. New York: Basic.

Fiedler, C. R. (1994). Inclusion: Recognition of the giftedness of all children. *Network, 4*(2), 15–23.

Fiedler, C. R. (2000). *Making a difference: Advocacy competencies for special education professionals*. Boston: Allyn & Bacon.

Floyd, F. J., & Gallagher, E. M. (1997). Parental stress, care demands, and use of support services for school-age children with disabilities and behavior problems. *Family Relations, 46*(4), 359–372.

Fujiura, G. T., Roccoforte, J. A., & Braddock, D. (1994). Costs of family care for adults with mental retardation and related developmental disabilities. *American Journal on Mental Retardation, 103*(3), 225–235.

Friedrich, W. N., Wilturner, L. T., & Cohen, D. S. (1985). Coping resources and parenting mentally retarded children. *American Journal of Mental Deficiency, 90*, 130–139.

Gerdel, P. (1985). *Who are the researchers and why are they saying these horrible things about me?* Unpublished manuscript, Topeka, KS.

Gowen, J. W., Johnson-Martin, N., Goldman, B. D., & Appelbaum, M. (1989). Feelings of depression and parenting competence of mothers of handicapped and nonhandicapped infants: A longitudinal study. *American Journal on Mental Retardation, 94*, 259–271.

Hague, W. J. (1995). *Evolving spirituality.* Edmonton: University of Alberta, Department of Educational Psychology.

Harris, V. S., & McHale, S. M. (1989). Family life problems, daily caretaking activities, and the psychological well-being of mothers of mentally retarded children. *American Journal on Mental Retardation, 94*, 231–239.

Hawkins, N. E., & Singer, G.H.S. (1989). A skills training approach for assisting parents to cope with stress. In G.H.S. Singer & L. K. Irvin (Eds.), *Support for caregiving families: Enabling positive adaptations to disability* (pp. 71–83). Baltimore: Brookes.

Hill, R. (1949). *Families under stress.* New York: Harper.

Hill, R. (1958). Generic features of families under stress. *Social Casework, 49*, 139–150.

Holroyd, K. A., & Lazarus. R. S. (1982). Stress, coping, and somatic adaptation. In L. Golderger & S. Breznitz (Eds.), *Handbook of stress: Theoretical and clinical aspects* (pp. 21–35). New York: Free Press.

Hughes, R. S. (1999). An investigation of coping skills of parents of children with disabilities: Implications for service providers. *Education and Training in Mental Retardation and Developmental Disabilities, 34*(3), 271–280.

Jackson, Y., Sifers, S. K., Warren, J. S., & Velasquez, D. (2003). Family protective factors and behavioral outcome: The role of appraisal in family life events. *Journal of Emotional and Behavioral Discorders, 11*(2), 103–121.

Janoff-Bulman, R. (1992). *Shattered assumptions: Towards a new psychology of trauma.* New York: Macmillan.

Koegel, R. L., Schreibman, L., Loos, L. M., Dirlich-Wilhelm, H., Dunlap, G., Robbins, F. R., et al. (1992). Consistent stress profiles in mothers of children with autism. *Journal of Autism and Developmental Disorders, 22*(2), 205–216.

Krauss, M. W. (May, 1991). Theoretical issues in family research. Paper presented at the annual meeting of the American Association on Mental Retardation, Washington, DC. (ERIC Document Reproduction Service No. ED337923)

Kubler-Ross, E. (1969). *On death and dying.* New York: Macmillan.

Kupfer, F. (1982). *Before and after Zachariah.* New York: Delacorte.

Latson, S. R. (1995). Preventing parent burn out: Model for teaching effective coping strategies to parents of children with learning disabilities. Retrieved May 20, 2003, from http://www.ldonline.org

Lazarus, R. S., & Folkman, S. (1984). *Stress, appraisal, and coping.* New York: Springer.

Maton, K. I. (1989). The stress-buffering role of spiritual support: Cross sectional and prospective investigations. *Journal for the Scientific Study of Religion, 28*, 310–323.

McCubbin, H. I., & Patterson, J. M. (1982). Family adaptation to crises. In H. I. McCubbin, A. E. Cauble, & J. M. Patterson (Eds.), *Family stress, coping, and social support* (pp. 26–47). Springfield, IL: Thomas.

McCubbin, H. I., Thompson, A. I., & McCubbin, M. (1996). *Family assessment: Resiliency, coping, and adaptation.* Madison: University of Wisconsin System.

McCubbin, M. A., & McCubbin, H. I. (1993). Families coping with illness: The resiliency model of family stress, adjustment, and adaptation. In C. Danielson, B. Hamel-Bissell, & P. Winstead-Fry (Eds.), *Families, health, and illness* (pp. 21–63). New York: Mosby.

McCubbin, M. A., & McCubbin, H. I. (1996). Resiliency in families: A conceptual model of family adjustment and adaptation in response to stress and crises. In H. I. McCubbin, A. I. Thompson, & M. A. McCubbin (Eds.), *Family assessment: Resiliency, coping, and adaptation* (pp. 1–64). Madision: University of Wisconsin System.

McDonald, L., Kysela, G. M., & Reddon, J. (March, 1987). Stress and supports to families with a handicapped child and adjustment of families with handicapped children. Paper presented at the Alternative Futures for the Education of Students with Severe Disabilities Conference, Edmonton, Canada. (ERIC Document Reproduction Service No. ED310578)

Melnyk, B. M., Feinstein, N. F., Moldenhouer, Z., & Small, L. (2001). Coping in parents of children who are chronically ill: Strategies for assessment and intervention. *Pediatric Nursing*, 27(6), 547–557.

Moses, K. (1987, Spring). The impact of childhood disability: The parent's struggle. *Ways*, pp. 6–10.

Murphy, D. L., Behr, S. K., & Summers, J. A. (August, 1990). Do something about it—Think! Cognitive coping strategies and stress and well-being in parents of children with disabilities. Paper presented at the annual meeting of the American Psychological Association, Boston. (ERIC Document Reproduction Service No. ED331247)

Muscott, H. S. (2002). Exceptional partnerships: Listening to the voices of parents of children with disabilities. *Preventing School Failure*, 46(2), 66–69.

Neef, N. A., & Parrish, J. M. (1989). Training respite care providers: A model for curriculum design, evaluation, and dissemination. In G.H.S. Singer and L. K. Irvin (Eds.), *Support for caregiving families: Enabling positive adaptation to disability* (pp. 175–188). Baltimore: Brookes.

Office of Special Education Programs. (2001). Improving family involvement in special education. *Research Connections in Special Education*, 9, 1–8.

Olson, D. H., McCubbin, H. I., Barnes, H., Larson, A., Muxen, M., & Wilson, M. (1983). *Families: What makes them work*. Beverly Hills: Sage.

Palfrey, J. S., Walker, D. K., Butler, J. A., & Singer, J. D. (1989). Patterns of response in families of chronically disabled children: An assessment in five metropolitan school districts. *American Journal of Orthopsychiatry*, 59, 94–104.

Palus, C. J. (1993). Transformative experiences of adulthood: A new look at the seasons of life. In J. Demeck, K. Bursik, & R. Dibiase (Eds.), *Parental development* (pp. 39–58). Hillsdale, NJ: Erlbaum.

Parish, S. L., Pomeranz-Essley, A., & Braddock, D. (2003). Family support in the United States: Financing trends and emerging initiatives. *Mental Retardation*, 41(3), 174–187.

Park, J., Turnbull, A. P., & Turnbull, H. R. (2002). Impacts of poverty on quality of life in families of children with disabilities. *Exceptional Children*, 68(2), 151–170.

Patterson, J. M. (1988). Families experiencing stress. The Family Adjustment and Adaptation Response Model. *Family Systems Medicine*, 6, 202–237.

Patterson, J. M. (1989). A family stress model: The Family Adjustment and Adaptation Response. In C. Ramey (Ed.), *The science of family medicine* (pp. 95–117). New York: Guilford Press.

Patterson, J. M. (1993). The role of family meanings in adaptation to chronic illness and disability. In A. P. Turnbull, J. M. Patterson, S. K. Behr, D. L. Murphy, J. G. Marquis, & M. J. Blue-Banning (Eds.), *Cognitive coping, families, and disability* (pp. 221–238). Baltimore: Brookes.

Peterson, R. A. (August, 1982). Stress management for parents of developmentally disabled people. Paper presented at the annual convention of the American Psychological Association, Washington, DC. (ERIC Document Reproduction Service No. ED225075)

Roach, M. A., & Orsmond, G. I. (1999). Mothers and fathers of children with Down syndrome: Parental stress and involvement in childcare. *American Journal on Mental Retardation*, 104(5), 422–436.

Salisbury, C. L. (1987). Stressors of parents with young handicapped and nonhandicapped children. *Journal of the Division for Early Childhood*, 11, 154–160.

Santelli, B., Poyadue, F. S., & Young, J. L. (2001). *The Parent to Parent handbook: Connecting families of children with special needs*. Baltimore: Brookes.

Schilling, R. F., Kirkham, M. A., Snow, W. H., & Schinke, S. P. (1986). Single mothers with handicapped children: Different from their married counterparts? *Family Relations*, 35, 69–77.

Schwab, L. O. (1989). Strengths of families having a member with a disability. *Journal of the Multihandicapped Person*, 2, 105–117.

Scorgie, K., & Sobsey, D. (2000). Transformational outcomes associated with parenting children who have disabilities. *Mental Retardation*, 38(3), 195–206.

Scorgie, K., Wilgosh, L., & McDonald, L. (1996). A qualitative study of managing life when a child has a disability. *Developmental Disabilities Bulletin, 24*, 68–90.

Scorgie, K., Wilgosh, L., & McDonald, L. (1999). Transforming partnerships: Parent life management issues when a child has mental retardation. *Education and Training in Mental Retardation and Developmental Disabilities, 34*, 395–405.

Selye, H. (1980). The stress concept today. In I. L. Kutash, L. B. Schlesinger, & Associates (Eds.), *Handbook on stress and anxiety* (pp. 127–143). San Francisco: Jossey-Bass.

Shapp, L. C., Thurman, S. K., & Ducette, J. P. (1992). The relationship of attributions and personal well-being in parents of preschool children with disabilities. *Journal of the Multihandicapped Person, 16,* 295–303.

Sherman, B. R. (1995). Impact of home-based respite care on families of children with chronic illness. *Children's Health Care, 24*, 33–45.

Simons, R. (1987). *After the tears: Parents talk about raising a child with a disability.* San Diego: Harcourt Brace Jovanovich.

Simpson, R. L. (1996). *Working with parents and families of exceptional children and youth: Techniques for successful conferencing and collaboration.* Austin, TX: Pro-Ed.

Singer, G.H.S. (1993). When it's not so easy to change your mind: Some reflections on cognitive interventions for parents of children with disabilities. In A. P. Turnbull, J. M. Patterson, S. K. Behr, D. L. Murphy, J. G. Marquis, & M. J. Blue-Banning (Eds.), *Cognitive coping, families, and disability* (pp. 207–220). Baltimore: Brookes.

Sloper, P., & Turner, S. (1991). Parental and professional views of the needs of families with a child with a severe disability. *Counseling Psychology Quarterly, 4*, 323–330.

Spiegle, J. A., & van den Pol, R. A. (1993). *Making changes: Family voices on living with disabilities.* Cambridge: Brookline.

Stinnett, N., & DeFrain, J. (1989). The healthy family: Is it possible? In M. J. Fine (Ed.), *The second handbook on parent education: Contemporary perspectives* (pp. 53–74). San Diego: Academic Press.

Tanner, J. L., Dechert, M. P., & Friedan, I. (1998). Growing up with a facial hemangioma: Parent and child coping and adaptation. *Pediatrics, 101,* 446–452.

Taunt, H. M., & Hastings, R. P. (2002). Positive impact of children with developmental disabilities on their families: A preliminary study. *Education and Training in Mental Retardation and Developmental Disabilities, 37*(4), 410–420.

Taylor, S. E. (1983). Adjustment to threatening events: A theory of cognitive adaptation. *American Psychologist, 38*, 1161–1173.

Thames, B. J., & Thomason, D. J. (January, 1998). Building family strengths: Overview. *Clemson Extension Family Relationships,* 1–4.

Trute, B., & Hauch, C. (1988). Building on family strength: A study of families with positive adjustment to the birth of a developmentally disabled child. *Journal of Marital and Family Therapy, 14*, 185–193.

Turnbull, A. P., Patterson, J. M., Behr, S. K., Murphy, D. L., Marquis, J. G., & Blue-Banning, M. J. (1993) (Eds.). *Cognitive coping, families, and disability.* Baltimore: Brookes.

Turnbull, A. P., & Ruef, M. (1997). Family perspectives on inclusive lifestyle issues for people with problem behavior. *Exceptional Children, 63*(2), 211–227.

Turnbull, A. P., & Turnbull, H. R. (1985). *Parents speak out: Then and now* (2nd ed.). Columbus: Merrill.

Turnbull, A. P., & Turnbull, H. R. (2001). *Families, professionals, and exceptionality: Collaborating for Empowerment* (4th ed.). Upper Saddle River, NJ: Merrill/Prentice Hall.

Vohs, J. (1993). On belonging: A place to stand, a gift to give. In A. P. Turnbull, J. M. Patterson, S. K. Behr, D. L. Murphy, J. G. Marquis, & M. J. Blue-Banning (Eds.), *Cognitive coping, families, and disability* (pp. 51–66). Baltimore: Brookes.

Walsh, J. (2003). The psychological person: Relationship, stress, and coping. In L. Hutchinson (Ed.), *Dimensions of human behavior: Person and environment* (2nd ed., pp. 185–218). Thousand Oaks, CA: Sage.

Weisner, T. S., Beizer, L., & Stolze, L. (1991). Religion and families of children with developmental delays. *American Journal on Mental Retardation, 95,* 647–662.

Wilton, K., & Renault J. (1986). Stress levels in families with intellectually handicapped preschool children and families with nonhandicapped preschool children. *Journal of Mental Deficiency Research, 30,* 163–169.

Winkler, L. M. (1988). Family stress theory and research on families of children with mental retardation. In J. Gallagher and P. M. Vietze (Eds.), *Families of handicapped persons: Research, programs, and policy issues* (pp. 167–195). Baltimore: Brookes.

Wolfensberger, W. (1994). A personal interpretation of the mental retardation scene in light of the "signs of the times." *Mental Retardation, 32,* 19–33.

Zeitlin, S., & Rosenblatt, W. P. (April, 1985). Family stress: A coping model for intervention. Paper presented at the annual convention of the Council for Exceptional Children, Anaheim, CA. (ERIC Document Reproduction Service No. ED258388)

CHAPTER 6
Identifying and Accessing School Support Services for Parents and Families

● ○ ○ ○ ○

In this chapter, you will understand:

- How to identify school-related needs of parents and families.
- The rationale and need for identifying and serving a range of parent and family needs.
- The rationale and need for parents and families to be able to receive community and nontraditional school services within schools.

- The implications of school-based family support programs and services on desired family outcomes and professional–parent relationships.

Family Perspective: The Websters

Katharine and William Webster describe themselves as "conservative" individuals who value and support education. They were themselves relatively successful students while in public school and are of the opinion that when parents and teachers work together and support one another, the students under their care make the best progress. They both grew up in homes where their parents were supportive of teachers and school policies. Thus, relative to their own children, they consider themselves to be continuing a well-established family value. In this connection, they have stated on numerous occasions that they are strong supporters of their children's teachers and school programs, even when they were not totally in agreement with their decisions. For example, on one occasion, their daughter's third-grade teacher assigned additional homework for the entire class related to poor performance by several children on a cooperative group project, even though their daughter's cooperative group completed its project with no difficulty. The Websters indicated that they supported their child's teacher's decision related to this matter.

The Websters' third child, Timothy, was diagnosed with Down syndrome shortly after birth. This was particularly upsetting to both parents and grandparents because Timothy was their first boy and because he reportedly was the first child in either family who had a significant disability. Initially the Websters openly stated that Timothy's birth was a "gift" and "God's will." They also initially believed that their family was "strong-minded" and that this strength, along with their strong belief in the power of education, would be sufficient to satisfy whatever challenges might confront Timothy and their family.

While generally positive about Timothy's educational program, the Websters were surprised and dismayed by the stress and negative impact that Timothy's disability had on the family. In spite of Timothy's appearing to make satisfactory educational progress, the family have increasingly found themselves confronted with a host of unmet emotional and support needs. Mr. and Mrs. Webster quickly discovered that they were expected to have considerably more involvement in their son's program than they had experienced with their normally developing and achieving daughters. That they wanted to satisfy the school's expectations for involvement created considerable frustration related to their confusion about how best to participate. Mr. Webster has recently become particularly outspoken in this regard, observing that school personnel appear to want him and his wife to participate in various decisions and "team meetings," without the benefit of school personnel educating them about their perceived duties and role or even the nature of the meetings they are invited to participate in. Timothy's development and behavior have also been frustrating to his family. For instance, while Timothy's teachers report that he is able to use the toilet independently at school, his family reports that he continues to require considerable assistance with toileting at home. The parents have attempted to not overly burden their daughters with Timothy's care, believing that placing this responsibility onto their other children would be detrimental to their emotional health and social opportunities and experiences. These circumstances have been the source of significant frustration and distress for Mr. and Mrs. Webster. As a result, the parents have sought counseling and other supports through their church and from the county mental health organization. Regrettably, they report that neither organization has been successful in meeting their needs.

The Websters are confused and frustrated over how to best meet their growing list of needs related to having a son with a disability. This confusion is particularly acute related to the role and capacity of their public school system in assisting them in meeting their needs. Given the various community and other support options with which they are familiar, the Websters are most comfortable and confident in their public school district and its personnel as a source of support for the family relative to their son's disability. Accordingly, their wish is for an integrated system that will assist them in identifying and meeting a variety of needs that are outside of what the superintendent of schools for their district refers to as "the boundaries of what a public school can provide to a family."

<u>Reflecting on the Family Perspective</u>

1. What strategies can school personnel use to identify the needs of the Webster family?
2. What are the responsibility and role of school personnel in helping the Webster family respond to their unmet emotional and support needs?
3. How can school personnel assist Mr. and Mrs. Webster in identifying an appropriate level of involvement in their son's program?

The present chapter addresses the role of schools in providing school-based educational and family support services. We discuss common needs of parents and families along with the role of school personnel and systems in meeting these needs. We provide a rationale and discussion of an integrated service model wherein school and community services are provided within the structure of school organizations. Chapter 7 presents a rationale and discussion of community-based support services.

THE ROLE OF SCHOOLS IN SUPPORTING PARENTS AND FAMILIES

The role of schools in meeting the needs of parents and families of students with disabilities has changed substantially over the decades. These changes are the result of numerous economic, political, demographic, and societal trends and events as well as enactment of legislation and accompanying advocacy movements that have affected the rights and treatment of persons with disabilities (Cuban & Usdan, 2003; Fine & Simpson, 2000; O'Day, 2002; Turnbull & Turnbull, 2001). Enactment of the Education for All Handicapped Children Act in 1975 and subsequent amendments and reauthorizations of IDEA have had profound effects on special-needs children and youth. Significant among the elements of this legislation is the ever-increasing emphasis on parent and family involvement and family needs. Indeed, a salient feature of the most recent IDEA reauthorization is the need for improved parent–professional partnerships, meaningful parent and family involvement in students' education and education-related decision making, and coordination of school and school/community resources in meeting parent and family needs.

Regrettably, in spite of these significant legislative and accompanying policy changes, there remains strong evidence that parents and families have been unable to work in meaningful partnership with professionals. Moreover, there is strong evidence to support the contention that parents' and families' needs routinely fail to be identified and effectively addressed (Simpson, 1996; Wright & Stegelin, 2003). Indeed, in spite of stronger and stronger language mandating parent and family involvement in educational decision making, and identification of the potential benefits and rationale for coordinating support and related services through schools (Lawson & Sailor, 2000), parents and families all too frequently report being isolated and restricted from active school-team participation. Parents and families have also consistently voiced concern that needed school and community resources and services are unavailable, that they lack quality and reliability, and that they are difficult to use (Fine & Nissenbaum, 2000). Recognizing the benefits and necessity of parent–professional partnerships and involvement and the role of school personnel and organizations in assisting parents in meeting the many needs that accompany the myriad challenges associated with raising and supporting a child with a disability is the first step in addressing the aforementioned problems.

This chapter presents an analysis of common parent and family needs and a model for addressing these needs. In addition, the chapter focuses on planning for and individualizing parent and family school involvement and participation. Included is a rationale for school and community service integration as a means of coordinating efforts to address parent and family needs within the boundaries of school organizations.

UNDERSTANDING AND PLANNING FOR PARENT AND FAMILY NEEDS

The heterogeneous and dynamic needs and situations of parents and families, including those whose members have disabilities, defy a simple and universally reliable needs classification system. Nevertheless, a school-based service delivery system for parents and families requires an identification of basic and common needs of parents and families. Accordingly, for purposeful planning and development of a global and generalized infrastructure for addressing parent and family needs, we recommend that school programs plan their programs around five basic need elements (shown in Table 6.1): (a) effective programming for students, including a qualified teacher and support personnel; (b) regular and ongoing opportunities for parents and professionals to exchange information; (c) participation, advocacy, and partnership opportunities and activities; (d) training programs for parents who seek skills needed to implement home-based skill-training, management, and tutoring programs with children; and (e) problem solving, coping, and emotional and psychological supports for parents and family members. Further information on how school professionals can support families of children with disabilities in meeting these identified needs are addressed in chapters 3 (emotional support needs), 5 (coping support needs), 8 (advocacy support needs), 9 (behavioral support needs), and 10 (educational support needs).

Table 6.1   Parent and Family Model of Commonly Experienced Needs.

- Effective programming for students
- Regular and ongoing opportunities for parents and professionals to exchange information
- Participation, advocacy, and partnership opportunities and activities
- Training programs for parents who seek skills needed to implement home-based skill-training, management, and tutoring programs
- Problem-solving, coping, and emotional and psychological supports for parents and family members

High-Quality and Effective Programs for Students with Disabilities

Designing high-quality, effective programs for students with disabilities is a need that is not specific to parent and family involvement. Yet, because it is so basic to supporting parents and families, we include it as a foundation component that schools must first satisfy before they can respond to other needs. An effective program for parents and families, including qualified teachers and support personnel, has no universally accepted operational definition. However, in spite of this difficulty and the variability that surrounds the exact meaning of an effective program and qualified personnel, there is general agreement that it involves assuring parents and others that students are enrolled in schools that are physically and emotionally safe; that teachers and staff are qualified and committed to providing each student an effective educational experience; that teachers are using proven effective-practice curricula and strategies; and that students demonstrate appropriate progress and outcomes on important educational measures. Finally, this baseline element includes the important caveat that parents and family members are empowered to take action and are otherwise involved in making important educational decisions. A checklist of items that parents, families and professionals may wish to use in their assessment of potential school programs is shown in Communication and Collaboration Tips Box 6.1. While neither comprehensive nor standardized, these items may help professionals and parents/families focus attention on factors that are connected to an effective program and that bode well for students' success.

COMMUNICATION AND COLLABORATION TIPS   **BOX 6.1**

Program Quality Assessment Items for Parents, Families, and Professionals

While neither comprehensive nor standardized, the items listed below may assist professionals and parents/families in focusing attention on factors that are connected to an effective program and that bode well for students' success. It is recommended that this informal and subjective assessment tool be used as a 5-point rating scale, with 1 corresponding to "Excellent" and 5 corresponding to "poor." It is also recommended that the raters be given a choice of "not observed/no information" for items on which they have no information. Finally, it is recommended that this instrument be used by professionals to evaluate themselves; and that parents be encouraged to cooperatively work with school personnel when evaluating school programs.

1	2	3	4	5	NA
EXCELLENT				POOR	NO INFORMATION

1. Teachers and support staff have appropriate licensure and training for their respective jobs.
2. Teachers and support staff appear to have command of their respective subject matter and successfully communicate and teach their subjects.
3. Teacher gives evidence of being an effective instructor and classroom manager.
4. Teacher and support staff give evidence of having a classroom atmosphere that is positive and inviting.
5. Teacher and support staff demonstrate an understanding of students' cognitive and social development and needs.
6. Teacher and support staff use developmentally appropriate activities and assignments.

(continued)

COMMUNICATION AND COLLABORATION TIPS (Continued)   Box 6.1

7. Teacher and support staff adapt assignments and classroom activities in accordance with students' individual needs.
8. Teacher and support staff communicate with students, other adults, and parents and families in an appropriate fashion, including with sensitivity to individuals' culture, exceptionality, and personal needs.
9. Teacher and support staff demonstrate instructional awareness and sensitivity to students' needs, including monitoring their learning and adapting assignments and activities.
10. Teacher and support staff give evidence of having prepared in advance for students, including having necessary materials, structure, and instructional aides.
11. Teacher and support staff use appropriate resources and supportive instructional activities in their teaching, including computers, assistive technology, and experiential learning opportunities.
12. Teacher and support staff demonstrate effective and efficient management of students' instructional time, including supporting students' on-task attention and related learning activities.
13. Teacher and support staff include application opportunities for students to apply, practice, and generalize newly acquired skills and knowledge.
14. Teacher and support staff actively facilitate students' learning by explaining lesson content through providing information, citing examples, asking questions, demonstrating skills, and providing relevant practice activities.
15. Teacher and support staff appropriately provide individual, small-group, and classwide instruction, relative to students' needs.
16. Teacher and support staff are actively involved in classroom activities.
17. Teacher and support staff provide students with ongoing individualized feedback and evaluative information.
18. Teacher and support staff manage students' behavior using appropriate positive and supportive classwide and individual behavior intervention plans.
19. Teacher and support staff demonstrate fairness and consistency in managing students' problems.
20. Teacher and support staff give evidence of collaborating and communicating regularly and effectively with parents and families.

Ensuring an effective and high quality program for students, including those with disabilities, can be expected to overshadow other parent and family needs. That is, unless parents and family members consider their children's program to be at a minimum adequate, they will most likely be unable to fully focus on other areas of parent and family need. Case Illustration 6.1 addresses this important issue.

Regular, Ongoing Opportunities for Parents/Families and Professionals to Exchange Information

Subsequent to ensuring parents and families an adequate educational program, we believe that all parents and families have a need for regular and ongoing opportunities for parents/families and professionals to exchange information. The amount and nature of such interplay will vary from family to family. Nonetheless, we consider it essential that school personnel and community professionals take the initiative to

CASE ILLUSTRATION 6.1

Delores and Walter Pickell moved from Chicago to a small community in Michigan to assist with care of elderly parents and to have the support of family members for their five children, including their 16-year-old daughter, who has mental retardation and a significant hearing loss. In spite of their optimism, general positiveness, and sense of certitude in deciding to "come home," both parents candidly revealed that until they were assured that their "special-needs daughter" had a "good educational program" with a "caring and competent teacher" in a setting "where the other kids would accept Sissy," they were unable to be comfortable and confident that their decision to move was in the best interests of their family.

create and nurture convenient and efficient methods of regularly keeping parents and families informed, and of allowing parents and families to share information with school and school-based community personnel. Initially meeting informational needs frequently involves sharing information with parents and families and answering questions about assessment findings and implications. Many parents of students with disabilities have reported difficulties in obtaining an appropriate assessment for their child and a subsequent accurate diagnosis (Kohler, 1999; Myles & Simpson, 2003). Moreover, once a diagnosis has been given, many parents and family members will want additional information about the condition (Melynk, Feinstein, Moldenhouer, & Small, 2001; Simpson, 1996). Accordingly, topics and needs associated with assisting parents and family members in understanding diagnostic information and its implications should be expected to be a common element of initial meetings and information exchanges among parents, family members, and school and community professionals.

In addition to exchanging preliminary and basic information with parents and introducing parents and families to students' programs, initial contact meetings between professionals and families are designed to establish rapport and create the conditions that foster and sustain collaborative working relationships. As discussed in chapters 3 and 5 these efforts are also beneficial to parents and families relative to their potential to provide psychological and emotional supports and stress reduction. Furthermore, positive initial contacts with parents and family members not only bode well for conditions that support ongoing information exchanges but also students' school and community success (Dunst, Trivette, & Snyder, 2000; Simpson, 1996; Wright & Stegelin, 2003). Decades ago, Duncan and Fitzgerald (1969) reported that establishing positive relationships with parents prior to pupils' beginning junior high school increased parents' interest in school matters and improved students' attendance, grade-point averages, dropout rates, and disciplinary referrals. Similarly, others (Bailey, 2001; Bauer & Shea, 2003; Christenson & Cleary, 1990) have reported that parents and families who are most involved in their child's education are most apt to positively perceive schools and school personnel, and that student outcomes are closely connected to parent and family involvement.

Accordingly, initial positive professional initiations and continual follow-up with parents appear to facilitate parent and family members' willingness to work with and exchange information with school and other school-based professionals, including in development of students' IEPs.

Initial contacts between parents and family members and school personnel will at least in part focus on securing from families important factual and attitudinal information needed to serve individual students. We contend that professionals should assume that parents and family members have information that is otherwise unavailable to them. Indeed, parents and families will commonly be the most reliable long-term source of information about students' histories and functioning. Many school-based professionals rely on a structured interview format to obtain needed information during initial contact meetings with parents and families (see, e.g., Simpson, 1996). Such structure permits school personnel to efficiently secure information about parent/family members' perception of students' needs, students' developmental histories, school-related histories and parent/family member perspectives, parent/family members' goals and expectations for students, and demographic information.

Initial contacts will also typically involve giving parents and family members information about the educational and related programs a learner with special needs will be provided. Such information supports future collaboration and communication and assists in satisfying families' basic need for information and discussion opportunities. Moreover, it creates the communication supports that facilitate ongoing communication and information exchanges between families and professionals. Included in the information disseminated in these preliminary and initial meetings is an interpretation of assessment and diagnostic procedures and findings, a description of the educational program to be used with learners, the manner in which a learner's progress will be assessed and communicated to parents, and school and community resources and problem-solving options available to parents and family members. Communication and Collaboration Tips Box 6.2 identifies additional information that parents and families may find useful.

That parents and family members are sometimes overwhelmed by diagnostic and related evaluation information associated with a learner's disability is well documented (Reeve & Cobb, 2000). Accordingly, many initial parent and family needs for information will relate to interpretations of diagnostic findings and their implications. Additional information related to providing such interpretations and otherwise facilitating an understanding of previously disseminated diagnostic information is shown in Communication and Collaboration Tips Box 6.3.

Parents and family members can be expected to have a need for information related to the educational program their children will be receiving. Such information relates to school and classroom schedules; the teacher's and school's overall philosophies of education and related programs; general and specific curricula and behavior-management strategies scheduled for use; and related generic services and programs such as meal programs, transportation options, and so forth. These initial contacts are also opportunities for teachers and other school-based professionals to discuss with parents procedures for communicating student progress and options for maintaining an ongoing exchange of information. Recent advancements in

---

COMMUNICATION AND COLLABORATION TIPS   **BOX 6.2**

Information for Dissemination to Parents and Families

✔ Description of students' educational programs
✔ School and class schedules and routines, including students' individual activity schedules
✔ Curriculum information, including the manner in which an adapted or special education curriculum connects to the general district and school curricula
✔ Management and discipline programs, procedures, and policies
✔ Procedures for assessing students' progress and disseminating this information to parents and families

---

COMMUNICATION AND COLLABORATION TIPS   **BOX 6.3**

Format for Providing Diagnostic Information and Otherwise Facilitating Parent and Family Members' Understanding of Diagnostic Information

Clarify the Purpose, Background, and Expectations for the Diagnostic Evaluation This initial step of the interpretation of findings conference involves discussing and clarifying the reasons for the evaluative referral and the purposes and expectations for the evaluation.

Discuss the Assessment Methods and Procedures Subsequent to clarifying the purposes and expectations for the evaluation, parents and family members should be provided a description of the tests and other methods used in the assessment process. Specific examples of test items and other procedures used in the assessment are advised to ensure comprehension of the process.

Discuss the Assessment Findings Along with Their Implications This step of the interpretation process involves discussing with parents the salient findings and other elements of the evaluation. Most information shared with parents and family members will generally fall under the categories of (a) intellectual/cognitive findings; (b) educational, achievement, and vocational findings; (c) emotional, behavioral, and personality findings; (d) physical, medical, sensory, and motor findings; and (e) other findings. Identifying educational implications associated with each element of the interpretation is a mandatory element of this process.

Opportunities for Parents and Family Members to Ask Questions and Otherwise Discuss Assessment Findings and Their Implications Parents and family members can be expected to have questions regarding the information relating to their child's functioning and performance. Often implication-related queries will be in the form of issues that the interpreter will be unable to definitively answer, such as "Will his children have the same problem?" "Can he go to college?" "Will she marry?" Regarding these complex issues, it is recommended that interpreters seek to clarify the nature and meaning of the question; attempt to determine if the family member(s) who raised the question is seeking an answer or is more interested in offering his or her perspective

(continued)

COMMUNICATION AND COLLABORATION TIPS (Continued)   **BOX 6.3**

---

on the matter; permit parents and family members time and ample opportunities to comprehend and consider information provided; and permit parents and family members opportunities to share their feelings about the information.

Summarize for Parents and Family Members Salient Assessment Findings, Their Implications, and a General Overview of How the Student's Needs Will Be Addressed This element of the feedback and interpretation process will serve as a means of capturing for parents the key elements of the diagnostic findings and shifting the conference toward a consideration of the child's educational and other needs, goals connected to these needs, and the manner in which the educational program will generally need to be crafted to best meet a student's individual needs.

---

technology-based communication such as e-mail and school Web sites, along with more traditional phone and note systems, allow parents and educators a variety of options for maintaining these important regular contacts.

Informed professionals can significantly enhance the self-education process related to the disability or condition of a family member that many parents and family members go through. That is, many parents and families of students with disabilities will seek out information from books, Web sites, conferences and seminars, experts in the field, and other sources. Although there is abundant information available to parents; some of this information may be lacking in accuracy. When professionals offer parents recommendations for suitable and reliable information, especially when their recommendations are based on an analysis of scientific literature, they are assisting in satisfying a common need while building trust and rapport between home and school and community professionals and organizations (Dunlap, 1999; Lambie, 2000; Schalock & Alonso, 2002).

As discussed previously, educators and community professionals are most effective in serving the needs of students and families when bolstered by current information. Parents and family members not only have a significant impact on children's functioning, they also usually know more than anyone else about the child and the child's living condition. Therefore, an open and ongoing relationship between home and school wherein regular updates about children, families, and related matters are provided is crucial. Ideally, the same rationale also extends to the need for school and community professionals to exchange information about children and families. Although confidentiality policies and related requirements and protocol are obviously associated with this process, there is a recognized need for ongoing information exchange among families and the professional groups that are involved in working with them. Accordingly, we consider it essential that educational professionals assume that all parents and families require opportunities for ongoing information sharing and communication, as well as having similar exchange opportunities themselves. Thus, just as parents and families benefit from an effective educational program for their children, significant benefit is derived from ongoing communication exchanges with the professionals who work with their children (Bailey, 2001; Bauer & Shea, 2003).

Participation, Advocacy, and Partnership

Some parents and families can be expected to have needs connected to permitting them to be more skilled and participatory in working with professionals to develop, implement and evaluate programs for students with special needs. As discussed in chapter 8 of this book, we consider these participation, advocacy, and partnership needs to be essential for parents and families wishing to be actively involved in ongoing decision making and advocacy relative to their children. That is, rights and privileges granted to parents and families through various enactments and policy statements have proven to be of limited value to individuals who lack the knowledge and skills necessary to be legitimate educational partners and advocates. Accordingly, in conjunction with apprising parents of their responsibilities and advocacy role relative to working with professionals to support students with disabilities is the school's role in training and supporting interested and motivated parents and family members in these activities. Without such training and support, few parents will be effective partners and participants in the various meetings and decisions they are expected to participate in. Thus, untrained and unsupported parents and families can be expected to be less efficient and effective student and program advocates than those individuals who receive training and support.

Specific action steps connected with participation, advocacy, and partnership needs include helping parents and family members understand the protocol and procedures associated with participating in various school-related activities and meetings such as IEP conferences, progress report meetings, and so forth. Such training also includes sharing rights and responsibilities with parents and families. Similarly, this process includes preparing and empowering parents and families to be advocates by making them better consumers of community, school, and organizational services and resources. For example, parents who receive training on accessing community and state respite care services can be expected to be more effective in using such services to support their families than those who lack such training.

School-based professionals have numerous strategies for ensuring parent and family participation in IEP and other conferences and meetings. First, school personnel can strive to clarify federal, state, and district protocol connected with interpretation and operational practice of fulfilling various legal and administrative requirements. While schools, agencies, and district administrators must follow various guidelines and requirements related to serving learners with disabilities, these procedures should be no more bureaucratic and onerous than necessary, including paperwork, formality of meetings, vocabulary and shared language, and so forth. Second, concerted efforts should be undertaken to ensure that parents and families are not intimidated by professionals in these meetings. Because the development of learners' IEPs along with other staffing meetings may necessitate wide representation of professionals, parents and families may find themselves participating in meetings about which they have little understanding, with a number of unfamiliar individuals. Accordingly, parents and families should be made to feel as comfortable as possible. Steps to achieve this include limiting meetings to only essential professionals; apprising parents and family members ahead of time about the nature, protocol, and agenda of meetings; maintaining a professional albeit informal atmosphere for meetings; encouraging parents and family members to bring friends or advocates to meetings; ensuring that parents know at least one professional who will be at the meeting, and so forth. Finally, as discussed elsewhere in this book, training can facilitate parent and family participation and collaboration. When participants are trained to actively engage and participate in meetings, their contribution becomes more productive and their capacity to fulfill their responsibilities as confident and informed advocates for their child, enhanced.

All parents have been granted authority and are expected to be involved in the education of their children with special needs. However, the form of their involvement will vary significantly. We recommend that all parents and families have opportunities for participation, advocacy, and partnership training. Yet, not all parents and families will perceive themselves to want or need such training. Therefore, as described in Case Illustration 6.2, we consider participation, advocacy, and partnership training to be ultimately subject to parents' and families' choosing to be a part of such activities and opportunities.

CASE ILLUSTRATION 6.2

Even dating back to her college days, Ruth Tidwell described herself as a "fighter," especially for her family. This self-proclaimed "enforcer of what's right" has been closely involved in the education and treatment of her son with autism. A single parent with no family in her community, Ruth became involved in conflicts with school personnel almost immediately on her child's entrance into a preschool program. While the conflicts varied in regard to specific issues, they generally related to her understanding of her child's rights under IDEA. These conflicts continued until school personnel made the decision to conduct a series of workshops for parents on IDEA. The trainer, an independent contractor associated with a community mental health center, who did not have a prior relationship with the school district, provided information on the nature, meaning, and intent of the various IDEA components; advocacy strategies for parents and families; policy-related responsibilities of parents and school districts; and problem-solving strategies. Related to approving the training, the school's board of education members were ambivalent about "giving more ammunition to a few problem parents." However, subsequent to providing the workshops, the number and severity of conflicts with parents, including Ruth Tidwell decreased, and parents generally reported that they perceived themselves to be better able to support and advocate for their children.

Training Parents to Implement Skill-Training, Management, and Tutoring Programs at Home

A fourth area of parent and family need for which we recommend that school and school-based community personnel offer services and resources involves training parents to implement skill-training, management, and tutoring programs with their children at home. As is the case with participation, advocacy, and partnership, not all parents and families will consider this to be a need, and some parents who may recognize the potential value of home-based program implementation may decline participation related to time, resources, and other issues. Under such conditions, we recommend that school and school-based community professionals honor parent and family preferences to not participate. However we do recommend that professionals communicate to parents and families the availability of parent training opportunities, along with the advantages of home-based skill-training, management, and tutoring programs. Still, unless parents and family members request or agree to participate, we consider it essential that school personnel and other professionals not thrust on parents the obligation to implement programs at home and other nonschool settings.

While not a universal need among parents and families, and in our opinion a need that should primarily be based on parent and family preferences, there is clear evidence that parents and families can be effectively trained to implement a variety of intervention and training programs with their children (Kohler, 1999; Maag, 2004; Simpson, 1996). That parents and families historically have generally not received the training necessary to effectively apply home-based interventions (Zirpoli & Melloy, 2004) in no way negates the importance of this need and the corresponding services that satisfy it. Indeed, empowering parents and family members to participate in a therapeutic alliance by training them to implement utilitarian programs in multiple settings is a significant example of collaboration.

Many of the most successful home-based parent- and family-operated student management programs are based on behavioral or applied behavior analysis methodology (Maag, 2004; Mundschenk & Foley, 2000; Sulzer-Azaroff & Mayer, 1977; see chapter 9). In accordance with these methods, parents and others are instructed to focus on observable and measurable target behaviors, and to manipulate environmental conditions and apply various consequences to modify the frequency, intensity, and duration of target responses. For example, parents may be instructed to reduce the frequency of a child's tantrums by systematically ignoring crying and reinforcing more appropriate behaviors. Such programs have proven to be among the most successful ways of extending scientifically based strategies into home and community settings (Webber, Simpson, & Bentley, 2000). Additional information for assisting parents and family members implement behavior-management programs is provided in Communication and Collaboration Tips Box 6.4. Moreover, this topic is explored in depth in chapter 9.

In a manner similar to parent/family-applied behavior management and skill acquisition and maintenance programs, parents and family members have also been successfully trained to serve as tutors and academic supporters for their children (Vernon, Walther-Thomas, Schumaker, Deshler, & Hazel, 2000). In addition to empowering parents and families by allowing them to be active educational participants, these methods also give students increased opportunities to respond and thereby increase students' chances to practice and learn. We believe that schools and community agencies have an obligation to apprise parents and families who desire to be treatment and intervention agents of training opportunities. Likewise, school and other professionals have a responsibility to provide suitable training and ongoing support and follow-up for parents and families interested in participating as home- and community-based intervention and treatment agents. This theme is described in Case Illustration 6.3. (See also chapter 10.)

COMMUNICATION AND COLLABORATION TIPS   BOX 6.4

Format for Assisting Parents and Family Members in Implementing a Home-Based Behavior-Management Program

Procedural Steps	Activities
Identify and define one or more target behaviors for intervention	List and operationally define parent/family concerns about specific problem behaviors
	Rank parent/family concerns
	Identify and discuss the child's strengths and adaptive responses, particularly as related to the perceived problem response
	Select one target response for modification
Identify environments, situations, and related antecedent variables wherein the target behavior occurs	Identify individuals, times, activities, circumstances, and related factors that may be related to or causing the problem response
Identify possible functions or motivators for the target behavior	Conduct a functional assessment of the target behavior, including the antecedent variables, responses, and reactions of others subsequent to the occurrence of the problem behavior, including attention, avoidance of a disliked activity, and so forth
Help parent(s) and family members to identify, observe and record the target response	Identify and demonstrate an appropriate observation system and recording procedure record for parent/family use
	Assist the parents/family members in reliably using the selected measurement procedure to assess the target behavior
	Make necessary adjustments to the observation and recording system based on parent/family and other feedback
Subsequent to at least 1 week's acquisition of baseline data, train parents/family members to chart and inspect the target response data	Train parents/family members to use appropriate graphs or other visual displays to chart and analyze the target response
Subsequent to at least 1 week's acquisition of baseline data, train parents/family members to record, chart, and analyze daily observations	Train parents/family members to chart and analyze the target response data, including variability and trends

---

COMMUNICATION AND COLLABORATION TIPS (Continued)   **BOX 6.4**

Subsequent to training parents/families to chart, inspect, and analyze target response, assist parents/families in developing intervention procedures and performance goals	Assist parents/families in selecting suitable positive behavioral supports, including consequences, environmental modifications, and other variables
	Assist parents/family members in establishing suitable expectations and outcome goals for the target behavior
	Train parents/family members to apply the intervention program at home or in another nonschool setting
	Train parents/family members to continue observing, recording, charting, and analyzing the target behavior and target behavior data subsequent to introducing the intervention program
Subsequent to the above, continue follow-up meetings with parents and family members as needed, including contacts related to observing, recording, and analyzing the target behavior data; making changes in the recording, charting, and intervention procedures; and encouraging and consulting with parents and family members regarding program progress	Implement program modifications and other amendments as needed
	Maintain a follow-up schedule for parent/family feedback related to program progress
	Encourage parent/family collaboration and program application

---

Problem-Solving, Coping, and Emotional and Psychological Support

Consistent with the overall theme of this book, a fifth area of significant need that many parents and families of children with disabilities experience relates to problem solving, coping, and emotional and psychological support. These topics are discussed in depth in chapters 3 and 5. We consider schools and communities to have a shared responsibility to help parents and families address their need for emotional and psychological supports, counseling, and related assistance. Accordingly, cooperative school and school-based community programs are particularly utilitarian in addressing these needs. Thus, both school and community professionals must accept responsibility for providing these services.

As is the case with participation, advocacy, and partnership needs and needs relating to training parents to implement skill-training, management, and tutoring programs, not all parents and families of children with disabilities will require problem-solving, coping, and emotional and psychological support services. Yet, these needs are relatively

CASE ILLUSTRATION 6.3

Paula and Leroy Mason are the parents of four children ranging in age from 3 to 12. Both parents work full-time outside the home. The Masons describe their home life as "comfortably chaotic." That is, in addition to their busy work schedule, they frequently get together with friends and family and often attend soccer matches, baseball games, and other events in which their children participate. When approached by their son's teacher about using a three-time-per-week academic tutoring program, the parents and grandparents gave the matter considerable attention. However, after lengthy discussion, the parents decided to decline participating in the program because they judged the program to take away time from other family functions and choices. They also made the decision to not be a part of the formal tutoring program based on the evening time that was regularly devoted to helping each of their children, including their oldest son, who had a learning disability, with their respective homework assignments.

In contrast, the Warren family chose to participate in the academic tutoring program that was offered to the Mason family. The Warrens' 11-year-old son had been diagnosed with ADHD and a learning disability in the third grade and had reportedly "struggled with academics throughout his years in school." This child's academic problems were particularly significant in reading. As a result, Mr. and Mrs. Warren decided that they would commit to spending approximately 15 to 20 minutes five evenings per week working with their son using a word flashcard program developed by his teacher. Mr. and Mrs. Warren reported to the teacher that administering the program required significant discipline and scheduling on their part. However, they also indicated that the progress shown by their son in reading was worth the effort and sacrifice.

common (Reeve & Cobb, 2000; Schalock & Alonso, 2002), albeit frequently neglected. Indeed, many parents and families of children with special needs will, at a minimum, periodically require emotional support, psychological counseling, and other clinical and social assistance. This area of need also includes crisis intervention; conflict resolution; and consultation regarding developmental, personal, and related matters, thus making it all the more a service that demands school and community professionals' consideration and resources. Many parents and families of children with special needs will periodically experience crises, conflicts, and the need for problem-solving support and other resources. Without question, this frequently unattended area of parent and family need connects to a wide range of support services that affect a significant number of individuals (Epstein, 1995; Schalock & Alonso, 2002).

Generally, many parents and families with members who have disabilities can be expected to need informational, emotional, and psychological support services related to the exceptional reciprocal and interactive family-based expectations, relationships, and roles that occur as a function of members' disabilities. That is, within families, as well as systems in general, individuals, including children and adolescents, assume various dynamic roles and responsibilities and are expected to live up to various expectations. These assignments are based on age, gender, unique skills and training, tradition, societal roles and expectations, and countless other related factors. Family systems, and the ways in which family units function, tend to be highly unique and individualized based on the aforementioned variables, in combination with factors such as ethnic background, religious beliefs, and educational and economic factors. These myriad variables, in combination with countless other sociological factors, combine to form highly unique family structures, beliefs, patterns of functioning, relationships, and so forth. These factors, and their permutations and combinations, create the experiential context wherein families take on their unique and individual persona. Related to this development and functioning, the occurrence of untoward and stressful events such as raising a child with a disability often disrupt, impede, or otherwise change the functioning and relationships of families. Accordingly, families of children with disabilities may experience additional stress and a disruption in ordinary family functioning, roles, assignments, and expectations. Although some families may choose to respond to these conditions using internal resources, other family units require the support and intervention of outside professionals to adjust and adapt. As observed decades ago by Buscaglia (1975), "a disability is not a desirable thing and there is no reason to believe otherwise. It will, in most cases, cause pain, discomfort, embarrassment, tears, confusion and the expenditure of a great deal of time and money" (p. 11). Thus, even though some families may choose to deal with experiences and conditions associated with a child with a disability on their own, there is no reason to believe that this will be an easy process. Many families benefit from the support of counselors, mediators, trained problem solvers, and other professionals who are knowledgeable and skilled in techniques for bolstering, counseling, and otherwise helping parents and family members understand and contend with the difficult circumstances that oftentimes accompany a disability (Bauer & Shea, 2003; Fine & Nissenbaum, 2000). Indeed, even the healthiest, strongest, and most functional families will be affected by a child with a disability, and otherwise healthy families may benefit from professional counseling and related supports.

As noted above, it is our assumption that many parents and families of children with disabilities will at least periodically have a need for emotional and psychological support. Yet, this commonly accepted assumption has long lacked scientific support and sophistication related to specific parent and family needs and corresponding supports (see, e.g., Buck, 1950; Gorham, 1975; Love, 1973). That is, many professionals have developed their parent-related activities and programs around a number of unsupported generalities and oversimplifications connected to the assumed effects of a child with a disability on families, and on the assumed process that parents and families go through relative to learning to accept and accommodate a family member with special needs. It is not unusual for professionals to incorrectly assume that parents and families will have predictable and common reactions to a child with a disability, that they will traverse a common set of sequential stages, and that they will have similar emotional experiences and needs subsequent to raising a child with a disability. Commenting on this practice, researchers have reported that although there are broadly defined patterns of parent and family adaptability to children with disabilities, there are also prominent individual person and family differences (Blacher, 1984; O'Shea, O'Shea, Algozzine, & Hammitte, 2001; Schalock & Alonso, 2002). Researchers have also reported that reactions and experiences of parents and families related to children with special needs are associated with a number of factors, including the availability of resources and supports, two-parent versus one-parent families, economic conditions, severity and nature of a child's disability, family strengths, and myriad related variables (Barnett & Boyce, 1995; Dyson, 2003; Fewell & Gelb, 1983; Schilling, Kirkham, Snow, & Schinke, 1996; Turnbull & Turnbull, 2001). We, too, consider it mandatory that professionals refrain from the practice of using broadly defined and scientifically unsupported generalizations to attempt to understand and support the process that "typical" families will follow in adjusting and responding to a member with special needs. In our opinion and experience, there is no common course of experience and need for parents and families. Furthermore, it is our contention that parents and families cannot reliably and effectively be served using models that assume that parents and families have common and predictable service needs. Thus, while we understand and support the need for broadly based service models that plan for commonly experienced parent and family needs, we contend that implementation of such models must be based on an analysis of specific individual parent and family needs and preferences.

A variety of theoretical and procedural options exists for helping parents and families respond to their need for counseling, support, and crisis intervention, including humanistic, cognitive, behavioral, psychodynamic, and family system analysis. Each of these approaches has its own assumptions and procedural guidelines, and practitioners who rely on these options follow a generally consistent methodology. Many school-based professionals (e.g., counselors, school psychologists) tend to be eclectic and pragmatic. Thus it is common to see practitioners and programs that combine various styles and approaches to best respond to the needs of their clientele. For instance, a school-based mental health provider (e.g., clinical psychologist) who primarily relies on a cognitive approach could be expected to use strategies that recognize the assumed connection between thoughts and emotions, and the need to assist individuals experiencing psychological difficulties in identifying patterns of faulty thinking to positively influence their behavior, problem-solving capacity, and coping skills (Zionts, Zionts, & Simpson, 2002). Teachers and other school personnel not primarily trained as emotional support or counselors, but who nevertheless assist parents and families through emotional support and problem-solving activities, can be expected to operate in a more short-term and informal fashion than mental health practitioners do.

Independent of the theoretical approach and the roles of the various school-based professionals who assist parents, basic emotional support and problem-solving elements are needed. These basic elements include creating an appropriate listening environment wherein effective communication and problem-solving can occur, creating an empathetic atmosphere wherein parents and family members feel that their concerns are being actively listened to and their perceptions and perspectives are respected and understood, accepting and supporting parent and family values and beliefs whenever possible, cultivating and accommodating active parent and family partnership relationships, and working to ensure that parents and families have a trusted professional to confide in and to share sensitive information with.

PARENT AND FAMILY NEEDS AND PARTICIPATION ASSESSMENT

Active parent and family participation in children's educational and other life experiences bodes well for their development and school and community success. We firmly believe (and our belief is supported by research) that there is a direct correlation between parents' and families' opportunities for collaborative partnerships with school and community professionals and parent and family empowerment to support members with special needs (Bailey, 2001; Wehman, 1999; Wright & Stegelin, 2003). Equally important, children themselves generally experience optimal growth and opportunities for achievement of desired outcomes when educational experiences occur within an ecology of family–professional cooperation and reciprocal participation (Berry & Hardman, 1998; Friend & Cook, 2004; Trivette, Dunst, & Hamby, 1996; Vernon et al., 2000).

The importance of family–professional partnerships and family participation in school programs for students with disabilities is widely accepted (Fiedler & Swanger, 2000). Yet, to be most effective, such involvement clearly needs to be individualized. As noted earlier, it is all too common for school and community professionals to plan for parent and family involvement based on the assumption that there is little need for program variability. Thus, even in situations where schools and other organizations strive to make parents active participants in educational activities and decision making, efforts to facilitate their involvement often mistakenly fail to recognize the heterogeneous needs of families for different levels and types of involvement.

In response to this problem, we recommend that, at a minimum, professionals consider two basic issues when considering the participation needs of parents and families. First, and most fundamentally, there should be recognition of the variable and unique needs and preferences of parents and families. As noted earlier, family units will vary in accordance with needs, time available for program participation, motivation for involvement, knowledge and skills required for various forms of participation, and so forth.

The second issue that directly follows the first consideration is that professionals offer parents and families a range of participation options. Professionals should openly and actively discuss with parents and families the fact that they may have different requirements, and that professional–parent relationships are most effective when these differences are recognized and accommodated. Subsequent to this discussion of uniqueness, a range of participation options should be offered. While not intended to serve as a rigid inventory or a formal bill of fare, this process does allow parents and families to consider how their unique circumstances best connect with the need for and the advantages of professional–parent involvement. Notable in this discussion process is the notion that increased levels of parent and family involvement do not necessarily equate with more effective involvement. Indeed, there are countless examples of parents and family members who demonstrate high-quality interactions and relationships with school and community professionals within select areas of involvement.

There are multiple descriptors and classifications for conceptualizing option levels for parent/family–professional participation. Within this range is the option of limited involvement and participation. Although we consider such a level undesirable, it is preferable to denying parents and families their right to decline participation and program involvement. That is, when parents and families prefer, for whatever reason, minimal participation with school personnel, we consider it appropriate for professionals to honor that preference. In this context, we use the term *honor* to refer to professionals' allowing parents to make such choices without efforts to make them feel guilty or obligated to defend their decision. At the same time, in such circumstances, we advise that all parents, including those who request minimal participation in school and community programs, be provided ongoing updates of their children's progress, be invited to participate in basic meetings such as IEP planning sessions, and be apprised of the availability of school and community resources, in case there are changes in family needs or changes in attitudes relative to participation. We consider it essential that parents who choose limited participation and involvement be provided the name of key school and school-based community personnel who can serve as referral sources, and that these individuals offer these parents an assessment of available resources that may be drawn on to address their family and child-related needs.

Our contention that it is essential that parent and family involvement be individualized is directly connected to their aforementioned heterogeneous nature, including variability in interests, time, resources, knowledge, and skills related to school-based involvement. Individualization of parent and family member involvement also fits with a family systems theory approach, wherein family elements are interrelated and issues and factors affecting one member affect other family members as well (Fine & Nissenbaum, 2000; Seligman & Darling, 1997; Turnbull & Turnbull, 2001).

A range of degrees of parent and family involvement necessitates that professionals (and others such as parent advocates) be able to conceptualize and describe involvement options at different levels. Shown and discussed below are four possible parent/family involvement levels that are offered as options for permitting parents and family members to participate in a child's education on an individualized basis. These potential levels of involvement are not hierarchical. That is, a higher level of involvement is not necessarily superior to less active involvement. Rather, needs, time, and other resources, interests, and family-specific variables are the basis for identifying the most suitable involvement for a particular family or individual. The four levels of potential involvement are discussed relative to providing a structure for assisting parents and families in selecting an involvement level that most effectively meets their needs.

Level 1: Awareness, Attendance, and Basic Participation

This baseline level of parent and family involvement involves school personnel providing information about a child's special needs, the educational program that has been crafted to respond to these needs, and the personnel who are hired to support student and family participation and needs. Level 1 involvement assures that parents and family members are given opportunities to become familiar with school and community programs that may be needed to support students and families, information about a student's educational services and programs, invitations to attend and participate in conferences such as IEP and progress report meetings, and opportunities to receive and provide information relevant to a child's school and school-related performance.

Level 2: Ongoing Communication, Information Sharing, and Basic Program Involvement

Ideally, all parents and families will be involved in ongoing communication and information sharing. A free-flowing exchange of information bodes well for professionals, families, and the students themselves. Thus, through formal and informal ongoing exchanges of information and participation in conferences and other school-related activities, students' support is maintained while creating an interpersonal atmosphere that nurtures trust, mutual respect, and a foundation for ongoing reciprocal support.

Level 3: Advocacy and Collaborative Program Involvement

This more advanced level of involvement assumes that parents and families are involved in ongoing communication and information sharing and a relationship that is generally mutually supportive and trusting. Building on this Level 2 involvement, parents and family members with expressed or perceived needs for collaborative involvement in goal identification, program strategy analysis, and program implementation and progress analysis are offered avenues for direct program participation. This level of involvement is also provided for parents and families who desire to serve as advocates for their children and for those who desire to implement collaborative home and community programs such as tutoring, behavior management, and so forth.

Level 4: Collaboration and Partnership Participation

This most advanced level of involvement builds on Level 2 and Level 3 assumptions. That is, Level 4 involvement sees parents and families maintaining ongoing communication and collaboration with school and community professionals along with collaborative advocacy and program application involvement. However, parents and families who function at a partnership level are those who have the skills, knowledge, motivation, and other resources that permit them to function on an equal basis with professionals. That is, they generally have equal knowledge and skills when compared with professionals and thus are able to engage in joint and independent programming and related activities. Parents and family members who function at a level of collaborative and partnership participation also are commonly involved in activities supportive of other children and families, such as taking part in advocacy programs and other advisory, volunteer, and service programs.

A MODEL FOR ADDRESSING PARENT AND FAMILY NEEDS WITHIN SCHOOL ORGANIZATIONS

Consistent with our theme that schools should take greater responsibility and leadership in responding to the pluralistic needs of parents and families of children and youth with disabilities, is the notion that schools should be structured to serve as sites for delivery of social, medical, mental health, and other parent/family support services. That is, the creation of full-service schools wherein there are school-based partnerships with community organizations appears to be both a logical and cost-effective mechanism for helping parents and families address a variety of needs that may be traditionally perceived to fall outside of school boundaries. Such services acknowledge that parents and families, including but not limited to those who deal with members with special needs, require a variety of support services and programs. Moreover, this model acknowledges that although school personnel are aware and sensitive to these needs, they are frequently unable to provide the array of support services required by parents and families without assistance in the form of partnerships with community agencies and related programs. The collaborative partnerships that ensue from community–school operations bring the promise of building better partnerships with families, schools, and communities; improving communication among families, school professionals, and community agencies; and improving both school and nonschool organizations' ability to accommodate a wide range of student and family needs.

While community-school reform models have recently received increased attention (Rones & Hoagwood, 2000; Sailor & Skrtic, 1996), the concept is not new. Tyack (1992) reported that in the early 1900s, progressive reformers in the United States used public schools to facilitate a variety of social reforms. Thus, exploitation of immigrant and poor children and families was reduced via compulsory education and child labor laws. Schools were also used as sites for meal distribution and summer enrichment programs. As precursors to modern-day full-service schools, these programs hired personnel to link needy and struggling families with community resources, and vocational guidance counselors were hired to assist students and families in finding employment. School clinics were also established to ensure that children received immunizations, medical evaluations, instruction in proper hygiene, and dental care. Unfortunately many of these early reforms were denounced as being contrary to a free-economy system and accused of promoting socialized medical and related services. Moreover, even the most successful school-based community programs were reported to be notoriously noncollaborative (Tyack, 1992). That is, families were generally perceived to be ignorant and unable to serve as collaborative decision makers and participants in identifying and meeting their needs. As a result, many parents and families were reported to view these early efforts as not being in their or their children's best interests.

Over time, many of these early reform movements continued in schools, albeit in a far different form than originally implemented. Disadvantaged and poor families have for decades been offered state and federally supported nutrition, medical, social, employment, and educational resources and opportunities. Yet, as suggested by a number of critics of these efforts (Lawson & Sailor, 2000; McKnight, 1995), there continued to be a pervasive pattern of using "top down" models wherein families and individuals who needed or received services were thought of as passive recipients of professionally determined decisions and given few collaborative opportunities to interact with professionals.

Notwithstanding the back-to-basics and traditional-school movements that have characterized the educational landscape of recent years, there appears to be renewed awareness of the need to link community and school programs and services. Unlike with previous movements, however, there appears to be greater recognition of the need for school and community personnel to support parents and families in being partners in these operations, and in permitting parents, family members, and students themselves to have a significant voice in making decisions related to service choices and delivery. Indeed, a number of professionals (Hays, Lipoff, & Danegger, 1995; Rones & Hoagwood, 2000; Wright & Stegelin, 2003) have observed that making parents equal partners in decisions related to school-based educational and community programs and services required to meet family and students' needs and basing these services on unique family characteristics, including family strengths, are fundamental requirements for program success.

Full-service schools in which school and community-based professionals work together in support of parents and families appear to have the potential to effectively address each of the areas of parent and family need identified in this chapter. However, success will require legitimate and meaningful partnerships among parents and families, school professionals, and individuals who work for community agencies. Shared governance, wherein partners who participate in school-based community programs are each empowered to be an equal partner and where meaningful and ongoing communication is nurtured and expected, is mandatory. Such a culture ensures that school personnel and agency professionals will not fall into the trap of simply coexisting in the same building without communicating or collaboratively working to achieve mutually beneficial goals; and without making parents and families partners in the communication and decision-making process. Thus, (a) delivery of effective educational services must be based on shared input of parents and families and school and community professionals; (b) ongoing communication and information exchange must involve regular interactions among all partners (within the parameters of ethical, legal, and confidentiality requirements); (c) participation, advocacy, and partnership and skill-training, management, and tutoring program needs can be undertaken with equal input from each of the three partners, with parents and families in many instances being permitted to take leadership roles; and (d) problem-solving, coping, and emotional and psychological support programs that are shared by community and school professionals, with equal decision-making authority by parents and family members, have the greatest potential for success.

Prominent and obvious among the roles that agencies and agency professionals can play in full-service schools are services and programs that address parent and family emotional and psychological needs. The authors of the Policy Leadership Cadre for Mental Health in School (2001) sagely observed that "mental health in schools" should "encompass considerations of the school's role related to both positive mental health (e.g., promotion of social and emotional development) and mental health problems (psychosocial concerns and mental disorders) of students, their families, and school staff" (pp. 5–6). This observation clearly recognizes the need for services that focus on a wide range of consumers, and that are crafted to promote preventive programming rather than being exclusively designed to address only problems of students and families. Clearly the goal of effectively and efficiently addressing parent and family needs for support is one that cannot be accomplished by independent efforts of mental health or school professionals, particularly without meaningful partnerships with parents and families. Such cooperative programming assists families in traversing the inconvenience and bureaucracy so common in social service and mental health programs, and in capitalizing on the shared resources of schools and community agencies.

While the importance and necessity of collaboration and a shared vision among school and community professionals is obvious, it is also obvious that each entity operates under different guidelines. Thus, as we discuss in chapters 7 and 11, effective school-based partnerships are not easy to form or maintain. Social service and mental health programs typically are the responsibility of city, county, and state governments. In many states, the various programs that constitute so-called mental health services (e.g., substance abuse, developmental disabilities, and juvenile judicial and child protective services) operate under different organizational structures. Moreover, community social and mental health services may range from for-profit to nonprofit organizations. This variability makes the process of establishing and operating effective partnerships among school and community professionals, with equal partnership status for parents and families, even more complex. Yet, this approach has the best chance of providing effective preventive and direct services to parents and families, including those with a child with a disability. Indeed, this approach appears to be the most efficient and cost-effective way of creating "a seamless web of supports and services that 'wrap around' children and families and to bring an end to the current fragmentation and categorical separation of school agency-directed programs" (U.S. Department of Education, 2000, p. 9) that is advocated by the U.S. Department of Education and called for in the No Child Left Behind Act of 2001. An example of a comprehensive school-based and family-centered cooperative program is described in Case Illustration 6.4.

CASE ILLUSTRATION 6.4

The Rayville Public Schools, in cooperation with a community mental health organization, designed and implemented a family-centered and comprehensive, cooperative school-based program. The program provided an array of services for students and their families, including children with disabilities. The goal of this family-focused program was to support families and build on family strengths. That parents were active decision-making members of the program's advisory and directory boards ensured that a collaborative professional–family partnership was a foundational element of the organization. Moreover, parents and families were supported in providing a number of services as a part of the program, including advocacy, training, and informational services.

Included in the Rayville program were multiple family-centered services that were aimed at satisfying an array of needs and that allowed multiple levels of parent and family participation. Programs included referrals for social and community-based services, including welfare, social security, medical care, respite care, and vocational counseling. The program also offered case management services, wherein a team of school-based community mental health providers and school personnel cooperatively worked with school IEP teams to identify and address parent, family, and student needs. Skill-building programs were also an element of the program, thus allowing parents and family members to learn about home-tutoring and management programs along with programs designed to enhance family members' capacity to actively participate in IEP and other decision-making conferences. Finally, the Rayville program supported an ongoing information library on various aspects of disability and special education as well as parent and family support groups, opportunities for short-term counseling, and a sibling support program and network.

The Websters Revisited

Katherine and William Webster continue to be supportive and to have generally positive perceptions toward their children's teachers and schools. Relative to Timothy's program, there have been improvements in their perceptions and attitudes. They attribute these developments to improved communication with Timothy's teacher and program team, including a brief daily "parent–school" report and weekly phone visits with the teacher. Moreover, they report feeling more comfortable and empowered related to having greater control over their level of involvement in their son's program. For instance, due to discussions with Timothy's school team related to clarifying their involvement in various school activities, they now feel more comfortable in selectively choosing which activities to participate in. They chose not to participate in a home-tutoring training program; however, they decided to participate in a toilet-training program that was designed to teach them to replicate the successful toileting procedures used at school.

Mr. and Mrs. Webster have also benefited from a cooperative school district and county mental health information and support group for parents of students with disabilities. They attend approximately half of the weekly meetings and report that connecting with other parents of students with disabilities has been helpful. They have also joined a national organization that supports individuals with Down syndrome, and they indicate that they feel empowered by their association with this group.

SUMMARY STATEMENTS

- Parents and families with members with disabilities will have variable needs.
- For general planning purposes, school and community personnel should conceptualize and plan for addressing basic and common needs of parents and families.
- Individualization is essential for parent and family involvement and participation in school and community programs.
- School and community cooperative partnership programs are an efficient and effective means of addressing parent and family needs.

QUESTIONS FOR DISCUSSION

1. Use the *Parent and Family Model of Commonly Experienced Needs* in Table 6.1 to analyze the perceived needs of a family of a student with a disability.
2. Relative to the above needs analysis, identify and discuss resources and activities associated with the four levels of participation involvement discussed in this chapter.
3. Relative to the above needs analysis, discuss the services that would be most appropriate and suitable for the family within a collaborative school-based school–community partnership program.

RESOURCES FOR IDENTIFYING AND ACCESSING SCHOOL SUPPORT SERVICES

- **National Dissemination Center for Children with Disabilities**
  (www.nichcy.org)

This organization is a central source of information on a variety of disability matters affecting infants, toddlers, children, and youth, including IDEA, the No Child Left Behind enactment, and effective educational practices.

- **Disabilities Studies and Services Center**
  (www.dssc.org)
  The Disabilities Studies and Services Center (DSSC) is a unit of the Academy for Educational Development. It provides information, technical assistance, and training to professionals and programs that serve individuals with disabilities and their families.

- **Council for Exceptional Children**
  (www.cec.sped.org)
  The Council for Exceptional Children is primarily an international organization for professionals who are involved with students with disabilities, gifted students, or both. It has a variety of resources and information for parents and families, including governmental policies, professional standards, advocacy, and effective professional practices.

- **National Mental Health Consumers' Self-Help Clearinghouse**
  (www.mhselfhelp.org)
  This Web site has multiple sources of information, including consumer information and referrals, consultation, a consumer library, a newsletter, and a consumer-supported nationwide networking movement.

- **Pacer Center: Parent Advocacy Coalition for Educational Rights**
  (www.pacer.org)
  This site provides a variety of user-friendly materials and resources, including resource links and publications.

- **Parents Helping Parents: The Parent-Directed Family Resource Center for Children with Special Needs**
  (www.php.com)
  This Web site provides a variety of resource ideas and options for families with children with special needs.

- **_Exceptional Parent_ magazine**
  (www.eparent.com)
  This publication and site offer information and resources for parents and families of persons with disabilities, including siblings.

REFLECTION ACTIVITIES

1. Request that one or more members of a family of an individual with a disability apply the Parent and Family Model of Commonly Experienced Needs (Table 6.1). As part of the activity, identify recommendations for most efficiently and effectively

addressing these perceived needs. Ask the family member(s) to also recommend how his or her perceived needs might best be addressed by school and community professionals, and then compare the two sets of recommendations.

2. Based on the needs analysis information in Item 1, discuss the services that could be delivered via a collaborative full-service school program. As part of this activity, identify challenges and barriers to developing such a program, along with strategies for addressing these challenges.

REFERENCES

Bailey, D. B. (2001). Evaluating parent involvement and family support in early intervention and preschool programs. *Journal of Early Intervention*, 24(1), 1–14.

Barnett, W., & Boyce, G. (1995). Effects of children with Down syndrome on parents' activities. *American Journal on Mental Retardation*, 100, 115–127.

Barry, J. O., & Hardman, M. (1998). *Lifespan perspectives on the family and disability*. Boston: Allyn & Bacon.

Bauer, A. M., & Shea, T. M. (2003). *Parents and schools: Creating a successful partnership for students with special needs*. Upper Saddle River, NJ: Merrill/Prentice Hall.

Blacher, J. (1984). Sequential stages of parental adjustment to the birth of a child with handicaps: Fact or artifact? *Mental Retardation*, 22, 55–68.

Buck, P. (1950). *The child who never grew*. New York: Day.

Buscaglia, L. (1975). *The disabled and their parents: A counseling challenge*. Thorofare, NJ: Slack.

Christenson, S. L., & Cleary, M. (1990). Consultation and the parent-education partnership: A perspective. *Journal of Education and Psychological Consultation*, 1, 219–241.

Cuban, L., & Usdan, M. (Eds.). (2003). *Powerful reforms with shallow roots: Improving America's urban schools*. New York: Teachers College Press.

Duncan, L., & Fitzgerald, P. (1969). Increasing the parent–child communication through counselor–parent conferences. *Personnel and Guidance Journal*, 48, 514–517.

Dunlap, G. (1999). Consensus, engagement, and family involvement for young children with autism. *The Journal of the Association for Persons with Severe Handicaps*, 24, 222–225.

Dunst, C. J., Trivette, C. M., & Snyder, D. M. (2000). Family–professional partnerships: A behavioral science perspective. In M. J. Fine & R. L. Simpson (Eds.), *Collaboration with parents and families of children and youth with exceptionalities* (pp. 27–48). Austin, TX: Pro-Ed.

Dyson, L. L. (2003). Children with learning disabilities within the family context: Comparisons with siblings in global self-concept, academic self perception, and social competence. *Learning Disabilities Research and Practice*, 18, 1–9.

Education for All Handicapped Children Act of 1975, 20 U.S.C. & 1400 et seq.

Epstein, M. (1995). School-family-community partnerships: Caring for the children we share. *Phi Delta Kappan*, 76(9), 701–712.

Fewell, R., & Gelb, S. (1983). Parenting moderately handicapped persons. In M. Seligman (Ed.), *The family with a handicapped child: Understanding and treatment* (pp. 175–202). Orlando, FL: Grune & Stratton.

Fiedler, C. R., & Swanger, W. H. (2000). Enpowering parents to participate: Advocacy and education. In M. J. Fine & R. L. Simpson (Eds.), *Collaboration with parents and families of children with disabilities* (pp. 437–464). Austin, TX: Pro-Ed.

Fine, M. J., & Nissenbaum, M. S. (Eds.). (2000). The child with disabilities and the family: Implications for professionals. In M. J. Fine & R. L. Simpson (Eds.), *Collaboration with parents and families of children with disabilities* (pp. 3–26). Austin, TX: Pro-Ed.

Fine, M. J., & Simpson, R. L. (Eds.). (2000). *Collaboration with parents and families of children with disabilities*. Austin, TX: Pro-Ed.

Foster, M. (1988). A systems perspective and families of handicapped children. *Journal of Family Psychology, 2,* 54–56.

Franklin, C., & Streeter, C. (1998). School-linked services as interprofessional collaboration in student education. *Social Work, 43*(1), 67–69.

Friend, M., & Cook, L. (2004). *Interactions: Collaboration skills for school professionals.* White Plains, NY: Longman.

Gorham, K. A. (1975). A lost generation of parents. *Exceptional Children, 41*(8), 521–525.

Hays, C., Lipoff, E., & Danegger, A. (1995). *Comprehensive service initiatives: A compendium of innovative programs.* Washington, DC: Finance Project.

Individuals with Disabilities Education Act Amendments of 1997, 20 U.S.C. & 1400 et seq.

Kohler, F. (1999). Examining the services received by young children with autism and their families: A survey of parent responses. *Focus on Autism and Other Developmental Disabilities, 14,* 150–158.

Lambie, R. (2000). Working with families of at-risk and special needs students: A systems change model. *Focus on Exceptional Children, 32*(1), 1–22.

Lawson, H. A., & Sailor, W. (2000). Integrating services, collaborating, and developing connections with schools. *Focus on Exceptional Children, 33*(2), 1–22.

Love, H. D. (1973). *The mentally retarded child and his family.* Springfield, IL: Thomas.

Maag, J. (2004). *Behavior management: From theoretical implications to practical solutions.* Belmont, CA: Thomson/Wadsworth.

McKnight, J. (1995). *The careless society: Community and its counterfeits.* New York: Basic Books.

Melynk, B. M., Feinstein, N. F., Moldenhouer, Z., & Small, L. (2001). Coping in parents of children who are chronically ill: Strategies for assessment and intervention. *Pediatric Nursing, 27*(6), 547–557.

Mundschenk, N., & Foley, R. (2000). Building blocks to effective partnerships: Meeting the needs of students with emotional or behavioral disorders and their families. In M. J. Fine & R. L. Simpson (Eds.), *Collaboration with parents and families of children*

and youth with exceptionalities (pp. 369–387). Austin, TX: Pro-Ed.

Myles, B. S., & Simpson, R. L. (2003). *Asperger syndrome: A resource for parents and professionals.* Austin, TX: Pro-Ed.

O'Day, J. (2002). Complexity, accountability and school improvement. *Harvard Educational Review, 72*(3), 293–329.

O'Shea, D. J., O'Shea, L. J., Algozzine, R., & Hammitte, D. J. (2001). *Families and teachers of individuals with disabilities.* Boston: Allyn & Bacon.

Policy Leadership Cadre for Mental Health in School, (2001). *Mental health in schools: Guidelines, models, resources and policy considerations.* Retrieved November 12, 2004 from http://smhp.psych.ucla.edu/pdfdocs/policymakers/cadreguidelines.pdf.

Reeve, R. E., & Cobb, H. C. (2000). Counseling approaches with parents and families. In M. J. Fine & R. L. Simpson (Eds.), *Collaboration with parents and families of children with disabilities* (pp. 177–193). Austin, TX: Pro-Ed.

Rones, M., & Hoagwood, K. (2000). School-based mental health services: A research review. *Clinical Child and Family Psychology Review, 3,* 223–241.

Sailor, W., & Skrtic, T. (1996). School–community partnerships and educational reform: Introduction to the special issue. *Remedial and Special Education, 17*(5), 267–283.

Schalock, R. L., & Alonso, M.A.V. (2002). *Handbook on quality of life for human service practitioners.* Washington, DC: American Association on Mental Retardation.

Schilling, R., Kirkham, M., Snow, W., & Schinke, S. (1996). Single mothers with handicapped children: Different from their married counterparts? *Family Relations, 35,* 69–77.

Seligman, M., & Darling, R. B. (1997). *Ordinary families, special children: A systems approach to childhood disability.* New York: Guilford Press.

Simpson, R. L. (1996). *Working with parents and families of exceptional children and youth.* Austin, TX: Pro-Ed.

Sulzer-Azaroff, B., & Mayer, G. R. (1977). *Applying behavior analysis procedures with children and youth.* New York: Holt, Rinehart & Winston.

Trivette, C. M., Dunst, C. J., & Hamby, D. W. (1996). Characteristics and consequences of help-giving practices in human services programs. *American Journal of Community Psychology, 24,* 273–293.

Turnbull, A. P., & Turnbull, H. R. (2001). *Families, professionals and exceptionality: Collaborating for empowerment* (4th ed.). Upper Saddle River, NJ: Merrill/Prentice Hall.

Tyack, D. (1992). Health and social services in public schools: Historical perspectives. *Future of Children,* 2(1), 19–31.

U.S. Department of Education. (2000). *Twenty-second annual report to Congress on the implementation of the Individuals with Disabilities Education Act.* Washington, DC: Author.

Vernon, S., Walther-Thomas, C., Schumaker, J. B., Deshler, D. D., & Hazel, J. (2000). A program for families of children and youth with learning disabilities. In M. J. Fine & R. L. Simpson (Eds.), *Collaboration with parents and families of children with disabilities* (pp. 277–302). Austin, TX: Pro-Ed.

Webber, J., Simpson, R., & Bentley, J. (2000). Parents and families of children with autism. In M. J. Fine & R. L. Simpson (Eds.), *Collaboration with parents and families of children with disabilities* (pp. 303–324). Austin, TX: Pro-Ed.

Wehman, T. (1999). A functional model of self-determination: Factors contributing to increased parent involvement and participation. *Focus on Autism and Other Developmental Disabilities,* 13(2), 80–86.

Wright, K., & Stegelin, D. A. (2003). *Building school and community partnerships through parent involvement.* Upper Saddle River, NJ: Merrill/Prentice Hall.

Zionts, P., Zionts, L., & Simpson, R. (2002). *Emotional and behavior problems: A handbook for understanding and handling students.* Thousand Oaks, CA: Corwin Press.

Zirpoli, T. J., & Melloy, K. J. (2004). *Behavior management: Applications for teachers.* Upper Saddle River, NJ: Merrill/Prentice Hall.

CHAPTER 7
Partnering to Provide Community Support Services for Parents and Families

●●●●●●●●●●●●●●●●●●●●○○○○

In this chapter, you will understand:

- The typical community support needs of families of children with disabilities.
- The key components of full-service schools.
- The issues associated with families accessing support services in the adult services system, including income support, health care, housing options, employment training, and family support programs.

- The benefits of school–community support services for children with disabilities and their families, school professionals, and schools.

Family Perspective: The Newtons

Sean Newton is a 15-year-old boy who has received special education services since he was 7 years old based on his serious emotional and behavioral problems. Sean can get along with his classmates, but he is often temperamental. He taunts others when things do not go his way. He frequently berates and intimidates female students. School staff have set goals with the family and expressed hope that the parents could overcome their marital difficulties enough to help Sean in several academic and behavioral areas. Mr. Newton had expressed a willingness to assist his wife in gaining control over Sean's defiance at home, but he works long hours and is seldom home. Basically, Mrs. Newton is unable to control Sean at home and is afraid of his frequent behavioral outbursts. Sean is an angry young man with an extremely low self-image. His lack of academic progress has exacerbated his poor image.

A growing problem in the Newton household is Sean's alcohol abuse. The problem is getting so bad that Sean has been suspended from school on three occasions in the past two months because he came to school "under the influence." Sean has also recently been arrested and charged by the district attorney with burglary and vandalism to a local school. There will be a juvenile court hearing in a couple of weeks to determine the disposition of Sean's case. The school is advocating for placement in a juvenile detention center. Both the school staff and the parents feel that Sean's behaviors, poor motivation to attend school, and possible alcohol addiction make it impractical to maintain Sean at home and in a regular school setting.

Reflecting on the Family Perspective

1. How could the school assist the Newtons in keeping Sean in the community and within a regular high school setting?
2. What kinds of community support services would be necessary to aid Sean and his family?

There are three all-too-familiar and undeniable realities impacting families of children with disabilities and schools in this first decade of the 21st century. First, there are increasing and pervasive societal circumstances that create risks for families. These risk factors include, among others, job market volatility, economic instability, increased substance abuse problems, mental health problems, family violence, poverty, neighborhood disintegration, increased feelings of alienation and learned helplessness, and fragmented and inadequate support services (Anderson & Mohr, 2003; Powell, Batsche, Ferro, Fox, & Dunlap, 1997; Summers, McMann, & Fuger, 1997). Second, school professionals cannot exert much influence and control over some of the most important factors that influence student learning (e.g., family and community systems, peer networks; Lawson & Sailor, 2000). This reality creates a double bind for school professionals, who are, nevertheless, held accountable for demonstrating improvement in students' learning and academic achievement. Third, schools alone cannot overcome the effects of these influences given the inadequate resources allocated to schools to deal with increasingly complex student and family problems (Adelman & Taylor, 2002).

These three realities require increasingly integrated and comprehensive support services for families of children with disabilities. In an effort to address these support needs of families, schools and school professionals are forming partnerships with various community service agencies. As discussed later in this chapter, these school–community partnerships take various forms, but these collaborative relationships involve both professional and organizational challenges. Most school professionals have been trained to act relatively autonomously and in isolation from other professionals, especially professionals working outside of school settings (Mostert, 1996). From an organizational perspective, school and community-based services are too often inadequate, inflexible, and fragmented (Osher & Hanley, 2001). School–community linkages call for new professional and organizational ways of doing business. To the extent that schools and school professionals can effectively meet these new challenges, children with disabilities and their families will be better served.

This chapter discusses the emerging role and responsibility of school professionals as collaborative partners with a variety of community service providers in offering comprehensive and coordinated support services to families of children with disabilities. We start by discussing families' needs for community support services. Further, we describe examples of full-service or community schools and some of the related service delivery models often referred to as school-linked services or wraparound services. Finally, this chapter also discusses some of the key adult community services for individuals with disabilities and their families.

FAMILIES' NEEDS FOR COMMUNITY SUPPORT SERVICES

Families frequently report that they need information about available community resources and supports (Gowen, Christy, & Sparling, 1993; Odom & Wolery, 2003). The task of adjusting to the challenges of raising a child with a disability can be daunting, and parents, quite naturally, look to support from the most obvious place: their local school (Arellano & Arman, 2002). Support needs vary from family to family and could include a multitude of services designed to address daily living needs. Turnbull and Turnbull (2001) categorized the impact of a child's disability on the family functions or the family's ability to satisfactorily address their needs in the following areas: affection, self-esteem, spiritual, economic, daily care, socialization, recreation, and education. A helpful resource with a large listing of Web sites for various supports and services designed to benefit children with disabilities and their families is *The Special Education Yellow Pages* (2000) by Pierangelo and Crane. Communication and Collaboration Tips Box 7.1 provides examples of typical community support services in each of the family needs and functions areas identified by Turnbull and Turnbull.

A useful instrument in assessing a family's needs for services is the Family Needs Scale by Dunst, Cooper, Weeldreyer, Snyder, and Chase (1987). This instrument measures a family's need for different resources and support. The scale includes 41 items categorized into nine distinct factors. Each item is rated on a 5-point Likert scale ranging from almost never (1) to almost always (5) a need. The nine factors are as follows:

- Factor I includes basic resources such as furniture, clothing, child care, health care, transportation, food, utilities, and employment.

COMMUNICATION AND COLLABORATION TIPS   BOX 7.1

Family Need Areas	Examples of Community Support Services
Affection	• Parent education programs • Parent support groups • Family counseling • Child abuse prevention agencies
Self-esteem	• Community recreation programs • Youth groups (e.g., boys/girls clubs, Scouts) • Parent training and information centers • Mental health agencies
Spiritual	• Religious organizations • Parent support groups
Economic	• Public assistance agencies • Social Security Administration • Medicaid • Family support programs • Vocational rehabilitation agencies • Estate planning services from attorneys or disability organizations • Health care organizations
Daily Care	• Medicaid—Katie Beckett program • Respite care agencies • Home health care agencies • Independent adult living centers • Child care organizations
Socialization	• Sibling support groups • Parent support groups
Recreation	• Special summer camps • Community recreation programs • Local libraries • YMCA
Education	• Protection and advocacy agencies • Parent training and information centers • Assistive technology organizations • Early childhood agencies • Postsecondary education institutions

- Factor II assesses specific child care items such as specialized dental and medical care, respite care, adapted equipment, and having someone to talk with about their children.

- Factor III involves personal and family growth issues such as doing things together, educational opportunities, family travel/vacation, and saving for the future.
- Factor IV measures the family's need for financial and medical resources such as paying for special child necessities and family health care.
- Factor V assesses a family's needs in their child's education, including adequacy of current and future educational placements, child care, and child therapy.
- Factor VI measures family needs revolving around meal preparation, such as time to cook, help with feeding the children, and adapted equipment.
- Factor VII measures the family's need for future child care items such as respite care, child care, and the child's future vocation.
- Factor VIII assesses the family's financial budgeting needs.
- Factor IX measures the family's need for household support items.

FULL-SERVICE SCHOOLS

In an effort to address the increasingly diverse and complex needs of children with disabilities and their families, schools in many communities are restructuring to become full-service or community schools. Schools can serve as the hub for delivery of or connection to a variety of services that complement and support education. Dryfoos (1994) described full-service schools in the following manner:

> The vision of the full-service school puts the best of school reform together with all other services that children, youth, and their families need, most of which can be located in a school building. The educational mandate places responsibility on the school system to reorganize and innovate. The charge to community agencies is to bring into the school: health, mental health, employment services, child care, parent education, case management, recreation, cultural events, community policing, and whatever else may fit into the picture. The result is a new kind of "seamless" institution, a community-oriented school with a joint governance structure that allows maximum responsiveness to the community, as well as accessibility and continuity for those most in need of services. (p. 12)

There are several provisions in IDEA that serve as legal bases for requiring schools to provide or link families up with community support services. First, there is substantial overlap between some of the core values of a community-based system of care for children with disabilities and their families and key components of IDEA, including parent participation, individualized educational planning, and placement in the least restrictive environment (Anderson & Matthews, 2001). Second, IDEA transition requirements emphasize collaborative linkages between schools and community agencies (Blalock, 1996). Third, Part C of IDEA, which mandates services for infants and toddlers with disabilities, requires education programs to coordinate a comprehensive set of interdisciplinary services that address the needs of all children and families (Summers, Steeples, et al., 2001). Fourth, there are several examples of related services that schools are legally required to provide children with disabilities and their families if those services are necessary to assist the child in benefiting from special education (DePaepe, Garrison-Kane, & Doelling, 2002). Examples of related services include school health services, counseling, and parent training and counseling. Finally, a recent U.S. Supreme Court decision in *Olmstead v. L.C.* (1999) held that inappropriate restrictive placements of individuals with disabilities constitute discrimination under Title III of the Americans with Disabilities Act (ADA). Bullock (2002) maintained that the *Olmstead* decision has implications for schools under IDEA. Specifically, under the transition-planning requirements of IDEA, students with disabilities are to move smoothly from secondary schools to postschool activities that maximize their independence. This would seem to place a legal obligation on schools to address the needs of children with disabilities in residential treatment facilities, detention centers, and other segregated settings. Barriers to implementing the *Olmstead* decision could largely be overcome through greater collaboration between school and community support services.

When schools help children and families to become more resilient in the face of family, school, and community stressors, the children's academic achievement levels increase (Arellano & Arman, 2002). The community schools movement seeks to establish relationships with other professions and community organizations (Lawson, 1999). This school movement simply acknowledges that children cannot learn if they are hungry, ill, abused, or facing problems at home. As noted by Walther-Thomas, Korinek, and McLaughlin (1999), most communities have services such as public and private day care, public health, mental health, social services, parks and recreation, vocational rehabilitation, juvenile justice, and a host of United Way referral services. Full-service schools tap into these community agencies and form collaborative partnerships by encouraging some community service providers to relocate to schools while other agency partners remain housed in the community but firmly linked to schools through established communication and referral networks. Full-service schools provide services based on the needs of students and their families, not on what kind of services are conveniently available (Cessna & Skiba, 1996).

School professionals are instrumental in identifying students and families who may need services, sharing information with service providers, and ensuring delivery of services. Indeed, as recognized by Lindle (1996), school professionals are the most important link in community service efforts because of their unique relationships and daily contact with students. School professionals working in full-service schools assume new roles and responsibilities, as stated by Bucci and Reitzammer (1992):

> Although the primary responsibility of the teacher will be the academic development of the students, greater attention will go to the health and social factors that affect student learning. The teacher will need to develop a greater understanding of the variety of services that are available to address the health and social service needs of the child. The teacher will become part of a team of professionals working to help children to become successful and contributing members of society. (p. 292)

Examples of the new roles and responsibilities of school professionals include:

- Learning about school-linked comprehensive services for children and families
- Developing an expanded view of responsibilities that extends to each student's academic development, health, and social well-being
- Identifying areas of student and family needs
- Learning about social service agencies in the community

- Participating in professional development to learn how to identify and refer children and families who are in need of services
- Advocating an expanded role for the school in working with families and social service agencies
- Establishing collaborative partnerships with community agencies and service providers

In this section, we discuss the foundation of full-service schools, interprofessional and interagency collaboration, and we describe examples of supports provided by full-service schools. These examples include school-linked service integration and wraparound services.

Interprofessional and Interagency Collaboration

As stated at the beginning of this chapter, there are both professional and organizational challenges to establishing effective school–community partnerships. The greatest professional challenge is reversing the traditional tendency of school professionals to operate in relative isolation from other professionals and to act autonomously. There are many definitions of interprofessional collaboration. One defines interprofessional collaboration ". . . as a mutual, reciprocal effort among professionals, families, and other caregivers to deliver effective interventions to children for their increased physical, emotional, and academic well-being" (Mostert, 1996, p. 135). Lawson and Sailor (2000) stated it simply: "Every professional working with the same child, adult, and family has to be on the same page" (p. 10). Interagency collaboration involves organizational linkages between schools and various community agencies in an effort to respond to the needs of children with disabilities and their families that extend beyond the capabilities of typical school services (Walther-Thomas et al., 1999). To systematically analyze interprofessional and interagency collaborative support services, it is useful to consider the different levels of collaboration that are involved. Bruner (1991) outlined four levels of collaboration necessary for a successful full-service school model. Each of these levels of collaboration will be briefly discussed, with a focus on the key characteristics or issues associated with effective delivery of support services to students with disabilities and their families.

Collaboration Among Administrators   This level of collaboration provides the necessary institutional support for an effective school–community program. Interagency collaboration is fostered when there is shared leadership among the participating community agencies; a clear and coherent vision of comprehensive school-linked community services; comprehensive planning to establish goals, roles, and responsibilities; adequate resources to provide the necessary services; sustained implementation to work through the inevitable growing pains associated with major change initiatives; and continuous evaluation mechanisms to assess the effectiveness of services provided (Walther-Thomas et al., 1999). Communication and Collaboration Tips Box 7.2 identifies some of the key issues associated with each of the elements of collaboration between administrators identified above.

Collaboration Among Community Service Providers and School Professionals   In a real sense, successful family support services are provided not by agencies but by individual staff members. These professionals are responsible for making the day-to-day work of the interagency collaborative team function smoothly and effectively. Lawson and Sailor (2000) identified several concepts necessary for effective interprofessional collaboration. First, there must be *interdependence* between two or more professions. Any one profession depends on other professions in achieving its goals of meeting the complex needs of children with disabilities and their families. Second, collaborative professionals understand that there is *conditional equality* in their relationship. Power and expertise are shared as democratic relationships evolve. Third, a *unity of purpose* emerges when different professions begin to acknowledge their interdependence and engage in holistic planning and intervening to address the whole child and the entire family system. Fourth, as a clear unity of purpose develops, collaborative professionals assume *shared responsibility for results* and, in general, become more results oriented as data collection systems are established. The fifth concept recognizes that busy professionals must have some incentive for taking the time to meet and making the effort to provide the necessary services. In other words, collaborative professionals must possess *enlightened self-interest*. They must recognize that through joining forces, they will gain a collaborative advantage and, thus, experience a greater sense of efficacy in their interventions. Sixth, when collaborative professionals recognize they will likely be more successful through their joint efforts, they become more willing to share and develop common grounds for working together. A sense of *reciprocity* emerges.

> Professionals who collaborate share missions, goals, and objectives. They also share definitions of "the problem(s)," including what's wrong that needs fixing and what's good and right that needs strengthening. They develop shared language, problem-solving protocols, and barrier-busting strategies. They also learn to share resources and supports. They develop shared governance structures. Thus, true interprofessional collaboration is durable; it tends to have sticking power and staying power. (Lawson & Sailor, 2000, p. 11)

Finally, professional collaborative relationships experience *generativity*; that is, they become more innovative in their problem solving and develop a real commitment to the work being done on behalf of children with disabilities and their families.

Collaboration Among Members of a Participating Agency   Both school professionals and community service providers must be able to work successfully with other staff members within their own organization. Effective intraorganizational staff collaboration ensures a collegial atmosphere in the interagency collaborative team. Interagency collaborative members will function more effectively as a team if those members have previously experienced success as a team member within their own organization. Teaming is recognized as a critical ingredient in collaborative problem solving. Fleming and Monda-Amaya (2001) conducted a Delphi study to identify and validate a list of critical process variables that support team efforts and effectiveness. They identified 49 critical process variables selected from six categories. The critical-variable categories for effective teaming include (a) team goals, (b) team roles and membership, (c) team communication, (d) team cohesion, (e) team logistics, and (f) team outcomes.

COMMUNICATION AND COLLABORATION TIPS   **BOX 7.2**

Issues Associated with Collaboration Among Administrators

Assessing Shared Leadership

❏ Are interagency members clear about their roles and responsibilities?
❏ Did each agency administrator actively involve direct services staff in planning efforts?

Assessing the Vision

❏ Do all interagency members share family-centered beliefs about families of children with disabilities (e.g., treat families with dignity and respect, identify and work with family strengths, actively involve families in decisions about services, provide individualized family support services, adhere to culturally responsive practices)?
❏ Do all interagency members share responsibility for the success or failure of family support services?
❏ Can interagency members articulate common values and goals?

Assessing Comprehensive Planning

❏ Do comprehensive plans guide resource allocation, professional development, personnel assignments, and staff schedules?
❏ Does the interagency team regularly share information and allow input from families on proposed changes in the provision of school–community support services?

Assessing Resources

❏ Do the agency administrators provide policies, materials, personnel, and other resources to support school–community service delivery?
❏ Are caseloads of direct support services staff reasonable to allow for effective school–community collaboration?
❏ Is common planning time provided to allow interagency staff to regularly meet?

Assessing Implementation

❏ Is ongoing professional development provided to ensure the continuous skill development of support services staff in effective interagency collaboration?

Assessing Evaluation Efforts

❏ Are student and family supports the key elements in interagency decision making?
❏ Are student and family outcomes assessed and monitored on an ongoing basis?
❏ Do interagency evaluation plans foster program review, systematic improvement, and replication as appropriate?

Source: Adapted from Walther-Thomas, C., Korinek, L., & McLaughlin, V.L. (1999). Collaboration to support student services. *Focus on Exceptional Children, 32*(3), 1–18.

Some examples of critical process variables under each identified category will be briefly presented. *Team goals* include process variables such as clear team purpose, goals are regularly reviewed, goals are supported by the family, goals are attainable, and the team goals are prioritized. Examples from the *team roles and membership* category are commitment to the team process by each member, accountability to the team, an unbiased team leader, and team roles are perceived as important by team members. *Team communication* addresses decision-making efforts. Decisions are made for the good of the student and his or her family, decisions are alterable, and decisions are reached by consensus. *Team cohesion* fosters a sense of trust and safety in sharing ideas. Team cohesion is also cultivated by taking the time to celebrate team successes, demonstrating respect for team members, permitting disagreement among team members, and recognizing the efforts of team members. *Team logistics* involve an internal evaluation of progress by the team members and clearly understood team procedures. Finally, *team outcomes* include process variables such as solutions are practical, the team reviews the impact of their plan of services, parent satisfaction is part of the evaluation, modifications are made as necessary, and members are committed to implementing the plan of services.

Collaboration Among School Professionals, Community Service Providers, and Families

This level of collaboration is where community support services are actually provided. Effective interagency collaborative initiatives emphasize the point of contact among service providers and families. School professionals help families obtain the services they need, and as community service providers make contact with families who need their services. Giangreco (2000) enumerated three essential dispositions of school professionals in their collaborative interactions with community service providers and families. First, school professionals must be continual learners so that they are willing to learn from other professionals and from families. Second, school professionals must embrace family-centered beliefs, values, or assumptions in their efforts to support children with disabilities and their families. Finally, school professionals must uphold a keen awareness of the importance of supporting families of children with disabilities. Ultimately, as noted by Giangreco, the key issue is whether the professional efforts and services provided contribute to a better life for students with disabilities and their families. Park, Turnbull, and Turnbull (2002) defined quality of life for families as having their needs met, enjoying life together as a family, and pursuing opportunities and achieving goals that are meaningful to the family. Interprofessional collaboration contributes to family quality of life by enhancing the effectiveness of programs and services designed to address the needs of families of children with disabilities (Mostert, 1996; Myers, Sweeney, & White, 2002; Shoffner & Briggs, 2001; Walther-Thomas et al., 1999).

A key skill for school professionals in their collaborative interactions with families is to carefully listen to the family's story and goals (Smith & Prelock, 2002). One technique for assisting the family in telling their story and identifying community support needs is to use an ecomap. An ecomap is an information-gathering strategy that can be used with families in an initial attempt to understand their environment. Ecomaps were originally used to help social workers assess individual family needs. These maps portray the child's developmental contexts, showing the interactions of family members with outside resources, including extended-family members, schools, various community services, friends, and work. The ecomap depicts the nature and flow of the relationships between family members and outside resources. It identifies areas of stress and support within the family system as well as where individual and family needs are unmet. See Communication and Collaboration Tips Box 7.3 on how to develop an ecomap.

COMMUNICATION AND COLLABORATION TIPS   **BOX 7.3**

Example of a Family Ecomap

To develop an ecomap, the school professional sits with the family group around a large piece of paper or a posterboard and asks nonintrusive questions such as "Who are the people who live together in your family?" "What kinds of relationships do you have with those individuals?" Different types of lines can be used to illustrate the types of relationships involved. For example, **bold,** solid lines can signify good, supportive relationships. Wavy lines can identify tenuous or problematic relationships. Ecomaps provide considerable information on the family's social environment, significant sources of stress, and available used and unused sources of support.

Fields Family Ecomap

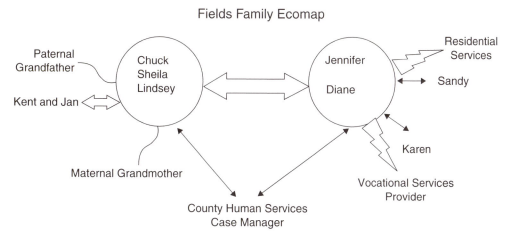

Support Conclusions from Ecomap

1. The parents, Chuck and Sheila Fields, live with their youngest daughter, Lindsay. Their daughter Jennifer, who has severe and multiple disabilities, lives in her own home with a roommate, Diane.
2. The parents receive little emotional or practical support from either grandparent (represented by wavy lines).
3. The parents have Kent and Jan as their best friends and receive a lot of natural support from that couple.
4. The county human services case manager provides solid support to both the parents and to Jennifer.
5. The level of support from both the vocational and residential services providers is problematic. These are areas in which the family could use assistance.
6. Jennifer receives solid and regular support from her job coach, Sandy, and her home health aide, Karen.

Barriers to Interprofessional and Interagency Collaboration

A variety of barriers to interprofessional and interagency collaboration exist (Mostert, 1996). Collaborative teams often fail due to communication problems. Sometimes this miscommunication is caused by different professions being unfamiliar with each other's terminology and distinct language base. For instance, special education teachers can quickly turn off general education teachers through their excessive use of special education jargon and acronyms (i.e., IDEA, LRE, FAPE, IEE, PLEP, and on and on). Miscommunication can also occur due to the difficulties of finding sufficient time to conduct meetings to coordinate services. Many professionals find meetings aversive, especially if viewed as nonproductive and excessive. In some instances, interprofessional collaboration fails because the members did not possess the necessary sustained commitment. Establishing trust and an operational structure does take time. In addition, providing supports and services to meet the multifaceted and complex needs of families is challenging work and rarely is effective with a quick-fix mentality. Interprofessional and interagency collaboration require dedication and commitment over a sustained period of time and during situations in which the professionals involved may be experiencing more setbacks than successes. Collaborative teams have dissolved when one or more professional members were dragged into the effort without the necessary personal commitment to the team's goals and efforts. Effective collaboration must be voluntary and based on a strong sense of mutuality and interdependence. A strength of interprofessional collaboration is that professionals can learn from members of a different profession who bring diverse perspectives, knowledge, and skills. This strength can also become a weakness if collaborative team members resist the point of view of another profession. For example, an educational program for a child with autism was severely hindered when the special education teacher refused to implement any of the sensory integration intervention recommendations offered by the occupational therapist. Finally, collaborative efforts suffer when the team members' roles and responsibilities are not clearly defined, resulting in role confusion or ambiguity.

FULL-SERVICE SCHOOLS: PRINCIPLES AND PROCEDURES

Full-service schools are embodied in approaches referred to as school-linked services integration or wraparound service systems. In these approaches, the available human support service systems in a community are brought together in a fully integrated arrangement. Individual services and support are "wrapped around" students and their families (Skrtic, Sailor, & Gee, 1996). As noted by Skrtic et al.,

> Under such an arrangement, virtually all community human support systems—including public education, employment, housing, religion, community health systems, social welfare, mental health, parks and recreation, probation, child protective services, juvenile justice, early childhood, aging, and so forth—are coordinated and fitted to the needs of a particular client family. (p. 149)

Lawson and Sailor (2000) identified a number of goals or purposes often associated with the full-service schools movement, including:

(1) improving the service system; (2) maximizing the efficient use of limited resources; (3) maximizing the independence of families by freeing them from long-term dependence on the government; (4) rebuilding and restoring the capacities of families and local communities; (5) expanding economic and social development and increasing parental employment; (6) improving outcomes for children and families; (7) contributing to improvements in school performance; (8) improving professionals' working conditions, efficacy, performance, and job satisfaction; and (9) revitalizing and empowering local neighborhood communities to mobilize effectively for collective action and to facilitate democratic participation. (p. 5)

Principles

School-linked services integration or wraparound approaches are based on a number of fundamental principles or values (Anderson & Matthews, 2001; Anderson & Mohr, 2003; Bullis & Cheney, 1999; Osher & Hanley, 2001; Summers et al., 1997; VanDenBerg & Grealish, 1996). VanDenBerg and Grealish (1996) summarized the philosophical foundation on which wraparound services are based:

- Wraparound efforts must be based in the community.
- Services and supports must be individualized to meet the needs of the children and families and not designed to reflect the priorities of the service system.
- The process must be culturally competent and build on the unique values, strengths, and social and racial makeup of children and families.
- Parents must be included in every level of development of the process.
- Agencies must have access to flexible, noncategorized funding.
- The process must be implemented on an interagency basis and be owned by the larger community.
- Services must be unconditional. If the needs of the child and family change, the child and family are not to be rejected from services. Instead, the services must be changed.
- Outcomes must be measured. If they are not, the wraparound process is merely an interesting fad (p. 9).

There are some common themes amongst the various lists of key principles associated with school-linked services integration or wraparound services. One of those themes is *empowerment*. Services are provided to families in an effort to enhance their own capacities for problem solving. The key to such a school–community service system is to lessen family dependence by enhancing their natural support networks and building on their strengths. Another fundamental theme is *nonjudgmental, unconditional support*. When interventions are not successful with a particular family, the professional focus and effort is not on blaming the family for the failed services. Instead, the professionals focus on refining the services provided to be more successful in their efforts to aid the family. A prime example of a traditional "victim blaming" perspective is offered by Franz (2003). He tells the story of a young man named Clarence. When Clarence was five, an uncle repeatedly raped him. School personnel thought that Clarence's escalating behaviors at school were due to his cognitive disability and poor expressive language skills. When Clarence's parents requested therapy from the school, the school social worker responded, "How are you supposed to do therapy with a kid like that?" When Clarence became a teenager, he was involved in a number of sexually aggressive incidents against younger children. School officials sought his expulsion from school, while the assistant district attorney pursued a correctional placement for Clarence. During the juvenile court hearing, an exasperated judge refused to give up on Clarence by simply removing him from the community. Instead the judge ordered the school and other community service agencies to develop a comprehensive service plan to address the needs of Clarence and his family. The judge ended by stating, "I want no more Clarences in my courtroom" (p. 244). Quite simply, the judge was trying to break the negative cycle of blaming Clarence for his sexually aggressive behaviors. Instead, the judge was seeking to garner the necessary support resources to address Clarence's challenging behaviors.

A final common theme in principles undergirding full-service schools is *respect*. Professionals working with families at risk in full-service schools are respectful of their circumstances and treat parents as collaborative partners, not as clients. This respect cultivates trust between the family and professionals.

Procedures

The operational procedures of full-service schools include a number of distinct procedural steps. For brevity purposes, this section will illuminate four key procedural stages: (a) resource coordination, (b) identification of the child and family support team, (c) strengths discovery, and (d) development of a support plan (Franz, 2003; VanDenBerg & Grealish, 1996). Once a child and family are determined to be in need and eligible for services, a case manager or resource coordinator is assigned to identify key individuals or organizations in the child's and family's lives, to facilitate team meetings, to identify services needed by the child and family, to assess training needs of team members, to arrange implementation of services and supports not presently in existence, to identify and manage funding sources, to evaluate outcomes of services and supports provided to the child and family, and to develop transition plans (Sewell, 1990). Because the case manager position is a critical role, it is essential that the professional serving in that capacity possess broad knowledge of community resources, interpersonal communication skills to facilitate relationships with families and other service providers, and a nonjudgmental perspective toward families and their diverse situations.

The child and family support team usually consists of 4 to 10 members. The team's primary responsibilities are to develop a support plan, monitor the implementation of that support plan, and evaluate the outcomes of the services and supports provided to the child and family. The support team consists of the child and family and others who are close to the family. VanDenBerg and Grealish (1996) recommended that the support team consist of both professionals and nonprofessionals (i.e., extended family members, friends, neighbors). The value of nonprofessionals on the support team is that they are likely to be aware of informal resources and natural supports that professionals may not know about.

As stated previously in this chapter, full-service community schools maintain a focus on the strengths of children with disabilities and their families. In fact, individualized service and support plans are based on the strengths of the child and family. As noted by VanDenBerg and Grealish (1996), the strengths-discovery approach of full-service schools differs from the assessment and planning procedures associated with categorical services delivery models. In a categorical delivery model, service agencies focus on disabilities and deficits in an effort to determine if the child or family qualifies for a particular service. Considering the importance of building on clients' strengths in achieving positive support plan outcomes, the development of strength models is a critical component in the operational procedures of full-service schools (Duchnowski & Kutash, 1993).

The strengths-discovery process is accomplished through a "strengths chat" as identified by VanDenBerg and Grealish (1996). This involves professionals' engaging in a conversation with the child and family about what they perceive to be their strengths. Strengths-discovery questions are designed to help professionals identify existing family resources, family preferences and values, and how family members view themselves (Community Partnerships Group, 1995). Another example of an instrument that assesses family strengths and resources is the Family Functioning Style Scale (Deal, Trivette, & Dunst, 1988). This 26-item instrument is designed to determine the extent to which individual family members believe their family is characterized by various strengths and capabilities. Specifically, this instrument measures family strengths and resources identified by five factors. The first factor assesses the *Interactional Patterns* (i.e., spending time together, listening to all points of view, sharing concerns and feelings) of the family. The second factor, *Family Values*, involves issues such as taking pride in accomplishments of family members, making personal sacrifices for the benefit of the family, and valuing family relationships over material possessions. The third factor measures intrafamily *Coping Strategies* (i.e., looking for the bright side of issues, not worrying about events beyond one's control, forgetting overwhelming problems). The fourth factor is *Family Commitment*. This factor looks at issues such as trying to solve family problems before seeking outside assistance and depending on other family members. The final factor, *Resource Mobilization*, measures the extent to which the family uses extrafamily support.

The final procedural step critical to the success of full-service schools that we will discuss is the development of the individualized services and support plan for families. To focus the support team on potential needs of the family, the following life domain areas provide a structure for developing the family support plan (VanDenBerg & Grealish, 1996).

1. **Living Situation**—Consider the family's living arrangement, space, privacy, comfort, stability of placement, and safety of physical environment.

2. **Crisis**—Consider the child's crisis and the family's methods of crisis management in the home, school, and community.

3. **Basic Needs/Financial**—Consider the family's access to shelter, food, transportation, child care, respite care, and financial resources, and their money management skills.

4. **Family**—Consider the family constellation, relationships among members, extended family resources, social support network, values, and strengths.

5. **Emotional/Psychological**—Consider any significant psychological histories of the child or other family members.

6. **Social/Recreational**—Consider the social interactive skills of family members, identify formal and informal social relationships, and describe activities within the family and in the community.

7. **Community Resources**—Consider the community resources the child and family currently uses, needs, or wants.

8. **Cultural**—Consider any ethnic or national traditions and discuss the family's access to and affiliation with those traditions.

9. **Vocational/Educational**—Consider the child's academic and behavioral functioning, educational grade level and placement, school attendance, and work experiences or employment skills and interests.

10. **Spiritual**—Consider any religious or spiritual beliefs, values, practices, and support.

11. **Legal**—Consider any significant involvement with the legal system.

12. **Medical**—Consider physical health, mental health, alcohol/drug abuse, significant past medical information, medication regimen, and health and health equipment needs of family members.

After a discussion of each of the above-mentioned life domains (with the child, parents, and other family members participating in this review and discussion), the family support team prioritizes the life domain areas in which the child and family are experiencing the most needs. Each life domain is rated by the team as being an area of no needs or mild, moderate, or great needs. Further, specific strengths of family members are identified for each life domain area. The family support team next brainstorms as many options as possible for addressing each of the prioritized needs. After this brainstorming process, the team identifies what options are most likely to be effective and develops a support plan around those options. The family support plan is organized by the life domains in which the prioritized needs were identified. "The ideal plan should focus more on informal supports than on formal services, as services will eventually end while informal supports such as friendships and family support will likely continue indefinitely" (VanDenBerg & Grealish, 1996, p. 15). Figure 7.1 provides an overview of the procedural steps in providing wraparound services.

Full-service schools involve coalitions of community-based service providers. Some providers may locate their services at schools whereas other community-based service providers remain located in the community, but those provider agencies are firmly linked with schools through established communication channels and referral networks (Lawson, 1999). Full-service schools provide both formal support and informal or natural support to children with disabilities and their families.

Families may receive a variety of formal support services provided by professionals, involving myriad local, state, and federal programs. Some of the formal support services provided by community agencies linked with full-service schools include

Figure 7.1 *Procedural steps in providing wraparound services.*

health screening and services; dental services; family planning; individual counseling; substance abuse treatment; mental health services; nutrition/weight management; basic services such as housing, food, clothing; recreation; mentoring; family welfare services; parent education; literacy training; child care; employment training; case management; and crisis intervention (Dryfoos, 1994). Communication and Collaboration Tips Box 7.4 provides suggestions on how school professionals can develop a family-friendly community resource directory.

Informal or natural supports mean personal associations and relationships typically developed in the community that enhance the quality of life for individuals with

---

COMMUNICATION AND COLLABORATION TIPS   **BOX 7.4**

Developing a Family-Friendly Community Resource Directory

❏ Organize listing of community organizations by family functional needs (e.g., affection, self-esteem, spiritual, economic, daily care, socialization, recreation, education).

❏ Include a welcoming letter at the beginning of the directory. Explain why you have developed the directory and how parents can use the directory, and invite parents to ask questions.

❏ Include a table of contents.

❏ Develop a consistent format for reporting organization information.

❏ Important information to include about each organization:
   1. Name of contact person at the organization
   2. Brief description of services provided
   3. Eligibility criteria (if any)
   4. Fees (if any)

---

disabilities and their families. Natural supports may include family relationships, community friendships, associations with fellow students or employees, and associations developed through participation in community organizations and activities (Nisbet, 1992). Natural supports are often more effective than formal supports because the assistance or support is provided by individuals who live and interact with the individual with a disability and his or her family on a day-to-day basis (Fabry, Reitz, & Luster, 2002). In addition, natural supports offer the following advantages over formal supports provided by professionals:

- Professional service providers come and go, whereas natural support persons typically remain more constant in an individual's or family's life.
- Professional support providers often isolate and focus on differences of the individual with disabilities.
- Natural supports foster a sense of belonging and inclusion.
- Natural supports provide more diverse experiences and opportunities than could ever be programmed by a professional service provider.

School professionals can assist children with disabilities and their families in developing natural supports in a number of ways. For example, using an ecomap, school professionals can help parents focus on their neighborhood and potential support allies in the local community (see Box 7.3). School professionals can also identify organized groups that exist in the community.

Community groups or organizations can help welcome individuals who have been routinely excluded from their communities. School professionals foster greater natural supports by paying attention to natural cues and systematically fading the level of formal support and allowing a natural support structure to emerge. For example, a teacher of students with severe disabilities had been assisting one of her students with self-feeding skills during lunchtime in the school's cafeteria. The teacher noticed that several nondisabled female students sitting nearby started taking an interest in the female student with severe disabilities. Gradually over two weeks, the teacher coaxed and encouraged the nondisabled students to assist the student with a disability during lunchtime. Eventually, the teacher completely removed herself from the cafeteria as nondisabled peers provided the natural support to assist the student with a disability during lunchtime. Of course, school personnel need to monitor the provision of those supports at lunch to ensure appropriate feeding techniques are being followed by the peer assistants.

ACCESSING FAMILY SUPPORTS WITHIN THE ADULT SERVICES SYSTEM

Effective school–community support services address child and family needs during the school years. But what about the needs of families and their *adult* sons and daughters with disabilities? There is a basic difference between education and adult services. Public education is an entitlement program, meaning that once a child is identified as a "student with a disability" under IDEA, that child is entitled to special education services. Public education services must be provided to eligible students with disabilities regardless of funding problems. Conversely, in the adult services system, individuals may meet eligibility requirements for a particular service but may not receive those services if funding problems restrict the amount of services provided. An eligible individual may be placed on a waiting list for services and may begin receiving services when funding permits. Many adult services involve eligibility programs where waiting lists are prevalent. In this section, we will briefly describe some common adult services for individuals with disabilities that provide income support, health care, housing options, employment training, and family support.

Income Support

Many families are concerned about the financial security of their adult member with a disability. The long-term responsibility of meeting the financial needs of an adult family member with a disability is a daunting prospect for most low-or modest-income families. Further, if the individual with a disability is able to work, will his or her employment income be enough to support him or her? There are two major federal sources of income support for low-income individuals with disabilities and their families: Social Security Disability Insurance (SSDI) and Supplemental Security Income (SSI). Both programs are administered by the Social Security Administration. The SSDI program pays benefits to individuals with disabilities who have worked and paid Social Security taxes on their earnings. Further, dependents of a worker who has retired, become disabled, or died are eligible for SSDI benefits. The amount of benefits depends on how long the insured worker was employed, how much money the person earned, and how many people are being paid from the worker's account. The SSI program pays benefits to individuals with disabilities whose income and resources are below set limits. Under SSI, the individual does not have to have a work history. SSI eligibility automatically qualifies the individual for Medicaid benefits. Children with disabilities under 18 whose families are low income will likely qualify for SSI. Further, SSI serves as a principal source of income support for many adults with disabilities.

To receive SSDI or SSI benefits based on a disability, a person must meet the following requirements:

- A medical professional must determine that the person has a physical or mental impairment;
- The impairment must be severe and be expected to last at least 12 months or to result in death; and
- Due to the impairment, the person must not be able to engage in any "substantial gainful activity" (a job that pays more than approximately $750 per month).

To be eligible for SSI payments, the individual with a disability must not own more than $2,000 in countable resources. There are numerous resources that are excluded from counting as a resource for SSI benefits, including: SSI and Social Security back payments, disaster relief payments, a home in which the person lives, household goods and personal effects up to an equity value of $2,000, an automobile, money or property that is part of a plan to achieve self-support, the cash value of life insurance, and burial spaces. Often friends and family members want to assist an individual with a disability who is receiving SSI but they do not want to jeopardize that person's receipt of SSI payments. Despite the income and resource limitations to qualify for SSI, friends and family members can provide the following kinds of assistance:

1. Paying someone to provide a service to the person on SSI.
2. Paying bills for things that cannot be resold and are not food, clothing, or shelter (e.g., cable TV bills, bills for fuel and maintenance on an automobile).
3. Gifts of excluded resources such as a car, furniture, items needed by the person for a trade or business.
4. Gifts of airline tickets and paying for hotels, meals, and a companion while the person is traveling.
5. Making a contribution of money or property to a plan to achieve self-support.
6. Putting money or property into a supplemental needs trust.
7. Assisting the person in becoming a home owner or providing housing at reduced rent (Froemming, 2001).

Health Care

Adults with disabilities are often unable to afford private health care insurance. Further, families of children with extraordinary health care costs often experience financial devastation due to large medical bills. The Medicaid program, also known as medical assistance, is a federal–state program authorized by Title XIX of the Social Security Act. Medicaid is the basic medical and health care assistance program for low-income individuals, including those with disabilities. There are income and resource limitations imposed upon individuals and families to qualify for Medicaid funds. Medicaid is funded jointly by the state and federal governments. The federal government's share is recalculated every year and is based on a state's per capita income compared to the national figure. In most states, individuals with disabilities who receive SSI are automatically eligible for Medicaid without submitting a separate application.

In 1971, Congress amended Medicaid rules to permit federal funds to flow to states to improve the living conditions of individuals with disabilities residing in institutions. So, under these provisions, individuals with disabilities residing in institutional settings are deemed income eligible for Medicaid based only on their income and resources. The income and resources of the individual's parents are not counted in determining eligibility for Medicaid. To respond to what many critics felt was an inherent bias in favor of institutional placements for individuals with disabilities, in 1981, Congress approved a new program, the Home and Community-Based (HCBS) Waiver Program (Turnbull & Turnbull, 2001). This waiver program allowed states to use Medicaid funds to address the needs of individuals with disabilities who would otherwise require institutional care if not for the community-based services. The HCBS Waiver Program led to the Katie Beckett Program, which provides support for children with long-term disabilities who live at home. Previously under Medicaid provisions, the child's parents' income and resources would be counted in determining eligibility for funding. Under the Katie Beckett Program, children with long-term disabilities living at home are deemed eligible for Medicaid funds based on their care needs rather than on their parents' income and assets (Hall, 2001). A child is eligible for Medicaid under the Katie Beckett Program if the following criteria are met:

- Child is under 19 years old and living at home.
- Child qualifies as disabled under the standards in the Social Security Act.
- Child requires a level of care at home that is typically provided in hospital or nursing facilities.
- Child requires care that can be provided safely and appropriately in the family home.
- Child has income and assets within the Medicaid program guidelines.
- Child has home care costs that do not exceed what Medicaid would pay if the Child were in an institution.

Medicaid funds cover a broad range of medical, rehabilitative, and support services. In most states, Medicaid pays for physician services, medically necessary hospital services, inpatient care in a skilled nursing facility, home health services (i.e., assistance with dressing, bathing, doing laundry, food shopping, meal preparation), skilled nursing services, respiratory care, therapies (i.e., physical, occupational, and speech), audiology services, outpatient treatment for mental illness, substance abuse treatment, drugs, medical supplies and equipment (i.e., corrective shoes, braces, oxygen equipment, artificial limbs, hearing aids, wheelchairs), dental services, vision care services, transportation to get to Medicaid-covered services, immunizations for children, and case management. There are, however, a number of issues related to receiving some of the aforementioned Medicaid-funded services. For example, many states cover dental services but individuals with disabilities often have difficulty in finding a dentist who will accept Medicaid funds because the reimbursement rates are below their actual costs (Hall, 2001). Another implementation problem area is prior authorization. For many Medicaid services, a provider must first ask the regulating agency to authorize payment for the services before it is provided. This process often creates administrative delays in receiving needed services.

Housing Options

It is safe to say that many families of children with disabilities worry about three critical questions as their children leave school and enter adulthood. First, where will my child live? Second, where will my child work? And third, to what extent will my child participate in community and social activities? This section will offer some information on the first question, and the subsequent section will address the second question. The third question is addressed in Chapter 11 on transition planning and programming. Most families and professionals these days are advocating for community-based, supported living options located in residential neighborhoods for individuals with disabilities. In terms of living options outside of the parent(s)' home, three models are most typical: group homes, semi-independent homes and apartments, and foster family care (Berry & Hardman, 1998).

Group homes may be small, with two to four individuals living in a house, or large, with eight or more residents. Group homes have live-in staff who provide training and assistance to the residents in daily living skills. During the day, group home residents are typically involved in work activities, ranging from competitive employment without supports to supported employment to traditional sheltered workshop activities. Some residents with more severe disabilities may spend their days in adult day care settings where daily living skills and recreational activities are stressed.

Berry and Hardman (1998) identified three variations of semi-independent homes and apartments. First, *apartment clusters* involve several apartments located in close proximity to each other, with a residential supervisor living in one of the apartments in the cluster. Residential support staff assist individuals with disabilities in all of the activities associated with maintaining a household—cleaning, laundry, grocery shopping, meal preparation, paying bills, balancing checkbooks, and other similar day-to-day tasks. A second type of semi-independent housing option is described as a *single coresidence home or apartment*. In this model, a residential staff member shares living space with a roommate who is disabled. The final type of semi-independent living arrangement is a *single home or apartment*. In this model, the person with a disability owns or occupies a home or apartment and is assisted on an as-needed basis by a nonresident staff person. Fiedler (2000) discussed how a vision for semi-independent living for his daughter with severe and multiple disabilities was realized shortly after she turned 18 years old. With the assistance of a county low-income home ownership program and an interest-free home rehabilitation loan, the Fiedlers' daughter, Jennifer, was able to purchase her own home. Jennifer is supported in her home with the assistance of a live-in residential support person.

The third housing model is foster family care. In this living arrangement, an individual with a disability is placed into a surrogate family home. The surrogate family assists the person with daily living skills. The foster family receives compensation from the state or county to provide such services.

Funds for housing assistance are typically allocated at the local level (city and county), so there are significant variations in eligibility, housing priorities, types of funds, loan conditions, and timelines (Brost, 2001). Most of these funding sources have upper income eligibility limits and many place a cap of 80% of county median income, adjusted for family size. Individuals with disabilities on SSI or working at low-wage jobs find it difficult to afford decent housing. Housing resources can assist individuals with disabilities and their families, often in the form of a loan that can be used to pay part of the rent; assist with the down payment for a home; modify structures for health, safety, and accessibility; aid in rehabilitation and repair; and make weatherization improvements and a variety of other structural improvements.

The primary federal housing subsidy program is Section 8, created in 1974. Under the Section 8 program, the United States Department of Housing and Urban Development (HUD) pays a portion of the housing costs incurred by eligible households. Housing assistance eligibility is limited to families or individuals whose income is below 80% of the median income in the county of residence. County median income adjusted by family size and other Section 8 information can be obtained from the HUD. A family or individual eligible for a Section 8 housing subsidy is expected to pay 30% of their adjusted income for housing, defined as rent and utilities. The Section 8 program is administered locally by a public housing authority.

Many local governments and not-for-profit agencies administer public funds in the form of no-interest or low-interest loans that assist individuals with disabilities with a down payment to purchase a home or help with home rehabilitation and accessibility improvements (Brost, 2001). Individuals contemplating the purchase of a home in need of repair or accessibility modifications should consult their local housing organization to determine if that particular home is a sound purchase and how to make repairs a part of the overall purchase price.

Employment Training

It is well established that many adults with disabilities are unemployed or under-employed (Berry & Hardman, 1998). Steady employment is critical to the long-term support of individuals with disabilities. Beyond the obvious monetary rewards of employment, a job that pays a decent wage provides a person with a disability a sense of identity, fosters interaction with nondisabled peers, enhances community connections, and promotes a positive image of people with disabilities. A principal source of employment training for individuals with disabilities is the vocational rehabilitation (VR) program authorized by the federal Vocational Rehabilitation Act and the Workforce Investment Act of 1998. Congress established the VR program to empower individuals with disabilities and to maximize their employability and economic self-sufficiency. Eligibility for VR services is based on (a) a documented disability and (b) the need for VR services to obtain employment. Employment outcomes range from full- or part-time competitive work to supported employment to other employment opportunities consistent with a person's interests, abilities, and strengths (Fuller & Hlavacek, 2001). To be eligible for VR services, the disability need not be so severe as to qualify the person for SSDI or SSI. The disability must only serve as a substantial impediment to employment. Individuals receiving VR services must be able to benefit from those services, so if the VR agency claims that an individual is too severely disabled to be capable of employment, the agency has the burden to prove that the person cannot benefit from services. If a state does not have sufficient resources to provide VR services to all eligible individuals, the state must establish priorities for limited services or what is called an "Order of Selection." In fact, individuals with the most severe disabilities are to receive top priority for VR services.

Once eligibility for VR services is established, an individualized plan of employment (IPE) is developed for the person with a disability. This plan is developed in concert with the individual, family members, and agency personnel. The IPE must include:

- Specific employment outcomes
- Specific VR services to be provided
- Timeline for providing services and achieving employment outcomes
- Specific agencies chosen by the person with a disability to provide the VR services
- Criteria for evaluating progress toward the employment outcomes
- Responsibilities of the VR agency, the person with a disability, and other participating agencies
- Any costs that the person with a disability will be responsible for
- Projected need for postemployment services, if necessary (Fuller & Hlavacek, 2001)

Whatever services an individual needs to overcome barriers to employment may be offered in the IPE. Available VR services include the following: (a) assessment to determine eligibility; (b) counseling, guidance, and job placement services; (c) vocational training, including higher education and the purchase of tools, materials, and books; (d) diagnosis and treatment of physical or mental impairments to reduce or eliminate employment obstacles; (e) transportation, including training in the use of public transportation; (f) personal assistance services; (g) interpreter services for individuals who are deaf and orientation and mobility services for individuals who are blind; (h) occupational licenses, tools, equipment, and supplies; (i) technical assistance for individuals interested in self-employment or small business operation; (j) rehabilitation technology, including vehicle modification, telecommunications, and other technological aids; (k) transition services for students with disabilities; (l) supported employment; (m) services to the family to assist an individual with a disability to achieve employment outcomes; and (n) postemployment services.

Family Support

Almost one half of the states have developed family support programs that are designed to assist families of children with disabilities (often children with more severe disabilities) to meet their basic needs (Turnbull & Turnbull, 2001). Another goal of family support programs is to provide in-home support so that families will be able to raise their children with severe disabilities at home. Family support programs vary from state to state, but typically, families receive a financial payment to purchase needed services that they choose, or the families receive a voucher that they can redeem for services. A key component in family support programs is the respect accorded to parents by allowing them to make the decisions on what services to purchase. A wide variety of services has been provided by family support programs, including case management, respite care, day care, homemaker services, home health care, therapeutic services, assistive technology, vehicle and home modifications, parent education and training, counseling, and numerous other types of services (Bergman & Singer, 1996).

To date, research findings on family satisfaction with family support programs have been positive. For example, families report that their ability to care for their child with disabilities at home has been enhanced (Agosta & Melda, 1995). In addition, families experience less stress and have more time for themselves (Herman & Marcenko, 1997). Perhaps the true value of family support programs was best expressed by Turnbull and Turnbull (2001) when they stated, "The bottom line is that when you link families to economic and family support resources, you are being an empowering agent" (p. 221).

In Wisconsin, the family support program is administered at the county level. Families are eligible for support services if they (a) have a child under 21 with a severe disability living at home and (b) will be able to take care of their child at home if needed supports are provided (Hanna, 2001). The severe disability must limit the child's daily living activities in self-care, learning, communication, mobility, and self-direction. Eligibility for the program is not limited by family income; however, higher income families may pay for some services based on a sliding fee scale. The experience to date in Wisconsin has been that the counties do not have sufficient funding to provide support services to all of the families requesting funding, so families are placed on waiting lists. Families are limited to a maximum of $3,000 annually in funding support.

BENEFITS ASSOCIATED WITH SCHOOL–COMMUNITY SUPPORT SERVICES

In this chapter, we have argued for a full-service school model to address the increasingly complex needs of children with disabilities and their families. Schools must collaborate with community agencies because no one profession (e.g., educators), or its organization (e.g., schools), can fulfill its goals and meet the needs of students with disabilities and their families without the support of other professions (e.g., child welfare professionals, health professionals, family support professionals) and their organizations (e.g., respite care organizations, community health clinics, social services agencies). Interprofessional and interagency collaboration is a practical necessity in the 21st century. As noted by Lawson and Sailor (2000), the most important school-, peer-, family-, and community-related factors for student success in school are the same factors predictive of success in the child welfare, juvenile justice, mental health, health, and employment sectors. In this section, we identify some of the benefits associated with school–community collaborative support services as experienced by children with disabilities, families, school professionals, and schools.

In several studies, wraparound services for students with emotional disorders, behavioral disorders, or both have improved mental health services for those children and reduced the usage of out-of-area, restrictive placements (Anderson & Mohr, 2003; Martin, Tobin, & Sugai, 2002; Summers et al., 1997). Enhanced services in the students' home communities improve the long-term prognosis for students with emotional disorders, behavioral disorders, or both. As an example, it has been found that collaborative services programs decrease the number and duration of restrictive out-of-home placements of children with emotional disorders, behavioral disorders, or both (Arellano & Arman, 2002). School–community support services augment students' resiliency, a critical factor in school success and healthy development (Anderson & Mohr, 2003). For example, Rosenblatt and Attkisson (1997) reported academic gains and high levels of school attendance for students with emotional disorders, behavioral disorders, or both served by a full-services school model. Finally, in a collaborative initiative designed to address the needs of children with special health care issues, school nurses had access to information and technical support from a health consultation program established by a regional children's hospital. This school–community support service improved school attendance of children with special health care needs, increased child self-care abilities, and contributed to a higher quality of care for both the children and their families (Neff & Villareale, 2003).

Strength-based school–community support services for families focus not just on the physical and safety needs of families but also on family members' needs for belongingness and love, self-esteem, and self-actualization. This strength-based approach fosters family independence by assisting families in identifying and building on their adaptive skills within each family member (Powell et al., 1997). Parents become empowered as they start to see themselves as individuals who are capable of not only addressing their own needs but helping others facing similar challenges. Parents learn to view themselves as individuals who can make a difference in other people's lives by sharing their expertise in resolving family problems. School–community family support services increase the knowledge and skills of parents so they can be more proactive in preventing future problems, are better equipped to nurture their children's development, and can promote family stability and a better quality of life (Dunst & Deal, 1994). When school professionals and community service providers actively involve families in decision making surrounding the identification and delivery of support services, parents report higher levels of satisfaction with the services they receive (Rosen, Heckman, Carro, & Burchard, 1994; Trivette, Dunst, Boyd, & Hamby, 1995). There are also studies demonstrating that strength-based, family-centered school–community support services contain costs, improve family economic conditions, contribute to family cohesion, increase parental skills and emotional well-being, and enhance parental self-efficacy (Allen & Petr, 1995; Lee, 1995; Rivera & Kutash, 1994).

School professionals have reported benefits from their participation in school-linked community support services programs. For example, through increased interprofessional collaboration, school professionals commented that their judgments and decision making were more effective because they considered different and multiple perspectives to problems as they interacted on a regular basis with individuals from different professions (Mostert, 1996). Golan and Williamson (1994) conducted a study of 462 teachers in school-linked service efforts in 77 California schools and concluded, "When teachers become involved in school-linked services (that is, when their job changed to support the meeting of students' noneducational needs), they had more contact with parents and service agency staff, felt more efficacious concerning their own abilities to help students, and perceived greater involvement in and effectiveness of program services" (p. 7). The job satisfaction of school professionals improves as their feelings of self-efficacy increase (Lawson & Sailor, 2000).

The benefits to schools from increased collaboration with community service providers are multiple and diverse. The interprofessional and interagency collaboration contributes to collegiality and increased sharing of ideas among school professionals (Coben, Thomas, Sattler, & Morsink, 1997). In addition, these researchers also noted improved skills and attitudes for school professionals. A "can do" attitude prevails in schools that are committed to school-linked community support services for students and families. Other benefits to schools have been identified, including:

- Improvements in the physical conditions and resources that support student learning
- Increases in the number and kinds of people who support school efforts
- Improvements in the attitudes and expectations of parents, school personnel, and students
- Improvements in the depth and quality of the learning experiences of students, school professionals, and parents (Dryfoos, 1998; Hatch, 1998)

The Newtons Revisited

Sean's special education teacher worked closely with the coordinator of the county's wraparound program, and Sean was enrolled in an after-school outpatient alcohol treatment program. In addition to the alcohol treatment program, the local mental health center collaborated with the school counselor in running an anger management group three times per week at Sean's school. Slowly, Sean started to develop more insight into the causes of his aggressive behaviors. The wraparound program team coordinator convinced the juvenile court intake worker to recommend to the judge that Sean's case enter a new deferred-prosecution program that gave Sean 6 months to pay off the $1,200 damages he caused during the vandalism at one of the local elementary schools. Knowing that Sean was not motivated to continue in school in a traditional, academically-oriented program, the special education teacher modified Sean's school schedule so every afternoon Sean attended a vocational program in automotive technology at a nearby technical college. This vocational program had an apprenticeship component that allowed Sean to work 10 hours per week at an automobile service shop. In 6 months, Sean earned $800 to make restitution on his vandalism case. The court granted Sean a 4-month extension to make restitution of the remaining $400, which Sean paid off in 3 months.

The school social worker referred Sean's mother to a parent support group for families of children with challenging behaviors. This support group bolstered Mrs. Newton's confidence that she could set behavioral expectations and household rules for Sean. The special education teacher worked with Mrs. Newton to set up a positive behavioral support plan at home for Sean. One of the elements of the support plan allowed Sean to earn coupons for the local go-kart track. This reinforcement program also brought Sean's father back into a more central role in his life because Mr. Newton and Sean would go to the go-kart track together.

SUMMARY STATEMENTS

- Given the increasingly diverse and complicated support needs of children with disabilities and their families, it is imperative that schools collaborate with community service providers in the provision of a broad array of support services.
- Full-service schools serve as the hub for delivery of or connection to a variety of community services that complement and support education.
- Full-service schools embrace several key principles, including empowering families; engaging in nonjudgmental, unconditional support for families; and demonstrating respect in forming collaborative partnerships with families.
- Families of students with disabilities must be able to effectively access a variety of supports in the adult services system, including income support, health care, housing options, employment training, and family support.

QUESTIONS FOR DISCUSSION

1. Provide a rationale why schools should become full-service schools.
2. What do you see as the critical differences in philosophy and operation of full-service schools versus traditional schools?
3. Describe the changing roles and responsibilities of school professionals working within full-service schools.

RESOURCES FOR PROVIDING COMMUNITY SUPPORT SERVICES

- **Research and Training Center on Family Support and Children's Mental Health**
  (www.rtc.pdx.edu)

  This center is devoted to providing effective services for families and their children with emotional, behavioral, or mental health disorders. This Web site contains information on the National Wraparound Initiative and promoting mental health education in the schools.

- **United Cerebral Palsy Association**
  (www.ucpa.org)

  This national advocacy organization provides information on legislation and resources related to employment, housing, health and wellness, transportation, parenting, sports and leisure, and other relevant topics for individuals with disabilities.

- **Office of Vocational and Adult Education**
  (www.ed.gov/about/offices/list/ovae/index.html)

  This site serves as a clearinghouse on postsecondary education for young adults with special learning needs.

- **U.S. Equal Employment Opportunity Commission**
  (www.eeoc.gov)
  This governmental agency enforces civil rights employment laws.

- **U.S. Social Security Administration**
  (www.ssa.gov)
  This Web site provides information on disability and SSI benefits for individuals with disabilities.

- **Centers for Independent Living**
  (www.jik.com/ilcs.html)
  This Web site provides information on independent living centers in every state.

REFLECTION ACTIVITIES

1. To determine your knowledge of available community resources (federal, state, local) in your geographical area, assume that a family you are working with has an identified need in the following respects. For each identified need, what resources exist in your area to support a family?

   - Information on services for children with special health care needs
   - Developmentally appropriate toys that they can try out before deciding to purchase
   - A break from the day-to-day demands of caring for their child with a disability
   - Information on how to increase their advocacy skills
   - Information on how to enhance greater self-esteem for family members
   - Assistance in addressing daily care tasks once their child with a disability is living in his own apartment
   - Information on housing options for individuals with disabilities
   - Support groups for parents
   - Information and support to address the concerns of nondisabled children in the family
   - Support for parenting a child with emotional and behavioral problems
   - Information on how to impact the state legislature on disability-related issues
   - Information on health insurance options or how to advocate for health benefits
   - Financial assistance to support families of children with disabilities
   - Information on assistive technology
   - Availability of intensive in-home intervention services for children with autism

2. Work with the family of a child with a disability and (a) identify family strengths and (b) determine domain areas in which the family and child require support services.

REFERENCES

Adelman, H. S., & Taylor, L. (2002). School counselors and school reform: New directions. *Professional School Counseling, 5*(4), 235–248.

Agosta, J., & Melda, K. (1995). *Supplemental security income for children with disabilities.* Washington, DC: Human Services Research Institute.

Allen, R. I., & Petr, C. G. (1995). *Family-centered service delivery: A cross-disciplinary literature review and conceptualization.* Lawrence, KS: Beach Center on Families and Disability.

Anderson, J. A., & Matthews, B. (2001). We care . . . for students with emotional and behavioral disabilities and their families. *Teaching Exceptional Children, 33*(5), 34–39.

Anderson, J. A., & Mohr, W. K. (2003). A developmental ecological perspective in systems of care for children with emotional disturbances and their families. *Education and Treatment of Children, 26*(1), 52–74.

Arellano, K. M., & Arman, J. F. (2002). The children first program: A school-based mental health collaborative. *Journal of Humanistic Counseling, Education and Development, 41,* 3–13.

Bergman, A. I., & Singer, G.H.S. (1996). The thinking behind new public policy. In G.H.S. Singer, L. E. Powers, & A. L. Olson (Eds.), *Redefining family support: Innovations in public–private partnerships* (pp. 435–464). Baltimore: Brookes.

Berry, J. O., & Hardman, M. L. (1998). *Lifespan perspectives on the family and disability.* Boston: Allyn & Bacon.

Blalock, G. (1996). Community transition teams as the foundation for transition services for youth with learning disabilities. *Journal of Learning Disabilities, 29,* 148–159.

Brost, M. M. (2001). Housing resources and strategies. In Wisconsin Coalition for Advocacy (Ed.), *Rights and reality II: An action guide to the rights of people with disabilities in Wisconsin* (pp. 231–235). Madison, WI: Author.

Bruner, C. (1991). *Thinking collaboratively: Ten questions and answers to help policy makers improve children's services.* Washington, DC: Education and Human Services Consortium. (ERIC Document Reproduction Service No. ED338984)

Bucci, J. A., & Reitzammer, A. F. (1992). Collaboration with health and social service professionals: Preparing teachers for new roles. *Journal of Teacher Education, 43*(4), 290–295.

Bullis, M., & Cheney, D. (1999). Vocational and transition interventions for adolescents and young adults with emotional or behavioral disorders. *Focus on Exceptional Children, 31*(7), 1–24.

Bullock, M. (2002, Fall). A systems approach to the provision of services to individuals with disabilities. *Educational Horizons, 81*(1), 21–26.

Cessna, K. K., & Skiba, R. J. (1996). Needs-based services: A responsible approach to inclusion. *Preventing School Failure, 40,* 117–123.

Coben, S. S., Thomas, C. C., Sattler, R. O., & Morsink, C. V. (1997). Meeting the challenge of consultation and collaboration: Developing interactive teams. *Journal of Learning Disabilities, 30,* 427–432.

Community Partnerships Group. (1995). *Training manual on the wraparound process.* Pittsburgh, PA: Authors.

Deal, A. G., Trivette, C. M., & Dunst, C. J. (1988). *Family functioning style scale: An instrument for measuring family strengths and resources.* Asheville, NC: Winterberry Press.

DePaepe, P., Garrison-Kane, L., & Doelling, J. (2002). Supporting students with health needs in schools: An overview of selected health conditions. *Focus on Exceptional Children, 35*(1), 1–24.

Dryfoos, J. (1994). *Full service schools.* San Francisco: Jossey-Bass.

Dryfoos, J. (1998). *Safe passage: Making it through adolescence in a risky society.* New York: Oxford University Press.

Duchnowski, A. J., & Kutash, K. (1993, October). *Developing comprehensive systems for troubled youth: Issues in mental health.* Presented at the Shakertown Symposium on Developing Comprehensive Systems II, Shakertown, IL.

Dunst, C. J., Cooper, C. S., Weeldreyer, J. C., Snyder, K. D., & Chase, J. H. (1987). *Family Needs Scale.* Asheville, NC: Winterberry Press.

Dunst, C. J., & Deal, A. G. (1994). A family-centered approach to developing individualized family support plans. In C. J. Dunst, C. M. Trivette, & A. G. Deal (Eds.), *Supporting and strengthening families, Vol. 1: Methods, strategies and practices* (pp. 90–104). Cambridge, MA: Brookline.

Fabry, B. D., Reitz, A. L., & Luster, W. C. (2002). Community treatment of extremely troublesome youth with dual mental health/mental retardation diagnoses: A data based case study. *Education and Treatment of Children, 25*(3), 339–355.

Fiedler, C. R. (2000). *Making a difference: Advocacy competencies for special education professionals.* Boston: Allyn & Bacon.

Fleming, J. L., & Monda-Amaya, L. E. (2001). Process variables critical for team effectiveness: A delphi study of wraparound team members. *Remedial and Special Education, 22*(3), 158–171.

Franz, J. P. (2003). No more Clarences: Creating a consistent and functional multisystem resource for children with complex needs and their families. *Journal of Disability Policy Studies, 13*(4), 244–253.

Froemming, R. (2001). Social security disability insurance and supplemental security income. In Wisconsin Coalition for Advocacy (Ed.), *Rights and reality II: An action guide to the rights of people with disabilities in Wisconsin* (pp. 10–37). Madison, WI: Author.

Fuller, T., & Hvalacek, T. (2001). Vocational rehabilitation. In Wisconsin Coalition for Advocacy (Ed.), *Rights and reality II: An action guide to the rights of people with disabilities in Wisconsin* (pp. 223–230). Madison, WI: Author.

Giangreco, M. F. (2000). Related services research for students with low-incidence disabilities: Implications for speech-language pathologists in inclusive classrooms. *Language, Speech, and Hearing Services in Schools, 31,* 230–239.

Golan, S., & Williamson, C. (April, 1994). *Teachers make school-linked services work.* Paper presented at the annual meeting of the American Educational Research Association, New Orleans.

Gowen, J. W., Christy, D. S., & Sparling, J. (1993). Informational needs of parents of young children with special needs. *Journal of Early Intervention, 17*(2), 194–210.

Hall, L. (2001). Medicaid and BadgerCare. In Wisconsin Coalition for Advocacy (Ed.), *Rights and reality II: An action guide to the rights of people with disabilities in Wisconsin* (pp. 38–62). Madison, WI: Author.

Hanna, J. (2001). Family support program. In Wisconsin Coalition for Advocacy (Ed.), *Rights and reality II: An action guide to the rights of people with disabilities in Wisconsin* (pp. 125–126). Madison, WI: Author.

Hatch, T. (1998). How community action contributes to achievement. *Educational Leadership, 55*(8), 16–19.

Herman, S. E., & Marcenko, M. O. (1997). Perceptions of services and resources as mediators of depression among parents of children with developmental disabilities. *Mental Retardation, 35*(6), 458–467.

Lawson, H. A. (1999). Two frameworks for analyzing relationships among school communities, teacher education, and interprofessional education and training programs. *Teacher Education Quarterly, 26*(4), 9–30.

Lawson, H. A., & Sailor, W. (2000). Integrating services, collaborating, and developing connections with schools. *Focus on Exceptional Children, 33*(2), 1–22.

Lee, I. (1995). *Family-centered practices in early intervention: Literature, evaluation, and validation studies.* Lawrence, KS: Beach Center on Families and Disabilities.

Lindle, J. C. (1996). The wisdom of teacher involvement in school-linked social services: Some pros and cons for teacher involvement. *Journal for a Just and Caring Education, 2*(2), 164–167.

Martin, E. J., Tobin, T. J., & Sugai, G. M. (2002). Current information on dropout prevention: Ideas from practitioners and the literature. *Preventing School Failure, 47*(1), 10–17.

Mostert, M. P. (1996). Interprofessional collaboration in schools: Benefits and barriers in practice. *Preventing School Failure, 40,* 135–138.

Myers, J. E., Sweeney, T. J., & White, V. E. (2002). Advocacy of counseling and counselors: A professional imperative. *Journal of Counseling and Development, 80*(4), 394–402.

Neff, J., & Villareale, N. (2003). The center for children with special needs: Creating system changes through a collaborative, family-centered approach. *Exceptional Parent, 33*(11), 50–54.

Nisbet, J. (Ed.). (1992). *Natural supports in school, at work, and in the community for people with severe disabilities.* Baltimore: Brookes Publishing.

Odom, S. L., & Wolery, M. (2003). A unified theory of practice in early intervention/early childhood special education: Evidence-based practices. *The Journal of Special Education, 37*(3), 164–173.

Olmstead v. L. C., 527 U.S. 581 (1999).

Osher, D., & Hanley, T. V. (2001). Implementing the SED national agenda: Promising programs and policies for children and youth with emotional and behavioral problems. *Education and Treatment of Children, 24*(3), 374–403.

Park, J., Turnbull, A. P., & Turnbull, H. R. (2002). Impacts of poverty on quality of life in families of children with disabilities. *Exceptional Children, 68*(2), 151–170.

Pierangelo, R., & Crane, R. (2000). *The special education yellow pages.* Upper Saddle River, NJ: Merrill/ Prentice Hall.

Powell, D. S., Batsche, C. J., Ferro, J., Fox, L., & Dunlap, G. (1997). A strength-based approach in support of multi-risk families: Principles and issues. *Topics in Early Childhood Special Education, 17,* 1–26.

Rivera, V. R., & Kutash, K. (1994). Case management services and individualized care. In V. R. Rivera & K. Kutash (Eds.), *Components of a system of care: What does the research say?* (pp. 115–140). Tampa, FL: University of South Florida, Florida Mental Health Institute, Research and Training Center for Children's Mental Health.

Rosen, L. D., Heckman, T., Carro, M. G., & Burchard, J. D. (1994). Satisfaction, involvement and unconditional care: The perceptions of children and adolescents receiving wraparound services. *Journal of Child and Family Studies, 3,* 55–67.

Rosenblatt, A., & Attkisson, C. C. (1997). Integrating systems of care in California for youth with severe emotional disturbance IV: Educational attendance and achievement. *Journal of Child and Family Studies, 6,* 113–129.

Sewell, R. (1990). *What are some principal functions performed by an AYI Coordinator?* Juneau, AK: Department of Health and Social Services.

Shoffner, M. F., & Briggs, M. K. (2001). An interactive approach for developing inter-professional collaboration: Preparing school counselors. *Counselor Education and Supervision, 40,* 193–202.

Skrtic, T. M., Sailor, W., & Gee, K. (1996). Voice, collaboration, and inclusion: Democratic themes in educational and social reform. *Remedial and Special Education, 17,* 142–157.

Smith, V. K., & Prelock, P. A. (2002). A case management model for school-age children with multiple needs. *Language, Speech, and Hearing Services in Schools, 33,* 124–129.

Summers, J. A., McMann, O. T., & Fuger, K. L. (1997). Critical thinking: A method to guide staff in serving families with multiple challenges. *Topics in Early Childhood Special Education, 17,* 27–52.

Summers, J. A., Steeples, T., Peterson, C., Naig, L., McBride, S., Wall, S., et al. (2001). Policy and management supports for effective service integration in early Head Start and Part C programs. *Topics in Early Childhood Special Education, 21*(1), 16–29.

Trivette, C. M., Dunst, C. J., Boyd, K., & Hamby, D. W. (1995). Family-oriented program models, help-giving practices, and parental control appraisals. *Exceptional Children, 62,* 237–248.

Turnbull, A. P., & Turnbull, H. R. (2001). *Families, professionals, and exceptionality: Collaborating for empowerment* (4th ed.). Upper Saddle River, NJ: Merrill/Prentice Hall.

VanDenBerg, J. E., & Grealish, E. M. (1996). Individualized services and supports through the wraparound process: Philosophy and procedures. *Journal of Child and Family Studies, 5*(1), 7–21.

Walther-Thomas, C., Korinek, L., & McLaughlin, V. L. (1999). Collaboration to support students' success. *Focus on Exceptional Children, 32*(3), 1–18.

CHAPTER 8
Fostering Effective Parent and Family Educational Advocacy

● ●

In this chapter, you will understand:

- The need for parental advocacy in special education.
- Common barriers to active parent participation and advocacy in their children's special education programming.
- Advocacy training elements for parents to assume a role as an effective advocate for their child with disabilities.

- The essential attitudes/dispositions, knowledge bases, and skills for parents to serve as advocates for their children with disabilities. Essential knowledge bases include knowledge of special education law and procedures and the dispute resolution mechanisms in special education. Essential skills include interpersonal communication skills, collaboration skills, advocacy skills, organizational and documentation skills, IEP meeting participation skills, and conflict resolution skills.

Family Perspective: The Runnels

Ron and Elizabeth Runnels have two children. Their son, Matt, was born with cerebral palsy and severe mental retardation. Matt is now in the third grade. His sister, Ann, is a sixth grader and is developing normally. Mr. and Mrs. Runnels are both employed full-time—Ron is an automobile mechanic and Elizabeth is a dental hygienist. Although the parents are concerned about their children's education, they are overwhelmed by deciding what is best for meeting Matt's significant educational needs.

Matt has been described by school professionals as cognitively functioning at about a 4-year-old level. Due to his cerebral palsy, Matt's speech is very limited and he uses a wheelchair to move around. Matt spends his entire school day in a self-contained special education classroom. His IEP contains goals and objectives designed to increase his daily living and adaptive skills. Although Matt has been making steady progress in his functional skills in the past 3 years, his parents wonder if he is being sufficiently challenged at school. Matt is a very personable child and clearly enjoys interacting with other children. The school has a "special buddy" program whereby nondisabled third and fourth graders spend some time each day in the special education classroom. Unfortunately, this program has not stimulated any out-of-school friendships between Matt and nondisabled peers.

At the last IEP meeting to discuss Matt's progress and to review his current goals and objectives, the special education teacher, Mrs. Murray, presented the Runnels with a draft IEP for next year. Although Mrs. Murray stressed that the parents could make any changes they desired in the draft IEP, the Runnels did not know where to start. The parents did have some concerns about Matt's current educational programming. First, they wondered why he could not spend any time in a general education third-grade classroom. Although he would need to have adapted educational goals, the parents felt a general education classroom would provide Matt with more social interaction and communication opportunities. Another concern of the Runnels was Matt's communication program. His speech was inconsistently intelligible and the school staff used a picture communication board. Matt has some control over his arms and hands, so he can point to pictures on his communication board. This, however, was a laborious process. The parents had questions about a computerized communication system for Matt. Finally, the parents wanted to be more actively involved in developing IEP goals and objectives, but they did not know how to integrate their concerns and desires into the right "IEP language." Basically, Mr. and Mrs. Runnels were anxious and intimidated at every IEP meeting they attended. They acknowledged the school professionals were experts and they did not want to step on anyone's toes by complaining or disagreeing with what the educators recommended for Matt.

Reflecting on the Family Perspective

1. How can school personnel empower the Runnelses to exercise their rights as educational decision makers?

2. What specific knowledge about special education rights and procedures should school personnel be prepared to provide to Mr. and Mrs. Runnels?

⊙   ⊙   ⊙

As many parents of children with disabilities can attest, the rights of students in special education are not always self-enforcing. That is, the existence of state and federal special education legal rights and procedural protections are no automatic guarantee that school districts will adhere to the letter of the law. Therefore, there is an increasing need for educational advocacy on behalf of children with disabilities (Fiedler & Antonak, 1991; Simpson, 1996; Turnbull & Turnbull, 2001), especially during the current public education climate where resources are limited due to local, state, and federal governmental budget deficits. Fiedler (2000) identified five reasons supporting the need for educational advocacy on behalf of children with disabilities: (a) the historical discrimination experienced by individuals with disabilities; (b) the frequent denial of educational rights of children with disabilities; (c) the fact that schools are political and bureaucratic entities, meaning school organizations are conservative by nature and resistant to change; (d) the lack of effective parental advocacy; and (e) the findings from special education outcomes research, which strongly indicate that many graduates of special education programs are not employed, not living on their own, not integrated into their communities, and in general, not very satisfied with their lives. Simply stated, effective educational advocacy is necessary to address each of the above-mentioned issues. The lack of parental advocacy can be addressed by school professionals' assuming responsibility for training and supporting parents to enable them to become effective advocates for their children.

There are many definitions of advocacy. In general, an advocate is one who speaks on behalf of another person or group of persons to bring about change (Anderson, Chitwood, & Hayden, 1997). In the context of this chapter, the discussion will focus on parents speaking on behalf of their children with disabilities. More specifically, advocacy can be defined as ". . . intervention when needed services are not accessible; are not available; are not appropriate; are not effectively provided; or when the voice of a child is not being heard" (Herbert & Mould, 1992, p. 118). This chapter will address reasons why parents cannot always rely on school professionals to serve as advocates for their children, thus increasing the importance of parents assuming the role of child advocate. Typical barriers to active parent participation in educational decision making will be identified. The majority of the chapter will focus on the most important elements or competencies for effective educational advocacy by parents. These advocacy competencies will be categorized into essential attitudes/dispositions, knowledge, and skills (Fiedler, 2000).

PROFESSIONAL RELUCTANCE TO SERVE AS EDUCATIONAL ADVOCATES

Although numerous school professionals have historically been willing to function as advocates for students with disabilities and their families, there is a pervasive reluctance by many school professionals to assume this role and responsibility. Fiedler

(1986) speculated on the reasons why so many school professionals are reluctant to be child advocates: "Special education professionals have historically avoided advocacy responsibility because of insufficient training, legal ramifications, pressure from superiors, and competing time and energy demands" (p. 7). Many school professionals are intimidated by the potential legal ramifications of challenging the services offered by their school district. Indeed, this advocacy dilemma results from a school professional's dual role as an advocate for children with disabilities and a school employee (Frith, 1981; Rock, Geiger, & Hood, 1992). Frith defined this advocacy dilemma "as a conflict that arises when a professional must decide whether to actively defend a child's rights when doing so would contradict the stated or implied directives of the professional's employing agency" (p. 487). This advocacy dilemma causes school professionals to contemplate whether their primary loyalty rests with their employing school district or with the children they serve. In terms of professional ethical obligations as enunciated by organizations such as the Council for Exceptional Children (CEC; 1993) and the National Association of School Psychologists (2000), that advocacy dilemma is clearly resolved on the side of advocating for the child. Unfortunately, some school administrators and boards of education perceive a "good school employee" as someone who does not challenge the organization. With this perspective, professional advocacy is viewed as aberrant radical behavior instead of behavior that fulfills a professional ethical obligation.

Functioning as an advocate requires school professionals to extend their typical job descriptions and expectations. As noted previously, many school professionals avoid their advocacy responsibilities because of competing time and energy demands. Indeed, many school professionals feel overwhelmed by basic job and family demands that preclude advocacy work (Kagan, 1989). In interviews conducted with school professionals, Fiedler (1997) indicated that the most frequent reason mentioned for not serving as a child advocate was the excessive time and energy demands required in being an advocate. Other reasons offered for professional reluctance to serve as an advocate included:

- Fear of reprisals from school administration
- Different perceptions on what being a child advocate is all about
- Belief that being an advocate is not part of their job responsibilities
- The fact that advocacy can be exhausting, frustrating, and emotionally draining work
- Professional burnout
- Lack of necessary advocacy skills
- Intimidation from potential legal implications
- Possibility that advocacy may lead to "inconvenient outcomes" for individual educators
- Assumption that advocacy is solely a parental responsibility
- Personality traits—being an advocate is easier for individuals who are outspoken and assertive
- Feeling overwhelmed with regular job duties—tendency to focus only on personal needs, not the needs of others

- Uncomfortable with taking risks
- Uncomfortable with change
- Lack of administrative support to serve as an advocate
- Insufficient patience
- Lack of professional passion in one's work (Fiedler, 2000, pp. 5–6).

Although school professionals are encouraged to function more directly as child advocates, this chapter advances an indirect way for professionals to fulfill their advocacy responsibilities. School professionals are clearly serving as advocates when they support parents in acquiring the necessary knowledge and skills for effective advocacy on behalf of their own children with disabilities. Again, there is an acknowledged professional obligation to provide this kind of training and information to parents. For example, the CEC's Standards for Professional Practice require special educators to (a) extend opportunities for parent education, utilizing accurate information and professional methods, and (b) inform parents of the educational rights of their children and of any proposed or actual practices that violate those rights (CEC, 1993). Further, the principles for professional ethics adopted by the National Association of School Psychologists (2000) mandate that "School psychologists encourage and promote parental participation in designing services provided to their children. When appropriate, this includes linking interventions between the school and the home, tailoring parental involvement to the skills of the family, and helping parents gain the skills needed to help their children" (pp. 623–624).

THE IMPORTANCE OF PARENTAL ADVOCACY

IDEA clearly recognizes that parents are their children's first and best advocates. This legislative acknowledgement is found in the empowering of parents to be active educational decision makers by bestowing the following rights:

- Guarantee of a free appropriate public education for children with disabilities
- Notification whenever the school proposes to evaluate a child, wants to change a child's educational program, or refuses a parent's request for an evaluation or a change in placement
- The ability to initiate a special education evaluation if the parents think their child is in need of special education or related services
- Requirement of informed parental consent prior to the initial evaluation and placement of a student in special education
- Power to obtain an independent education evaluation if parents disagree with the outcome of the school's evaluation
- Right to review all educational records
- Requirement that the school must fully inform parents of all rights that they have under the law
- Participation in the development of an IEP for a child in special education
- Requirement that children with disabilities be educated in the least restrictive environment

- Ability to request a due process hearing to resolve differences with the school that could not be resolved informally (Simpson, 1996; Yell, 1998).

Parents are natural advocates because they know their child better than anyone else. In addition, there is a strong correlation between active parent participation in their child's education and increased child development (Stoecklin, 1994). Friesen and Huff (1990) identified additional reasons why parents should function as educational advocates: (a) parents have been given this social and legal responsibility, (b) parents have an emotional investment in their child's welfare that goes well beyond the emotional investment of professionals, (c) parents are more constant in their child's life than professionals are, (d) parents can be persuasive advocates because they have direct, firsthand experiences with the school system, (e) parents' advocacy motivation is less likely to be viewed with suspicion than are the possibly self-serving motives of some professionals, and (f) parents do not have potential conflicts of interest as professionals sometimes do; they are more free to speak out.

BARRIERS TO ACTIVE PARENT PARTICIPATION

For parents to become active participants and advocates in their children's education, school professionals must recognize the barriers that operate to restrict active parent participation. As Fiedler and Swanger (2000) noted, "These barriers either operate indirectly by damaging parent–professional interactions and, ultimately, their relationship, or have a direct adverse impact on parents' participation by limiting their time, energy, knowledge, and psychological support, which are necessary for their active participation and advocacy" (p. 441). Fiedler and Swanger identified these barriers to active parent participation: cultural and language differences, poverty, parental lack of knowledge about special education procedures to assist them in their educational decision making, negative professional attitudes toward parents, parental burnout, and parental alienation and isolation. Each of these barriers will be briefly discussed.

Cultural and Language Differences

In a study to determine the perceived level and importance of parent participation in specific school-to-community transition activities, Geenen, Powers, and Lopez-Vasquez (2001) surveyed four groups of culturally diverse parents of children with disabilities: African American, Hispanic American, Native American, and European American. In addition, school professionals serving the students and families targeted for this study were also surveyed. The parent and professional surveys identified 10 different transition activities parents may engage in to prepare their children with disabilities for life after high school. The survey findings revealed several differences between culturally and linguistically diverse (CLD) parents and European American parents. CLD parents placed significantly more importance than did European American parents on talking to their children about transition, helping their children prepare for postsecondary education, teaching their children to engage in self-care activities related to their disability, teaching their children about the family's culture, and teaching their children how to use transportation independently. On the other hand, European American parents reported significantly more participation in school-based transition meetings. School professionals perceived CLD parents as significantly less involved than European American parents on a majority of the identified transition activities. In particular, professionals described the involvement of CLD parents in school-based planning meetings as low.

This study points to the importance of school professionals' recognizing that culturally diverse families have a variety of values that contribute to their educational involvement in myriad ways other than the traditional manner of attendance at school-based planning meetings. In addition, school professionals must realize that they typically interact with parents only within the context of school and, consequently, have limited awareness of family activities, beliefs, and values within other contexts such as community, extended family, and religion. One final caveat is that school professionals must be very careful not to form generalized conclusions about culturally diverse groups, even when those opinions are informed by research findings. Ultimately, school professionals must recognize and respect the uniqueness of each family.

Latino parents also have distinct perceptions about their participation in educational decision-making activities. Levine (1999) reported that Latino parents want to participate in school-related activities for their children with disabilities. However, as Pappas (1997) noted, many Latino parents may have specific beliefs about their rights and responsibilities in regard to educational decision making and, consequently, leave those responsibilities solely to school professionals. Some of this reluctance to assume an active role in education decisions may certainly be related to lack of English proficiency and failure to understand the school system and parents' roles. Consequently, some Latino parents assume a passive role in the educational decision-making process (Turnbull & Turnbull, 2001). In fact, many CLD parents may perceive school professionals as experts whose opinions cannot be opposed (Harry, Allen, & McLaughlin, 1995). In a survey of 100 Latino parents, Lian and Fontanez-Phelan (2001) found that a majority of the respondents understood their rights in the IEP process (85%) and agreed they were responsible for ensuring appropriate educational services for their children with disabilities (71%), while 64% of the parents revealed they would challenge school officials if their children's rights were being violated. However, those Latino parents expressing reluctance to be active educational decision makers reported a lack of confidence to assume such responsibility due to their educational level (e.g., no high school diploma) and their poor English proficiency.

In terms of recommendations for school professionals, Latino parents indicated a need for school workshops on cross-cultural issues, including an honest discussion concerning the expectations of European American teachers compared to those of Latino parents. In addition, Lian and Aloia (1994) suggested that school professionals determine the level of educational participation each parent prefers. Perhaps the best advice for school professionals emerged from a study of family and professional preferences for relationship building conducted by Summers and her colleagues (1990). Both parents and professionals revealed they wanted "a process that evolves much like a friendship: using conversation and mutual self-disclosure, avoiding formal measures of any kind, and proceeding at a pace that is unhurried and with an attitude that is nonjudgmental, supportive, and caring" (p. 97).

Kalyanpur, Harry, and Skrtic (2000) argued that the cultural underpinnings of the legal mandate for parent participation in special education decision making are based on three core values: equity, individual rights, and freedom of choice. Further, they maintain that one reason for limited parental participation in educational decision making is that these three core values may be antithetical to the beliefs and values of many culturally and linguistically diverse families of children with disabilities. For example, many Asian American families do not place a high value on equity, instead viewing professionals as experts with unquestionable knowledge. With this cultural expectation, parents do not expect to be active decision makers, and they will be reluctant to disagree with professionals' recommendations. In terms of individual rights, many Asian American families favor social obligations over individual rights. Therefore, such families may be uncomfortable with the prevailing culture of individual rights on which special education mandates are based. Finally, the value of individual choice is not universally shared across all cultures. For some culturally diverse families, individual choices are not highly valued and, thus, parents would not expect to be presented with educational options or decisions by school professionals.

Poverty

A disproportionate number of students with disabilities are raised by families of lower SES. Family poverty or financial difficulties impose a number of logistical barriers that restrict parent participation in educational decision making. For example, long work hours, limited transportation availability, limited access to communication aids (e.g., telephones or computers) and lack of affordable child care restrict low SES parents' opportunities to participate in IEP meetings (Salend & Taylor, 1993). In a comparative study of the advocacy efforts of parents of high and low SES with children in special education, Coots (1998) found that high SES parents were able to supplement their children's educational experiences if some needs were not adequately met by the school. For example, high SES parents could afford to hire a tutor to enhance their children's education. Conversely, low SES parents were not in a position to hire additional services for their children and continued to demand services from the school. For their efforts, the low SES parents were often labeled as difficult or noncompliant parents by school officials. Finally, low SES parents typically lack access to elaborate networks of support and information that high SES parents have at their disposal (Fine, 1993). This lack of information and support hampers the advocacy efforts of low SES parents.

Lack of Knowledge About Special Education Procedures

Parent participation and educational decision making are restricted by limited knowledge of special education rights and procedures, and many parents lack this basic understanding (Geenen et al., 2001). As an example, Sontag and Schacht (1994), in a survey of the needs of parents of young children with disabilities, determined that approximately one half of the parents wanted to know more about services available for their children and how the educational system works. It is understandable that, without this knowledge, parents feel uncomfortable and intimidated at school-based meetings. School professionals must remain mindful of how confusing and anxiety-producing IEP meetings can be for even knowledgeable and confident parents, let alone parents who lack sufficient knowledge of special education rights and procedures.

Related to the issue of lack of parental knowledge of special education rights and procedures is evidence that suggests school professionals often fail to provide parents with sufficient information to enhance their educational decision-making role. For example, Katsiyannis and Ward (1992) surveyed parents of students in special education programs and determined that approximately 10% of the parents reported they did not receive a written statement of their educational rights and 13% did not get an explanation of those rights. Further, League and Ford (1996) reported that fathers of children with disabilities revealed they frequently did not receive the type of communication they needed from school professionals to empower them to participate in their children's education in terms of managing misbehavior, advocating for appropriate services, and encouraging academic performance.

Negative Professional Attitudes Toward Parents

Historically, many school professionals have viewed parents as mere recipients of educational decisions (Turnbull & Turnbull, 2001). This disempowering perspective neither encourages nor supports parents in their educational advocacy efforts. Research findings suggest school professionals often communicate this attitude in interactions with parents. For example, Sontag and Schacht (1994) reported parents of young children with disabilities were told by school professionals what their child's problem was and what could be done about it, without any attempt to solicit input into the educational decision-making process. Surprisingly, given this professional perspective, over half of the parents indicated they helped make decisions about their child's educational program anyway. Kalyanpur et al. (2000) confirmed that little effort is made by many school professionals to seek families' input when making decisions about their child's education. When parents are not viewed by school professionals as full and equal partners in evaluation and educational programming decision making as required by law, parents are more prone to perceive themselves as mere recipients of educational decisions made by professionals, they are less likely to attend IEP meetings, and they feel their input is discounted and they are unable to influence outcomes (Harry, Allen, & McLaughlin, 1995). When this becomes the prevailing school professional attitude and parent interaction style, the main activity of an IEP meeting is to secure a signature rather than to promote collaboration. It is not surprising then that IEP meetings often last an average of only 20 to 30 minutes under these conditions (Fiedler & Swanger, 2000).

As noted above, poor parental participation may be caused by school systems that do not encourage parents to actively engage in educational decision making (Lian & Fontanez-Phelan, 2001). Parents may even initially possess the motivation, knowledge, and skills to serve as effective advocates for their children with disabilities, but the school climate may disempower them (Harry, Rueda, & Kalyanpur, 1999).

CLD parents are at even greater risk of school professionals' negative attitudes because many professionals perceive them as having low enthusiasm and commitment for their children's education (Warger & Burnette, 2000).

Parental Burnout

Families experiencing a crisis situation or chronic stress often have their time and energy consumed and are thus unable to expend any additional time and energy on educational advocacy (Fiedler, 2000). As stated by Fiedler and Swanger (2000),

> Evidence suggests parents may become less involved over time in educational processes such as IEP meetings. They may become weary following years of struggle at home, with school personnel, and with various other professionals. In effect, parents may suffer "burnout" and as a consequence might not attend IEP meetings or other parent-teacher conferences. (p. 443)

In addition, parents often report feeling less community acceptance and greater isolation as their children with disabilities grow older (Brotherson, Berdine, & Sartini, 1993). Indeed, it is understandable that parents of secondary students with disabilities are generally perceived as less involved in educational decision making than are parents of younger children (Lynch & Stein, 1982).

Parental Alienation and Isolation

Professional insensitivity and lack of encouragement for parental participation in educational decisions may cause parents to feel disengaged and isolated from schools (Adams & Welsch, 1999). This parental disengagement and disenfranchisement is fostered by frustration at not being able to collaborate in meaningful ways with school professionals. For example, Harry, Allen, and McLaughlin (1995) found that low- to low-middle-income African American parents of students with disabilities and parents of nondisabled peers who were entering urban public schools initially possessed high expectations for their children and positive views regarding their participation in educational decision making. Over time, however, parent participation became perfunctory for parents of students with disabilities compared to the level of participation demonstrated by parents of nondisabled students. Parents of the students with disabilities became disillusioned, isolated, and alienated in their interactions with school professionals. Parents of children with disabilities experience increasing difficulties over time in understanding and effectively interacting with the special education system in schools (Lynch & Stein, 1987).

ELEMENTS OF EFFECTIVE PARENT EDUCATIONAL ADVOCACY

What knowledge and skills must parents possess in their desire to be effective educational advocates for their children with disabilities? Fiedler (1991) argued that school professionals should focus on two broad topics: legal rights and enhancing parent participation in the IEP decision-making process. Simpson (1996) advanced a model of family educational advocacy training that consisted of three basic topics: (a) training in parent rights and responsibilities under IDEA; (b) training in participation in IEP, progress report, and other family–school conferences; and (c) training related to identifying and using school and community resources. Spiegel-McGill, Reed, Konig, and McGowan (1990) developed an advocacy skills training program for parents of children with disabilities entering special education preschool programs from home-based infant developmental education programs. Their advocacy skills training program consisted of: (a) understanding the effects of transitions on the family's lives; (b) knowing one's child (understanding functional skill levels); (c) understanding program options and services, including the roles and responsibilities of various professionals; (d) using effective communication skills; (e) knowing educational rights and procedures; and (f) putting the puzzle together (preparing for IEP meetings, getting assistance from community resources and parent organizations). Finally, Turnbull and Turnbull (2001) described the advocacy training provided parents by federally funded Parent Training and Information Centers. These centers assist families in understanding the nature and needs of their child's disability; learning about special education legal rights and procedures; monitoring their child's educational programs; training in effective communication skills; participating in educational decision-making processes; and providing information on how to access national, state, and local resources.

The parent educational advocacy training program promoted in this chapter follows the general organizational scheme advanced by Fiedler (2000). School professionals can empower parents to become effective educational advocates for their children with disabilities by focusing on *essential attitudes/dispositions, essential knowledge bases*, and *essential skills*. Effective parental advocacy requires certain advocacy attitudes that will be discussed in this section. Second, parents must become knowledgeable of special education legal rights and special education dispute resolution mechanisms (e.g., mediation, due process hearings, and IDEA complaint procedures). Finally, parent advocates need specific skills, including interpersonal communication skills, collaboration skills, advocacy skills, organizational and documentation skills, IEP meeting participation skills, and constructive conflict resolution skills.

Essential Attitudes/Dispositions

Effective parent advocates possess certain attitudes/dispositions and personal characteristics. Dispositions reflect the values and attitudes of parents in terms of their commitment, sense of responsibility, and behaviors on behalf of their children with disabilities. Some of the biggest challenges parents face are their fears, anger, and attitude about advocacy and the schools. School professionals can promote essential attitudes/dispositions within parents by serving in an emotional support capacity and encouraging self-reflection. There are three key values inherent in an advocacy disposition: purpose, passion, and hope (Hargreaves & Fullan, 1998). School professionals instill a greater sense of purpose in parents by empowering them. Advocacy is a primary vehicle for empowering parents. "Empowering parents . . . means interacting with all of them more extensively. Listening to them more sincerely, soliciting their opinions and feedback, more determinedly, and involving them in curriculum development and in decisions about their own children's learning more widely—all on a regular basis" (Hargreaves & Fullan, 1998, p. 46). Second, parents are, quite naturally, passionate about their children's development and future. This passion when it spills forth in negative ways may impair the parent's ability to function as an effective advocate. School professionals can empower parents in educational decision making by assisting an emotional parent in clearly articulating his or her vision for the child. In addition, speaking up passionately about an educational injustice makes a parent vulnerable to frustration, disillusionment, and exhaustion. School professionals can foster parental passion by functioning, again, as a source of emotional support. Finally, school professionals need to cultivate a sense of hope in families of children with disabilities. Hope fuels parental advocacy efforts. In fact, as noted by Goleman (1995), there are emotional benefits of maintaining a hopeful attitude:

> From the perspective of emotional intelligence, having hope means that one will not give in to overwhelming anxiety, a defeatist attitude, or depression in the face of difficult challenges or setbacks. Indeed, people who are hopeful evidence less depression than others as they maneuver through life in pursuit of their goals, are less anxious in general, and have fewer emotional distresses. (p. 87)

In addition to the advocacy values discussed above, there are other critical attitudes or characteristics of effective parent advocates. Packer (2002) identified flexibility and determination as two key advocacy characteristics. Parents must remain flexible when advocating for their children's educational rights. On most issues, there are multiple responses to deal with any challenge. If a parent locks into only one way to address a problem, she is more likely to engender resistance on the part of school professionals. Maintaining flexibility requires an open mind and effective listening skills. School professionals can model this characteristic in their regular interactions with parents. Determination involves persistence or a sustained effort over time. Advocacy can be taxing, draining, and time-consuming work that requires a sustained commitment over a long period of time. However, this kind of determination must be tempered by a pragmatic assessment of how important a particular issue is and whether, as Packer (2002) puts it, you are willing to "die on this particular hill" (p. 8). An effective advocate carefully chooses his battles, because not all battles are worth fighting.

Essential Knowledge Bases

Special Education Legal Rights   To ensure appropriate educational services for their children with disabilities, parents must know special education laws and procedures. IDEA is the federal special education law. This law was last reauthorized and revised in 1997 and most recently in 2004 with the passage of the Individuals with Disabilities Education Improvement Act (20 U.S.C. Sec. 1400 et seq.). A basic understanding of special education law can be obtained by knowing the legislative purposes of these six major principles: zero reject, nondiscriminatory evaluation, free and appropriate public education (FAPE), least restrictive environment (LRE), procedural due process, and parent participation (Turnbull & Turnbull, 2000). A brief explanation of each major principle of special education law will be followed by a series of questions identified by Fiedler (2000) that special education advocates must be able to answer if they are to become effective advocates. These questions set the training agenda for school professionals seeking to empower parents as effective educational advocates. In addition, significant IDEA 2004 revisions as they pertain to specific major principles of special education law will be briefly highlighted.

Zero Reject The constitutional foundation for the zero reject principle of special education law is the equal protection clause of the Fourteenth Amendment, which provides that no state may deny to any person within its jurisdiction equal protection of the laws (Turnbull & Turnbull, 2000). This principle is philosophically rooted in the democratic ideal that every person is valuable and entitled to equal education opportunities to develop his or her full potential. Zero reject means that *all* students with disabilities eligible for services under IDEA are entitled to a free appropriate public education.

Parents should be able to answer the following questions related to the zero reject principle:

- Who is eligible for special education services under IDEA?
- Are some children so severely disabled that they are totally ineducable and therefore not entitled to protection of IDEA?
- Are school districts obligated to pay for residential placements of students with disabilities?
- Are public school districts obligated to provide special education services to students with disabilities whose parents enroll them in private schools?
- Does the Constitution permit public schools to use funds for special education services to students with disabilities attending private parochial (church-affiliated) schools?
- Do school districts who deny graduation diplomas to students in special education who fail to pass the state's minimum competency test deprive such students of a free appropriate education?
- What disciplinary sanctions are legally permissible and do not require due process procedural protections?
- What disciplinary sanctions are legally permissible provided the school practices appropriate procedures in implementing such sanctions?
- What is the legal status of corporal punishment as a form of discipline?
- Can a student with a disability be suspended on a long-term basis or expelled from a public school?
- Are schools required to continue special education services during long-term suspension or expulsion?
- What are legally permissible procedures for schools to use when dealing with students with disabilities who present a danger to themselves or others?
- Does IDEA provide any disciplinary protection to students not yet determined eligible for special education?

- What are the requirements under IDEA for including behavior management plans in IEPs?

The statutory provisions pertaining to children with disabilities who are placed by their parents in private schools have been revised. The public school district's responsibility to consult with private school representatives and parents of children with disabilities in private schools during the design and development of special education and related services has been clarified (20 U.S.C. Sec. 1412 [10]). Further, a private school official has a right to file a complaint with the state educational agency that the local public school district did not engage in consultation that was meaningful and timely. Another revision was designed to reflect more recent U.S. Supreme Court decisions on whether special education public school services may be provided to students attending private religious schools without violating the First Amendment's establishment of religious clause. The IDEA 2004 statute provides that special education and related services may be provided to parentally placed students in private religious schools as long as those services are secular, neutral, and nonideological.

Nondiscriminatory Evaluation To ensure that school districts engage in appropriate assessment activities in determining a student's eligibility for special education, IDEA is highly prescriptive of specific evaluation procedures to conduct fair and comprehensive educational evaluations. If the eligibility evaluation procedures are inadequate, resulting educational placement and programming decisions will likely be inappropriate as well. Yell (1998) summarized the nondiscriminatory evaluation procedures under IDEA as containing these provisions: (a) tests are administered in the child's native language or mode of communication; (b) standardized tests must be validated for the specific purposes for which they are intended; (c) standardized tests are administered by trained professionals in conformity with the test's instructions; (d) the evaluation is tailored to assess the child's specific areas of educational need, including parent information; (e) evaluators must use technically sound instruments that assess multiple areas and factors; (f) no single procedure is used as the sole criterion for determining special education eligibility; (g) the evaluation team includes at least one person who is knowledgeable in the child's suspected area of disability; and (h) the child is assessed in all areas related to the suspected disability.

Parents should be able to answer the following questions related to the nondiscriminatory evaluation principle:

- Is parental consent required for a preplacement special education evaluation?
- What is the effect of prereferral evaluations and interventions on IDEA preplacement evaluation requirements?
- Can a school ignore a special education referral or decide not to conduct an IDEA preplacement evaluation?
- Who is required to be a member of the multidisciplinary evaluation team?
- Can IQ tests be used in making special education placement decisions of CLD students?
- What are the multidisciplinary evaluation team's decision-making responsibilities?
- What are the reevaluation requirements for students in special education?

In the 2004 reauthorization of IDEA greater concern was placed on the issues of mislabeling and high dropout rates among minority children. Also, in the findings section of the statute, it was noted that a disproportionately high number of minority students were being placed into special education (20 U.S.C. Sec. 1400 [c] [11–14]). In another eligibility determination issue, IDEA 2004 provides that no child shall be determined to be a child with a disability if the determinant factor is lack of appropriate instruction in reading (20 U.S.C. Sec. 114 [b] [5]).

Free and Appropriate Public Education (FAPE) If students with disabilities are not receiving an appropriate public education, they are being functionally excluded from a meaningful educational experience. Functional exclusion is an education that lacks meaning or significance for a student. IDEA defines special education as "specially designed instruction, at no charge to the parents or guardians, to meet the unique needs of a child with a disability" (IDEA, 20 U.S.C. Sec. 1404 [a] [16]). The FAPE principle has both procedural and substantive aspects (Guernsey & Klare, 1993). Numerous procedural protections ensure parent and student participation in educational decision making. The substantive right to a FAPE consists of

> special education and related services which (A) have been provided at public expense, under public supervision and direction, and without charge, (B) meet standards of the state educational agency, (C) include an appropriate preschool, elementary, or secondary school education in the state involved, and (D) are provided in conformity with the Individualized Education Program. (IDEA, 20 U.S.C. Sec. 1401 [18] [C])

Even with this legislative guidance on the definition of a FAPE, this principle has proven to be elusive in its understanding and evolving in its application.

Parents should be able to answer the following questions related to the FAPE principle:

- Are costs of providing a student with a FAPE a relevant factor in educational decision making?
- Is the IEP a legally binding contract?
- What is the *Rowley* standard for determining a FAPE?
- What is the effect of a procedural violation in developing a student's IEP on the receipt of a FAPE?
- Is there a denial of a FAPE when the parents object to a particular instructional approach or methodology?
- Are some students with disabilities entitled to extended-school-year programming?
- What are the IDEA requirements for placement decision making in providing a FAPE?
- Who are the required IEP team members?
- What are the parental participation requirements in developing the student's IEP?
- Can the school district conduct an IEP meeting in the parents' absence?
- What happens when the parents do not agree with the IEP?
- Does the public school district have any IEP responsibilities for students the district places in private schools?

- What are some of the substantive requirements of an IEP that courts have scrutinized in judging the legal validity of an IEP?
- What are the IDEA requirements for revising IEPs?
- Are there any potential legal consequences if a teacher decides not to abide by the contents of the IEP in terms of goals, objectives, and services provided?
- What is the IDEA definition of related services and what are listed related services under the law?
- What are the U.S. Supreme Court's criteria for determining whether a service qualifies as a "related service" that the school is legally obligated to provide?
- How have courts decided on other specific requests for related services such as transportation, school health services, complex health services, assistive technology, and counseling and psychological services?
- Is it legally permissible for school districts to seek reimbursement from third-party payers for the cost of related services?

IDEA 2004 incorporated many of the accountability provisions of the No Child Left Behind Act (NCLB) of 2001. For example, to improve the academic performance of children with disabilities, school personnel should have the skills and knowledge to use *scientifically based instructional practices* (20 U.S.C. Sec. 1400 [c] [5]). Further, the NCLB requirement that all teachers be *highly qualified* was adopted by IDEA 2004 (20 U.S.C. Sec. 1401 [10] and Sec. 1412 [a] [14]). For special education teachers who are primarily responsible for teaching core academic subjects to their students, they must demonstrate subject matter competence in those academic areas to be considered *highly qualified*. It is likely that most states will require as a part of their teaching licensure process that special education teachers pass a subject matter content examination.

Another NCLB accountability provision was added to IDEA 2004 requiring that states establish goals for the performance of children with disabilities that are the same as the definition of *adequate yearly progress* for nondisabled students (20 U.S.C. Sec. 1412 [a] [15]). In addition, all children with disabilities shall be included in all general state- and districtwide assessment programs, with appropriate accommodations and alternate assessments where necessary and as indicated in their individualized education programs (20 U.S.C. Sec. 1412 [a] [16]).

The definition of related service was modified by IDEA 2004. Interpreting services and school nurse services were added to the list of potential school-provided related services (20 U.S.C. Sec. 1401 [26]). Further, related services were defined to exclude surgically implanted devices such as cochlear implants.

IDEA 2004 also prohibits state and local educational agencies from requiring that a student obtain a prescription for medication as a condition of attending school or receiving special education services (20 U.S.C. Sec. [a][25]). Presumably this provision was included in the reauthorized statute to address parental fears that school districts could mandate that parents medicate their children with attention deficit hyperactivity disorder as a school attendance requirement.

Finally, in statutory changes that impact the FAPE principle, greater emphasis and accountability was placed on a school district's responsibility to provide effective transition services to promote successful post-school employment or education of students with disabilities (20 U.S.C. Sec. 1400 |c||14|). In another transitional services requirement, for students with disabilities whose eligibility terminates due to graduation or age, the local school district shall provide the student with a summary of the student's academic achievement and functional performance along with recommendations to assist the student in meeting postsecondary goals (20 U.S.C. Sec. 1414 |c||5|).

Least Restrictive Environment (LRE)   LRE requires that

> to the maximum extent appropriate, children with disabilities, including children in public or private institutions or other care facilities, are educated with children who are not disabled, and that special classes, separate schooling, or other removal of children with disabilities from the regular educational environment occurs only when the nature or severity of the disability is such that education in regular classes with the use of supplementary aids and services cannot be achieved satisfactorily. (IDEA, 20 U.S.C. Sec. 1412)

The LRE principle can be viewed as a civil rights mandate to ameliorate over 200 years of societal segregation of individuals with disabilities from the mainstream (Fiedler, 2000). In addressing the valid and legally mandated governmental responsibility of providing special education services to students with disabilities, school districts should restrict access to mainstream educational environments only as necessary to meet their educational needs. The LRE principle has sparked much litigation to apply its standard on a case-by-case basis and has fueled the debate over inclusion.

Parents should be able to answer the following questions related to the LRE principle:

- Are the terms *mainstreaming* and *inclusion* legal concepts in IDEA?
- What is the relation between the legal principles of LRE and FAPE?
- Are school districts legally required to educate students with disabilities in their neighborhood schools?
- Does the LRE requirement apply to nonacademic settings and programming?
- What are some of the most significant judicial standards enunciated by the courts for determining the extent of the right of students with disabilities to be educated with nondisabled peers in general education classrooms?

Procedural Due Process and Parent Participation   The final two principles of special education law are discussed together because they jointly operate to ensure that schools comply with IDEA requirements. Procedural due process safeguards afford parents a basic right of protest when they disagree with the educational decisions and actions of the school district. In addition, the parent participation principle guarantees that parents have equal educational decision-making rights with school professionals. Coupled, these two principles serve as the enforcement mechanisms of special education law.

Parents should be able to answer the following questions related to the procedural due process and parent participation principles:

- What are the notice requirements in IDEA?
- When is parental consent required?

- What access rights do parents have to their children's educational records?
- What is a "surrogate parent" and when must the school district appoint one?
- What are the IDEA independent educational evaluation requirements?
- Does IDEA provide for mediation when parents and school districts are in dispute over a student's special education?
- What is a due process hearing and when may it be requested?
- What are the parents' basic due process hearing rights?
- What is the Handicapped Children's Protection Act?
- What happens to the student's educational placement during the pendency of the due process hearing?
- What is the role of the due process hearing officer?
- What are the due process hearing appeal rights of the parties?

A significant change in IDEA 2004 is its emphasis on encouraging the use of positive and constructive ways to resolve disagreements between parents and school (20 U.S.C. Sec. 1400 [c] [8]). For example, prior to proceeding to a due process hearing, either party must provide notice of their complaint to the other party and they may not proceed to a due process hearing until a complaint notice has been filed. The local educational agency must provide a response to the parent's complaint notice that explains the actions taken and options considered by the school district (20 U.S.C. Sec. 1415 [b] [7]). The intent of this provision is to narrow the issues being litigated and to encourage more settlements. Another revision allows the state educational agency to establish procedures for parents and schools that choose not to use mediation. In such circumstances, parents and schools may be offered an opportunity to meet with a disinterested party (e.g., a parent training and information center, community parent resource center, or an alternative dispute resolution entity) to encourage the use and explain the benefits of mediation to the parents (20 U.S.C. Sec. 1415 [e] [2] [B]). Finally, the IDEA 2004 allows for a resolution session prior to the start of a due process hearing. During this resolution session, the school district shall convene a meeting with the parents and the other IEP team members in a last attempt to reach a mutual resolution of the dispute (20 U.S.C. Sec. 1415 [f] [1] [B]).

IDEA 2004 included several revisions to IEPs and the IEP team decision-making process. First, in an effort to reduce some of the paperwork burdens associated with special education processes, IEPs no longer require benchmarks or short term objectives. It is sufficient for an IEP to contain a statement of *measurable annual goals* including academic and functional goals (20 U.S.C. Sec. 1414 [d] [1] [A]). In a further attempt to reduce paperwork demands, IDEA 2004 establishes a multiyear IEP demonstration where no more than 15 states may pilot longterm planning by offering the option to parents and schools to develop a comprehensive multiyear IEP not to exceed three years (20 U.S.C. Sec. 1414 [d] [5] [A]). This multiyear IEP is designed to coincide with natural transition points for a student (e.g., transition from preschool to elementary grades, from elementary grades to middle school, from middle school to high school, or from high school to postsecondary activities).

In addition to the changes noted above regarding the contents of an IEP, IDEA 2004 allows for more flexibility in determining IEP team attendance. For example, an

IEP team member may be excused from attending an IEP team meeting if parents and school agree that the attendance of that particular team member is not necessary because that team member's expertise or curricular area is not being modified or discussed at the meeting (20 U.S.C. Sec. 1414 [d] [1] [C]). Further, parents and the school may agree not to convene an IEP meeting for the purpose of discussing changes in the IEP and, instead, develop a written document to amend or modify the student's IEP (20 U.S.C. Sec 1414 [d] [3] [D]). Finally, parents and the school may agree to use alternative means of conducting an IEP meeting such as video conferences and conference calls (20 U.S.C. Sec. 1414 [d] [7] [f]).

A final set of IDEA 2004 revisions impact procedure due process protections of parents. First, there is now a two-year statute of limitations for parents to prosecute a formal complaint against the school district. That is, the alleged violation must have occurred not more than two years before the date the parent or local educational agency knew or should have known about the alleged action that forms the basis of the complaint (20 U.S.C. Sec 1415 [b] [6] [B]). Second, the losing party in a due process hearing has 90 days from the date of the hearing officer's decision (or if the state has a timeline for such actions, as prescribed by state law) to file a lawsuit in state or federal court (20 U.S.C. Sec [i] [2] [B]). Finally, it is important that parents are aware of a new provision that allows school districts to recover attorney's fees from the parent and the attorney of the parent who files a frivolous complaint or litigates for an improper purpose, such as to harass, to cause unnecessary delay, or needlessly increase the cost of litigation (20 U.S.C. Sec. 1415 [i] [3] [B]).

Special Education Dispute Resolution Mechanisms   Effective parental advocacy requires knowledge of the formal dispute resolution mechanisms in place in special education. Without this knowledge, parents will be unable to pursue their advocacy actions when a dispute reaches an impasse. This section will briefly discuss three formal dispute resolution mechanisms that are available to parents embroiled in a dispute over their child's special education services: mediation, due process hearing, and IDEA complaint process.

Mediation   Mediation is a voluntary process that allows parents and school districts to informally work out differences that they have about a child's special education services, with the help of a neutral third person—a mediator. The following are key elements of mediation: (a) it is a nonadversarial process, (b) it engages the involved parties in a collaborative problem-solving process, and (c) the process is led by an impartial third party (Dobbs, Primm, & Primm, 1991). The 1997 amendments to IDEA require all states to operate a special education mediation system (IDEA 20 U.S.C. Sec. 1415). It should be noted, however, that mediation is not suitable for all family–school dispute situations. For example, Engiles, Peter, Baxter Quash-Mah, and Todis (1996) identified four situations where mediation is inappropriate: (a) one or both parties requires a legal interpretation of IDEA or other applicable law, (b) the parents' goal is a personnel change, (c) one of the parties to the dispute is unwilling to participate in a collaborative problem-solving process, and (d) there is an imbalance between the parties in terms of ability to negotiate and problem solve (e.g., one of the parties is suffering from an illness that diminishes his or her mental capacity).

Mediation rests on several principles and inherent goals. First, as stated above, the mediation process is collaborative. Parents and school professionals must work together to create solutions that meet their respective mutual needs and interests. Second, the parties to a mediation are empowered to serve as the ultimate decision makers. The mediator does not possess the authority to impose decisions on the parties as a hearing officer or judge could. Third, mediation does not focus on finding blame or fault with any of the parties. Instead, mediation focuses on finding mutually determined solutions through communication and collaborative problem solving. Fourth, through nonjudgmental communication and problem solving, mediation fosters greater trust and respect between the parties. Finally, mediation is future oriented because the past is relevant only as a guide and background for developing agreements about future interactions between the parties (Engiles et al., 1996).

Parents need to be given information so that they have an idea of what to expect from a mediation session. A typical special education mediation session includes the following phases:

- In the opening phase, the mediator asks both parties to introduce themselves and their representatives (attorneys may participate in mediation session if both parties agree), explains the purposes of the mediation session, describes the mediator's role, explains the steps in the mediation process, reviews the due process rights of the parties, explains the implications and impact of reaching a settlement agreement, and establishes basic ground rules for the mediation session.
- The mediator explains the agreement-to-mediate form and asks both parties to sign it.
- The mediator asks each participant to explain his or her viewpoint of the situation.
- The mediator may ask questions to clarify, brainstorm, or encourage the parties to create possible solutions.
- As proposed solutions are being generated and discussed, either one or both parties may have a need to caucus. During a caucus, the parties meet separately, with the mediator acting as a facilitator to clarify concerns and determine what each party is willing to consider as a solution.
- A mediation session may be short (e.g., 1 hour or less) or last for more than 1 day. The parties determine how many times they need to meet to pursue mutually satisfactory solutions.
- There are three possible outcomes of mediation: (a) the parties reach an agreement that is committed to writing in a document called a mediation agreement, (b) the parties fail to reach a mutually agreeable solution and decide that further mediation sessions would not be productive, and (c) both parties agree to meet again after gathering and considering additional information (Schrag, 1996).

Due Process Hearing   A due process hearing is a more formal process than a mediation session and is, by nature, adversarial. An impartial hearing officer is appointed to conduct the hearing. A hearing officer opens the hearing with a statement on the following: (a) the legal authority to conduct the hearing, (b) the purposes of the hearing, (c) the role of the hearing officer, (d) information on the due process rights of the parties, and (e) hearing procedures and rules. Following the hearing officer's introduction, both parties are allowed to make opening statements, outlining their arguments. After the opening statements, the formal presentation of evidence commences. The school will present its evidence first through documents (e.g., evaluation reports, IEPs, behavioral records, progress reports) and testimony of witnesses. The parents may cross-examine the school's witnesses. The hearing officer may also ask questions of any witness. After the school presents its case, the parents present their evidence. The parents may also submit documentary and testimonial evidence. The school may cross-examine the parents' witnesses. After completion of the parents' evidence, both parties may make closing statements summarizing their positions. The hearing officer closes the hearing and indicates when a written decision will be rendered. The appeal rights of the parties are also explained by the hearing officer.

Given the adversarial nature of due process hearings, parents must engage in a thorough consideration of the potential advantages and disadvantages of initiating a due process hearing request. Fiedler (2000) identified a number of potential negative consequences and limitations of the due process hearing model, including (a) the excessively adversarial nature of due process hearings, (b) the perceived unfairness of the hearing process, (c) the time-consuming nature of hearings, (d) the financial and emotional costs to both parents and school professionals, (e) the removal of the decision-making authority from the parties in dispute, (f) the inaccessibility of the hearing system (e.g., primarily available to middle to higher income and well-educated parents), (g) the overlegalization of the hearing system and special education, and (h) the negative effects on the child with disabilities whose parents participate in a due process hearing. School professionals can assist parents in their analysis of whether to enter into a due process hearing situation by encouraging parents to consider the factors discussed in Communication and Collaboration Tips Box 8.1.

COMMUNICATION AND COLLABORATION TIPS   **BOX 8.1**

Factors to Consider Before Requesting a Due Process Hearing

1. Understand the school district's position.
2. Know what is wrong with the school district's position/actions.
3. Know what you want from the school district.
4. Weigh your position against the school district's position.
5. Know where you want your child educated while the dispute is being resolved.
6. Decide who will represent you at a due process hearing.
7. Weigh the benefits/costs of going to a due process hearing.

Source: Adapted from *Negotiating the special education maze: A guide for parents and teachers* (pp. 41–45) by Winifred Anderson, Stephen Chitwood, and Deidre Hayden, 1997, Bethesda, MD: Woodbine House.

IDEA Complaint Process An individual or organization may file a signed written complaint with the state department of education alleging a procedural or substantive violation of special education law. The state department of education must investigate and resolve the complaint within 60 days of receipt of the written complaint. If a violation is found, the state department of education will require the school district to submit a corrective action plan outlining the steps the district will take to correct the violation(s). Appeals of the state department of education's decisions may be taken to the OSEP of the U.S. Department of Education.

Suchey and Huefner (1998) maintained that, in comparison to mediation and due process hearings, the IDEA complaint process has several potential advantages. First, the scope of a complaint can cover the same full range of either procedural or substantive issues that are addressed in a due process hearing. Second, the costs of the complaint process are borne by the state agency, not the local school district or parents. Third, attorneys do not typically participate as representatives for the parties in the complaint process. And finally, corrective action plan orders of the state department of education are enforceable in court, similar to due process hearing decision orders.

Essential Advocacy Skills

Pardeck (1996) identified a number of advocacy skills that are necessary for parents to advocate effectively for their children with disabilities:

- Parents must believe in their rights.
- Parents must have a clear vision.
- Parents must have good organizational skills.
- Parents must be able to prioritize.
- Parents must possess a good understanding of their children's disabilities.
- Parents must know the laws.
- Parents must follow the chain of command.
- Parents should be informative.
- Parents should offer solutions.
- Parents must be principled and persist.
- Parents must learn to communicate effectively.
- Parents must let others know when they are pleased.
- Parents must develop endurance.
- Parents must follow through.
- Parents need a sense of humor.

This next section will focus on essential advocacy skills, including interpersonal communication skills, collaboration skills, effective advocacy skills, organizational and documentation skills, IEP meeting participation skills, and constructive conflict resolution skills.

Interpersonal Communication Skills Effective interpersonal communication skills advance parental advocacy efforts in a variety of ways. They establish interpersonal trust in a relationship; create a relationship of mutual acceptance and respect; convey empathy for another person's concerns; establish rapport by creating the conditions for a comfortable and unconditional relationship; set an atmosphere for mutual problem solving; establish a collaborative relationship; provide individuals with a catharsis by relieving tension, frustration, and anxiety in the process; and influence the attitudes and behaviors of another person (Fiedler, 2000). Several variables influence the quality of interpersonal interactions between parents of students with disabilities and school professionals. Fiedler (1986, 1993) identified these key interpersonal communication interaction variables as (a) different assumptions and expectations concerning the student's present abilities and future needs, (b) objectivity, (c) different opinions of the student's educational progress, (d) flexibility, (e) trust, and (f) effective and open communication. Each of these interpersonal communication interaction variables will be briefly discussed.

Different Assumptions and Expectations Concerning the Student's Present Abilities and Future Needs There are several reasons why parents and school professionals may possess different expectations about a student's abilities and needs. For example, parents and school professionals may have different values and attitudes regarding the implications of a child's disability. Some parents, for understandable reasons, may be overly protective of their child and, thus, have unrealistically low expectations of their child's capabilities. Alternatively, other parents, struggling with denial and acceptance issues, may maintain unrealistically high expectations of their children's future potential. Another reason for different expectations is parental beliefs that the school has committed insufficient attention to their concerns. This form of "professional dismissal" of parental concerns is not conducive to establishing collaborative partnerships. Simpson (1996) revealed that parents often consider their child's educational needs are met if school professionals listen and respond to their concerns. Finally, different expectations can arise when parents argue that the school's evaluation of their child was inaccurate, biased, or incomplete.

Objectivity Fiedler (2000) defines objectivity as ". . . the ability to refrain from personalizing a dispute and to concentrate on resolving a problem using facts and data without distorting information with personal feelings or prejudice" (p. 132). Interpersonal communication between two parties who are not able to remain objective is characterized by defensiveness and blaming behaviors. In discussing a student's educational needs, school professionals must set the tone and interpersonal communication style by being objective and data based in their documentation of student needs, instead of relying on subjective feelings of "what ought to occur" for the student. "Decisions and recommendations that are based on objective data force educational planners to articulate the basis for such decisions" (Fiedler, 1993, p. 274).

Different Opinions of the Student's Educational Progress Many adversarial situations are based on parental dissatisfaction with their child's educational progress, the effectiveness of which school professionals defend (Budolf & Orenstein, 1982). Without any attempt to have a meeting of the minds on how a student's educational progress will be objectively measured and communicated, there will be little motivation to engage in mutual problem solving. Parents who are dissatisfied with their child's

---

COMMUNICATION AND COLLABORATION TIPS   **BOX 8.2**

Steps in Describing a Student's Educational Progress

1. Organize information into broad categories.
2. Begin with positive information.
3. Cite specific examples related to informational categories.
4. Relate the information to the student's IEP.
5. Encourage parents to discuss each point in need of clarification.
6. Provide examples of the student's work.
7. Explain how student progress is evaluated.
8. Emphasize how instruction is individualized.

Source: Based on *Effective skills in parent/teacher conferencing* (pp. 23–32), by T. M. Stephens and J. S. Wolf, 1980, Columbus, OH: NCEMMH.

educational progress must be equipped to document their concerns. Stephens and Wolf (1980) urged the format in Communication and Collaboration Tips Box 8.2 in an attempt to avoid different opinions of the student's educational progress maintained by the parents and school professionals.

Flexibility Flexibility was identified earlier in this chapter as an essential advocacy characteristic of parents. Advocates who are inflexible are not receptive to new ideas, change, or alternatives. Inflexible individuals are not willing to compromise. As noted by Fiedler (2000), "When school professionals behave in an inflexible manner, parents feel impotent in their legitimate attempts to have input in the educational decision-making process. This causes feelings of frustration and engenders future conflict between families and schools" (p. 133).

Trust Interpersonal trust is a necessary ingredient for establishing a collaborative and problem-solving relationship between parents and school professionals. Simpson (1996) indicated that a trusting relationship is based on three basic elements: an atmosphere where a shared feeling of safety exists, reassurance and modeling of risk-taking behaviors, and reinforcement of both parties for risk-taking initiatives. The importance of trust in interpersonal relations was more extensively discussed in chapter 3.

Effective and Open Communication "Effective and open communication involves an interaction process in which parents and school are able and willing to listen and learn from each other, share ideas, and be understood" (Fiedler, 1986, p. 4). Interpersonal communication is facilitated by demonstrating the effective communication characteristics and employing the verbal communication skills identified in Communication and Collaboration Tips Box 8.3.

Collaboration Skills Parental advocacy is enhanced through effective collaboration with school professionals. Friend and Cook (2003) defined interpersonal collaboration

---

COMMUNICATION AND COLLABORATION TIPS   **BOX 8.3**

Interpersonal Communication Skills

Effective Communication Characteristics

- ❑ **Rapport**—It is important to take some time at the beginning of an interpersonal interaction to become acquainted with the other person or to share a positive comment. Establishing rapport can ease tension and anxiety in an advocacy situation.
- ❑ **Genuine**—In interactions with parents of students with disabilities, school professionals should minimize their use of professional jargon. Excessive use of professional jargon by school professionals communicates the message that the parents are not viewed as equals in this collaborative partnership.
- ❑ **Concrete**—Effective communicators are concrete or specific when describing situations or concerns to another person. Concrete communication reduces misunderstanding and confusion.
- ❑ **Confrontation**—Confronting another person during a communicative interaction can note discrepancies between verbal behaviors and actions or provide feedback about a person's behaviors. This form of confrontation can be effective in clarifying communicative intent or identifying hidden issues that need to be discussed.
- ❑ **Self-disclosure**—Self-disclosure fosters personal connections with another person through sharing feelings or experiences. Self-disclosure contrasts with the traditional aloof, detached demeanor maintained by many school professionals.
- ❑ **Immediacy**—Effective communicators maintain the focus on the present and the future and avoid extensive attention to a past that cannot be undone.

Effective Verbal Communication Skills

- ❑ **Door-opening statements**—These statements demonstrate interest and willingness to listen while encouraging the other person to continue talking. This verbal technique facilitates mutual problem solving by conveying the notion that the school professional values the parent's opinions and perspectives. Examples include "Then what?" "Can you tell me more about . . . ?"
- ❑ **Paraphrasing**—Paraphrasing involves the listener's restating in her own words what she thought the other person just stated. This verbal skill demonstrates you are an active listener and offers the chance to rectify possible misunderstandings. Examples include "What I hear you saying is . . . " and "In other words . . . "
- ❑ **Reflecting affect**—This communication skill involves the ability to sensitively perceive the other person's underlying feelings. Examples include "So, do you feel like . . . ?"
- ❑ **Clarifying statements**—Clarifying statements serve to reduce miscommunication by ensuring the listener accurately understands the intent of the speaker's message. Examples include "What do you mean?" "Could you elaborate?"
- ❑ **Questioning**—There are two types of questions: close ended and open ended. Close-ended questions seek specific factual information. Open-ended questions invite more discussion. Excessive use of close-ended questions can make an interaction seem like an interrogation. Further, be careful with using a lot of *why* questions. Such questions connote disapproval or condemnation and evoke defensive responses.
- ❑ **Summarization**—Summarizing statements review the key aspects of an interpersonal interaction and signal the close of discussion on one topic and a bridge to another topic.

as "a style for direct interaction between at least two coequal parties voluntarily engaged in shared decision making as they work toward a common goal" (p. 6). Friend and Cook went on to identify several common characteristics for effective collaboration, including: collaboration is voluntary, collaboration requires parity among participants, collaboration is based on mutual goals, collaboration depends on shared responsibility for participation and decision making, collaborators share resources, collaborators share accountability for outcomes, a collaborative interpersonal style is valued, collaborators must trust one another, and a sense of community evolves from collaboration.

Fiedler (2000) outlined a number of competencies for effective advocacy-oriented collaboration:

- Demonstrates genuine empathy and sensitivity to the needs and perspectives of others.
- Displays interest in and sensitivity to people.
- Understands one's own values.
- Displays an ability to learn from others.
- Exhibits an ability to respect others' input, opinions, and criticisms.
- Presents self as an ally.
- Is willing to take risks and make mistakes to learn.
- Models and promotes self-reflection.
- Demonstrates an ability to support the viewpoints of others.

Effective Advocacy Skills   This section will focus on principles for effective advocacy and critical steps in the advocacy process. According to Bootel (1995), there are several core principles for effective advocacy.

Ask for What You Want Parent advocates must possess sufficient confidence and assertiveness to request the desired changes they seek for their child's education. If parents appear uncertain or hesitant of what they want, school professionals are unlikely to take the parents' advocacy seriously or may assume the parents lack commitment and persistence in pursuing their advocacy goals.

Be Specific in Your Request If parents cannot clearly articulate what changes they are seeking in their child's educational program, they will be at a distinct disadvantage in their advocacy. Vague and overly general requests give the impression that the parents have not completely thought about what is wrong with their child's educational program. At this point, school professionals will be less motivated to engage in serious mutual problem solving.

Organize, Coordinate, Orchestrate At times, parental advocacy will revolve around organizing other parents or concerned individuals to join a coalition or group to seek widespread changes in school district policies or practices. The importance of coalition building is seen in the old adage about "strength in numbers." In building a coalition to advocate for a common concern, it is critical to take the necessary time and energy to reach a group consensus on advocacy goals and priorities. The added clout of having a coalition advocate on a particular issue can be quickly dissipated if that group does not speak in one clear and consistent voice.

Touch All the Bases Another basic principle of effective coalition building is to solicit support from as many groups as possible that have similar advocacy interests. Consider all the groups or constituents that may be impacted by the issue that is the current cause of coalition concern. In addition, a beginning coalition should also consider discussing its advocacy issue with groups or individuals that may appear as likely opponents. This allows an advocacy group to gauge the strength of the opponent's position and to identify specific objections.

Stay Flexible, Be Opportunistic Although advocates need to identify clear goals and develop a plan of action, they must remain flexible to seize unexpected opportunities. Fiedler (2000) cited an example of his own parental advocacy actions in requesting a meeting to express concern over some of the IEP goals and objectives for his daughter. At the IEP meeting, the school district offered to hire an outside consultant to conduct an independent educational evaluation of his daughter and to review her current program. Although this was not the Fiedlers' initial advocacy goal, they seized the opportunity to bring in an external expert to offer educational programming suggestions.

Keep It Simple Bootel (1995) encouraged advocates to state the reasons for their concerns and proposed solutions in 30 seconds. Advocates should strive to capture an audience's attention within the first few sentences of their message.

Assume the Perspective of Others An effective advocate carefully listens to the questions and comments of others to gain insight into their perspective. It is beneficial whenever advocates are able to illustrate a disability issue by personalizing it through sharing an anecdote on how a problem directly impacts a child with a disability and his family. This tactic puts a name and face to the advocacy issue and moves the discussion out of theoretical or abstract realms.

Build and Preserve Your Credibility As stated by Fiedler (2000), "Effective advocates recognize that their personal reputation for integrity, honesty, and credibility are important advocacy tools. To build and enhance these tools, advocates must (1) not mislead anyone in their advocacy actions, (2) not spring any unfair surprises on others, and (3) not promise more than they can deliver" (p. 197).

Never Burn Any Bridges Effective advocates strive to avoid making enemies in their advocacy actions. Advocacy alliances and oppositions can shift like ocean waves, depending on the issues under discussion. Bootel (1995) noted, "Remember, in advocacy, there are no permanent friends and no permanent enemies" (p. 20).

Follow Up To establish credibility and trust, advocates must be counted on to do what they say they will do. Therefore, advocates need to complete their agreed-on tasks within the designated time period.

Steps in the Advocacy Process   According to Hines (1987), there are five distinct steps in the process of engaging in effective advocacy: (a) problem definition, (b) information gathering, (c) action planning, (d) assertive action, and (e) follow-up.

The goal of the *problem definition* step is to specifically define the problem and state what is needed to resolve it. Once this is accomplished, the advocate can prioritize what issues to address. The following questions are useful in clarifying problems and possible solutions:

- How do you know there is a problem?
- Who is affected by the problem and how?
- When did the problem start?
- What kinds of changes would solve the problem?
- How will you know when the problem is solved?
- By what date should the problem begin to be resolved?
- What has been done to address the problem so far?
- Are there any ethical or legal guidelines that relate to the problem?

Gathering relevant and accurate *information* is critical to the success of any advocacy action. Communication and Collaboration Tips Box 8.4 provides parents with an information-gathering checklist.

The *action plan* identifies the step-by-step activities the advocate will employ to resolve the conflict. Typical elements of a comprehensive action plan include (a) a statement of the problem; (b) a description of the ideal resolution; (c) a list of acceptable compromise solutions; (d) a list of all of the information needed to pursue the desired advocacy goal, dividing this into information already obtained and information needed; (e) a description of potential benefits others could experience from the changes requested by the advocacy actions; (f) a description of the other party's needs and arguments in opposition to the requested changes and possible responses to each of the opponent's arguments; (g) a description of the advocacy strategies to be employed; (h) a timeline for completion of each step in the action plan; and (i) a discussion of possible actions to take if the advocacy actions are not successful.

In the *assertive action* step in the advocacy process, the advocate implements the action plan. Assertive actions are at the core of effective advocacy. But there is a fine line between being appropriately assertive versus being aggressive and making threats. An assertive advocate is a good listener, is respectful of others' perspectives, is able to control his or her emotions, and uses collaborative problem-solving skills. As an effective problem solver, the assertive advocate knows what she wants, does not blame or criticize school officials, protects the integrity of the parent–school relationship, seeks win–win solutions to problems, and makes every attempt to clearly understand the school's position (Wright & Wright, 2002).

In the final step of the advocacy process, the advocate *follows up* to ensure the implementation of agreed-on actions and changes. When agreed-on actions are implemented, a thank-you letter to those individuals responsible for taking the corrective actions should be sent. When changes are not forthcoming, a letter should be sent reminding the appropriate individual of the agreements reached, with a timeline for action. This letter should be copied to the next level in the agency chain-of-command structure.

Organizational and Documentation Skills   An effective parent advocate must be able to organize an array of information that is collected during the course of home–school problem situations. In addition, advocates must carefully and accurately document the

COMMUNICATION AND COLLABORATION TIPS   **BOX 8.4**

Information-Gathering Checklist
Responsible Agencies

Know what agency is responsible to provide the services requested.

Rights and Rights Procedures

Know your relevant legal rights and the complaint/appeals process.

If there is no legal provision clearly establishing a right to a particular service, you must use other arguments to persuade the agency to provide the requested services. Examples of such arguments include:

- ❑ My child's health and safety is being endangered.
- ❑ My child is not experiencing an educational benefit from the current services.
- ❑ My child's current services unnecessarily segregate or isolate my child from students without disabilities.

Agency Chain of Command

Know the administrative structure and chain of command of the agency.

Student Records

Review your child's educational records.

Policy Documents

Review school district policies and procedures.

Source: Making a difference: Advocacy competencies for special education professionals (p. 200) by Craig Fiedler, 2000, Boston: Allyn & Bacon. Adapted from *Don't get mad: Get powerful! A manual for building advocacy skills* by M. L. Hines, 1987, Lansing: Michigan Protection and Advocacy Service (ERIC Document Reproduction Service No. ED 354683).

content of advocacy interactions and the manner in which they occur (e.g., at meetings or in phone conversations). In terms of organizing school records, Anderson et al. (1997) developed a Four-Step Record Decoder process that includes (a) organize, (b) read, (c) analyze, and (d) evaluate. In the *organize* phase, all school records are sorted into two categories: documents describing the student (i.e., evaluation reports, IEPs, progress reports) and correspondence or administrative documents (i.e., meeting notices, consent forms, placement forms). Arrange documents in chronological order from oldest to most recent and include the name of the document, the date, and the reporting individual. In the second, *read*, stage, gather general impressions about the student's abilities and needs (both from the parent's and school's perspectives). The advocate should maintain a list of questions or concerns related to specific documents. In the *analyze* phase, list the student's strengths and weaknesses. Further, maintain a list of recommendations made by school professionals. Finally, analyze this information for trends. For example, are student strengths or weaknesses mentioned by more than one school professional? Are similar concerns repeated over multiple years? In the final, *evaluate*, step, these questions should be addressed by the parent advocate:

- Are the school's conclusions and recommendations about the student in agreement with the parent's?
- Are there any missing documents in the school records? Do all of the school reports contain all of the legally required components?
- Are school reports appropriately objective in describing the student's behaviors, skills, and needs?
- Are school evaluations appropriately comprehensive and culturally fair?
- Is the school report information sufficiently current to address present issues and concerns?
- Are there significant discrepancies between the conclusions or recommendations of various school professionals?

Good documentation is essential to advocacy. In their documentation of advocacy interactions, parents must be able to provide answers to who, what, why, when, where, and how, and to explain questions. Wright and Wright (2002) suggested that parents develop a contact log to document phone conversations with school professionals. This contact log includes the following parts: who, when, what you wanted, what you were told, and a section for notes. The Wrights also provide an example of how to document school problems. This problem report should include the date, a short description of the problem, a list of people involved, and facts. The facts portion of the problem report addresses these questions: What happened? When did it happen? Who was involved? Where did it happen? Why did it happen? Who witnessed? What action did school take? What action did you take? And any other facts.

Advocates should commit to writing summaries of any advocacy-based school meetings. In a meeting-summary letter to school professionals involved in the advocacy-based meeting, parents should ask for confirmation of the summary points. At the very least, this meeting-summary letter should (a) summarize the substance of the meeting discussion; (b) summarize any agreements reached or promises made; (c) articulate questions or information that need to be addressed or gathered; (d) describe the next tasks and individuals responsible for specific tasks, along with deadlines for completion of those tasks; and (e) establish future meeting dates if necessary (Fiedler, 2000).

In addition to writing letters to summarize school meetings, parents should write letters to request information, request action, provide information or describe an event, decline a request, or to express appreciation (Wright & Wright, 2002). The Wrights offer several suggestions for writing effective letters. First, use short sentences and paragraphs to make your message easier to read and understand. Second, inform the reader what you want in the first paragraph of the letter. Third, treat the letter recipient with courtesy and kindness. Fourth, your letter should prompt the recipient to act. At the end of your letter, restate what action you want the recipient to take. Finally, make it easy for the recipient to respond to your letter by providing contact information including your name, telephone number, address, fax number, and e-mail address at the end of the letter.

IEP Meeting Participation Skills   Initial discussions concerning parent–school disagreements and mutual problem solving typically occur in the context of an IEP meeting. Therefore, it is critical that parents are active and effective decision makers at IEP meetings. Whether the IEP meeting is to determine a student's eligibility for special education services or to develop an IEP, parents need to prepare for the meeting, and they should anticipate possible areas of disagreement with the school. Parents can prepare for an upcoming IEP meeting by using a premeeting worksheet developed by Wright and Wright (2002). In this premeeting worksheet, parents complete information on the time, date, location, purpose, and who requested the meeting. In addition, parents should consider the following:

- Who will attend the meeting?
- What do the parents want from this meeting?
- What does the school want from this meeting?
- What action do the parents want the school to take?
- How motivated is the school to give the parents what they want?
- What might prevent the school from giving the parents what they want?
- How can the parents alleviate the school's concerns?

During an eligibility determination IEP meeting, parents may feel that the school has not adequately assessed all of their child's educational needs. In situations like these, Packer (2002) has developed a chart to assist parents in organizing their thoughts and focusing their advocacy interactions during an IEP meeting. See Communication and Collaboration Tips Box 8.5. This kind of premeeting preparation can make the difference in successful IEP meeting advocacy.

Once a child has been evaluated and the IEP team has concluded that there is (a) a qualifying disability under the law and (b) that due to the child's disability, he is in need of special education services, the focus of the IEP team turns to developing an appropriate IEP. The IEP document must include the following components:

1. A statement of the child's present levels of educational performance, including a description of how the child's disability affects her involvement and progress in the general education curriculum.

2. A statement of measurable annual goals related to meeting the child's needs resulting from his disability to enable the child to participate in the general education curriculum, and to meet each of the child's other educational needs.

3. A statement of the special education and related services to be provided to meet each of the goals, including supplementary aids and services to support general education class participation if appropriate.

COMMUNICATION AND COLLABORATION TIPS   **BOX 8.5**

Organizing Parental Concerns During an IEP Eligibility Determination Meeting

List parent concerns	Evidence or indicators of problem	If parent knows what problem may be related to, indicate it here	If assessment is needed, what kind?	Accommodations or special services needed?	Agreements reached?

Source: Packer, L.E. (2002). *Education advocacy: A self-help tutorial for parents.* Retrieved November 21, 2003, from www.tourettesyndrome.net.

4. An explanation of the extent, if any, to which the child will not participate with nondisabled children in the general education classroom.

5. A statement of any individual modifications in the administration of state- or districtwide assessments of student achievement that are needed for the child to participate in the assessment, and if the IEP team determines that the child will not participate in a particular state- or districtwide assessment of student achievement, a statement of why that assessment is not appropriate for the child and how the child will be assessed.

6. The projected date for the beginning of the services and modifications described and the anticipated frequency, location, and duration of those services and modifications.

7. A statement of how the child's progress toward the annual goals will be measured and how the child's parents will be regularly informed, at least as often as parents are informed of their nondisabled children's progress.

8. A statement of transition services for a student 14 years or older.

9. A positive behavioral support plan if the child's behavior is an issue.

10. Consideration of assistive technology and services (Anderson et al., 1997).

Bateman and Linden (1998) advocated a useful three-step planning process for developing educationally useful IEPs. This process is particularly family-friendly because parent participation is encouraged from the beginning. The three steps include:

1. School professionals and family members list the student's unique educational needs and characteristics. After completing this list, similar needs and characteristics are clustered together.

2. School professionals and family members identify what school services would be necessary to address the prioritized educational needs/characteristics categories. These school services could include special education services, related services, or general classroom modifications.

3. School professionals and family members decide what student behavioral changes will signify that school services are effective. This information becomes the basis for developing IEP goals and objectives.

A final example of an educational planning process is Making Action Plans (MAPS; Falvey, Forest, Pearpoint, & Rosenberg, 1994). MAPS is an alternative to the traditional IEP meeting procedures and allows the family to engage in long-term vision and priority setting for their child with disabilities. At a meeting involving school professionals working with a student, the student's family members, community agency personnel (if applicable), and nondisabled friends, a facilitator leads the group through a series of seven questions. These questions are: (1) What is the student's history? (2) What are your dreams for the student? (3) What are your nightmares? (4) Who is this student? (5) What are the student's strengths, gifts, or talents? (6) What are the student's needs? and (7) What is the student's plan of action? This process is useful for providing a more positive climate to educational planning than commonly exists at many traditional IEP meetings. In addition, MAPS identifies family priorities and establishes educational priorities that can serve as the foundation for developing IEP goals and objectives.

Conflict Resolution Skills   Effective special education advocacy is constructive in that both parties to a dispute are satisfied with the outcomes and sense that they have benefited as a result of the conflict. On the other hand, destructive conflict resolution leaves the parties feeling dissatisfied with the outcomes and feeling they have lost as a result of the conflict (Deutsch, 1973). Whether conflict is constructive or destructive is largely determined by the skills and strategies employed by the parties engaged in a dispute. Constructive conflict resolution is advanced by the following behaviors or tactics: (a) minimize differences in goals and emphasize cooperative strategies, (b) emphasize the desirability of mutually satisfactory outcomes, (c) refrain from harmful actions or statements, (d) emphasize mutual dependencies, (e) ensure equal status in negotiations, (f) attempt to understand others' motives, and (g) maintain openness about intentions and rationale (Walton, 1969).

Constructive conflict resolution is fostered by employing a collaborative problem-solving process (Berry & Hardman, 1998; Fiedler, 1991; Simpson, 1996). In this process, both school professionals and parents must possess sufficient motivation to commit the time and energy necessary for engaging in this mutual course of action. There are five essential steps in collaborative problem solving. The first step is to *define the problem*. It is critical to define the problem from the perspectives of both parties. The second step involves brainstorming to *generate possible solutions*. In the next step, the parties must mutually *choose a solution* after weighing potential risks and benefits of each of the possible solutions identified in Step 2. At this stage, the parties must evaluate real-world constraints of time, energy, and resources to ensure that the chosen solution has a legitimate chance of succeeding. The fourth step requires the parties to *implement the chosen solution*. The final step of collaborative problem solving is to *evaluate the solution*. Both parties need to agree on the objective evaluation criteria that will be used to determine if the solution is successful or not. In addition, the parties must establish a timeline by which they will analyze the accumulated information and apply that data to the evaluation criteria.

The Runnels Family Revisited

Ron and Elizabeth Runnels contacted their state's Parent Training and Information Center. Within 1 week, that agency had identified a local parent advocate who met with the Runnelses to listen to their concerns about Matt's special education program. In terms of advocating for more general education classroom participation for Matt, the parent advocate knew several special education consultants and put the Runnelses in touch with one. The consultant met with Ron and Elizabeth and spent some time with Matt at home and in school. The consultant identified a number of functional skills that Matt could legitimately work on while in a general education classroom. At the next IEP meeting, Ron and Elizabeth, armed with the consultant's recommendations, felt more confident in advocating for general education inclusion for their son. In addition, the Runnelses requested that the school's assistive technology specialist assess Matt and determine his needs for augmentative communication. For the first time, Ron and Elizabeth left an IEP meeting with some optimism and a new determination to forge a partnership with school professionals in developing an appropriate educational program for Matt.

SUMMARY STATEMENTS

- Parents of students with disabilities are logical advocates for their children and, in recognition of this belief, special education law has empowered parents with significant educational decision-making rights.
- There are a number of barriers that limit active parent participation in their child's special education. These barriers include cultural and language differences, poverty, parental lack of knowledge about special education rights and procedures, negative professional attitudes toward parents, parental burnout, and parental alienation and isolation.
- School professionals can empower parents by providing them with special education advocacy training and support. Effective special education advocates possess specific attitudes/dispositions, knowledge bases, and skills.
- To function as effective advocates for their children with disabilities, parents must become knowledgeable of special education legal rights and special education dispute resolution mechanisms. In addition, parents need specific skills, including interpersonal communication skills, collaboration skills, advocacy skills, organizational and documentation skills, IEP meeting participation skills, and constructive conflict resolution skills.

QUESTIONS FOR DISCUSSION

1. Provide a rationale why parents are the logical and best advocates to represent their children's special education rights.
2. How can school professionals minimize or eliminate existing barriers to active parent participation in educational decision making?
3. Describe specific advocacy training and support activities that school professionals should be able to provide parents of children with disabilities.

RESOURCES FOR EDUCATIONAL ADVOCACY SUPPORT

- **Commission on Mental and Physical Disability Law, American Bar Association**
  (www.abanet.org/disability/home.html)

  This Web site contains a list of legal resources and governmental agencies that protect the legal rights of individuals with disabilities.

- **Wrightslaw**
  (www.wrightslaw.com)

  Pete and Pam Wright provide a wealth of information to assist special education advocates. Advocates can sign up for the Wrightslaw newsletter.

- **Parent Advocacy Coalition for Educational Rights (PACER)**
  (www.pacer.org)

  This national parent information and support organization offers a variety of advocacy information and assistance.

- **Office of Special Education and Rehabilitation Services (OSERS)**
  (www.ed.gov/about/offices/list/osers/index.html)

  This agency is part of the U.S. Department of Education and is responsible for special education programming and enforcement. A number of informational guides for parents are available at this Web site.

- **Disability Rights Education and Defense Fund, Inc.**
  (www.dredf.org)

  This is a national law and policy center dedicated to advancing civil and educational rights of individuals with disabilities. This Web site maintains a special education Web page with information on laws, the IEP process, Web resources and more.

- **National Disability Rights Network**
  (www.napas.org)

  Every state has a federally funded "protection and advocacy" agency designed to provide advocacy assistance to individuals with disabilities and their families. This Web site includes information and resources related to special education law.

REFLECTION ACTIVITIES

1. Conduct an analysis of existing barriers to active parent participation in special education decision making in a local school or school district. Develop a plan to reduce or eliminate those barriers.

2. Identify a local parent support group and form a committee to develop a parent advocacy training program. This committee, composed of school professionals and parents of children with disabilities, will identify parent advocacy needs in the local school district and develop an advocacy training curriculum and related activities.

REFERENCES

Adams, J. Q., & Welsch, J. R. (1999). *Cultural diversity: Curriculum, classroom, and climate.* Macomb: Illinois Staff and Curriculum Developers Association.

Anderson, W., Chitwood, S., & Hayden, D. (1997). *Negotiating the special education maze: A guide for parents and teachers.* Bethesda, MD: Woodbine House.

Bateman, B. D., & Linden, M. A. (1998). *Better IEPs: How to develop legally correct and educational useful programs* (3rd ed.). Longmont, CO: Sopris West.

Berry, J. O., & Hardman, M. L. (1998). *Lifespan perspectives on the family and disability.* Boston: Allyn & Bacon.

Bootel, J. A. (1995). *CEC special education advocacy handbook.* Reston, VA: Council for Exceptional Children.

Brotherson, M. J., Berdine, W. H., & Sartini, V. (1993). Transition to adult services: Support for ongoing parent participation. *Remedial and Special Education, 14*(4), 44–51.

Budolf, M., & Orenstein, A. (1982). *Due process in special education: On going to a hearing.* Cambridge, MA: Ware Press.

Coots, J. J. (1998). Family resources and parent participation in schooling activities for their children with developmental delays. *Journal of Special Education, 31,* 498–520.

Council for Exceptional Children. (1993). *CEC policy manual.* Reston, VA: Author.

Deutsch, M. (1973). *The resolution of conflict: Constructive and destructive process.* New Haven, CT: Yale University Press.

Dobbs, R. F., Primm, E. B., & Primm, B. (1991). Mediation: A common sense approach for resolving conflicts in special education. *Focus on Exceptional Children, 24,* 1–11.

Engiles, A., Peter, M., Baxter Quash-Mah, S., & Todis, B. (1996). *Team-based conflict resolution in special education.* Eugene, OR: Lane Education Service District. (ERIC Document Reproduction Service No. ED 40169)

Falvey, M. A., Forest, M., Pearpoint, J., & Rosenberg, R. (1994). Building connections. In J. S. Thousand, R. A. Villa, & A. I. Nevin (Eds.), *Creativity and collaborative learning: A practical guide to empowering students and teachers* (pp. 347–368). Baltimore: Brookes.

Fiedler, C. R. (1986). Enhancing parent–school personnel partnerships. *Focus on Autistic Behavior, 1*(4), 1–8.

Fiedler, C. R. (1991). Preparing parents to participate: Advocacy and education. In M. J. Fine (Ed.), *Collaboration with parents of exceptional children* (pp. 313–333). New York: Clinical Psychology Publishing.

Fiedler, C. R. (1993). Parents and the law: Conflict development and legal safeguards. In J. L. Paul & R. J. Simeonsson (Eds.), *Children with special needs: Family, culture, and society* (pp. 256–278). Fort Worth, TX: Harcourt Brace Jovanovich.

Fiedler, C. R. (1997). *Interviews with professional educators who serve as advocates for children with disabilities and their families: Findings and insights.* Unpublished manuscript.

Fiedler, C. R. (2000). *Making a difference: Advocacy competencies for special education professionals.* Boston: Allyn & Bacon.

Fiedler, C. R., & Antonak, R. F. (1991). Advocacy. In J. L. Matson & J. A. Mulick (Eds.), *Handbook of mental retardation* (pp. 23–32). New York: Pergamon Press.

Fiedler, C. R., & Swanger, W. H. (2000). Empowering parents to participate: Advocacy and education. In M. J. Fine & R. L. Simpson (Eds.), *Collaboration with parents and families of children with exceptionalities* (pp. 437–464). Austin, TX: Pro-Ed.

Fine, M. (1993). [Ap]parent involvement: Reflections on parents, power, and urban public schools. *Teachers College Record, 94,* 682–711.

Friend, M., & Cook, L. (2003). *Interactions: Collaboration skills for school professionals.* Boston: Allyn & Bacon.

Friesen, B., & Huff, B. (1990). Parents and professionals as advocacy partners. *Preventing School Failure, 34*(3), 31–37.

Frith, G. H. (1981). "Advocate" vs. "professional employee": A question of priorities for special educators. *Exceptional Children, 47,* 486–492.

Geenen, S., Powers, L. E., & Lopez-Vasquez, A. (2001). Multicultural aspects of parent involvement in transition planning. *Exceptional Children*, 67(2), 265–282.

Goleman, D. (1995). *Emotional intelligence*. New York: Bantam Books.

Guernsey, T. F., & Klare, K. (1993). *Special education law*. Durham, NC: Carolina Academic Press.

Hargreaves, A., & Fullan, M. (1998). *What's worth fighting for out there?* New York: Teachers College Press.

Harry, B., Allen, N., & McLaughlin, M. (1995). Communication versus compliance: African-American parents' involvement in special education. *Exceptional Children*, 61, 364–377.

Harry, B., Rueda, R., & Kalyanpur, M. (1999). Cultural reciprocity in sociocultural perspective: Adapting the normalization principle for family collaboration. *Exceptional Children*, 66, 123–136.

Herbert, M. D., & Mould, J. W. (1992). The advocacy role in public child welfare. *Child Welfare*, 70(2), 114–130.

Hines, M. L. (1987). *Don't get mad: Get powerful! A manual for building advocacy skills*. Lansing: Michigan Protection and Advocacy Service. (ERIC Document Reproduction Service No. ED 354683)

Individuals with Disabilities Education Act of 1997, 20 U.S.C. Sec. 1400 et seq.

Individuals with Disabilities Improvement Act, 20 U.S.C. Sec. 1400 et seq.

Kagan, S. L. (1989). The new advocacy in early childhood education. *Teachers College Record*, 90(3), 465–473.

Kalyanpur, M., Harry, B., & Skrtic, T. (2000). Equity and advocacy expectations of culturally diverse families' participation in special education. *International Journal of Disability, Development and Education*, 47(2), 119–136.

Katsiyannis, A., & Ward, T. J. (1992). Parent participation in special education: Compliance issues as reported by parent surveys and state compliance reports. *Remedial and Special Education*, 13(5), 50–55.

League, S., & Ford, L. (1996, March). *Fathers' involvement in their children's special education program*. Paper presented at the annual meeting of the National Association of School Psychologists, Atlanta, GA.

Levine, E. (1999). *Latino families: Getting involved in your children's education*. Cambridge, MA: Harvard Family Research Project.

Lian, M.-G. J., & Aloia, G. F. (1994). Parental responses, roles, and responsibilities. In S. Alper, P. J. Schloss, & C. N. Schloss (Eds.), *Families of students with disabilities: Consultation and advocacy* (pp. 51–93). Boston: Allyn & Bacon.

Lian, M.-G. J., & Fontanez–Phelan, S. M. (2001). Perceptions of Latino parents regarding cultural and linguistic issues and advocacy for children with disabilities. *Journal of the Association for Persons with Severe Handicaps*, 26(3), 189–194.

Lynch, E. W., & Stein, R. C. (1982). Perspectives on parent participation in special education. *Exceptional Education Quarterly*, 3(2), 56–63.

Lynch, E. W., & Stein, R. C. (1987). Parent participation by ethnicity: A comparison of Hispanic, Black, and Anglo families. *Exceptional Children*, 54(2), 105–111.

National Association of School Psychologists. (2000). *Principles for professional ethics*. Bethesda, MD: Author.

Packer, L. E. (2002). *Education advocacy: A self-help tutorial for parents*. Retrieved on November 21, 2003, from http://www.tourettesyndrome.net.

Pappas, G. (1997, March). Forging home–school partnership with Latino families. *LARASA Report*, 1–6.

Pardeck, J. T. (1996). Advocacy and parents of special needs children. *Early Child Development and Care*, 120, 45–53.

Rock, S. L., Geiger, W. L., & Hood, G. (1992). CEC's standards for professional practice in advocacy: Members' attitudes and activities. *Exceptional Children*, 58, 541–547.

Salend, J. S., & Taylor, L. (1993). Working with families: A cross-cultural perspective. *Remedial and Special Education*, 14(25), 32–39.

Schrag, J. A. (1996). *Mediation and other alternative dispute resolution procedures in special education*. Alexandria, VA: Project FORUM, National Association of State Directors of Special Education. (ERIC Document Reproduction Services No. ED 399736)

Simpson, R. L. (1996). *Working with parents and families of exceptional children and youth: Techniques for successful conferencing and collaboration*. Austin, TX: Pro-Ed.

Sontag, J. C., & Schacht, R. (1994). An ethnic comparison of parent participation and information needs in early intervention. *Exceptional Children, 60*(5), 422–433.

Spiegel-McGill, P., Reed, D. J., Konig, C. S., & McGowan, P. (1990). Parent education: Easing the transition to preschool. *Topics in Early Childhood Special Education, 9*(4), 66–77.

Stephens, T. M., & Wolf, J. S. (1980). *Effective skills in parent/teacher conferencing*. Columbus, OH: NCEMMH.

Stoecklin, V. L. (1994). Advocating for young children with disabilities. *Quarterly Resource, 8*(3), 1–35.

Suchey, N., & Huefner, D. S. (1998). The state complaint procedure under the Individuals with Disabilities Education Act. *Exceptional Children, 64*(4), 529–542.

Summers, J. A., Dell-Oliver, C., Turnbull, A. P., Benson, H. A., Santelli, B., Campbell, M., et al. Examining the individualized family service plan process: What are family and practitioner preferences? *Topics in Early Childhood Special Education, 10*, 78–99.

Turnbull, A. P., & Turnbull, H. R. (2001). *Families, professionals, and exceptionality: Collaborating for Empowerment* (4th ed.). Upper Saddle River, NJ: Merrill/Prentice Hall.

Turnbull, H. R., & Turnbull, A. P. (2000). *Free appropriate public education: The law and children with disabilities* (6th ed.). Denver: Love.

Walton, R. E. (1969). *Interpersonal peacemaking: Confrontation and third party consultation*. Reading, MA: Addison-Wesley.

Warger, C., & Burnette, J. (2000). *Five strategies to reduce overrepresentation of culturally and linguistically diverse students in special education* (Report No. ERIC/OSEP Digest E596). Arlington, VA: ERIC Clearinghouse on Disabilities and Gifted Education.

Wright, P., & Wright, P. D. (2002). *From emotions to advocacy: The special education survival guide*. Hartfield, VA: Harbor House Law Press.

Yell, M. L. (1998). *The law and special education*. Upper Saddle River, NJ: Merrill/Prentice Hall.

CHAPTER 9
Educational Support Services to Assist Parents and Families in Designing and Implementing Positive Behavioral Interventions

● ● ● ● ● ● ● ● ● ● ● ● ● ● ● ● ● ● ● ○ ○ ○ ○

In this chapter, you will understand:

- Historic interactions between families of children with behavioral challenges and school personnel and their outcomes for children with behavioral challenges.

- The rationale for the provision of educational support services for families involved in developing and implementing behavioral intervention plans (BIPs).
- The basic process of involving families in both functional behavioral assessment (FBA) and the development of behavioral intervention plans.
- Issues surrounding the educational support services to assist family participation in designing and implementing positive behavioral interventions.
- The benefits of different exemplar programs that provide educational support services to assist families in designing and implementing positive behavioral interventions.

Family Perspective: Jawna and Jake

"I am tired of talking about what's wrong with my kid! Each year we have these meetings and nothing ever changes. This is supposed to be special education. You're supposed to be the experts. Tell me, what are you going to do to help my son?"

Jawna was tired. She had sat through these meetings silently for years, listening to teachers tell her the list of things wrong with her son. It was frustrating. If they knew so much about what was wrong with Jake, why didn't they know how to help him? Jawna wondered if they would ever really understand Jake. They never seemed to mention his love of drawing, his interest in plants and animals. She knew so much more about Jake, but no one ever asked her. Each year they presented a new plan to stop his cursing and fighting. Sometimes it was the same plan they had used a few years ago, but no one except Jawna realized it. The plans never worked and Jake seemed to have fewer and fewer successes at school every year. Jake was smarter than they gave him credit for, she knew that, but her opinion about him didn't seem to matter much here. She could understand why Jake hated school. Jawna hated coming to these meetings just about as much as he hated his classes.

Reflecting on the Family Perspective

1. As a member of the school team, what would you do next?
2. What could have happened prior to this meeting to prevent this painful situation?

HISTORIC INTERACTIONS BETWEEN FAMILIES AND SCHOOL PERSONNEL WHEN DESIGNING AND IMPLEMENTING POSITIVE BEHAVIORAL INTERVENTIONS

Throughout recent history, a variety of classic studies demonstrated the power of family involvement and parent education and training on children's behavior (Berkowitz & Graziano, 1972; Forehand & Atkeson, 1977; Johnson & Katz, 1973; O'Dell, 1974). Although children who demonstrate significant behavioral issues can greatly benefit from the assistance and involvement of their family members with the interdisciplinary school team, families have historically been excluded from planning behavioral interventions (Lubetsky, Mueller, Madden, Walker, & Len, 1995). Unfortunately, the failure to involve families in interventions to address their children's behavioral issues has been another example of the research-to-practice gap. School professionals knew, and research demonstrated, the value of family education and involvement in the development of behavior interventions for children with behavioral challenges, and yet, it did not become the typical classroom practice.

Often, school personnel contacted family members only when a student had received a significant punishment from school personnel (e.g., suspension, expulsion; Karp, 1993; Stevenson & Srebnik, 1996). Since frequent contact was made only during times of crisis, the interaction between school personnel and family members centered around the student's problematic behaviors. Understandably, these negatively interactions were usually neither fulfilling nor helpful for the child, the family, or the school personnel. Over time, family members became increasingly disenchanted with the school system and despaired about the school's ability to help their child. This often led to diminished family participation in behavioral intervention planning. As families pulled out of the school team, school professionals' attitudes about parents and their perceptions of the families' interest in their children's education deteriorated. Thus, the relationship between the school personnel and the family members entered a downward spiral (Karp, 1993; Koyanagi & Gaines, 1993; Stevenson & Srebnik, 1996).

With the reauthorization of IDEA in 1997, improved relationships between school personnel and family members were encouraged as stronger responses to the needs of students with behavioral disorders were required. Although encouraging active participation of families has been a requirement since 1977 when the Education of All Handicapped Children Act (renamed IDEA in 1990) was enacted, the 1997 reauthorization of IDEA included additional content related to both children with behavioral issues and their families. Specific to children with behavioral issues, part of the IDEA 1997 requirement was a functional behavioral assessment (FBA). FBA is a collaborative multistep process that examines the students' behavior in the presence (and absence) of a variety of conditions. These conditions may be present in both school and nonschool (e.g., home, community) environments. IDEA 1997 was the first legislation to refer to FBA and behavior intervention plans (BIPs). The Office of Special Education Programs (OSEP; 2001) defined FBA as

> a systematic process for describing problem behavior, and identifying the environmental factors and surrounding events associated with problem behavior . . . [FBA] is used to a) define the problem behaviors, b) describe the settings under which problem behaviors are and are not likely to be observed, c) identify the function (the why) of the problem behaviors, and d) collect information from direct observation to support these outcomes. (p. 1)

Although experts in the field of behavioral issues argue that FBA and BIP should be used in a proactive manner at any point in program development, IDEA 1997 required completion of these two processes in two specific situations (Yell & Katsiyannis, 2000). The FBA and BIP procedures are required when (a) a student is being considered for an interim alternative educational setting due to drug violations, weapons charges, or danger to self or others or (b) it is the eleventh day of suspension within one school year of a student who has or is suspected of having a behavioral disorder (Fischer, 2003).

FBA also requires information from multiple people who are important in the child's daily life. The need to collect information from a variety of people increased the likelihood that families would be at least consulted regarding the behavioral issues their children demonstrated. The 1997 reauthorization of IDEA provided additional motivation for school professionals to include family members in the collaborative process. These additional motivations are reinforced with the continued FBA requirement in IDEA 2004. Parents must be informed of and invited to any meeting at which their child will be discussed. This change could be the perfect opportunity to involve families throughout all steps of the planning and implementation of positive behavioral interventions (Clark & Fiedler, 2003).

In addition to the requirements related to FBA, there are further expectations for school personnel who are involved with young children and the development of the Individual Family Service Plan (IFSP) as determined by Public Law 99–457. The IFSP must include, as desired by individual families, information regarding major outcomes and specific interventions. Even more strongly stated, PL 99–457 and IDEA 1997 require (when desired and appropriate) topical parent training.

The next section of this chapter will explain the processes of FBA and BIP as well as ways family involvement can enhance these processes. Subsequent sections of this chapter will describe educational supports that school professionals can provide to allow family members the most efficacious involvement in FBA, BIP, and the overall education of their child with behavioral issues.

RATIONALE FOR INCLUDING FAMILY MEMBERS IN DESIGNING AND IMPLEMENTING POSITIVE BEHAVIORAL INTERVENTIONS

This section will focus on the rationale for including family members' input in designing and implementing BIPs beyond what is implied by the process as it was developed. Five reasons for family involvement will be discussed, including (a) benefits of family member knowledge, (b) support for the family, (c) perceptual differences of children's behavior, (d) families as supports for school personnel, and (e) benefits for children.

Benefits of Family Member Knowledge

Parents possess a greater depth and breadth of knowledge about their child than any other team member does. Family members will spend more hours with the child and will interact with the child in more settings than any school professional will (Dunlop, Newton, Fox, Benito, & Vaughn, 2001). Families engage children in a large number of activities on an ongoing basis. It is estimated that children with behavioral challenges may be presented with and offered participation in upward of 150 different social and community activities with their family. Family members interact with their children in typical environments, rich with opportunities to practice skills far beyond those that can be experienced in the classroom. These environments are powerful in developing real-life prosocial skills that a child can use throughout his or her lifetime (Dunst, 2001).

The level at which a child with behavioral problems can be integrated into family routines, community environments, and general education is greatly dependent on the successful collaboration and consistency of behavioral strategies between school personnel and family members (Cordisco & Laus, 1993). In a recent study, when researchers controlled for students' gender, age, race, and family structure, they found that connectedness to family members reduced the prevalence, frequency, and severity of adolescent deviance (Dornbusch, Erickson, Laird, & Wong, 2001). If school personnel can work to enhance, support, and use the familial bonds to reinforce further prosocial activity, students with behavioral issues will be more successful.

Increased family involvement in behavioral assessment and intervention is in the best interests of families, children, and school personnel. Increased family involvement has provided a variety of benefits to intervention planning, including gathering better background information, increasing the families' ability to advocate for their child, and educating family members about behavioral solutions (Lubetsky et al., 1995). Since families have information about prior behavioral issues, previously implemented behavioral interventions, and a more longitudinal perspective on their children's development, family members' accounts can often provide a fuller history of the children than can be attained from school files. When family members are welcomed as fully participating team members, they can work collaboratively with school personnel to be certain that the most important skills and supports are included in their child's educational program. This proactive family involvement, when planned for by the team, is more positively received and easily incorporated than when families must work retroactively to get their ideas and concerns met after school personnel have predetermined a child's program. Families can assist teams in prioritizing the behaviors, skills, and goals that are most important for the student in a variety of nonschool environments.

Support for the Family

Children's behavior problems can have a negative impact on all different areas of family functioning. Problem behaviors may decrease a family's ability to spend time in the community, increase stress, and decrease time that can be spent with siblings or extended family members (Fox, Dunlap, & Philbrick, 1997). Beyond the actual behavioral issues a child presents, the emotional weight of possible behavioral issues creates great stress for family members. Families reported that as significant as their child's actual violent or disruptive behavior was, the fear, worry, and embarrassment associated with both the family members' and the public's view of their child's behavior were worse (Turnbull & Ruef, 1996). Including families in the process of developing BIPs reduces this stress and improves outcomes for students.

Family members reported challenges in all areas of dealing with their child's behavioral needs. Parents often turn to school personnel for up-to-date information about best practice in behavioral interventions. Information requested may regard both the child's behavior and the family's needs. Specifically, parents reported to Turnbull and Ruef (1996) requesting information, assistance, or both regarding (a) problem assessment, (b) developing structure and routines at home, (c) improving communication between the child and other family members, (d) expanding the child's relationships beyond the family circle, (e) increasing the child's positive control and ability to make choices, (f) de-escalating violent or stressful situations, and (g) maintaining a balance of attention given to other family members and to the child with behavioral needs.

Family members of children with autism described school personnel as their main source for information regarding behavioral interventions (Turnbull & Reuf, 1996). Family members may have limited or no access to research regarding behavioral interventions for children with behavioral needs. The research-to-practice gap between family interventions and research can be bridged by school personnel.

Educating the family about the behavioral intervention plans and involving them in the process of development allows families to experience reduced stress as the BIP is implemented in school and home. When parents know the procedure school personnel are following in response to their child's behavioral issues, they can work to react in the same way in nonschool environments. This consistency increases the possible success of BIPs. When the child succeeds, the parents' stress will be reduced as the tenor of school–home communication becomes more positive. Simultaneously, the parents will have positive behavioral tools, as well as a positive response plan, to prevent and react to their child's behavioral issues. This information can reduce stress at home for both the child and his or her parents. Programs that educate parents in proactive and positive behavioral strategies to use with their children who have behavioral issues have been found to reduce negative interactions between family members and the child with disabilities in both the home and community (Cheney, Manning, & Upham, 1997; Cordisco & Laus, 1993). This concept will be further discussed in the section describing exemplary programs. For example, many families of children who are participating in early intervention programs request information regarding skill-training programs to increase their child's prosocial behaviors (Cordisco & Laus, 1993). This provides the team with a broader perspective, which increases the likelihood that instruction at school will improve a child's life in multiple settings (Lubetsky et al., 1995).

Perceptual Differences of Children's Behavior

Families of children with behavioral issues often differ from school personnel in their perception of the type and level of disruptive behavior in which their child engages (Barnhill, Hagiwara, Myles, Simpson, Brick, & Griswold, 2000). Barnhill et al. found that parents perceived their children with Asperger's syndrome to be at risk for a greater number of social and behavioral deficits (e.g., aggression, depression, withdrawal) and to possess a greater number of behavioral and social deficits than the classroom teachers perceived. Although the reasons for the differences in the teachers' and family members' perceptions of the child's behavioral and social deficits are not completely understood, certainly the differences in structure, demands, and social climate of the home and school could be considered likely factors. Children with behavioral issues may be able to perform without incident for a certain length of time, but then need to let go of their continued self-monitoring/control. This release time may occur in either environment, making the child's behavior significantly different per environment. These different perspectives are important when determining a positive behavioral intervention: Because the behavior differs across settings, it will be necessary to look at behavior across settings to develop a fully effective BIP.

Families as Supports for School Personnel

Teachers face a dizzying array of possible interventions for children with behavior issues. The efficacy of these interventions is often unknown, and the recommendations of experts can be contradictory when examined against one another (Simpson, 1998). There is no single intervention that works for all children; therefore, the decision of which intervention to use for a specific child is daunting. Family members with their multiple deep and broad understandings of their child's behavioral patterns can be a great source of assistance in determining the best intervention to use with a student (Simpson, 1998).

To create and maintain daily harmony within the family schedule, it would be expected that family members of children with behavioral challenges will have developed a variety of preemptive strategies to avoid or reduce their child's behavioral problems during family routines. The types of environmental and behavioral adaptations the parents use are necessary to the family because these are used to lessen the impact of the child's behavioral issues on daily family functioning. These preventive measures used by families are a set of proven strategies to help the child in his daily environment. Assuming they are appropriate for school settings, the types of behavioral interventions used by family members in nonschool settings can be strong guides when developing interventions to decrease problem behavior and increase prosocial interactions. For these reasons, the family members are truly the team's experts about the child's behavior across time and context.

Benefits for Children

When families are involved in the team that supports their child, they are empowered and are more likely to follow through and feel responsibility for both home and school goals. Well designed, collaboratively developed BIPs can be implemented in multiple environments. Children whose families and school team have been collaborative and created a supportive environment have greater gains in behavioral and other areas of functioning (Lubetsky et al., 1995). Family members can provide support and continuity in accomplishing educational and behavioral change goals identified by school personnel (League & Ford, 1996). When family members are involved in the development of their child's BIP and the school has provided ongoing educational support, they are more comfortable using the tenets of best practice in behavioral intervention and following the BIP to prevent behavioral issues on the weekends, after school, and in a variety of nonschool settings. This carryover of the BIP can increase its efficacy and the child's generalization of the expectation of prosocial behavior.

Educational services to assist parents and families in designing and implementing positive behavioral interventions can and should occur throughout the processes of FBA and BIP. For example, information and skills related to observing and recording a child's behavior may be most helpful during the early stages of the FBA process, then training should continue with updates as needed throughout the rest of the processes. Conversely, information provision and skill building related to the implementation of a BIP would be most useful later in the process, when the function of the behavior is known. This will allow initial data collection, rather than the changing understanding of the parents, to determine the topography of the child's behavior.

Also, after the target behavior and function are known, the information and skill building can be better targeted to the family supporting that specific area of the child's behavior. The chronology of parent educational supports during the FBA and BIP development processes is described in the next section.

THE PROCESS OF INVOLVING FAMILY MEMBERS IN FBA AND THE DEVELOPMENT OF BIPS

The structured assessment of children's behaviors has a long history in the fields of psychology, medicine, and education. FBA has its historic roots in applied behavior analysis. Skinner (1953) outlined procedures for examining and understanding the function of human behavior. Many of these same procedures, updated and combined by generations of researchers, have developed into the current process of FBA. This process is used to determine the function of students' behavior issues and examine factors that increase or decrease the probability the problem behavior will occur. From this information, the collaborative team can develop a plan to support and teach alternative prosocial behaviors that will replace these behavioral issues. This plan is referred to as a BIP. Although the main content of the FBA and BIP processes is well accepted, there are some minor differences in definition and process, as described by a variety of professionals in the literature (Conroy, Clark, Fox, & Gable, 2000; Fischer, 2003; Nelson, Roberts, Mathur, & Aaroe, 1999). To be certain that both processes are understood, Figure 9.1 presents a graphic demonstration of the processes. Also, they are broken into steps in the next section (Fad, Patton, & Polloway, 1998; Liaupsin, Scott, & Nelson, 2000). After each step of the FBA and BIP is briefly described, plans to encourage family collaboration within each step are described.

Functional Behavioral Assessment (FBA)

Step 1: Collect Historical and Background Data   To begin the process of examining the behavior of a student who exhibits behavioral issues, it is important to have a full understanding of the evolution of this student's behavior. To provide a comprehensive view, there are two main tasks to complete in this step: review of records and completion of interviews.

   Family members can assist in several ways during this step in the FBA process. First, family members have had relationships with this child throughout the period described in the school records. Therefore, they can provide additional information that is missing from the child's files during records review. Second, family members can provide alternative, broader views of the child's history. The family members' views may include information beyond what the school was aware of at the time or may provide a perspective that is influenced by a different attitudinal mind-set. If both the perspectives of the school records and the family recollections are considered, this allows a more informed view of the child. Third, family members can be participants in the interview process. An example of a family interview structure is presented in Communication and Collaboration Tips Box 9.1. Finally, family members can provide their own archival record of the child's history, through pictures, artifacts, scrapbooks, and other familial records.

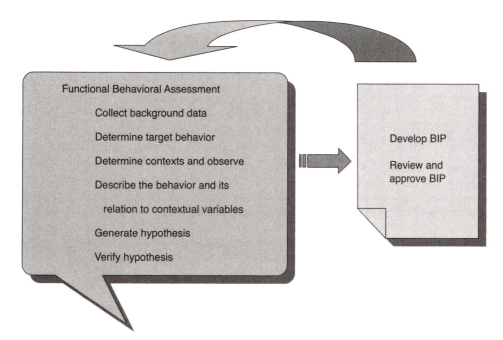

Figure 9.1 *The Process of* FBA *and* BIP.
Source: Content adapted from Liaupsin, C.J., Scott, T.M., & Nelson, C.M. (2000). Functional behavioral assessment: An interactive training module. User's Manual & Facilitator's Guide (Second Edition). Longmont, CO: Sopris West.

For family members to participate in the ways described above, they must have specific information and skills. They must be informed participants in the information-gathering process. For example, family members need information related to their rights and responsibilities as the child's advocate. This information includes (a) awareness of access to records, (b) confidentiality, (c) consent, and (d) voluntary participation in the process. The family members can be more helpful team members if they understand the entire process of FBA and BIP and the goal of each step. Providing specifics related to the family members' roles and the team members' expectations can assist family members in providing the information that will be most useful in the process. One example of an entertaining educational support could be to host a scrapbook night in which families come together with pictures and mementos of the child's history to create a mini-scrapbook that emphasizes the child as a whole person, rather than just a student. Information included in this packet could include the child's likes, dislikes, development, family history, hobbies, and so forth. In this way, the families can organize information that will be useful to the team, share their story with other families, and present their child in a more well-rounded way. This more expansive presentation of the child is important to the family, especially since it is occurring during a time that may be highly stressful due to both the child's problematic behavior and the feeling that all of the school team's energy is focused on the negative behavior of their child.

COMMUNICATION AND COLLABORATION TIPS   **BOX 9.1**

Example of a Family Interview Structure

What are your child's biggest strengths?
What activities, objects, or other items are most motivating to your child?
What behavior is most concerning to you?
Describe how the behavior happens.
How does this behavior affect you? Your family? Your child?
How often does this behavior occur?
How long has this behavior occurred?
When/where does it happen most/least frequently?
What can increase or decrease the probability of the behavior occurring?
What do you do in response to the behavior?
Have you experimented with any ways to decrease the behavior?
Is there anything you know that can prevent the behavior?
Why do you think your child does the behavior?
What would be a goal that would be comfortable for you regarding the intensity or frequency of the behavior?

Step 2: Determine the Target Behavior   During this second step in the process, it is necessary to determine the behavior that will be the focus of observation and intervention. This target behavior should be described in observable, measurable terms, and be of a high level of concern to all members of the team. The level of concern should be determined by the amount it impedes the student's safety, access, participation, and growth in a variety of environments.

While determining the target behavior, the family can be most involved in describing their level of concern related to the child's behaviors in different settings and in relation to the family. To accomplish this task, it will be necessary for the family to possess knowledge related to measurable and observable behaviors. Training related to sharing information about children's behaviors in observable and measurable terms could be extremely helpful at this point in the process.

Step 3: Make Direct Observations   After the team has explored the student's history and defined the target behavior, it is necessary to make direct observation of the student's behavior. A system of measurement should be determined, the contexts in which the student will be observed decided on, and the team members' access to those settings organized. Then, the team members should complete multiple observations.

Parents can be involved during this step of the process in a variety of ways. Family members can assist school professionals in gaining access to nonschool environments or, if direct observations are not possible in these environments, the family members can assist in the provision of alternative means for observation (e.g., videotape, use of Webcams). For some family members it may even be appropriate for them to act as additional observers.

Family members who collaborate during this step of the process must be provided educational supports related to types of data-collection systems and factors related to change in children's behavior.

Step 4: Generate a Hypothesis   A functional hypothesis should contain a description of the target behavior, an explanation of contextual variables that affect behavior, and a description of the function(s) of the behavior. The hypothesis is developed from the combination of the definition of the target behavior (determined in Step 2), an analysis of the data collected during the direct observations (acquired in Step 3), and a comparison of the current behavioral environment to events in the child's history (Steps 1 and 3).

Families can act as collaborative partners during this step by providing information related to long-range behavioral patterns and providing alternative hypotheses of the function of the behavior and contextual variables beyond school settings. To assist the team in this capacity, the family members should receive training related to the interpretation of behavior, the communicative intent of behaviors, and children's individual needs at specific developmental stages.

Step 5: Verify the Hypothesis, Including the Function of the Behavior   To determine if the hypothesis developed by the team is on track and useful, it is necessary to manipulate contextual predictor variables or observe the natural manipulation of these variables. Family members can assist in this process similarly to their participation as described in Step 3: direct observation. The family participation may include (a) procuring access to nonschool environments, (b) providing alternative means for direct observation, and (c) acting as an additional observer. The family can also act as an advocate to be certain that the outcomes of the variable manipulation as they relate to the child's problem behavior are done in an ethical manner that is least problematic for the child. If at any point the cost of manipulating the variables becomes too much of a risk or detriment to the child, the family member can advocate to alter the process.

To participate in this step of the process, family members need an understanding of the interactions among children, contextual factors, and the communicative intent of behavior as well as an understanding of FBA. For family members who have received training about the FBA process, the need to manipulate variables related to the child's behavior and its effect on the development of a BIP will be more understandable.

Behavioral Intervention Plan (BIP)

Step 1: Complete the FBA   This first step of the BIP is the connection to the previous process. Some authors have even stated that the sole purpose of an FBA is to generate a BIP (Fischer, 2003, Jolivette, Barton-Arwood, & Scott, 2000). Other authors connect these two processes (FBA and BIP) as one ongoing process (Fad, Patton, & Polloway, 1998). To reduce redundancy, description of the FBA process and examples of families' involvement in this process have been excluded here. Please review the previous section for details or see Figure 9.1. Table 9.1 provides a quick reference to the FBA and BIP

Table 9.1 FBA and BIP processes in review.

Step	Task	Family involvement opportunities	Educational supports for families
FBA 1: Collect historical and background data	Review records Complete interviews	Provide additional/missing info during records review Provide alternative/broader view to child's history Provide holistic overview of child's history Interview	Awareness of access to records, confidentiality, information, consent and participation in process Understanding of FBA and BIP processes
FBA 2: Determine target behavior	Develop a description of behavior Determine level of concern related to target behavior	Describe level of concern related to behavior in different settings and in relation to the family	Knowledge related to measurable and observable behaviors
FBA 3: Direct observation	Determine contexts Complete multiple observations	Provide access to nonschool environments Provide alternative means for direct observation Act as an additional observer	Awareness of types of data-collection systems Understanding of factors related to changes in behavior
FBA 4: Generate hypothesis	Describe the target behavior, contextual variables that affect behavior, and a function of behavior	Provide information related to long-range behavioral patterns Provide alternative hypotheses of the function of the behavior and contextual variables beyond school settings	Interpretation of behavior Understanding of communicative intent of behaviors Understanding of children's needs

FBA 5: Verify hypothesis	Manipulate contextual predictor variables or observe the natural manipulation of these variables	Provide access to nonschool environments Provide alternative means for direct observation Act as an additional observer	Understanding of interaction between children, contextual factors, and the communicative intent of behavior
BIP 1: Develop BIP	Create a plan that addresses the function of the behavior, provides instruction in replacement behavior, and considers contextual variables	Participate in development of BIP	Awareness of information related to various behavioral approaches and adaptations available to meet children's behavioral needs Parent training regarding behavioral correction and the instruction of prosocial behavior
BIP 2: Review and approve the BIP	Review current data on the child's behavior Determine the efficacy of the BIP Brainstorm changes to make the BIP more beneficial	Ongoing participation in decision making	Parent training related to various behavioral approaches and adaptations available to meet children's behavioral needs

processes, opportunities for family involvement, and educational support services that should be provided to allow maximum participation of family members.

Step 2: Write the BIP   Certainly, many team members view this step as the culmination of the processes, developing a plan to assist the child in improving his behavior. During this step, the team creates a plan that addresses the functions of the behavior, provides instruction in replacement behavior, and considers contextual variables. However, this step is not the final answer. The BIP is a working document that must be continually reevaluated and altered to be the most beneficial support and teaching tool possible for the individual.

Family members' participation in the development of the BIP is critical to its use and subsequent success. Parents can determine if the plan is plausible for a range of environments beyond school. Also, the plan must be practical and nontechnical enough to be implemented by family members and others beyond the school team.

For families to be most involved in this step of the process, they must be offered information related to various behavioral approaches and adaptations available to meet children's behavioral needs. Parent training regarding proactive behavioral supports, behavioral correction, and the instruction of prosocial behavior is also necessary. For families to be strong advocates for the most efficacious methods of behavioral intervention to be developed, they must also have access to currently accepted best practice in the field of behavioral intervention as well as new knowledge in the field (Fad, Patton, & Polloway, 1998).

Step 3: Review and Approve the BIP   The BIP itself becomes an ongoing process that must be continually revisited and updated to maintain its effectiveness as a tool for behavioral change. The family members must have access to the process of ongoing participation in decision making. Ongoing access to information related to various behavioral approaches and adaptations available to meet children's behavioral needs must also be available to family members throughout the process.

Table 9.1 provides a quick reference to the FBA and BIP processes, opportunities for family involvement, and educational support services that should be provided to allow maximum participation of family members.

PROVIDING EDUCATIONAL SUPPORT SERVICES TO ENHANCE FAMILY PARTICIPATION IN DEVELOPING POSITIVE BEHAVIORAL INTERVENTIONS

Cohesive Support Services

For students with behavioral challenges, IEP team members from the school may include the student, student's family members, general education teacher, special education teacher, speech and language therapist, child psychiatrist, or psychiatric social worker. Additionally, team membership may extend beyond school personnel to include health care providers, community counselors, and social services personnel (Lubetsky et al., 1995). Including community services in students' teams increases student support and provides greater knowledge and perspective. In the best-case example, these supports combine to provide wraparound support services. For example, Community Learning Centers are a set of federally supported, nationally recognized programs that provide care for at-risk children before and after school and facilitate access to county and city social services, school-based related services, community service organizations, and educational programs for both the children and their family members. Unfortunately, many school communities are not yet fully organized to provide these seamless services. Therefore, coordination of services is also critical, as the gaps or maze of systems may increase a family's stress (refer to chapter 5, where this will be discussed in detail). Families need assistance maneuvering through the complex system of support services to access those supports that will best meet their needs.

Professional Preparation for Offering Educational Support Services

School professionals have a responsibility to be prepared to collaborate with family members as partners. To prepare for this responsibility, school professionals should assess and further develop their collaborative skills. To act as a knowledgeable resource for families, school professionals should keep abreast of research and accepted best practice in the field, be aware of local resources, and develop a rapport with community supports for families and children. Even if the entire system is not ready to provide wraparound integrated services, service providers in and beyond the school can do a lot to provide greater knowledge of and accessibility to available services (Simpson & Carter, 1993).

Considerations for Providing Educational Support Services

When setting up the meeting, determine an interaction space that will be comfortable for all participants, not the school board room. Provide an agenda prior to the event. Include a list of team members invited along with the agenda. Be certain to have refreshments.

During the meeting, avoid jargon. If specific technical terms or programs will be discussed, include descriptions of these prior to the meeting, possibly with the agenda, and during meeting conversation as it becomes necessary. Check frequently for understanding. Provide opportunities for all members to make contributions. Determine and adhere to time limits. If additional meetings are needed, plan the next meeting at the end of the original meeting. Provide ground rules for each meeting. See Communication and Collaboration Tips Box 9.2 for an example set of ground rules. After the meeting, send out a set of minutes summarizing the meeting discussion and an action plan.

COMMUNICATION AND COLLABORATION TIPS   **BOX 9.2**

Team Meeting Rules

- ❏ Maintain confidentiality
- ❏ Use plain language
- ❏ Respect others' opinions
- ❏ Agree that it is okay to disagree
- ❏ Maintain a blame-free zone

Assessing Families' Needs and Readiness for Educational Support Services

The type and amount of educational support needed or desired by families whose children present challenging behavior cannot be predetermined. The services offered by the school must be individualized, based on the families' components, including values, goals, preferences, resources, routines, traditions, and activity patterns (Fox, Dunlap, & Philbrick, 1997; Simpson & Carter, 1993). These components are greatly determined by the family's ethnic, cultural, and religious beliefs. There is no specific set of components that exactly align with a culture or ethnicity, but the components and the family's background that informs them must be recognized and respected by all team members for the collaboration to be successful (Lubetsky et al., 1995). Time must be spent developing relationships. Just as the student's interventions cannot be predetermined, neither can the role or relationship between families and schools be assumed.

Family members may have a range of reactions to working with a team regarding their child's behavioral issues. Guilt, embarrassment, frustration, and pain are common as parents deal with the challenges brought on by their child's behavior. It is necessary for the team to be sensitive to and assist the family with these reactions or educational support may not be successful. The educational support must be offered as families and children are ready. The conversations regarding support development should describe the issues in a problem-solving mode and remain blame-free (Blechman, 1985).

Family members can receive information in a variety of ways. The way educational supports are provided depends on both the type of information needed and the family members' preferences. Educational supports can be delivered in three main formats: directive, interactive, or access. Directive is a more traditional in-service model in which an expert provides topical information, usually in a lecture format, to a group of family members. This method is most often used when providing background, introductory, or general knowledge about a topic. This method of delivery results in low participation by audience members and poor maintenance of information. Interactive presentations often are provided for small groups of family members or a student-based team. Frequently the topics are related to developing new skills. In this method of presentation there is a high expectation of audience participation. This method may be intimidating for some family members who have not yet become comfortable sharing their experiences with a group but could also lead to greater relationship development between

Table 9.2   Methods for educational support.

	Directive	Interactive	Access
Delivery mode	Expert as teacher	Collaborative sharing and practice	Library and referrals
Group size	Large group	Small group or team	Individual or family
Purpose	Introductory general knowledge	Skill development	Info beyond team ability
Differences	Family can remain fairly anonymous Low audience participation expected Not individualized Poor information maintenance	High expectation of audience participation Relationship building More likely to maintain skill	Unguided Anonymous

attendees. Finally, providing access to information is also an educational support service model. This is often the provision of access to a set of information, books, videos, other media, and referrals to community agencies related to family issues and children with behavioral issues. The information is often received apart from the team members. This method is generally unguided, with family members self-selecting the information they wish to access. This method may be helpful for families who are not interested in sharing a group experience but wish to gain some background knowledge. It can be problematic if the parents are uncertain what information will be beneficial, and therefore underutilize this resource. Table 9.2 provides a comparison of the three methods.

The next two sections of this chapter will provide information to prepare school professionals and team members for interactions during educational support services.

Attitudinal Approaches Conducive to Providing Educational Support Services

Parents report one of the biggest emotional supports is the hopefulness of others (Turnbull & Ruef, 1996). Not all teachers' roles are complex and energy intensive. Being positive and demonstrating care toward the child can be an immense energizer for family members during stressful times. One of the school personnel's roles is to prevent team interactions from being reduced to a remembrance of the child's past problems. This tendency to dwell on the child's past behavioral issues is a frequent pitfall for student-centered teams when proceeding through the FBA and BIP processes. Although the FBA does center on the conditions under which the problem behavior occurs, the interactions of the team members with each other as well as their interactions with both the child and the family must not deteriorate to such a single-minded focus. Rather, the team meetings should be structured around the entire child and, on entering the BIP process, should center on what strategies work to assist the child and build on the successes. School personnel should accentuate the progress the student has made as well as the initiative of family members and school personnel to problem solve and support the student with behavioral issues.

Emotional support and information sharing between school personnel and family members should not be misconstrued as therapy. Some school professionals have been remiss in their interactions when they neglect the affective side of the relationship with families, confusing such support for therapy services (Koyanagi & Gaines, 1993; Quinn & McDougal, 1998; Stevenson & Srebnik, 1996). Collaborative problem solving, development of collaborative relationships, information sharing, and educating parents are educational services. On the other hand, therapy is limited to personnel who possess mental health training credentials, is characterized by sharing of intimate information, and requires greater involvement in the dynamics of the family (Fine & Henry, 1989). The presence of community agencies connected with the school team can provide further assistance when supports in a school are well coordinated. Providing families access to support groups can also further assist families. Connecting parents with other parents who share their hopes, fears, and visions can be a powerful support (Turnbull & Ruef, 1996).

Preparing Families to Share Information

As discussed previously in this chapter, information sharing between school professionals and family members of children with disabilities can be mutually beneficial. Parents need easy access to information about behavioral interventions, strategies for improving the overall interactions between their child with behavioral issues and other family members, connections to local resources, and a variety of individually determined topics (Simpson & Carter, 1993). Conversely, school personnel need information about the child's life outside of school, behavioral patterns that have developed over time, history of past school performance, family and child goals, previous success of behavioral interventions, and family's cultural and individual values. All of this information can greatly affect the quality of the relationship between school personnel and families and, most importantly, provide effective supports and growth for the child. Prior to this informational exchange, there is an initial step that is critical for many families who have not previously experienced a true collaborative relationship with school personnel.

While developing relationships with families, it is critical to remember that they have heard negative information from professionals about their child on innumerable occasions (Dunst, 2001). In developing good relationships with families as well as developing successful BIPs, we need to recognize the positive image of the child. Parents may feel intimidated or overwhelmed when entering the collaborative educational team. Information and support in a variety of forms will help them to become more comfortable in this role. The families may need resources, information, and supports to become empowered advocates for their children (Simpson & Carter, 1993). Family empowerment for educational advocacy was discussed in depth in chapter 8.

Types and Examples of Educational Support Services Provided in Designing and Implementing BIPs

Common types of educational support services coordinated by school personnel include (a) sharing ideas and brainstorming solutions and coping techniques, (b) long-range personal futures planning, (c) family education in behavioral techniques, and (d) modeling and coaching of intervention techniques (Fox, Dunlap, & Philbrick, 1997).

Sharing ideas about behavioral issues, formulating proactive solutions to support the child's prosocial behavior, determining strategies to respond to problem behavior, and developing plans to teach prosocial behavior are at the heart of the FBA and BIP processes. This type of information sharing can happen informally between school personnel and family members during the course of a school day (e.g., when a parent drops a child off at school) or may occur as a highly planned and structured team meeting. Even if it is part of a planned event, the interaction can still remain family-friendly.

Long-range personal futures planning has been used to develop both goals for a child's educational career as well as team consensus regarding goals and team relationships. Given the right questions, family members can assist in providing a well-rounded, complete view of the child. Questions regarding the child's skills, interests, strengths, and hopes for the future can start to form this positive vision. From this positive complete vision, an intervention designed to reach the child's goals, rather than an intervention strictly focused on the abdication of negatively viewed behaviors, (Dunst, 2001).

School professionals also report experiencing more positive interactions with families and believe that their work is respected and understood better after such an event.

Children demonstrate behavioral problems for a wide range of reasons. For example, problematic behaviors can be understood as a response or communicative attempt at dealing with a social situation. The child's behavior may change if communication can be positively effected (Fox, Dunlap, & Philbrick, 1997). After determining the function of a child's behavior, it can often be effective to provide family education regarding behavioral techniques. This can range from simple practice sessions regarding increasing positive interactions between parents and children to a complex system of crisis avoidance and management. Family education efforts often focus on teaching parents behavior management strategies to implement with their children at home and in the community. Some programs are lecture and discussion based whereas others include "practice sessions" in which parents model certain behavioral strategies. During the practice sessions, parents receive critique from peers and the course leaders. Examples of the behavioral strategies include specific positive reinforcement of prosocial behavior and planned ignoring of minor misbehavior (Cordisco & Laus, 1993). Family members need this type of information not only to improve their child's behavior through the use of these techniques, but also to act as advocates who are able to scrutinize current educational and behavioral approaches used by the team.

Often, when a team determines a specific behavioral technique to be beneficial for a child, it is advantageous to have both the family members and school professionals receive training on this intervention technique. This type of educational support service should occur after the FBA has been completed so it is easier for all team members to determine if the technique will be useful (and worth the training time) to use with a specific student, based on the function of the behavior, the child's previous behavioral patterns, and the child's current life circumstance. The next section of this chapter will provide examples of educational support services.

EXAMPLES OF EDUCATIONAL SUPPORT SERVICES

Recently, there has been an increase in model programs to unite families, school personnel, and community supports in assisting students with their behavioral needs. In the best situation, service providers are both school and community based, the child's needs are explored, and supports and behavioral interventions are collaboratively negotiated; thus, all groups benefit (Lubetsky et al., 1995). In this section, a variety of different types of programs that include family members in the design and implementation of behavioral interventions for their children will be presented. None of these programs will be successful in *all* settings or for *every* child. It is critical that school personnel and families work together to develop a system that will work for them. The example programs in this section are to be used to inform practice, not dictate it.

In the classroom, school personnel can increase the modeling and demonstration of prosocial behavior by inviting moral mentors into the classroom (Honig & Wittmer, 1996). These individuals may be students' relatives or community members who demonstrate caring, support, volunteerism, inspiration, and generosity toward others. Movies or other forms of media used in the classroom should represent positive social and behavioral models as well as a diverse cast (Honig & Wittmer, 1996). Families should be provided with information regarding school efforts to include this programming in the school day. A parent newsletter and the school's family resource library are excellent places to provide information for parents regarding understanding child development, supporting children with challenging behavior, and teaching prosocial behavior.

It is often said that the best instruction parents provide for prosocial behavior is the way they model interactions in their children's presence. This can also be said for school personnel. To develop positive relationships with children and help develop prosocial behavior in students, school personnel must model empathic behavior when working with their students and their students' families.

A model program to support families of young children with severe behavioral issues was implemented by Fox, Dunlop, and Philbrick (1997). The program consisted of three phases: assessment, focused intervention, and follow-up. During assessment, a school facilitator assessed the family's needs and the child's behavioral issues and then conducted a futures plan. The intervention was intensive. The intervention phase included support from a variety of sources, including the community, local agencies, and familial assistance. During this phase, focusing on the goals determined in the planning session was paramount. Finally, the intervention was concluded with long-term follow-up. This program maintains the integrity of the FBA and the development of the BIP yet presents itself in a family-friendly manner and embraces long-term planning and relationships.

Parent skill training is best implemented when families and school personnel work together to determine the most important goals for the child, outcomes for the family, and appropriate methods for attaining these goals and outcomes (Cordisco & Laus, 1993). Training activities should build on skills family members already possess. The role of training is to assist the family in supporting the child's attainment of his or her goals. These desired goals, outcomes, and methods are best determined by interacting with the family and asking focused but informal questions. For example, a practitioner might inquire, "What changes would you want to see for your child as a result of our program?" "Are there specific places or activities that are most difficult for your child?" After the team has a strong understanding of the family-identified concerns, it should begin to develop an understanding of familial beliefs about parenting, family values, and current behavioral methods used by family members. This information, for younger children, is most often determined through observation, with follow-up conversations. For older children, it may be ascertained by questions within the same conversation that determined the family's concerns. Family concerns can and should be integral to the FBA. If appropriate, skills training then becomes part of the support plan. When all team members have duties or responsibilites to change their interactions and support to meet the direction of the BIP, family members are not singled out. Providing skills training for families at this point is also most expedient. Trainers are able to provide more specific information and practice that directly relate to the child's and family's needs. In contrast, generic training could be a hit or a miss when trying to target the skills-training needs.

At the University of South Florida, a group of researchers examining positive behavioral supports applied a participatory action research model to the development and implementation of interventions to assist children with significant problem behavior (Carr, 1997). In this project, the family was central in the assessment process. They were viewed as equal collaborators with the school staff and researchers. The family and staff completed ecological inventories collaboratively across all environments that the children utilized. The family and school staff implemented and altered the interventions as appropriate so that the child had the same supports and reactions across all settings. The outcomes of the study were measured in the amount of adult support required and lifestyle changes for both the child and the family. The children were successful in more environments than they were previously, required less assistance from adults, and had greater numbers of positive peer interactions.

Filial therapy provides direct instruction to parents while they interact with their children in a play setting (Montgomery, 1999). The parents are taught a variety of behavioral strategies, including proactive behavioral supports, positive strategies to react to problematic behavior, and ways to track their child's behavioral progress. Although the program is designed as an educational support, it has been found to reduce the parents' stress and increase their acceptance of their child (Montgomery, 1999). This type of intervention could be part of the BIP.

Education for parents should cover four areas: information sharing, skill building, improving self-awareness, and problem solving. Information sharing presents factual and conceptual information about behavioral interventions. Skill building is necessary to increase the probability that the information shared will generalize into the parents' routine with their family. Skill-building activities include role playing, modeling, and behavioral rehearsals to teach specific behavioral techniques. During self-awareness, family members develop specific goals for themselves and their interactions with their children with behavioral issues. Problem solving provides time for family members to develop a plan to incorporate these newly learned skills and meet their goals. This step will break down the changes to be made into subskills that family members view as accomplishable (Fine & Henry, 1989).

School personnel can demonstrate appropriate models of behavioral interventions while family members observe during school and meetings. Parents also can learn through positive reinforcement of their skills during these times (Blechman, 1985).

A school- or community-based child care referral system can be powerful in improving the social competence of all children, including those with behavioral issues. Honig and Wittmer (1996) found that children in high-quality child care were better able to cope in social situations, to interpret social cues from peers, and to maintain prosocial behavior during transition than were those from low-quality child care situations. Children with behavioral issues often end up in lower quality child care regardless of SES, specifically as a result of their behavioral efforts, thereby creating a vicious cycle. When students with behavioral disorders were placed in high-quality child care, there were significant improvements in their prosocial behavior (Honig & Wittmer, 1996). Access to information about high-quality community resources can be useful in providing families with greater options to find supportive environments for their child beyond the school.

A Special Note About Out-of-Home Treatment Programs

There has been a dramatic increase in the number of alternative residential and wildlife-based programs for children who are at risk or have behavioral disorders. Although these programs have had success changing behavior during the program, many programs lack the ability to instill behavioral change that can generalize back to the home environments (Pommier & Witt, 1995). Family member education during and follow-up after the child's participation in the alternative residential and wilderness-based programs have resulted in higher rates of long-range behavioral success for their participants. Unfortunately, the planned transition from the program back to home and school is highly variable. Some programs have defined procedures and support structures for follow-up, family education, and child support; others do not.

Jawna and Jake Revisited

Jawna's son Jake had a team that was stuck in a negative mind-set about the student. They were unable to break out of their conventional approach to children with behavioral disabilities and view Jake as a whole person. Greatly frustrated, Jawna met with an advocate and a representative from social services. These professionals had a different view of developing plans to meet Jake's needs. The social worker and advocate met several times with Jawna and Jake. They observed Jake's behaviors, noted his interests and motivations, and talked to Jawna about her most significant concerns. Then, the advocate met with Jake's teacher. The meeting went well. The teacher was so overwhelmed by the amount of time that had been spent planning for Jake, without result, that she was ready to try anything. Together, with the information collected from Jake and Jawna, they developed a BIP that would meet the needs underlying Jake's behavior; accentuate his talents and abilities; and be successful in home, school, and community settings.

Supports from school personnel and those from social services became collaborative, and the bridge between home and school strengthened. Communication between school personnel and Jawna was structured to address both positive and negative issues. Over time, the teacher began to see Jake as a student rather than a problem. Jake started to realize that school could be something other than the horrific experience it had been. Jawna and Jake still struggle with his behavioral issues, but now there are some solutions to try and supports to lean on as Jake grows and becomes more in control of his life.

SUMMARY STATEMENTS

- Family members possess information and access to teachable moments that are crucial in addressing behavioral challenges.
- The design of positive behavioral interventions must meet the child's needs and be feasible considering the context. The implementation of a strong, individualized, and proactive intervention plan improves students' and family members' social and emotional well-being.
- Although school personnel have not historically included family members in the process of designing and implementing positive behavioral interventions, there are tools, legislation, exemplar programs, and research that support a high level of family member input throughout this planning.

QUESTIONS FOR DISCUSSION

1. What has been the previous relationship between school personnel and families of children who require behavioral supports?
2. Why should school personnel involve family members in the development of BIPs?
3. What is the process of involving families in both the FBA and the development of BIPs?

RESOURCES FOR EDUCATIONAL SUPPORT SERVICES TO ASSIST IN DESIGNING AND IMPLEMENTING BIPs

- **Family Village School**
  http://www.familyvillage.wisc.edu/education/pbs.html
  This Web site provides an extensive list of links to sites for family members regarding collaboration with schools to develop positive behavior support plans.

- **Positive Behavioral Supports: Information for Educators**
  http://www.naspcenter.org/factsheets/pbs fs.html
  This Web site provides information for family members to be active as school personnel work with them to develop positive behavior support plans.

- **Early Childhood Behavior Project**
  http://ici2.umn.edu/preschoolbehavior/
  This Web site provides information for family members and school personnel to collaborate while developing positive behavior support plans specifically for young children.

- Lucyshyn, J. M., Dunlap, G., & Albin, R. W. (1992). *Families and positive behavior supports: Addressing problem behavior in family contexts.* Baltimore, MD: Brookes.

REFLECTION ACTIVITIES

1. Create an introductory guidebook of the FBA and BIP processes to assist families beginning this collaborative process as members of their child's school team.

2. Develop a set of materials describing resources available for families of children with emotional and behavioral disorders in the community.

3. Define three newly researched behavior intervention strategies. Can you fully describe the strategy, determine the situation in which it can be used, and state the reason it is currently accepted practice? Are you able to describe it in plain English, without the use of jargon?

REFERENCES

Barnhill, G. P., Hagiwara, T., Myles, B., Simpson, R. L., Brick, M. L., & Griswold, D. E. (2000). Parent, teacher, and self-report of problem and adaptive behaviors in children and adolescents with Asperger syndrome. *Diagnostique*, 25(2), 147–167.

Berkowitz, D. P., & Graziano, A. M. (1972). Training parents as behavior therapists: A review. *Behaviour Research and Therapy*, 10, 297–317.

Blechman, E. A. (1985). *Solving child behavior problems at home and at school.* Champaign, IL: Research Press.

Carr, E. (1997). The evolution of applied behavior analysis into positive behavior support. *The Journal of the Association for Persons with Severe Handicaps*, 22(4), 208–209.

Cheney, D., Manning, B., & Upham, D. (1997). Project DESTINY: Engaging families of students with emotional and behavioral disabilities. *Teaching Exceptional Children* 30(1), 24–29.

Clark, D., & Fiedler, C. R. (2003). Building family-school relationships during the assessment and intervention process. In M.J. Breen & C. R. Fiedler (Eds.), *Behavioral approach to assessment of youth with*

emotional/behavioral disorders: A handbook for school-based practitioners (pp. 561–586). Austin, TX: Pro-Ed.

Conroy, M. A., Clark, D., Fox, J. J., & Gable, R. A. (2000). Building competence in FBA: Are we headed in the right direction? *Preventing School Failure* 44(4), 169–173.

Cordisco, L. K., & Laus, M. K. (1993). Individualized training in behavioral strategies for parents of preschool children with disabilities. *Teaching Exceptional Children*, 25(2), 43–47.

Dornbusch, S. M., Erickson, K. G., Laird, J., & Wong, C. A. (2001). The relation of family and school attachment to adolescent deviance in diverse groups and communities. *Journal of Adolescent Research*, 16(4), 396–422.

Dunlap, G., Newton, J. S., Fox, L., Benito, N., & Vaughn, B. (2001). Family involvement in functional assessment and positive behavior support. *Focus on Autism & Other Developmental Disabilities*, 16(4), 215–221.

Dunst, C. J., Bruder, M. B., Trivette, C. M., Hamby, D., Raab, M., & McLean, M. (2001). Characteristics and consequences of everyday natural learning opportunities. *Topics in Early Childhood Special Education* 21(2), 68–92.

Education of the Handicapped Act Amendments of 1986. Public Law No 99-457100 stat. 1145.

Fad, K. M., Patton, J. R., & Polloway, E. A. (1998). *Behavioral intervention planning: Completing a functional behavioral assessment and developing a behavioral intervention plan*. Austin, TX: Pro-Ed.

Fine, M., & Henry, S. (1989). Professional issues in parent education. In M. J. Fine (Ed.), *The second handbook on parent education* (pp. 7–20). San Diego: Academic Press.

Fischer, T. A. (2003). Conducting functional behavioral assessment and designing behavior intervention plans for youth with emotional/behavior disorders. In M.J. Breen & C. R. Fiedler (Eds.), *Behavioral approach to assessment of youth with emotional/behavioral disorders: A handbook for school-based practitioners* (pp. 73–122). Austin, TX: Pro-Ed.

Forehand, R., & Atkeson, B. M. (1977). Generality of treatment effects with parents as therapists: A review of assessment and implementation procedures. *Behavior Therapy*, 8, 575–593.

Fox, L., Dunlap, G., & Philbrick, L. A. (1997). Providing individual supports to young children with autism and their families. *Journal of Early Intervention*, 21(1), 1–14.

Honig, A. S., & Wittmer, D. S. (1996). Helping children become more prosocial: Ideas for classrooms, families, schools, and communities. *The National Association for the Education of Young Children*, 51(2), 62–70.

Johnson, C. A., & Katz, R. C. (1973). Using parents as change agents for their children: A review. *Journal of Child Psychology and Psychiatry*, 14, 181–200.

Jolivette, K., Barton-Arwood, S., & Scott, T. M. (2000). Functional behavioral assessment as a collaborative process among professionals. *Education and Treatment of Children* 23(3), 298–313.

Karp, N. (1993). Collaboration with families: From myth to reality. *Journal of Emotional and Behavioral Problems* 1(4), 21–23.

Koyangi, C., & Gaines, S. (1993). *All systems failure: An examination of the results of neglecting the needs of children with serious emotional disturbance: A guide for Advocates*. National Mental Health Association, Alexandria, VA.

League, S. E., & Ford, L. (1996, March). *Fathers' involvement in their children's special education program*. Paper presented at the Annual Meeting of the National Association of School Psychologists, Atlanta, GA.

Liaupsin, C. J., Scott, T. M., & Nelson, C. M. (2000). Functional behavioral assessment: An interactive training module. *User's Manual & Facilitator's Guide* (Second Edition). Longmont, CO: Sopris West.

Lubetsky, M. J., Mueller, L., Madden, K., Walker, R., & Len, D. (1995). Family-centered/interdisciplinary team approach to working with families of children who have mental retardation. *Mental Retardation*, 33(4), 251–256.

Montgomery, M. J. (1999). *Building bridges with parents: Tools and techniques for counselors*. Thousand Oaks, CA: Corwin Press.

Nelson, J. R., Roberts, M. L., Rutherford, R. B., Mathur, S. R., & Aaroe, L. A. (1999). A statewide survey of special education administrators and school psychologists regarding functional behavioral assessment. *Education and Treatment of Children* 22(3), 267–279.

O'Dell, S. (1974). Training parents in behavior modification: A review. *Psychological Bulletin*, 81, 418–433.

Office of Special Education Programs (OSEP). (2001). *Improving family involvement in special education*. Reston, VA. (ERIC Document Reproduction Service No. ED 457625)

Pommier, J. H., & Witt, P. A. (1995). Evaluation of an outward bound school plus family training for the juvenile status offender. *Therapeutic Recreation Journal*, 29(2), 86–103.

Simpson, R. L. (1998). Behavior modification for children and youth with exceptionalities: Application of best practice methods. *Intervention in School and Clinic*, 33(4), 219–226.

Simpson, R. L., & Carter, Jr., W. J. (1993). Comprehensive, inexpensive, and convenient services for parents and families of students with behavior disorders. *Preventing School Failure*, 37(2), 21–25.

Skinner, B. F. (1953). *Science and human behavior*. New York: Macmillan.

Stevenson, J., & Srebnik, D. (1996, Feb. 26–28). *Congruence between parent-professional ratings of level of functioning: Relationships to collaboration and satisfaction*. Paper presented at A system of care for children's mental health: Expanding the research base proceedings of the 9th annual research conference, Tampa, FL. Document available through ERIC ED 460 493 EC306 869.

Turnbull, A. P., & Ruef, M. (1996). Family perspectives on problem behavior. *Mental Retardation*, 34(5), 280–293.

Yell, M. L., & Katsiyannis, A. (2000). Functional Behavioral Assessment and IDEA '97: Legal and practice considerations. *Preventing School Failure* 44(4), 158–162.

CHAPTER 10
Educational Support Services for Designing and Implementing Academic Intervention Programs

●●●●●●●●●●●●●●●●●●●●●●●●●●●○○○○○

In this chapter, you will understand:

- Reasons educators should invite family members to participate in a child's academic program.

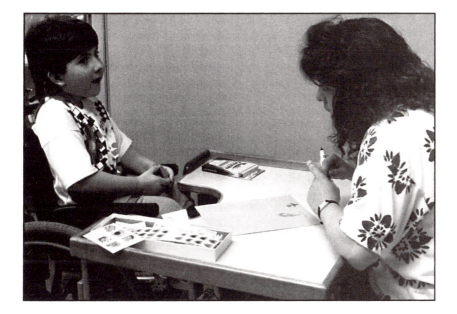

- Factors affecting family members' level of participation in a child's academic program.
- The process of empowering parents to be involved in academic decision making and daily academic activities.
- Reasons why parents don't tutor/teach their child at home.
- Why parent-as-tutor/teacher programs have often failed.
- Practices that allow for positive experiences for families when parents act as tutors.
- Examples of well-planned and implemented parent-as-tutor programs.

Family Perspective: Expectations of Tomas

"I can just see Tomas falling farther behind. He has all but given up reading when he is in the large group; when I hear him read to his peer buddy, it is painful even for me to listen to. He's never going to make it out of high school with a regular diploma, never mind college," said Jennifer, a fourth-grade general education teacher, during a meeting with her coteacher, Barb.

"I have been working with him every day on his reading. There's only so much we can do in the day. We aren't miracle workers. I send home all of his worksheets, the book club slips never get signed, and I keep telling his parents that he'll never get anywhere in his academics if they don't help him at home," replies Barb, Tomas's special education teacher.

Jennifer attempts to explain the parents' lack of interest in their son's reading: "Well Barb, what can you expect? His parents are never around, they've got all those kids in the house, and have you ever tried to read his absence excuse notes? I can't imagine how either of his folks got out of high school. Let's face it, Tomas needs more help than we can give him. He's going to end up working in the mill just like his parents."

Reflecting on the Family Perspective

1. What are the current barriers to collaboration between Tomas's family and his school team?

2. If you were a member of this team, what would you do to improve this situation?

These two teachers were having a common reaction to poor teaming between families and schools—frustration. However, the pain they saw Tomas experience as well as their own frustration made it impossible for them to see how they were contributing to Tomas's failure and his family's lack of involvement. This conversation clearly demonstrates that there are several weaknesses in Barb's and Jennifer's ability to work with families regarding academic decision making and involvement in daily academic activities that have not been addressed. Barb and Jennifer have certain values that may or may not reflect the parents' values. First, they communicate negative attitudes toward the size of Tomas's family and the jobs that his parents hold to provide for their family. Attitudinally, Barb and Jennifer view Tomas's parents' academic abilities through the deficit model, speaking only of what they perceive them to be unable to do. They are unaware or have flagrant disregard for his parents' abilities, his parents' interest in their own learning, and his parents' concern for their children's learning. These two teachers also make assumptions about the family's literary abilities based on incomplete information. Imagine if the literacy skills of each one of us were judged by an excuse note dashed off during the flurry of a busy family's hurried morning routine. In addition to their negative attitudes, Barb and Jennifer are using practices to increase Tomas's family involvement in academic activities that are known to have a low success rate.

Alternatively, the conversation between the teachers demonstrates that they possess several values that can help to increase Tomas's academic success and engage his parents in a collaborative partnership to maintain this academic success. First, Barb and Jennifer clearly value literacy. This is an area of academic skill that has consistently been linked to overall academic success, higher student motivation, and greater social acceptance (Cairney & Munsie, 1993; Douville, 2000; Lancy & Bergin, 1992). Second, there is a sense that what happens at home can have a strong impact on a child's ability to perform in school. Research and practical knowledge have demonstrated this fact over the last few decades. Family involvement in homework can be an effective tool to increase students' success ("Family Member Collaboration to Improve Academic Outcomes," 2001).

It is necessary for Barb and Jennifer to examine their attitudes and practices, seek information, and alter their teaching behavior based on this self-reflection and learning. If the coteachers can accomplish this change, Tomas has a much greater chance of academic success and his parents also have a greater chance at seeing school personnel as helpful and understanding their needs.

REASONS TO INVOLVE FAMILY MEMBERS IN THEIR CHILD'S ACADEMIC LIFE

Family members are the first teachers in a child's life (Al-Hassan & Gardner, 2002). Family members and children interact at an intimate level, often individually with each child. This level of individual attention is not possible in a class with 30 students. Family members have a long-term investment in, and spend a greater amount of time with, their children. When family members expend time and energy on academic endeavors, the value of academic pursuits is demonstrated to the children. Family members play a strong role in the success of students with disabilities in academic areas in general and homework specifically (Jenson & Sheridan, 1994). As compared to parents' discussions with children about the importance of education, their actions related to learning are even stronger determinants of their children's values related to education. Involving family members in academic endeavors that relate to school activities increases students' emotional and social adjustment in school environments (Johnson & Jason, 1994). Beyond their attitudes and modeling of the importance of education, there are practical implications that suggest family member involvement is critical to student learning.

Many children with disabilities have difficulty generalizing new skills and information from school to other environments (e.g., community, home). Family members can act as a catalyst to improve generalization of academics to alternate environments. They can provide time in alternative settings to practice concepts learned in school. These opportunities for generalization may be as formal as at-home tutoring or as informal as reading a story at bedtime. Children with disabilities also have difficulties applying information they perceive as school information or academic knowledge to experiences in their daily life. Again, parents can act as a catalyst to this application. Family members can integrate academic concepts into many daily routines, including setting the dinner table, shopping, cooking, planting a garden, or reading directions. As children notice that the academic gains they make in school improve their abilities to participate in environments outside of school, they are more motivated to be engaged during academic times in school. When family members provide structure and model study skills at home, the children will integrate these positive work habits. Children who have a high level of academic support from family members experience greater independence and success in academic endeavors as they advance through their educational career (Johnson & Jason, 1994).

EMPOWERING FAMILY MEMBER INVOLVEMENT IN CHILDREN'S EDUCATION

Whether family members decide to provide structured additional academic opportunities at home or they choose to spend their energies pursuing other familial activities, there are several ways that school teams are responsible for providing information about academic progress and determination of priority academic goals. In chapter 8, parental involvement in the Individualized Education Plan (IEP) process was discussed in great detail. However, several points related to academic goal setting, program development, and implementation are relevant to this discussion. Using accessible language rather than educational jargon when writing students' current level of educational performance and academic goals is a necessary first step. Some districts require that the IEP be written using terminology specific to the curricular benchmarks or published curriculum. This practice can distance family members during the discussion of academic progress of their child, as family members feel they lack either the necessary context or inside information to be a participant in the discussion. Accessible language in all reports, especially the IEP, minimizes barriers to family members' involvement and the perception of school personnel's superiority in the decision-making process regarding academics (Al-Hassan & Gardner, 2002).

Beyond students' progress and academic goals, school personnel must become comfortable describing and defending their curriculum and the pedagogical methods used to impart this knowledge. Certainly teachers have an educational and experiential background in pedagogy and curriculum. This expertise is not to be overlooked or underutilized. However, family members can share insights into their own child's learning process. In addition, when family members are welcomed as participants into discussions about academics, they also become more active listeners and become more open to reinforcing the school's pedagogical practices in the home. When parents act as instructors for their children at home, they should be encouraged to use research-based methods.

Parents are presented with educational fads and miracle cures for their child's disability on a daily basis. When family members have been made aware of best practice and have a way to evaluate methods that are presented, they become better consumers of education. In this way, they are better able to make decisions and assist in the implementation of teaching through methods that are complementary to those used in school (Martin & Hagan-Burke, 2002).

In addition to the collaborative opportunities during official processes such as IEP development, families can be provided a significant amount of information about their child and the academic program to which he or she is being exposed. There are many opportunities to inform family members of students' progress and academic activities throughout the school year. During meetings with family members, whether conducted during open house, individual conferences, home visits, pre-IEP meetings, or other face-to-face opportunities, school personnel can explain and model the techniques they use to assist and instruct the student. Family members should be apprised and given examples of the types of adaptations that are being made to the general education curriculum to provide access for the student.

Specific overtures to parents of children with disabilities must be included in all invitations to academic-related school events. Often invitations to open house or Meet the Teacher night do not address the issue of children who receive special education services and spend some or all of their daily life in general education classes. Family members are more likely to meet with the special education teacher than general education teachers, since they have had a greater amount of contact with the special education teacher. Invitations should explicitly state that family members should visit not only the child's special education teacher, but all of the general education teachers who interact with their child as well. The schedule of the event must also allow for these multiple interactions.

When family members are welcomed into all classroom settings, they can get a much greater sense of what is expected by each general education teacher. There are several issues important to the success of students with disabilities in general education classes. Since students with disabilities are sometimes absent from the general education classroom when scheduled for therapies or academic support, they may miss some experiences and information the general education teacher provides. These meetings also make general education teachers more aware that the students with disabilities in their class need information to complete the assignments that are expected of them. Arranging tours of the classrooms that the child participates in and providing an awareness of their child's daily schedule can also model the environment that could be set up for the child in the home. The family will get a better understanding of their child's academic progress and how this level of growth compares to his or her nondisabled peers. To advocate for their child's academic outcomes, family members should be encouraged to have a set of questions ready to ask school personnel. Likewise, teachers should be prepared to provide specific information regarding academic progress, expectations, and homework to families (Buck & Bursuck, 1996). Communication and Collaboration Tips Box 10.1 provides specific questions to be addressed proactively by all school personnel.

The responses to all of these questions provide family members with a deeper understanding of their child's academic abilities, learning styles, age-appropriate

---

COMMUNICATION AND COLLABORATION TIPS   **BOX 10.1**

Questions for School Personnel to Consider

To provide information and be prepared to collaborate with family members regarding academic issues, consider:

- ❏ What goals does the student have for each academic area?
- ❏ How will the student's in-class requirements, homework assignments, tests, and projects be adapted to meet the child's ability and goals?
- ❏ Who will complete these adaptations?
- ❏ How will communication about assignments be provided to all involved team members?
- ❏ How will grading of these assignments occur and who will be responsible for this grading?
- ❏ What level of participation will family members have in the completion of homework?
- ❏ What other skills will the student be taught to improve his ability to meet homework and classwork expectations?

---

expectations, and rate of progress. This will allow family members to be informed team members during decision making and to provide supports and instruction at home.

SUPPORTING FAMILY MEMBERS WHO ACT AS TEACHERS OR TUTORS TO THEIR CHILDREN

This section of the chapter will explore (a) reasons family members don't tutor or teach their child at home, (b) reasons to assist parents in working with their child's academics at home, (c) why family-member-as-tutor/teacher programs have often failed, (d) factors to consider when talking to family members about their ability to tutor their child, (e) the process of empowering family members to be their child's tutor or teacher, (f) factors that allow for positive experiences for families when parents act as tutors, and (g) examples of well-planned and implemented family-member-as-tutor programs.

Homework has been defined as tasks assigned by teachers to be completed in environments other than the classroom. These environments may include libraries, study halls, and after-school programs, but most assignments are expected to be completed at home during nonschool hours (Cooper, 1989; Stokes & Baer, 1977). Homework is intended to provide: (a) increased practice, (b) opportunities for personal development, (c) an enhanced level of parent–child relationship, (d) information to family members about their child's academic abilities, and (e) fulfillment of expectations (Epstein, 1988; Jenson & Sheridan, 1994). Unfortunately, it has also been used as punishment or implemented to fulfill administrative requirements (Epstein, 1988). The practice of assigning homework for these last two purposes has resulted in (a) lower motivation to engage in assigned homework, (b) decreased completion of homework assignments, (c) decreased interest in academic activities, (d) lower student and teacher morale, and (e) lower parental confidence in the abilities of school personnel to meet the needs of their children (Buck & Bursack, 1996). Besides homework, expectations for students outside of school include long-term projects, enrichment activities, and test preparation. To be as inclusive as possible, the term *daily academic activities* will be used when referring to homework and all other expectations for work outside of the school.

An understanding of current levels of academic activities is necessary to understand the requirements of students with disabilities and their family members in relation to daily academic activities. The use of daily academic activities as an instructional strategy is on the rise in response to pressure for students to demonstrate higher performance on state and national standardized tests (Bursuck, Harniss, Epstein, Polloway, Jayanthi, & Wissinger, 1999). The amount of daily academic activities assigned to students each day has increased consistently over the last 15 years as greater amounts of curriculum have been forced into each grade level (Polloway, Bursuck, & Epstein, 2001). Concurrently, students with disabilities are being included in both general education curriculum and high-stakes tests at an ever-increasing rate. Daily academic activities have been demonstrated to be an effective strategy to enhance the educational outcomes of all students, including those with disabilities (Austin, 1979; Goldstein, 1960; Jenson & Sheridan, 1994; Keith, 1987).

Beyond expectations for students without disabilities, there are greater challenges to meet these increased demands of daily academic activities for students with disabilities. Researchers and student team members recognize that children with learning and behavioral disabilities struggle greatly with daily academic activities and spend an average of twice the time completing assignments compared to those without disabilities, while having less successful completion rates (Jenson & Sheridan, 1994). Students with learning disabilities spend a large portion of daily academic activities time off-task and produce poorer quality homework products than their peers without disabilities do (Polloway et al., 2001).

Students with disabilities report favorable attitudes toward daily academic activities when they have a support system of teachers, family members, and peers who can provide assistance and reinforcement (Kay & Fitzgerald, 1994). Enjoyment and engagement are two frequently cited factors that allow for high rates of student success in classrooms. These same two factors are predictive of the level of success that daily academic activities tutor programs at home will experience (Douville, 2000; Lancy & Bergin, 1992). Thus, family members must be comfortable acting as a tutor or teacher for their child and have the energy and time to do this in a way that is enjoyable and engaging for the child and family member. Research has revealed a set of specific variables that support students with disabilities' success in daily academic activities (Bursuck et al., 1999). First, teachers (both general and special education) and family members must take an active daily role in monitoring students and communicating about daily academic activities. If students are to make daily academic activities a priority, the students' educational team must model this behavior. Second, schools need to find ways to provide teachers the time to plan, adapt, and assess the daily academic activities performance of students with disabilities. Third, instructional technology must be utilized to support and enhance communication with students and families regarding daily academic activities expectations. Homework hotlines, school and class Web sites, computerized student progress reports, and materials available on-line have all been used with success in improving daily academic activities outcomes (Bursuck et al., 1999). Fourth, students must be taught organizational techniques and a sense of responsibility for their own academic performance. Finally, special and general educators must continually communicate about the needs and accommodations appropriate for each student with disabilities (Buck & Bursack, 1996).

Reasons Family-Member-as-Tutor/Teacher Programs Fail

Family members need teachers to provide a greater level of communication, support, and recognition of the assistance they provide for their child than has been traditionally received (Kay & Fitzgerald, 1994). Traditionally, school personnel provided a student with an assignment or project and expected parents to help when the student had difficulty. This assumption is a certain failure for family member involvement in academics. The ambiguity of the family members' role as assistant and the sparse directions set parents up to feel underprepared and incapable of completing the task. Often, parents report that the assignments do not fit their child's abilities. Both the family member and the student are too frustrated to complete work that is not tailored to the students' abilities (OSERS, 2001). Frequent outcomes of this teacher recommendation include the family member's inadvertently completing the daily academic activities for the child, the family member's ignoring or having no involvement since he or she doesn't know how to begin, or the family member's providing continual prompts to the child to "do your work," which results in an eventual argument between child and family member when the child is unable or unwilling to complete the daily academic activities independently (Barbetta & Heron, 1991). Through these events, the parent and child both become resistant to trying daily academic activities work at home.

In this example, it is possible to begin to understand the role that school personnel have in the success or failure of academic tutoring at home. Family members who are insecure in the school setting and fearful about participating in school programs have their negative views of interactions with school personnel and perceptions of themselves as outsiders reinforced (Cairney & Munsie, 1993). Some family members feel intimidated by school and school faculty prior to the expectation that they be involved in their child's daily academic activities. When family members' level of academic abilities and comfort with the curriculum are not addressed, they will either retreat or become defensive about the daily academic activities. Parents often report feeling unprepared to assist their children with homework (Olympia, Jensen, & Neville, 1994). Parents who have not received adequate guidance from their child's teacher rely on the traditional (and minimally effective) methods that were used to instruct them when they were in school, such as overdrilling of fragmented facts, memorization of unrelated lists of spelling words or vocabulary, use of phonics instruction to the exclusion of all other reading approaches, and requiring excruciatingly perfect oral readings (Douville, 2000). Beyond lack of assistance and personal rapport with school personnel, cultural differences also can affect the level of family member involvement.

Cultural differences regarding the acceptance and involvement of family members in daily academic activities exist. Many family-members-as-tutor/teacher programs have focused on populations described as underperforming. It is often the school professional's lack of cultural awareness about children from different cultural backgrounds or low SES that has created this inequity. Further highlighting the inequity of educational opportunity given to students of differing cultural backgrounds serves to further alienate these groups. When an academically based home tutoring program focuses on a specific ethnic or socioeconomic population, this demonstrates that the student's own school team believes the cultural-deficit model that is so prevalent in society (Al-Hassan & Gardner, 2002). For example, Kermani and Janes (1997) initiated a project designed to assist low-income Latino family members in increasing their child's English literacy, and they lost 130 of the 180 families that originally agreed to be part of the project. The family members who quit the program felt that the purpose of the program was assimilationist and not sensitive to nonmainstream literacy patterns. To assist families with nonmainstream literacy patterns, Kermani and Janes were eventually successful in implementing their program through an alteration in their training process that included books without text, three-dimensional supplemental reading materials, parent-created books, and dictated stories.

FACTORS THAT AFFECT FAMILY MEMBERS' LEVELS OF PARTICIPATION IN THEIR CHILDREN'S ACADEMIC GROWTH

Family members have multiple roles in child development. Certainly, family members act as a child's first teacher, but many other familial functions demand the time and energy of family members. Family members must respond to other areas of daily need and development, such as providing social and recreational opportunities, working to meet household costs, attending to daily chores and household duties, as well as maintaining relationships with other family members. Successful inclusion of academic tutoring or teaching by family members requires careful consideration and planning by the entire school team so that family members are not overextended and stressed by the additional responsibility of tutoring. Several key factors are central to the decision to add academic instruction and support to a family member's responsibilities, including (a) the needs of the child, (b) the interests and goals of the family members, (c) the presence and level of other demands competing for time, (d) the abilities of the child and family member to work together in an instructive setting, and (e) the amount of professional support available (Barbetta & Heron, 1991). Familial resources and values also affect family members' amount of interaction with their children's academic progress (DiPrete, 1981).

Johnson and Jason (1994) developed an assessment scale to determine family members' interest in acting as positive academic instructors for their children, and their socioemotional ability to do so. This scale, comprising 27 items that the family member answers yes or no to, can act as a springboard for discussion between school personnel and families. The items on the assessment address time constraints, relationship equity between siblings, stress, competence in acting as a tutor, and ability to be positive while providing guidance and correction.

WORKING WITH FAMILY MEMBERS TO PROVIDE ACADEMIC SUPPORT AT HOME

As discussed previously in relation to factors to consider regarding family assistance with daily academic activities, there are different levels of involvement that a family member may be comfortable with or able to provide. This first level of support includes providing a space in the home that can be used for the child to complete daily academic activities (Olympia et al., 1994). Ideally, a desk or office area that is specifically designed for use as the child's work area could be provided. However, space problems are an issue for many families. The space allotted for daily academic activities can be multipurpose (e.g., the kitchen table) if there isn't enough space to provide a separate area. However, during the time the child and/or child–family member team is using the space, it should be as free of distraction and alternate activities as possible. Once this area is set up and discussed among family members, it requires minimal expenditure of energy or attention by the family member. An environment that provides appropriate supplies (e.g., paper, pencils, calculators) and resource materials (books, newspapers, educational toys) is also beneficial (Jenson & Sheridan, 1994). Indirectly related, providing time for daily academic activities may occur if family members can provide adult supervision and regulated television viewing.

A second level of involvement that has proven considerably more difficult for families to provide, yet contributes to academic success, is a consistent schedule for the completion of daily academic activities. For example, completion of daily academic activities is to take place every day directly after school or from 5:00 to 6:00 p.m. When family members are able to provide this consistent time, it demonstrates the family's commitment to academics as a daily activity and provides structure for the child. When this routine segment of time is scheduled and provided, students begin to expect that they will spend time working on academics at home. Children may become more organized regarding assignments and academic materials. For example, students may begin bringing more appropriate materials home and increasing the consistency and accuracy of their daily academic activities documentation.

The third level of family member involvement is when the family member facilitates and models organized daily discussion about the work expectations and subjects currently occurring in school. Parents may begin an interaction with the child, asking, "So, what did you learn in school today?" Unfortunately, however, routinely accepting a minimal response to this question from the school-aged child results in minimal interaction. In contrast to that traditional interaction, the family member who asks explicit questions about the academic activities of the day has a context for more meaningful discussion with the child. The family member has the background and understanding of the child's daily school life. Thus, the student can describe what happened at school that day without the necessity of a long explanation to contextualize the events.

The fourth level of family member involvement would be when the family member is expected to support the student when a part of the assignment is confusing or difficult. In some ways, this is the most difficult role for many family members. Family members must be able to recall processes, curriculum, or both from specific grade levels that they have had little or no involvement with over time. If family members are not provided the appropriate structure and information necessary to interact as supporters, the expectation is comparable to a game of Trivial Pursuit, wherein the family members must recall specific facts or processes on demand and in total disconnection from any curricular context. For family members to be successful in providing this level of support, school personnel must provide a general understanding of the expectations for completion of daily academic activities, examples of similar tasks, background information about the curriculum, access to the material, and possibly access to the answers to homework problems. Similar to Level 3 family member involvement, this will provide context for family members and increase the possibility that they can successfully assist the child. Two issues have been raised about this method of family member academic support. Unfortunately, researchers report that as the academic difficulty of homework assignments increases during middle school and high school, teachers place lower priority on communication with family members regarding academic progress in general and daily academic activities specifically (Polloway et al., 2001). Even with the context of the curriculum provided, the family member may not have the academic abilities to assist the child. This happens with increasing frequency as the child enters middle school and high school and encounters more challenging curricula. Faced with this more demanding work, the child may feel frustrated and incapable. A family member beginning support at this point may then become the target of these negative feelings, making teaming between the family member and child a negative experience.

The fifth level of family member involvement in academics, which requires a considerably higher level of energy and commitment, is parent as tutor. In this scenario, the family member–child team is provided with specific information to review. This may include basic arithmetic facts, spelling, or a writing assignment. The family member sits with the student, providing emotional support and guidance as needed during the activity. Tutoring is an oft misunderstood process and is frequently implemented incorrectly. It is important for family members to have specific instruction and examples of the process of tutoring if this model is to be used.

The sixth level is family member as teacher. This level of family member involvement occurs most frequently in literacy instruction (Cairney & Munsie, 1993; Lancy & Bergin, 1992). However, the approach can be applied to any academic discipline. In this model, the family member is instructing the student in academics that have not been provided in school. Many family members act as teacher completely separate from school activities. Activities in this instance may include teaching reading; providing geological, historical, sociological, or archaeological information while traveling; or reminiscing about family history. Although families may complete this type of instruction independent of school, it is a highly successful model when family members and school personnel work together to determine curriculum and pedagogy. This model has demonstrated benefits to the family members' parenting skills and the child's social and academic progress as well as supplementing the academic growth and cultural awareness of other students in the child's class. An example of the effect on the cultural awareness of the child's class might be to have a child who has learned to read a book offer to read it to the class, thus extending the knowledge of other classmates. Another example is when a child who returns from a trip presents artifacts related to a cultural studies lesson. In this example, the experiences of the child not only impact the specific child but are offered to his or her classmates.

FACTORS THAT ALLOW FOR POSITIVE EXPERIENCES FOR FAMILIES WHEN PARENTS ACT AS TUTORS

There are many documented approaches that provide opportunities for family members and students to have ongoing academic activities at home with positive cognitive and emotional outcomes. Before examining ways that family members can be assistive in daily academic activities, it is important to examine current daily academic activities. The quality of the assignment is highly correlated with the students' level of engagement and success with daily academic activities (Bryan & Sullivan-Burstein, 1997). First set up assignments that follow best practice. See Table 10.1 for tips on assigning homework.

After providing this level of support to students, it is also important to assess the appropriateness of the assignment for the class, and for students with disabilities in particular. Table 10.2 provides a set of activities teachers can use to evaluate their homework assignments.

After reviewing the quality and pertinence of the homework, teachers may then turn their attention to the relationship between school personnel and family members. As described previously, some families want to be more highly involved in their children's ongoing academic activities. Programs that provide materials and support to prepare the family members can significantly improve children's academic performance (Jayanthi, Bursuck, Epstein, & Polloway, 1997; Johnson & Jason, 1994). See Communication and Collaboration Tips Box 10.2 for specific suggestions related to

Table 10.1   The assignment matters.

- Assign tasks directed at the students' level.
- Assign small consistent amounts of homework.
- Provide clear written directions with the assignment.
- Suggest allowed learning tools (e.g., calculator).
- Provide examples.
- Allow students to begin the assignment during class.
- Provide a set of answers for the family members.
- Construct a help station where students and family members can receive clarification and assistance.
- Distribute homework policies and procedures regarding the level of independence that is expected, extra credit, allowable adaptations, and information about missed or late assignments.
- Check homework and provide feedback.

Source: Adapted from OSERS, 2001b. Homework practices that support students with disabilities. *Research Connections in Special Education, 4,* 1–8.

Table 10.2   Evaluating efficacy of homework assignments.

- Keep a log of assignments that includes your expectations for length of time for completion and level of achievement. Compare these results to students' grades and comments about length of assignment.

- Talk to other teachers about their assignments and policies regarding homework. Then, using this information, begin working with teachers to align expectations and procedures.

- Institute homework planners that can be accessed by the special education teacher, general education teacher, student, and parent. This provides a longitudinal record.

- Teach students to graph their progress on homework completion and accuracy. Examine the outcomes of these graphs for ways to meet the homework abilities of all students.

Source: Adapted from Bryan, T. & Sullivan-Burstein, K. (1997). Homework how-to's. *Teaching Exceptional Children, 29*(6), 32–37.

COMMUNICATION AND COLLABORATION TIPS   BOX 10.2

- ❏ Provide information in the beginning of the school year regarding assignments, procedures, and communication guidelines.
- ❏ Increase ongoing, informal communication with family members (e.g., school events, when children are dropped off or picked up at school).
- ❏ Realize that homework may be a lower priority for some families when compared to other familial needs.
- ❏ Develop comprehensive systemwide, and classroom procedures for homework and home–school communication.
- ❏ Provide informational programs for family members who want to increase their involvement in their child's daily academic activity.
- ❏ Provide a list of teachers, their contact information, and best times to contact them so family members can more easily contact school personnel.
- ❏ Make assignments and class materials available in a variety of public venues (e.g., homework hotline answering machines, Web sites, local libraries).
- ❏ Keep the school library open at night for family members to bring their children to this space.

Source: Adapted from Jayanthi, M., Bursuck, W., Epstein, M.H., & Polloway, E.A. (1997). Strategies for successful homework. *Teaching Exceptional Children*, 27(9); 538–550.

strategies teachers can use to support homework help at home. Allowing textbooks to go home with students is another step toward allowing family members access to their child's education.

Successful academic tutoring programs involve five parts, including determining likely parent–child teams, providing information and training for the parent, implementing the academic tutoring program in the home, supporting parents who implement the in-home academic tutoring program, and assessing the positive and

Table 10.3   Necessary supports for collaboration regarding daily academic activities.

- School personnel and family members must make communication regarding homework a daily routine.
- School administration must support and provide teachers with easy ways to communicate with families (e.g., telephone in room or Web sites available).
- School personnel must learn about and utilize technological advances to assist in communicating with family members.
- Students must be taught organizational skills and lessons of responsibility regarding homework and academic engagement.
- Special and general education personnel must collaborate to appropriately support students with disabilities in academic activities that occur both in class and at home.

negative impacts of the program on the child's academic performance and the relationship between family members.

Bursuck et al. (1999) identified common supports necessary for strong ties between family members and teachers regarding daily academic activities (See Table 10.3).

EXAMPLES OF WELL-PLANNED AND WELL-IMPLEMENTED PARENT-AS-TUTOR PROGRAMS

When well-structured programs welcome parents as teachers or tutors, children, schools, and family members derive great benefits (Cairney & Munsey, 1993; Johnson & Jason, 1994). After implementation of the adapted TTALL Home Literacy Learning program (Cairney & Munsey, 1993), parents were better able to choose age- and level-appropriate books for their children. The parents had new literacy skills and increased their reading level. Parents' self-esteem and affective relationships were positively affected as measured via self-reports, and there was an increase in the self-reports of affective relationships between parent and child. Children's reading level increased along with an improvement in their attitudes toward reading.

Snow, Burns, and Griffin (1998) instructed parents to use the language experience approach and scaffolded writing at home. This approach allows families to incorporate events from daily life into literacy activities. Parents were taught to act as scribes for children as they described events from daily life. Parents were also instructed to complete multiple readings of picture books with their child and then write a text story of what the child has imagined is happening in the story. This allows children to make a clear connection between oral speech and text. Parents who used the language experience approach and scaffolded writing at home reported their children's reading abilities and interest in literacy activities increased. Considering that enjoyment and engagement are some of the strongest predictors of success and that most children with disabilities lack both enjoyment and engagement during the period of emergent literacy, this program overcomes some major obstacles for students who are at great risk of academic failure (Douville, 2000; Lancy & Bergin, 1992). These approaches were also universally successful with parents who had a first language other than English and those who had limited literacy skills (Douville, 2000).

Barbetta and Heron (1991) designed and implemented a summer home-based learning program for students with mild disabilities. They trained parents to assess their children's initial knowledge of words, then provided a step-by-step procedure for practicing spelling and writing. Parents were then instructed to keep data with their child as the child progressed. The data collection was presented as a game, with awards and visual representation of student learning. After this initial training, parents were taught a similar assessment and intervention procedure for math facts. All children acquired and maintained increased writing skills, spelling abilities, and math facts. Although some of the parent participants expressed discomfort and misgivings about their ability to act as a tutor for their child, all of the family member–child dyads completed the program. On a follow-up satisfaction survey (with 100% return rate), parents were highly satisfied with the program (Barbetta & Heron, 1991).

A research team from the University of Utah developed three programs to assist students with disabilities with academic success (Jenson & Sheridan, 1994). These packages explain research-validated practices in nontechnical terms for family members so they can facilitate their child's academic progress. One module focuses on positive reactions for academic engagement at home, family member tracking of the child's daily progress, and variable reinforcement systems to increase and maintain homework completion. The second module describes tutoring activities that the family member–child dyad can do to enhance the child's academic achievement. These include activities in all areas of curriculum (e.g., math, spelling, history). The third module is to be shared between the child's teacher and a family member. This module describes ways the child's teacher and the family member can communicate to keep the student organized and on track with assignments, to measure the child's academic progress, and to discuss specific areas that may need alternative supports of instructional programs. The modules are presented by a consultant who is on call to assist the family member while he or she begins to work as a tutor or teacher for the child (Jenson & Sheridan, 1994).

Tomas's Family Revisited

Concerned about low test scores and falling personnel morale, Sue Shancey, the principal of Tomas's school, decided to institute two new programs. First, she began working with high school students who needed community service hours. After training, these students acted as tutors for students recommended by family members or teachers. Second, she began providing 1 day per month release time for teachers who would conduct home-visit conferences with families. Tomas's special education teacher, Barb, recommended Tomas for the tutor program and asked to have release time to visit with Tomas's family. His parents were excited and nervous to have Tomas's teacher come to their house. The school had never reached out to them in this way before. Tomas liked his tutor and began to be more motivated to complete even the difficult assignments. After the home visit, Barb had a better understanding of Tomas, the love his family demonstrated, and their sincere interest in his well-being. His family, now having a model to follow, set up a schedule and a place for Tomas to complete his daily assignments.

SUMMARY STATEMENTS

- There are many reasons why family members are reluctant or unsuccessful tutors of their children.
- School personnel must recognize and value different levels of family member participation in academics.
- For successful interaction between family members and school personnel in regard to academic support, there must be clear discussion and examples of expectations of family member roles and student outcomes.

QUESTIONS FOR DISCUSSION

1. What should school personnel expect from family members related to students' academic activities? Why?
2. Why has there been such a long history of failed programs to engage family members as tutors or teachers?

RESOURCES FOR COLLABORATION REGARDING ACADEMICS

- **Teaching Parents to Teach Their Children to Be Prosocial**
  http://www.ldonline.org/ld indepth/behavior/prosocial.html
  This Web page discusses strategies teachers can use to encourage parents of children with learning disabilities to teach communication skills at home.

- **Teach a Child to Read: Literacy Web Sites for Parents and Teachers**
  http://www.succeedtoread.com/resources.html
  This Web site lists a number of Web sites related to parents teaching literacy skills at home.

REFLECTION ACTIVITIES

1. Develop your own set of homework rules, procedures, and expectations.
2. Write a letter to family members describing your philosophy regarding homework.
3. Collect homework policies and other academic-related expectations for students and families from schools in your area. Compare the expectations. How and why are there differences?

REFERENCES

Al-Hassan, S., & Gardner, R. (2002). Involving immigrant parents of students with disabilities in the educational process. *Teaching Exceptional Children,* 34(5), 52–58.

Austin, J. D. (1979). Homework research in mathematics. *School Science and Mathematics,* 79, 115–121.

Barbetta, P. M., & Heron, T. E. (1991). Project Shine: Summer home instruction and evaluation. *Intervention in School and Clinic*, 26(5), 276–281.

Bryan, T., & Sullivan-Burstein, K. (1997). Homework how-to's. *Teaching Exceptional Children*, 29(6) 32–37.

Buck, G. H., & Bursuck, W. D. (1996). Homework-related communication problems: Perspectives of special educators. *Journal of Emotional & Behavioral Disorders*, 4(2), 105–114.

Bursuck, W. D., Harniss, M. K., Epstein, M. H., Polloway, E. A., Jayanthi, M., & Wissinger, L. M. (1999). Solving communication problems about homework: Recommendations of special education teachers. *Learning Disabilities Research & Practice*, 14(3), 149–159.

Cairney, T. H., & Munsie, L. (1993, April). *Beyond tokenism: Parents as partners in literacy training.* Paper presented at the Annual International Roundtable Center on Families, Communities, Schools and Children's Learning Conference, Atlanta, GA.

Cooper, H. M. (1989). *Homework.* White Plains, NY: Longman.

DiPrete, T. A. (1981). *Discipline and order in American high schools.* Washington, DC: National Center for Education Statistics.

Douville, P. (2000). Helping parents develop literacy at home. *Preventing School Failure*, 44(4), 179–181.

Epstein, J. L. (1988). *Homework practices, achievements, and behaviors of elementary school students* (Report No. 26). Baltimore, MD: Johns Hopkins University, Center for Research on Elementary and Middle Schools.

Goldstein, A. (1960). Does homework help? A review of research. *Elementary School Journal*, 60, 212–224.

Jayanthi, M., Bursuck, W., Epstein, M. H., & Polloway, E. A. (1997). Strategies for successful homework. *Teaching Exceptional Children*, 30(1) 4–7.

Jenson, W. R., & Sheridan, S. M. (1994). Homework and students with learning disabilities and behavior disorders. A practical, parent-based approach. *Journal of Learning Disabilities*, 27(9), 538–550.

Johnson, J. H., & Jason, L. A. (1994). The development of a parent–tutor assessment scale. *Urban Education*, 29(1), 22–33.

Kay, P., & Fitzgerald, M. (1994). Making homework work at home: The parent's perspective. *Journal of Learning Disabilities*, 27(9), 550–561.

Keith, T. Z. (1987). Children and homework. In A. Thomas & J. Gromes (Eds.), *Children's needs: Psychological perspectives* (pp. 275–282). Washington, DC: NASP Publications.

Kermani, H., & Janes, H. A. (1997, March). *Problematizing family literacy: Lessons learned from a community-based tutorial program for low-income Latino families.* Paper presented at the annual meeting of the American Educational Research Association, Chicago, IL.

Lancy, D. F., & Bergin, C. (1992, April). *The role of parents in supporting beginning reading.* Paper presented at the annual meeting of the American Education Research Association, San Francisco, CA.

Martin, E. J., & Hagan-Burke, S. (2002). Establishing a home–school connection: Strengthening the partnership between families and schools. *Preventing School Failure*, 46(2), 62–65.

Olympia, D. E., Jensen, M., & Neville, M. (1994). Homework: A natural means of home–school collaboration. *School Psychology Quarterly*, 9(1), 60–80.

OSERS. (2001a). Family Member Collaboration to Improve Academic Outcomes. (2001). *Research Connections in Special Education*, 4, 1–8.

OSERS. (2001b). Homework practices that support students with disabilities. *Research Connections in Special Education*, 8, 1–10.

Polloway, E. A., Bursuck, W. D., & Epstein, M. H. (2001). Homework for students with learning disabilities: The challenge of home–school communication. *Reading & Writing Quarterly*, 17, 181–187.

Snow, C., Burns, S., & Griffin, P. (Eds.) (1998). *Preventing reading difficulties in young children.* Washington, DC: National Research Council. (ERIC Document Reproduction Service No. ED 416465)

Stokes, T. F., & Baer, D. M. (1977). An implicit technology of generalization. *Journal of Applied Behavior Analysis*, 10, 349–368.

CHAPTER 11
Educational Support Services to Assist Parents and Families in Transition Planning and Programming

In this chapter, you will understand:

- How the transition process works.
- Problems teams encounter during the transition process.
- Interaction between transition planning and adult outcomes.

- Ways to involve family members in each area of transition.
- School personnel's legal responsibility to provide transition services.
- Activities to allow for best practice in transition planning.

Family Perspective: Jessica's Dreams

Jessica is 17 years old and has learning disabilities. She doesn't know what she wants to do once she graduates, but she is glad school will be over soon. Jessica isn't certain about a job, but she wants to get her own place, and dreams of marrying her boyfriend, Scott. Jessica believes he will be a good provider because she interprets his job at the local gas station/mini mart as a strong career beginning. He has worked there a long time, almost 2 years. Jessica feels her parents nag her a lot about what she's going to do with her life. She is tired of their nagging. She's only 17, and she doesn't want to settle down and get a job yet.

Tammy and Brian are Jessica's parents. They are concerned about Jessica's future. Every time they ask Jessica questions about what she wants for her future, it ends in a big argument. Tammy has called Jessica's teacher several times about her concerns. It seems that because Jessica is on an academic track, there isn't time for instruction on shopping, organizing a home, learning the value of money, and evaluating the risks and responsibilities of parenthood. Both Tammy and Jessica's school team know that Jessica has no interest in attending college. It makes Tammy wonder if it was worth all the advocating she did to keep Jessica in the highly academic college-preparatory classes. What good will academics do her if she can't apply them to her real life? She has seen other students with Jessica's level of ability and can't believe there isn't a better combination of strong academics and preparation for daily responsibilities in the school system.

Will is Jessica's teacher. He sees that Jessica is stuck in the middle. With adaptation and extra instruction, she has maintained decent grades and will graduate from high school. However, she hasn't learned any real-life application of the skills she has been taught. In some ways, Jessica seems so smart, she should be able to manage life skills on her own. However, in the past few months, it has become obvious to Will that Jessica doesn't have a full understanding of work, money, or even personal safety skills such as the use of contraception that will allow her to achieve a quality adult life. When Will contacted vocational rehabilitation, the counselor said that her caseload was too full, but that Jessica could contact her once she turned 18. In the meantime, she suggested Will should get her into some job placements. Will knew he couldn't fit a job placement into Jessica's schedule. He needed to find a set of supports for Jessica and students like her who weren't interested in or ready for college, yet had some pretty high academic skills, communication skills, and independence. Will hopes that once Jessica turns 18, things will fall into place.

Reflecting on the Family Perspective

1. What should Will do for Jessica?
2. How do you intervene when a family member and young adult have different ideas about what is best for the student's adult life?

○   ○   ○

ADULT OUTCOMES OF INDIVIDUALS WITH DISABILITIES

With proper transition planning and support, adults with all types of disabilities are capable of gaining and maintaining employment, housing, and a positive quality of life. It is not, however, the general experience of people with disabilities. Adults with disabilities have lower rates of employment, continuing education, and independent living, and higher rates of underemployment (Murray, 2003). Researchers report between 68% and 82% of people with disabilities, depending on demographics and location, between the age of 16 and 64 are unemployed (Ferguson & Ferguson, 1996; Wagner, 1993). Over 90% of adults with significant disabilities lack employment (LaPlante, Kennedy, Kaye, & Wenger, 1996; Luecking & Certo, 2002). More than 90% of graduates of special education programs live below the poverty line (Affleck, Edgar, Levine, & Kortering, 1990). Adults with disabilities are prone to isolation and social exclusion after leaving high school (Cameron & Murphy, 2002). These factors further restrict access to jobs for adults with disabilities. For individuals with disabilities who are female or racial minorities or whose families are of low SES, the adult outcomes are even more limited (Murray, 2003). For example, researchers found that Native American students with learning disabilities are less likely to continue into postsecondary education, obtain a job, receive pay that exceeds minimum wage, achieve independence from social service organizations, assert choice and control in their lives, and avoid drug abuse when compared to their white peers with or without disabilities (Ramasamy, Duffy, & Camp, 2000). Altogether, the availability of transition planning and educational programming affects the entire range of students with disabilities' quality of life.

With the provision of appropriate transition planning and educational programs, many individuals with disabilities, especially those with mild learning, attentional, behavioral, and physical disabilities, are able to find and maintain employment without any special support services or with minor alterations to the work environment. This concept is defined as competitive employment. In contrast, supported employment is the provision of ongoing support, supervision, or both to find and maintain community employment (Missouri Deaf/Blind Project and Center for Innovations in Special Education, 1996).

Unfortunately, the inability to provide adequate transition services for students with disabilities results in those with mild disabilities being underemployed or being unable to attain competitive employment. Those with more significant disabilities who receive ineffective transition services never achieve supported employment, and usually are placed in segregated day-treatment facilities. These segregated day-treatment facilities provide negligible monetary rewards; few skills with which to advance to higher paying, more complex jobs; and minimal personal choice and control.

These statistics are by themselves disturbing to school personnel and family members of children with disabilities, but the poor adult outcomes for people with disabilities become even more shocking and painful when compared to the positive outcomes possible with good transition services. Individuals with severe disabilities can own and maintain a supported living home of their own. However, supported living is the exception. The more expensive group residential facilities that inherently deny the rights, choices, and individuality of people with severe disabilities are the current societal norm (Ferguson & Ferguson, 1996). The lack of quality transition planning and programming maintains negative adult outcomes for individuals with disabilities.

Transition has been recognized by researchers and those involved in best practices in special education services as a critical and necessary concept, process, event, and legal mandate for 15 years; however, school districts and individual teams have failed to plan and implement successful transitions to support adolescents with disabilities (Hughes, Hwang, Kim, Killian, Harmer, & Alcantara, 1997). In a recent study, 40% to 60% of families whose children have disabilities noted that school personnel did not prepare their children for careers, postsecondary education, transportation, recreational interests, or domestic responsibilities prior to their graduation (Roessler & Peterson, 1996).

In the K–12 educational system, programs for school-aged children with disabilities and community supports for families and children with disabilities are supported in policy and governmental sanctions in a way that programs for adults with disabilities are not. At the same time that young adults with disabilities are being expected to take on greater amounts of autonomy and self-responsibility, organized supports that would help them achieve this learning and kind of independence are being removed (Mallory, 1996).

TRANSITION ISSUES

Transition Definitions

For team members to provide quality planning and programming, it is first necessary to understand the meaning of transition. The definition of transition varies widely. Some researchers, philosophers, and school personnel define transition in terms that emphasize the global concept; others emphasize the individual. For example, a global definition is offered by a federal support agency: "The implication of movement and change" (Missouri Deaf/Blind Project and Center for Innovations in Special Education, 1996).

When theorists describe transition globally, they often emphasize transition as an event that occurs multiple times during one's life. In this context, transition has been defined as time periods in the lives of families or individuals when significant developmental, social, or economic changes occur (Center for Educational Research and Innovation, 1986).

Multiple researchers and theorists have defined transition more specifically as the time when high school is ending and adulthood is beginning. For example, one commonly used definition explains transition as a set of individualized support strategies and learning experiences developed and implemented by individuals with disabilities and their network of family, friends, community, and paid providers to allow for maximum participation in adult communities (Benz & Halpern, 1987; Halpern, 1985; Hasazi, Gorden, & Roe, 1985; McDonnell, Hardman, Hightower, Keifer-O'Donnell, & Drew, 1993; Rusch, DeStefano, Chadsey-Rusch, Phelps, & Szymanski, 1992; Will, 1984). In this chapter, transition is defined as the process of preparing and launching adolescent students with disabilities from school-based services into all aspects of adult society. This definition focuses the chapter on the transition from school to adulthood, is broad enough to cover all areas of life affected by transition, yet is simple enough to be easily described to all team members.

Different Perspectives on Transition

Relationships among adolescents with disabilities, their family members, and school personnel change dramatically during the transition process. It is important for school personnel to have a strong understanding of the transition process, the adult service system, and best practices in planning and implementing successful individualized transition services to meet the needs of adolescent students with disabilities and their family members. Transition is a stressful developmental change that is highly emotionally charged for adolescents with disabilities and their family members. This stress can be offset by allowing the student with disabilities and his or her family members to feel prepared for the transition process.

Different members of a student's team may also define the issues of transition in alternative and sometimes conflicting ways. For example, adolescents who are experiencing the transition process most often emphasize their future career, their own place, and social relationships, whereas family members' comments most frequently highlight the adolescent's strengths, past achievements, and safety (Cooney, 2002). In a further contrast, school personnel centered their ideas around transition about currently available support options, coping strategies, and realistic expectations (Cooney, 2002).

> The acquisition of "adult status" is a complex and problematic issue for many young people. For those with disabilities it is often made difficult by attitudes linking disability, dependence, independence, and eternal childhood. "Adult status" may be considered as an ideal goal that individuals may more or less reach; persons with disabilities are no exception—however, they must be given the legal right to work towards that goal. (Organisation for Economic Cooperation and Development [OECD], 1986, p. 8)

> A person's transition from childhood to adulthood is a gradual change in the relationship between that person and his or her parents (or caregivers). While there is a broad range of relationship patterns between parent and child during this transition process, achieving adulthood is some version of increased independence and self-determination. (Ferguson & Ferguson, 2000)

For students with more significant physical or cognitive disabilities, the transition to adulthood is even more complicated by team members who may not recognize the individual with a disability as leaving adolescence and becoming a young adult. "Being an adult and gaining the status of adulthood are not synonymous" (Ferguson & Ferguson, 1996, p. 55). For individuals with cognitive or severe physical impairments, the chronological markers of adulthood (e.g., 18th or 21st birthday, completing high school) may not signal the beginning of adulthood to school personnel and family members. Individuals who have significant needs for ongoing support and supervision by others may not be perceived to be reaching adulthood (Ferguson & Ferguson, 1996). For individuals with these higher care needs to be treated as adults, adulthood may need to be explicitly communicated. Part of the transition is the team members' responsibility. This awareness of an individual's adult status must be identified and spotlighted by all team members. Autonomy, choice, and control must be focused goals for all individuals as they reach adulthood, regardless of the person's level of disability.

For example, making choices of menu, body position, and sensory experience can be the beginning level of choice and control for the student with disabilities.

Age of Majority

The age of majority is the chronological age at which a person changes his or her citizen status from minor to adult and incurs the rights and responsibilities to make certain legal choices (e.g., voting). School personnel should know and inform family members of federal and state laws pertaining to the age of majority. In states where educational rights transfer to the child at the age of majority, the school team must inform the student and the family members of the impending transfer of authority 1 year prior to the age of majority. The age of majority differs between 16 and 21, depending on the state. At this point, in some states, the child can make educational (and other decisions) independent of his or her family members. Rights that transfer from the family member to the child at the age of majority include notification and attendance at IEP meetings, consent to evaluation or change in placement, mediation or due process rights, and any other right previously granted to the family members of children with disabilities. Unless guardianship has been prearranged, at this age marker, the student, not the parent, is the primary participant in the IEP team (National Center on Secondary Education and Transition, 2002a). A student could, for example, choose to leave school without transition services and then become ineligible for essential services. Guardianship and legal competence are determined at the state level. Each of these concepts is held on a spectrum of levels of control rather than an absolute dichotomy of who has choice for an individual. For example, an individual may gain some rights while the guardian maintains decision-making power in other areas.

School personnel must be able to interpret and balance these multiple levels of students' decision making along with family members' roles as current and possibly future care providers and legal guardians. One model that has been particularly helpful for students with more significant disabilities is to allow for a young adult's self-advocacy within the guardianship model. This model depends on the development of a set of individuals designated as personal support agents, who act as translators and who are active team members focused on the desires, interests, and demonstrations of adult status by the individual with a severe disability (Ferguson, 1994; Ferguson & Ferguson, 1996; Taylor, 1988). The role of these personal support agents is defined through the implementation of four key beliefs. For more information on the implementation of the personal support agent, see Table 11.1.

LEGAL RESPONSIBILITIES TO PROVIDE TRANSITION PROGRAMMING

Federal requirements for transition planning and services are explained in IDEA.

> The term "transition services" means a coordinated set of activities for a student with a disability that:
>
> (A) is designed within an outcome-oriented process which promotes movement from school to post-school activities, including post-secondary education, vocational

Table 11.1 Personal support agent beliefs.

This list of tenets of personal support agents provides insight into the role of this newly defined team member.

- "Family means family": *Family* is larger than the narrowly defined *parents* and is defined individually.
- "Transition is plural": The transition to adulthood is a set of events and processes that are overlapping yet distinct and happen not only to individuals with disabilities but also to their families and support systems.
- "Adulthood is a group act rather than another birthday": The process of transition represents an ongoing shift of the balance of control from the family to the individual.
- "Support means doing whatever it takes": The provision of support to allow for maximum autonomy, self-expression, and growth is an individually determined set of intertwined supports and responsibilities.

Source: Ferguson, P. M., & Ferguson, D. L. (1996). Communicating adulthood: The meanings of independent living for people with significant cognitive disabilities and their families. *Topics in Language Disorders, 16*(3), 63.

> training, integrated employment (including supported employment), continuing and adult education, adult services, independent living, or community participation;
>
> (B) is based on the individual student's needs, taking into account the student's preferences and interests; and
>
> (C) includes instruction, related services, community experiences, the development of employment and post-school adult living objectives, and, when appropriate, acquisition of daily living skills and functional vocational evaluation. 20 U.S.C. Section 1401 (30)

IDEA regulations further describe:

> Transition services for students with disabilities may be special education, if provided as specially designed instruction, or related services, if required to assist a student with a disability to benefit from special education. 34 C. F. R. Section 300.29 (b)

These requirements translate into requirements for the IEP that change its focus from academics to transition. This change in focus begins at age 16 (Individuals with Disabilities Education Improvement Act of 2004), then further intensifies during the final year of the student's school experience prior to the transition. Specifically, IDEA states:

> A student's transition plan is part of the student's IEP. Beginning no later than the first IEP to be in effect when the child is 16, and updated annually thereafter, the IEP must contain appropriate measurable post-secondary goals, based upon age appropriate transition assessments related to training, education, employment, and were appropriate, independent living skills; and the transition services (including courses of study) needed to assist the child is reaching those goals. (20 U.S.C. Section 1414 [d][1][A][i][vii])

IDEA 1990 (IDEA, PL 100–476) brought school responsibility for transitioning students from school-aged services to adult living into the spotlight. School personnel were required to provide planning and educational programs that allowed students with disabilities to achieve positive adult outcomes. These adult outcomes applied not only to employment, but to all areas of adult living, including housing, recreation, socialization, and continuing education (Center for Innovations in Special Education, 1999). In addition to providing planning and programs, school personnel must reach out to community agencies, adult services, and family members to provide a connection to a variety of supports during this transition (Roessler & Peterson, 1996; Wehman, 1992).

Unfortunately, transition policy developed from disability policy that assumed individuals with disabilities will need continual, lifelong support and thus be an ongoing burden to society. This unfortunate primary assumption leads transition planning and programming to become a system that leads to exactly that self-fulfilling prophecy. When students' transition teams strive only for legal compliance with the transition mandates, individuals with disabilities fail to achieve during adulthood (Cooney, 2002). Frequently, individuals with disabilities are not provided with the tools to gain skills and abilities to become more autonomous, but are instead relegated to a substandard supervised, segregated existence outside the mainstream culture (Biklen, 1988, 1992; Ferguson & Ferguson, 1993; Mallory, 1995; Palmer & Wehmeyer, 1998). However, planning that goes creatively beyond legal mandates to a celebration of the strengths and talents of adolescents with disabilities and is inclusive of naturally occurring familial and community supports can overcome the negative assumptions of legislation to allow for positive interdependent outcomes for adults with disabilities (Cooney, 2002; Ferguson, Ferguson, Jeanchild, Olson, & Lucyshyn, 1993; Lehman, Bassett, & Sands, 1999).

AREAS OF TRANSITION

Having a full, high-quality life involves more than having a job. To help students with disabilities prepare fully for adulthood, a transition plan would need to address (a) having and caring for a home, (b) experiencing quality vocational opportunities, (c) attaining personal management, (d) developing and maintaining relationships, (e) participating in active recreation and leisure, (f) understanding sexuality and family planning, (g) participating as a member of the community, (h) continuing education and training/lifelong learning, (i) attaining transportation, and (j) understanding financial responsibilities.

Having and Caring for a Home

Having and caring for a home involves decisions about living arrangements, economics, cleaning, organizing, and preparing meals. It is highly important to include family members in transition planning because they may play a significant role in the area of domestic responsibilities at both an economic and a daily practical level. After the transition plan is in place, the education about having and caring for a home should reflect the student's familial and cultural values. This is an area of transition planning in which it makes sense for the family to have a significant responsibility of education. However, that does not limit the responsibility of the school personnel.

The student may attend home and careers courses yet still need a significant amount of training in domestic skills. It is best if these skills can be taught in natural settings (e.g., a community apartment, the students' homes) so the skills are more directly generalized.

Career Education

Vocational skills and on-the-job behaviors (e.g., appropriate conversation with coworkers, typical behavior for lunch breaks) must be directly taught in natural settings. For students to find a career path that meets their interests and skills, there must be multiple opportunities to job shadow, explore, and try out different vocations (Browder, Bambara, & Belfiore, 1997; Dolyniuk, Kamens, Corman, DiNardo, Totaro, & Rockoff, 2002). Multiple vocational placements that are based on an individual's skills and interests are imperative before the student leaves the school support system. To plan these experiences, school personnel must first work with the student with disabilities to determine initial career interests. After this discussion, career exploration opportunities can be arranged via family contacts, local business leaders, and school district personnel.

Personal Management

Personal management includes organizing life and personal belongings to meet commitments as well as self-care, hygiene, health, choices related to drugs or alcohol, and nutrition. Similar to transition preparation related to having a home, students may learn some information in school, such as in a health class. But many students may need more direct personal instruction about this area. It is often assumed that students with mild disabilities can learn and apply this area of curriculum without additional supports or direct teaching; however, this is not the case. Education in natural settings that presents the family's values while allowing for the young adult's own choice is critical. In addition to this education, personal management is an area that requires school personnel and family members to make connections with service providers. Students with disabilities should receive support in making connections and organizing personal information regarding emergency numbers, medical and dental support services, adult service provider contacts, and social service requirements. Personal management is an area that can prove useful in teaching self-advocacy skills to obtain the desired level of support needed in the young adult's life.

Relationship Development and Maintenance

Relationship development and maintenance must frequently be directly taught to individuals with all types of disabilities. After high school, many individuals with disabilities lose their friendships from school and feel isolated in the adult world (Cameron & Murphy 2002; Sitlington, 1996). This loneliness can make them vulnerable to exploitation by individuals or groups. A network of friends is most easily developed if natural supports have been collaboratively built by the individual with disabilities, school personnel, and family members. Continued growth of social connections can be made by increased competency in the area of recreational skills.

Recreational Interest and Skill Development

Recreational interests and skill development can highly impact the quality of life of all individuals, including those with disabilities. For 70% of individuals with cognitive disabilities, the main recreational activities are passive in-home endeavors (Wehman, 1992). The most common form of recreation for adults with disabilities is watching television (Sitlington, 1996). Recreational activities should reflect the individual's past interests and allow for the introduction of new skills as well. Recreation should be a mixture of passive and active activities. There should not just be one area of recreation that is encouraged in an individual. Many different recreational activities should be explored and supported. When school personnel are providing instruction and support in recreational skills, this should be completed in one-on-one or small-group settings rather than with a large set of individuals with disabilities. When students transition to the community, it is hoped that they will be integrated into community-wide recreational activities. Thus, recreational skills should be taught and supported in context with people who represent this diversity. When recreational skills that can be accomplished in the home and within community settings are developed, the individual continues to grow cognitively, make social contacts, and become a stronger member of the community.

Understanding Sexuality and Family Planning

Sexuality is an oft-avoided topic in educational and familial settings. Similarly, sexuality education is avoided in transition planning as well. All students as they approach adulthood need information about their own bodies, sexuality, intimate relationships, sexual and gender identities, sexual rights and responsibilities, masturbation, self-protection against victimization and sexually transmitted diseases, private and public demonstrations of emotion and desire, contraception, family planning, pregnancy, childbirth, and parenthood. Students with mild disabilities are often excluded from appropriate instruction because they are so similar to their peers, it is assumed they have understood the same information provided to adolescents without disabilities. However, this is far from true. The language issues that surround most students' abilities can highly impact their understanding of all instruction, including in sexuality (Carter, 1999). On the other end of the spectrum, adolescents with more significant disabilities are often excluded from instruction on sexuality because they are viewed as nonsexual beings or individuals who are not yet "ready" for this adult level of conversation. Both of these views are problematic and potentially dangerous. All people are sexual beings. As adolescents with severe disabilities mature, they will experience many of the same sexual changes and feelings experienced by those without disabilities. This confusing time for all teens can be even more destabilizing for individuals with significant physical and cognitive disabilities. Even for families or school personnel who are not yet prepared to view a person with a significant disability as able to participate or interested in an adult sexual relationship, the topic should still not be avoided. For self-protection and self-awareness, the topic of sexuality needs to be part of the transition-planning discussion.

Instruction must be direct, systematic, individualized, and related to natural environments and real situations as much as possible, because the generalization issues that occur in individuals with disabilities will certainly cause a failure to apply information related to sexuality during highly emotional real-life situations. A classroom climate based on trust and nonjudgmental practice will allow for the development of values and beliefs to guide future intimate relationships. For school personnel who are not prepared to meet this challenge, the collaboration of community partners from the local health department, women's center, or gynecological clinic may be helpful. To maintain parental involvement and awareness of the instruction related to topics that are impacted by the family's values, homework assignments regarding sexuality that require family member participation have been suggested (Carter, 1999).

Community Participation

Full community participation can be achieved by only those who know all of their civic responsibilities and opportunities. Community participation may overlap with recreation when citizens use the public library, community concert series, and local workshops. There can also be overlap between community participation and economic stability, including interactions with social services and vocational rehabilitation. Self-advocacy and an understanding of local, federal, and state legal responsibilities may include registering young men with the armed services, understanding drug and alcohol laws, obtaining a driver's license and a work permit, and voting.

Continuing Education and Training/Lifelong Learning

Colleges and universities are beginning to respond to the needs of students with disabilities. Beyond the requirements of the Americans with Disabilities Act, social and academic supports are being provided for students with disabilities at many institutions of higher education. These supports increase the probability that students with disabilities can complete a college education.

In Vermont, there is an exemplary program that provides an inclusive college experience for students with severe disabilities who are not seeking a college degree (Newton, 2001). Living in the dorms, auditing classes, and experiencing college social life are facets of a semisupported environment where young adults can receive the supports they need in a more natural environment, with their peers. To demonstrate the built-in support structure of a college or university, consider that these institutions provide (a) residence-hall assistants and directors who oversee the dorm activities and safety, (b) bathrooms, and common areas are cleaned by dorm staff, (c) daily meals are purchased for an entire semester, and (d) a roommate can be provided a stipend to act as further daily support.

For those students who are not interested in pursuing higher education, community college lifelong learning courses can provide ongoing opportunities to improve or maintain skills, meet new people, and participate in the community (Gugerty, 1999). These courses often center on hobby, craft, and sport activities and are attended by community members with a wide variety of skills and experiences. School professionals should be open to possibilities other than ending school at the high school level for students with disabilities.

Attaining Transportation

Independent mobility greatly increases the independence of young adults with disabilities. The services available vary significantly, depending on the size, location, and political leadership of the community. Social interaction, job possibilities, recreational opportunities, and personal management are all dependent on the availability of transportation. It is critical to begin addressing this issue during the student's transition. Community safety skills, access to public transportation, and scheduling should be addressed to allow the student with disabilities the greatest level of independence.

Understanding Financial Responsibilities

Developing an understanding of the value of money and the cost of living is difficult for all young adults. Often, this age group has larger-than-life dreams of exiting high school, buying a sports car, and spending their income at the local shopping mall. American children grow up bombarded with the messages of our consumerist society. The shock of monetary reality and budgeting usually occurs at this critical transition from high school to adult life. For students with disabilities, money management can be complicated by difficulties with math and lack of understanding of the purchasing process. It is an unfortunate reality that a large number of Americans with disabilities live at or below the poverty line. This serious lack of monetary stability requires even more stringent budgeting to maintain a quality life. If students with disabilities can be well prepared for money management, they will require less support during their adult life. Also, the better they can manage their earnings (and other income), the more likely the adult will be to attain a working-class or even middle-class status.

In summary, the transition from external regulation to autonomy, self-responsibility, independence, and self-advocacy in each area of transition may happen gradually over time. Students whose school professionals and family members assist them in developing a transition plan that addresses the necessary life responsibilities and expectations may be thrust on the emerging adult world all at once (Knowlton, Turnbull, Backus, & Turnbull, 1988). For example, some young adults may graduate, move out of the familial home, be economically independent, and need a job all at the time of the transition out of school. For others, this level of autonomy may never be expected of them during their adult life. The differences in the abruptness or gradual expansion of responsibilities can be a function of the individual type or level of disability, familial SES, cultural history, social expectation, or individual choice (Mallory, 1996).

ROLES OF TRANSITION TEAM MEMBERS

Family members' involvement has been described as the most critical support for successful transition (Morningstar, Turnbull, & Turnbull, 1995/1996; National Center on Secondary Education and Transition, 2002b). Unfortunately, this collaborative relationship between family members and school personnel during the transition process is not commonly achieved (Morningstar, Turnbull, & Turnbull, 1995/1996). Analogous to the disconnect with families during this transition process is the overwhelming exclusion of students with disabilities during their own transition planning (Martin, Marshall, & Maxson, 1993; Van Reusen & Bos, 1990). One reason for the lack of student involvement in transition planning is that prior to discussing transition and adult life, adolescents with disabilities cannot see the imminence of their own adulthood. Since being an adult seems so far away, the teenage student does not prioritize involvement in planning. School personnel and family members, aware and concerned about the students' transition to adulthood, need to include students in the conversation so they realize the importance of transition planning to their life. Family members may also be reluctant at first to view their child with disabilities as moving into adulthood and thus may not impress on their child the importance of the child's involvement in transition planning. This change in understanding involvement, self-advocacy, and personal responsibility is a necessary step for the family and the child to transfer control for the child's life from the family to the emerging adult. Parenting doesn't end when a child becomes an adult, but the role of the parent is altered. One positive model of parenting a young adult is the parent as mentor (National Center on Secondary Education and Transition, 2002b). In this model, the parent acts as a mentor to teach, challenge, and support.

School personnel and family members are not solely responsible for transition to adult life. Transition is an interdisciplinary, collaborative process (Agran, Cain, & Cavin, 2002). Collaboration with the adult services available is critical. Important steps in this process include inviting representatives to transition IEP meetings and involving the adult service personnel with families and individuals with disabilities prior to graduation so that individuals with disabilities know about the services available to them as adults (Repetto, White, & Snauwert, 1990). One adult service provider to invite to collaborate on transition IEP teams would be a vocational rehabilitation (VR) counselor. Although past collaborative relationships between school personnel and VR agencies have been disappointing (deFur, 1999; Wehman, 1992), the services available, if coordination across school personnel and agency personnel is possible, allow for greater employment and supports for young adults (Agran et al., 2002). A student qualifies for VR if he or she has a mental or physical disability that impairs his or her employment and he or she can benefit from the services provided by VR. (More information on eligibility for VR services is provided in chapter 7.) Once a student is deemed eligible, a specific VR counselor will be assigned to work with the young adult, and he or she, with the family, will develop an individual written rehabilitation program (IWRP). This IWRP will describe the coordinated services that the young adult will receive to gain employment. Services available from VR are outlined in Table 11.2.

Table 11.2 VR services.

- Evaluation for eligibility
- Assessment of interests and strengths to assist in career determination
- Training to allow the student to adjust to working life
- Aids and services needed for the adolescent to benefit from VR services
- Vocational training
- Training related to independent living skills that allow for successful employment
- Placement and job search assistance
- A IWRP plan

Source: Content adapted from National Transition Network, Institute on Community Integration. (1996). *Rehabilitation services available for youth with disabilities.* Minneapolis, MN: National Transition Network.

The transition team consists of many individuals. Each person on the transition team has multiple and mutual responsibilities. Balancing the abilities and interests of the adolescent with disabilities, the expectations and desires of the family members, and the previous experience and beliefs of school personnel is a difficult achievement (Cooney, 2002). It is necessary for school personnel to allow and even encourage individual ideas and outcomes from transition planning. A balance between the need for ownership of the plan by the individual whose life it is and the need for input from family members who will most likely act as a long-term natural support must also be negotiated. A parental decision to allow for complete individual choice by the young adult with disabilities or provide for some level of guardianship should be determined prior to the adolescent's reaching the age of majority (Mallory, 1996).

What a Teacher Can Do

Generally, during transition IEP meetings, progress toward goals and grades is the main topic of discussion. Unfortunately, however, long-term goals such as finding a career or being involved in postsecondary education are often left out of the conversation (Roessler & Peterson, 1996). This exclusion is a legal problem, but more seriously, the result of this incomplete discussion is a student who has no preparation for long-term success. In those last years in the school system, the person with disabilities has the highest level of services available during his or her adult life (Roessler & Peterson, 1996). This time of transition provides the opportunity to set up programs, supports, and forms of instruction that will allow the individual a level of autonomy to be successful as they enter the world of adult services. In contrast to the school personnel's agenda at transition IEP meetings, family members' greatest concerns include their child's lack of a plan after graduation, lack of ability to protect and advocate for himself or herself, unpreparedness for the demands of adult life, and legal and interpersonal difficulties (e.g., being arrested, lacking friends, unplanned pregnancies) (Roessler & Peterson, 1996).

School personnel should plan and teach skills that will allow for a student to live, work, play, and have relationships in adult communities. To allow for greatest generalization and maintenance of skills, school personnel should teach students community skills in natural environments that will be accessed during adulthood (e.g., stores, apartments, community job placements, restaurants, public services) (Missouri Deaf/Blind Project and Center for Innovations in Special Education, 1996). School personnel should provide ties between academics and daily life skills, develop a plan for students to have community access, and educate students about public transportation or create an informal network of supports to meet transportation needs (e.g., carpool plan, barter system) (Roessler & Peterson, 1996).

It is imperative to encourage self-advocacy through the provision of choices, decision making, and experience of consequences and responsibilities. Self-advocacy skills—the ability to make choices and be self-determined—are critical for students entering transition-planning sessions. Regardless of level of disability, self-advocacy and choice making must be an ongoing part of school curriculum. Autonomy is linked to adulthood. If an individual cannot have a voice in transition planning, then there is no way for him or her to have control in his or her adulthood. Regardless of their level of disability, students can participate in their transition planning (Cameron & Murphy, 2002). Students must be provided time to determine their own goals, be instructed on how to participate in and lead their transition IEP meetings, and be empowered to self-advocate and problem solve (Warger & Burnette, 2003). Communication and Collaboration Tips Boxes 11.1 and 11.2 provide further suggestions for enhancing student participation in developing transition IEPs.

COMMUNICATION AND COLLABORATION TIPS   BOX 11.1

- ❑ Start instruction of self-determination and self-advocacy early.
- ❑ Work with students to discover their interests and talents.
- ❑ Be prepared to deal with sensitive issues.
- ❑ Be comfortable having students actively participate in or lead their own IEP meetings.

COMMUNICATION AND COLLABORATION TIPS   BOX 11.2

- ❑ Plan time for students to work on developing their future goals and ideas for IEP goals.
- ❑ Teach collaboration skills as a course integrated into the curriculum.
- ❑ Communicate with families about the transition process and changes that their child will be experiencing.

Source: Warger, C., & Burnette, J. (2000). *Planning student-directed transitions to adult life.* OSEP Digest E593. (ERIC Document Reproduction Service No. ED 447627).

EMOTIONAL ISSUES FOR YOUNG ADULTS WITH DISABILITIES AND THEIR FAMILY MEMBERS DURING TRANSITION

As students with disabilities reach later adolescence, their family members' anxiety about the future as well as their demands on the educational and community support systems increase. These increased demands are a result of a school system that has provided higher levels of supports during previous times of transition or stress (e.g., initial identification). This increased level of anxiety can be both positive and problematic (Stark, 1992; Thorin, Yovanoff, & Irvin, 1996). The anxiety may increase the involvement of family members in the transition process. However, family members may also have unrealistic expectations of the number and level of supports that are available to adults with disabilities. Since school-aged services are mandated, it is frequently a shock that there are no mandated services for adults with disabilities, and that the services that do exist will not be as plentiful as those for children (Smull & Bellamy, 1991).

This anxiety, confusion, and realization of contradictions in the levels of service compounds the emotional issues of family members whose children have disabilities. While most families are experiencing a change to lesser involvement as their child ages into adulthood, family members of children with disabilities are again required to step up to a higher level of team collaboration and advocacy for their child (Nisbet, Covert, & Schuh, 1992). Thorin et al. (1996) described a set of emotional predicaments experienced by family members during this time. First, family members want to provide situations in which their children can exercise independence, yet want the children's health and safety to be ensured. Second, family members want both to begin having a life beyond their child and to do all that is possible to assist him or her in succeeding. Third, family members want to maintain the predictable, stable home life while meeting the changing needs and schedule of their young adult. Finally, family members have already had a long history of advocating and being involved in their child's life. The family members want to begin transferring that power to the young adult. For school personnel, it is important to acknowledge the families' individuality and simultaneously explain that these current dilemmas surrounding involvement, autonomy, responsibility, and control are normal experiences for families of young adult children with disabilities.

The change in relationships between a growing young adult and his or her family members is often a difficult adjustment. However, for family members of children with disabilities, the transfer of responsibility for the young adult from the family to the individual with disabilities can be even more precarious. It is most common that children outlive their parents. Although no one likes to dwell on his or her inevitable demise, it is a necessity, sometimes painful, for family members to arrange supports for their children with disabilities for when they will no longer be able to provide these supports themselves (Bigby, 1996). School personnel should be respectful and assist in development of natural supports for young adults with disabilities that will allow for this change in the structure of support as parents age. Adequate planning regarding whatever supports the family have provided is necessary. Most common areas of need include financial responsibilities, housing, and general supervision.

TOOLS TO DEVELOP A QUALITY, INDIVIDUALIZED TRANSITION PLAN

Although it is accepted best practice as well as a legal mandate that each student's transition plan be individual, the process of developing this plan can be guided by published frameworks, sets of life domains, or planning process tools (Mallory, 1996).

Beginning the transition process is an emotionally charged time. To facilitate their involvement in the process, family members and the student must understand the process, expectations, and outcomes. Information about what transition planning is, what an IEP is, and what supports are available should be provided to each student in the beginning of the transition process. Person-centered planning is a vehicle to welcome students into their transition planning process. Examples of this process include MAPS (Forest & Pearpoint, 1992), Personal Futures Planning (Mount & Zwernik, 1988), Essential Lifestyle Planning (Smull & Harrison, 1992), and Group Action Planning (Turnbull, Turnbull, & Blue-Banning, 1994). School personnel can also provide more informal instruction and support for students in their transition-planning process. Examples of information designed to assist teachers in developing group communication and self-advocacy in adolescents with disabilities include IPLAN (Van Reusen & Bos, 1990) and Where Do I Go from Here? Getting a Life After High School (Drill, McDonald, & Odes, 2004).

BEST PRACTICES IN THE TRANSITION PROCESS

The lack of a comprehensive transition plan and the lack of involvement of family and community supports merge to form the most common reason that individuals with disabilities experience negative outcomes of their transition from adolescence to adulthood and achieve negative adult life outcomes (Mallory, 1996). Two years after IDEA (as reauthorized in 1990) required individual transition plans for youth exiting the special education system, 92% of students' IEPs had no mention of transition within the last 4 years before graduation or leaving school. Researchers defined three key features to transition planning and instruction (Ferguson & Ferguson, 1996; Ferguson, Hibbard, Leinen & Schaff, 1990). These included support and instruction that occur in natural contexts rather than in segregated contrived environments designed to warehouse individuals with disabilities. User-defined supports, based on the desires and choices communicated by the individual who is experiencing transition, are the second provision. Third, variation based on culture, local values, opportunities, and understandings is necessary for the individual's eventual acceptance by the larger adult community. Although these supports are key, there is no single variable that will allow for a student's successful transition, because his or her education and adult life are complex and require multifaceted planning, support, and instruction if he or she is to be successful (Bullis & Davis, 1995). A summary of essential supports for transition planning is offered in Table 11.3.

Table 11.4 describes a list of features that are present in successful transition programs that have been identified in the current research.

Table 11.3 Critical support strategies.

- Assess social skills.
- Specify both academic and functional goals.
- Start planning early and review the plan often.
- Identify current needs for support.
- Identify current and possible natural supports.
- Identify student's choices and preferences.
- Evaluate and continually monitor student's social acceptance.
- Instruct the student regarding self-management and independence.
- Teach choice making and decision making.
- Identify objectives related to independence.
- Provide ongoing real-life work experience.

Sources: Bullis, M., & Davis, C. (1995). Transition achievement among young adults with deafness: What variables relate to success? *Rehabilitation Counseling Bulletin,* 39(2), 130–150. Hughes, C., Hwang, B., Kim, J., Killian, D.J., Harmer, M., & Alcantara, P.R. (1997). A preliminary validation on strategies that support the transition from school to adult life. *Career Development for Exceptional Individuals,* 20(1), 1–14.

Table 11.4 Provisions of successful transition programs.

Teams and transition programs that assist in successful transition of young adults with disabilities

- Plan processes that identify students' individual goals, strengths, and interests.
- Teach to specific goals and identified interests of students in areas related to postschool outcomes.
- Collaborate with families and natural support networks.
- Provide a bridge to adult service support systems.
- Establish community-based classes for small numbers of students.
- Provide community-based employment opportunities in settings with generally nondisabled coworkers.
- Plan recreation activities in typical community settings.
- Provide student-skills-based employment opportunities.
- Devise individualized schedules based on student strengths and needed experiences.
- Collaborate to share cost with schools and community and service agencies.
- Establish paid work with supports from adult service agencies prior to exiting school.

Sources: Council for Exceptional Children. (2000). *Transition-related planning, instruction, and service responsibilities for secondary special educators.* Washington, DC: ED/OSERS. Luecking, R. G., & Certo, N. J. (2002). Integrating service systems at the point of transition for youth with significant disabilities. A model that works. *National Center on Secondary Education and Transition Information Brief.* 1(4), 3–5.

Table 11.5 Encouraging development of empowered adults.

- Include children's view on vacation plans and major family purchases.
- Provide practice for handling emergency situations (being lost, injured, in jeopardy).
- Involve your children in IEP meetings.
- Prepare your child for the IEP through informal conversation and role play.
- Model collaborative skills with school personnel.
- Allow choices of gradually increasing significance as the child grows.
- Discuss and plan for issues of guardianship and autonomy.
- Allow children to voice their opinions and desires to family and community members.

Source: National Center on Secondary Education and Transition. (2002). *Age of majority: Preparing your child for making good choices.* Minneapolis, MN: PACER Center.

Encouraging Best Practices by Other Team Members

Family members should begin teaching children household chores and responsibilities at an early age. Encouraging self-reflection and independence at the child's disability level is a strong foundation for adult self-advocacy abilities. Family members should enhance the student's development of recreational and leisure skills through family involvement in community events and allow children to be involved in extracurricular clubs and activities. Table 11.5 contains ways family members can encourage skills that will prepare their children for the transition to adulthood.

Involvement of individuals with disabilities in their own transition process is a necessity. However, the adolescent's role in his or her transition process is commonly limited to that of a recipient of information and decisions or a consumer being convinced to buy into a prescribed bill of goods (Cooney, 2002; Morningstar, Turnbull, & Turnbull, 1995/1996). Self-determination is a person's ability to make decisions and pursue goals. The self-determined adolescent is better able to self-advocate and be a strong force in his or her transition process. When the transition process centers on the individual who will be transitioning, rather than external assumptions about the outcomes for people with disabilities or other team members' assumptions about who the person is or what he or she should want, the likelihood of having positive long-range outcomes in adulthood is much higher (Lehmann, Deniston, Tobin, & Howard, 1996). To become full members of their own transition planning and programming process, people with disabilities must be provided ongoing support and instruction in choice making, decision-making skills, and understanding of choice and consequence. The ability to make choices becomes a necessity during transition planning, when the adolescent with disabilities will get his or her desired adult outcomes only if he or she is able to be an effective self-advocate (Pain, Dunn, Anderson, Darrah, & Kratochvil, 1998; Schloss, Alper, & Jayne, 1993). As initial information gathering is occurring, school personnel can determine team members' comfort in supporting full membership of the adolescent with disabilities as a transition team member. Markers of welcoming attitudes toward self-advocates on the transition

Table 11.6   Family activities to prepare youth to participate as active members of their IEP teams.

- Review your child's educational records, past IEPs, report cards, progress reports, and interest inventories with your child.
- Develop a portfolio or scrapbook with your child that consists of items that represent his or her accomplishments, strengths, and interests (this need not be focused on any one area alone but may include academics, hobbies, clubs and sports, volunteer experiences, etc.).
- Allow time for the child to show and explain the portfolio or scrapbook to other family members.
- Spend time with the child talking about careers and ask what careers he or she might enjoy.
- Coordinate job-shadowing days for your child during the summer, when (with employer permission) your child spends time with family members and family friends at their workplace.
- Allow your child to develop his or her own ideas about what he or she enjoys or dreams for his or her future.
- Make a list of all of the people who help and support your child and your family; have the child bring this list to the IEP.
- Allow your child to choose and invite members of the list to join the transition IEP team.

Source: Center for Innovations in Special Education. (1999). Parents role in transition to adult life. *Do You Know . . . .* 2(1), 3–6.

team include behavior and language that respect the adolescent, are interactive in a collaborative way, are responsive, and are supportive of the ideas of the adolescent with disabilities. When these behaviors are demonstrated, students who are self-advocates, as well as family members, can feel listened to, accept responsibility, try different options, and be rewarded for their opinions. If negative attitudes toward the involvement of the adolescent exist, then school personnel can arrange for sensitivity training to support the student's involvement as self-advocate and main member of the decision-making transition team (Lehmann et al., 1996). Family members, with the collaboration of school personnel, can prepare an adolescent to have a positive self-advocacy experience on the transition IEP team. For specific suggestions to prepare students to participate in transition IEP meetings, see Table 11.6.

Jessica's Family Revisited

Will, Jessica, and Tammy met one evening after school. Will started the meeting by describing all of the growth he had seen in Jessica during her high school years. Noting his style of introduction, Tammy also described the ways Jessica had matured in her responsibilities at home. After listing all of Jessica's strengths and growth, Will turned the conversation to Jessica's future. Will asked Jessica to describe her best realistic dream for her future. As Jessica spoke, Will wrote down each item she described, without editing or judging the ideas. After all of her dreams of the future were written down, Will and Tammy helped Jessica brainstorm what types of activities would prepare her for this future. After a lengthy discussion and negotiation, Will, Jessica, and Tammy created a list of items Jessica was interested in participating in because she saw them as valuable to her future. After the meeting, Will worked with the other members of Jessica's team, the guidance counselor, and some local businesses to determine a plan for Jessica. Jessica started a paid internship at the local day care in the evenings after school. She opened a checking account for her weekly earnings and worked on budgeting with Will during one study hall per month. Jessica spent time over spring break volunteering at the Department of Social Services. One afternoon, Will accompanied Jessica to the local technical college. They had a tour, met with a career counselor, and talked with several student representatives. One day after school, Tammy went apartment hunting with Jessica and Scott. Based on Jessica and Scott's income and what the two of them thought they could afford for monthly rent, they called several apartments advertised in the local paper. Each of these activities occurred with minimal time away from her classes. It was harder for Jessica to maintain her studies, but she was more motivated because she felt that her view of the future was now beginning to be considered in her transition plan. After visiting the apartments, beginning to budget, working with children, and seeing the struggles of many parents as they work to have a good life for themselves and their family, there was substantial change in Jessica. She had a more realistic view of what portions of her dream fit together and what parts would need to be revised to live her adult life as she wished.

SUMMARY STATEMENTS

- As adolescents transition to young adults, leaving school-aged services, and entering adult society, there are changes in the relationship between the young adult and his or her family that should be acknowledged throughout the planning process.
- For positive adult outcomes, students with disabilities and their families must be provided with early and ongoing transition planning and educational supports from school personnel, community agencies, and natural supports.

QUESTIONS FOR DISCUSSION

1. What is transition?
2. Describe ways family members can be involved in each area of transition.
3. What can be done to teach self-advocacy skills to students with disabilities while encouraging family member participation on the transition team?
4. At what age should transition begin? What should the initial steps toward transition look like?

RESOURCES FOR SUCCESSFUL TRANSITION

- **Disability Studies and Services Center**
  (www.dssc.org)
  Academy for Educational Development provides a variety of information regarding transition and adult services.

- **Family Village: A Global Community of Disability-Related Resources**
  (www.familyvillage.wisc.edu/sp/TRANS.HTML)

  Family Village provides up-to-date information regarding many topics, including transition. There are opportunities to interact with other families and a large list of links.

- Drill, E., McDonald, H., & Odes, R. (2004). *Where do I go from here? Getting a life after high school.* New York: Penguin.

- Wehmeyer, M. L., Morningstar, M., & Husted, D. (1999). *Family involvement in transition planning and implementation.* Austin, TX: Pro-Ed.

REFLECTION ACTIVITIES

1. Explore adult services that are available in your community. Make a list of contacts for each service.

2. Walk around the neighborhood where your school is located. List all the possible job opportunities that could be explored within walking distance of the school.

3. Know the local transportation system in your area. Make a list of all the options available for getting around town.

4. Become knowledgeable in one (or more) of the tools that are available to assist in planning transition. Set up a meeting and use one of these tools with a family who has a child of transition age.

5. Interview all members of a young adult's transition team to understand each member's perspective, hopes, and concerns about that young adult's transition.

REFERENCES

Affleck, J. Q., Edgar, E., Levine, P., & Kortering, L. (1990). Postschool status of students classified as mildly mentally retarded, learning disabled, or nonhandicapped: Does it get better with time? *Education and Training in Mental Retardation, 25,* 315–324.

Agran, M., Cain, H. M., & Cavin, M. D. (2002). Enhancing the involvement of rehabilitation counselors in the transition process. *Career Development for Exceptional Individuals, 25*(2), 141–155.

Benz, M. R., & Halpern, A. S. (1987). Transition services for secondary students with mild disabilities: A statewide perspective. *Exceptional Children, 62,* 390–413.

Bigby, C. (1996). Transferring responsibility: The nature and effectiveness of parental planning for the future of adults with intellectual disabilities who remain at home until mid-life. *Journal of Intellectual & Developmental Disabilities, 21*(4), 295–312.

Biklen, D. (1988). The myth of clinical judgement. *Journal of Social Issues, 44,* 127–140.

Biklen, D. (1992). *Schools without labels: Parents, educators, and inclusive education.* Philadelphia: Temple University Press.

Browder, D. M., Bambara, L. M., & Belfiore, P. J. (1997). Using a person-centered approach in community-based instruction for adults with developmental disabilities. *Journal of Behavioral Education, 7,* 519–528.

Bullis, M., & Davis, C. (1995). Transition achievement among young adults with deafness: What variables relate to success? *Rehabilitation Counseling Bulletin, 39*(2), 130–150.

Cameron, L., & Murphy, J. (2002). Enabling young people with a learning disability to make choices at a time of transition. *British Journal of Learning Disabilities*, 30, 105–112.

Carter, J. K. (1999). Sexuality education for students with specific learning disabilities. *Intervention in School & Clinic*, 34(4), 220–223.

Center for Educational Research and Innovation. (1986). *Transition to adult and working life for young people who are handicapped: Toward a unified concept of transition*. Paris: Organization for Economic Cooperation and Development.

Center for Innovations in Special Education. (1999). Parent's role in transition to adult life. *Do You Know . . .* , 2(1), 3–6.

Cooney, B. F. (2002). Exploring perspectives on transition of youth with disabilities: Voices of young adults, parents, and professionals. *Mental Retardation* 40(6), 425–435.

Council for Exceptional Children. (2000). *Transition-related planning, instruction, and service responsibilities for secondary special educators*. Washington, DC: ED/OSERS.

deFur, S. H. (1999). Transition planning: A team effort. *National Information Center for Children and Youth with Disabilities Transition Summary*. Washington, DC: Author.

Dolyniuk, C. A., Kamens, M. W., Corman, H., DiNardo, P. O., Totaro, R. M., & Rockoff, J. C. (2002). Students with developmental disabilities go to college: Description of a collaborative transition project on a regular college campus. *Focus on Autism and Other Developmental Disabilities*, 17(4), 241.

Drill, E., McDonald, H., & Odes, R. (2004). *Where do I go from here? Getting a life after high school*. New York: Penguin.

Ferguson, P. M. (1994). *The personal support agent: Fulfilling the promise of adulthood for individuals with disabilities and their families*. Eugene: University of Oregon Specialized Training Program.

Ferguson, P. M., & Ferguson, D. L. (1996). Communicating adulthood: The meanings of independent living for people with significant cognitive disabilities and their families. *Topics in Language Disorders*, 16(3), 52–67.

Ferguson, P. M., & Ferguson, D. L. (2000). The promise of adulthood. In M. Snell & F. Brown (Eds.), *Instruction of students with severe disabilities* (5th ed.) (pp. 629–656). Upper Saddle River, NJ: Merril/Prentice Hall.

Ferguson, P. M., Ferguson, D. L., Jeanchild, L., Olson, D., & Lucyshyn, J. (1993). Angles of influence: Relationships among families, professionals, and adults with severe disabilities. *Journal of Vocational Rehabilitation*, 3(2), 14–22.

Ferguson, P. M., Hibbard, M., Leinen, J., & Schaff, S. (1990). Supported community life: Disability policy and renewal of mediating strategies. *Journal of Disability Policy Studies*, 1, 9–35.

Forest, M., & Pearpoint, J. C. (1992, October). Putting kids on the MAP. *Educational Leadership*, 50(2) 26–31.

Gugerty, J. (1999). Serving students with significant disabilities in two-year colleges: A summary of six highly effective approaches. More news you can use. *Journal for Vocational Special Needs Education*, 21(2), 35–46.

Halpern, A. S. (1985). Transition: A look at the foundations. *Exceptional Children*, 51, 479–502.

Hasazi, S. B., Gordon, L. R., & Roe, C. A. (1985). Factors associated with the employment status of handicapped youth exiting high school from 1979 to 1983. *Exceptional Children*, 51, 455–469.

Hughes, C., Hwang, B., Kim, J., Killian, D.J., Harmer, M., & Alcantara, P.R. (1997). A preliminary validation on strategies that support the transition from school to adult life. *Career Development for Exceptional Individuals* 20(1), 1–14.

Individuals with Disabilities Act of 1990 (IDEA), PL No. 101–476 602a, 20 USC 1401.

Knowlton, H. E., Turnbull, A. P., Backus, L., & Turnbull, H. R. (1988). Letting go: Consent and the "Yes, but . . . " problem in transition. In B. L. Ludlow, A. P. Turnbull, & R. Luckasson (Eds.), *Transition to adult life for people with mental retardation: Principles and practices* (pp. 45–66). Baltimore: Brookes.

LaPlante, M., Kennedy, J., Kaye, S., & Wenger, B. (1996). Disability statistics |Abstract|. *Institute on Disability and Rehabilitation Research Abstracts*, 11, 1–4. Washington, DC: U.S. Department of Education.

Lehman, J. P., Bassett, D. S., & Sands, D. J. (1999). Students' participation in transition related activities: A qualitative study. *Remedial and Special Education*, 20, 160–169.

Lehman, J. P., Deniston, T. L., Tobin, R., & Howard, D. (1996). Sharing the journey: An individual and integrated systems approach to self-determination. *Career Development for Exceptional Individuals*, 19(1), 1–14.

Luecking, R. G., & Certo, N. J. (2002). Integrating service systems at the point of transition for youth with significant disabilities: A model that works. *National Center on Secondary Education and Transition Information Brief*, 1(4), 3–5.

Mallory, B. L. (1996). The role of social policy in life-cycle transitions. *Exceptional Children*, 62(3), 213–223.

Martin, J. E., Marshall, L. H., & Maxson, L. L. (1993). Transition policy: Infusing self-determination and self-advocacy into transition programs. *Career Development for Exceptional Individuals*, 16(1), 53–61.

McDonnell, J., Hardman, M. L., Hightower, J., Keifer-O'Donnell, R., & Drew, C. (1993). Impact of community-based instruction on the development of adaptive behavior of secondary-level students with mental retardation. *American Journal on Mental Retardation*, 97, 575–584.

Missouri Deaf/Blind Project and Center for Innovations in Special Education. (1996). *The future is around the corner! A parent handbook for successful transition*. ED 392212.

Morningstar, M. E., Turnbull, A. P., & Turnbull, H. R. (Dec–Jan 1995/96) What do students with disabilities tell us about the importance of family involvement in the transition from school to adult life? *Exceptional Children*, 62(3), 249–260.

Mount, B., & Zwernik, K. (1988). *It's never too early, it's never too late. A booklet about personal planning for persons with developmental disabilities, their families, and friends, case managers, service providers, and advocates*. St. Paul, MN: Metropolitan Council. (ERIC Document No. ED 327997)

Murray, C. (2003). Risk factors, protective factors, vulnerability, and resilience. *Remedial & Special Education*, 24(1), 16–26.

National Center on Secondary Education and Transition. (2002a). *Age of majority: Preparing your child for making good choices*. Minneapolis, MN: PACER Center.

National Center on Secondary Education and Transition. (2002b). *Parenting post-secondary students with disabilities: Becoming the mentor, advocate, and guide to your young adult needs*. Minneapolis, MN: PACER Center.

National Transition Network, Institute on Community Integration. (1996). *Rehabilitation services available for youth with disabilities*. Minneapolis, MN: National Transition Network.

Newton, P. (2001). We're going to college! TASH *Connections* (Vol. 27, pp. 2–12). TASH: Baltimore, MD.

Nisbet, J., Covert, S., & Schuh, M. (1992). Family involvement in the transition from school to adult life. In F. R. Rusch, L. DeStefano, J. Chadsey-Rusch, L. A. Phelps, & E. Szymanski (Eds.), *Transition from school to adult life: Models, linkages, and policy* (pp. 407–424). Sycamore, IL: Sycamore.

Organisation for Economic Cooperation and Development (OECD). (1986). *Young people with handicaps: The road to adulthood*. Paris: Author.

Pain, K., Dunn, M., Anderson, G., Darrah, J., & Kratochvil, M. (1998). Quality of life: What does it mean? *Journal of Rehabilitation*, 64(2), 63–72.

Palmer, S. B., & Wehmeyer, M. L. (1998). Students' expectations of their future: Hopelessness as a barrier to self-determination. *Mental Retardation*, 36, 128–136.

Ramasamy, R., Duffy, M. L., & Camp, J. L. (2000). Transition from school to adult life: Critical issues for Native American youth with and without learning disabilities. *Career Development for Exceptional Individuals*, 23(2), 157–171.

Repetto, J. B., White, W. J., & Snauwert, D. T. (1990). Individualized transition plans (ITP): A national perspective. *Career Development for Exceptional Individuals*, 13, 109–119.

Roessler, R. T., & Peterson, R. L. (1996). An exploratory analysis of parental satisfaction with transition services. *Rural Special Education Quarterly*, 15(2), 29–35.

Rusch, F. R., DeStefano, L., Chadsey-Rusch, J., Phelps, L.A., & Szymanski, E. (Eds.). (1992). *Transition from school to adult life: Models, linkages, and policy.* Sycamore, IL: Sycamore.

Schloss, P. J., Alper, S., & Jayne, D. (1993). Self-determination for persons with disabilities: Choice, risk, dignity. *Exceptional Children, 60,* 215–225.

Sitlington, P. L. (1996). Transition to living: The neglected component of transition programming for individuals with learning disabilities. *Journal of Learning Disabilities, 29*(1), 31–41.

Smull, M. W., & Bellamy, G. T. (1991). Community services for adults with disabilities: Policy challenges in the emerging support paradigm. In L. H. Meyer, C. A. Peck, & L. Brown (Eds.), *Critical issues in the lives of people with severe disabilities* (pp. 527–536). Baltimore: Brookes.

Smull, M., & Harrison, S. B. (1992). *Supporting people with severe reputations in the community.* Alexandria, VA: National Association of State Mental Retardation Program Directors.

Stark, J. (1992). Presidential address 1992: A professional and personal perspective on families. *Mental Retardation 30*(5), 247–254.

Taylor, S. J. (1988). Caught in the continuum: A critical analysis of the principle of the least restrictive environment. *Journal of the Association for Persons with Severe Handicaps, 13,* 41–53.

Thorin, E., Yovanoff, F., & Irvin J. (1996). Dilemmas faced by families during their young adults' transition to adulthood: A brief report. *Mental Retardation 34*(2), 117–120.

Turnbull, A. P., Turnbull, H. R., & Blue-Banning, M. J. (1994). Enhancing inclusion of infants and toddlers and their families: A theoretical and programmatic analysis. *Infants and Young Children, 7*(2), 1–14.

Van Reusen, A. K., & Bos, C. S. (1990). IPLAN: Helping students communicate in planning conferences. TEACHING *Exceptional Children, 22*(4), 30–32.

Wagner, M. (1993, June). *Trends in postschool outcomes of youth with disabilities.* Paper presented at the meeting of project directors of the Transition Research Institute at Illinois, Washington, DC.

Warger, C., & Burnette, J. (2000). *Planning student-directed transitions to adult life.* OSEP Digest E593. (ERIC Document Reproduction Service No. ED 447627)

Wehman, P. (1992). *Life beyond the classroom.* Baltimore: Brookes.

Will, M. (1984). OSERS *programming for the transition of youth with disabilities: Bridges from school to working life.* Washington, DC: Office of Special Education and Rehabilitation Services, U.S. Department of Education.

CHAPTER 12
Family Stories Illustrating School-Based Support

The central themes of this book are that optimal youth progress occurs when families and professionals cooperatively work together; that families are equally important to students relative to communication, support, and other needs; and that school personnel and community professionals must work together to effectively address the needs of parents and families of students with special needs. In this connection, we offer in this chapter illustrations of the most important elements of this book. That is, each chapter's salient components are illustrated via use of case study examples. Thus, the objectives of this concluding chapter are to offer examples of real-life parent and family circumstances along with a brief description of how school and community professionals dealt with these issues.

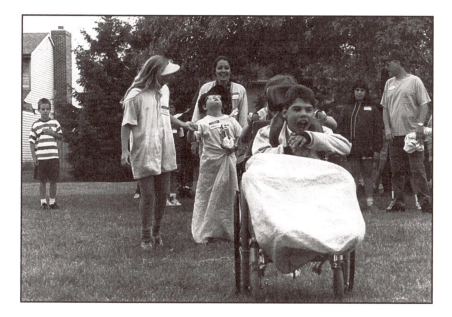

A common format is used for each illustration. A support need or related issue is first presented. Next, we offer illustrations of school and community professionals dealing with these issues in a realistic and effective manner. These illustrations were drawn from our collective work with parents and families. Thus, in most cases, these were actual situations in which we participated. Although names and other identifying facts were modified to ensure confidentiality, the major elements of the examples are factual.

These illustrations represent our optimism that there is great potential for positive and effective parent/family and professional involvement. At the same time, however, these illustrations represent the reality that much work remains to be done in the arena of parent/family and professional involvement.

SUPPORTING AN ETHNICALLY AND LINGUISTICALLY DIVERSE FAMILY

A Family's Need for Support

The Si family moved from the Philippines to the United States to receive medical assistance for their daughter Anna. She is the youngest of six children and Cora and Ric Si's only daughter. The family is very close and supportive of each other. Anna is 10 years old. She has severe multiple disabilities. Anna was diagnosed with dual sensory impairments, yet she has had no medical or educational support since her birth. The system of education and medicine in the Philippines is based on the idea that parents of children with disabilities are wholly responsible for their children with disabilities. Therefore, the Si family has received no guidance from the medical or educational systems that support children without disabilities.

Cora has fed Anna a mashed version of their meals through a bottle her entire life. Some of her physical issues are demonstrative of the results that occur when a family receives no support from service providers. From spending her days lying on her back on the family couch, Anna's legs are rigid and her hips remain in a splayed position. Cora and Ric had been told Anna would not live through her first year. The reality that Anna had lived so long was miraculous to Cora and Ric. They wanted the best for their daughter, and other than their love, they didn't know what that should look like.

Cora and Ric speak English but only in public. Chinese is the common language spoken in their home. On coming to the United States, they stayed with relatives in California, then later moved to Minnesota. In Minnesota, the Si family enrolled the boys in public school. Without any intervention from people who teach or support people with disabilities, Cora and Ric had no idea that Anna was as eligible as the boys were to attend school. Anna spent several months receiving medical assistance, including surgery on her hips, fittings for hearing aids, and surgery to insert a g-tube for nutritional support. When Anna came home from the hospital in her new wheelchair, the family threw a big party. The boys invited many of their school friends. When the teachers heard that the Si boys had a sister, they contacted the district special education coordinator, who called the Si family. This call changed the lives of Anna and her family forever.

An Example of School-Based Family Support

Ms. Jay, the middle school special education teacher, and Mrs. Hallondale, the district special education coordinator, invited Cora, Ric, and Anna for a visit and tour of the middle school special education program. Cora was amazed and delighted with the idea of Anna going to school. Ric was skeptical, believing that when the special education coordinator saw Anna, they would change their mind about services.

On the day Cora and Ric came to the middle school, Ms. Jay had arranged for an interpreter to accompany the group during the tour and visit. Cora and Ric were surprised at what they saw on their tour of the middle school and the supports the children received in the classes. They were introduced to a boy who had needs similar to Anna's. He spent his whole day in general education classes and his supports came into the classroom. He used a switch interface to access his communication system and his schedule consisted of tactile squares that represented different activities. The other children interacted with him in ways similar to how Anna's brothers interacted with her. It all seemed so normal. After the tour, Mrs. Hallondale spent time with the Si family, explaining Anna's and their rights through the assistance of the interpreter. The information was supplemented with written documents in both Chinese and English for Cora and Ric to take home. Ms. Jay stopped in at the end of the meeting to set up a home visit and IEP meeting to follow.

At the home visit, Ms. Jay and the interpreter worked with Cora, Ric, and their boys to develop long-range goals and possible annual goals for Anna. They based the questions on COACH (Giangreco, Cloninger, & Iverson, 1998). This assessment tool considered Anna's abilities, interests, routines, and needs. It allowed Cora, Ric, and the boys a great deal of input into Anna's IEP and daily school schedule.

To assist with Anna's transition to school, Ms. Jay planned with Cora and Ric to have Anna's lunch sent from home, along with some of her toys. Ms. Jay brought a Step-by-Step switch to the home visit. She asked each family member to say a calming phrase in Chinese that they frequently said to Anna. When Anna came to school, Ms. Jay used this to motivate Anna to touch the switch, and the familiar voices reassured her throughout the first few weeks of school. Although their request was unusual, Anna's older brothers were permitted to spend the day with Anna when she first entered school. They felt very protective of Anna and remembered how hard it was to get along in the first days in American schools. The boys really helped Anna's transition; they introduced Anna to her classmates, showed them her favorite toys, and taught them a few phrases in Chinese. Anna's teachers and therapists were glad to learn more about Anna so they could be able to work well with her even though she had limited communication. The communication devices Ms. Jay developed were programmed to speak phrases in Chinese when Anna activated them using a switch. Prior to coming to school, Anna had heard only Chinese, and because Anna had never left her home when the family lived in the Philippines, her exposure to English was minimal. Rather than overcoming Anna's communication issues and trying to bridge a language barrier simultaneously, the team had chosen to work on her communication goals in Anna's first language. So that the team could understand each phrase, Anna's communication device had a screen that displayed both the Chinese phrase and the English translation. The school personnel even found themselves learning multiple Chinese phrases using this mode of instruction.

In the months to follow, Anna made tremendous progress in her ability to interact. The set of services worked for Anna and her family because the school personnel worked with the family. The school personnel were eager to learn about the family and their hopes for Anna. The difference between the school culture and the family culture was a consideration in all the planning. The language differences also were approached with respect and understanding. When school personnel are open to learning about diversity in all its forms, children with disabilities can be more included in the community.

EMOTIONAL SUPPORTS FOR A FAMILY OF A DIFFICULT-TO-MANAGE YOUTH

A Family's Need for Support

Laila and Reginald Norris are the parents of Twila, an 18-year-old. Twila has received special education services since the age of 10. Initially diagnosed as having an emotional/behavioral disorder, she currently has an educational diagnosis of learning disability and a medical diagnosis of ADHD. While she primarily attends general education classes, her IEP provides for 1-hour daily support within a special education resource room and participation in a community work-study program 2 days per week. Twila's parents and teachers describe her as an impulsive youth who is socially and emotionally immature. At the same time, she is also described as an attractive and fun-to-be-with person who is eager to make friends and who regularly participates in various school and community activities.

Twila has two significantly older siblings who live with their mates and own children in other cities. As a result, Twila considers herself to be an "only child." Consistent with her perceived role as the only child in the family, she is extremely demanding of her parents. Mr. and Mrs. Norris often acquiesce to their daughter's whims because she is their "baby." Mr. Norris frequently travels in his work as a sales representative for an office-supply company; thus, he tends to give his daughter money to buy various things as an expression of his support and affection. His wife, in contrast, is an overly nurturing individual who enjoys spending a great deal of time with Twila. Thus, since Twila's birth, Laila has consistently been available to support her daughter's various social and other needs and wants.

The family dynamic changed about 6 months ago following Mrs. Norris's 82-year-old mother's being placed in a nursing home after falling and breaking her hip. Twila's grandmother also has dementia and has difficulty understanding why she is no longer able to live in her own home. In response to her mother's needs, Mrs. Norris has had to spend a great deal of time visiting and caring for her mother and her affairs. As a result, she has been less available to support her daughter, a circumstance that has caused Twila anguish, which she has not been shy in expressing.

Twila has become increasingly rebellious and defiant at home and school. Mrs. Norris's increased level of stress related to caring for her mother has been even further intensified by her daughter's recent outbursts. Twila's teachers have also recently expressed concern that Twila is more difficult to manage at school and that her noncompliance has resulted in several disciplinary referrals to the school's vice-principal. Only last week Mr. and Mrs. Norris discovered that Twila is in the early stages of pregnancy, a condition for which Twila insists she has no explanation.

An Example of School-Based Family Support

Although initially overwhelmed by the circumstances surrounding their family, especially their daughter's impending parenthood, the Norris family was able to secure support and referral services from school personnel. Laila and Reginald Norris had a good working relationship and an ongoing informal communication system with Twila's special education teacher and related service staff. Thus, the important initial process of creating and maintaining a trust-oriented relationship between the Norris family and school personnel was accomplished relatively easily.

The first step in the support process involved convening the members of Twila's IEP team and creating a modified IEP. The parents actively participated in the meeting, and Twila represented herself in the conference. The revision process included conducting an analysis of Twila's problem behaviors (i.e., the aforementioned rebelliousness, defiance, and noncompliance) and subsequently crafting a modified management, instructional, and parent–home communication plan. The revised IEP also included recommending that Twila attend the school district's student-mom program, wherein she would acquire skills and knowledge related to pregnancy, birth, and child care. The coordinator of that program also provided Twila and her parents with referral information related to obtaining medical care and counseling. The student-mom program coordinator advised the family that counseling was available to discuss postbirth issues, including adoption.

Even though the school personnel were unable to directly address the nonschool stress-related problems of the Norris family, they nevertheless recognized their responsibility in assisting them. Accordingly, they served as a referral source related to meeting this need. In this capacity, they recommended a collaborative community–school partner that provided mental health and social services. Personnel with whom the Norris family subsequently began working assisted them in addressing stress-related matters. They also initiated a family counseling program wherein they discussed Twila's pregnancy and how the family planned to deal with the baby. Finally, the social service personnel connected to the cooperative mental health–school district program served as a referral agent to help Mrs. Norris obtain elder-care and related services needed to more effectively assist her mother.

SUPPORTS FOR A SISTER OF A CHILD WITH AUTISM

A Siblings's Need for Support

Sheila Witherspoon is a single mother of two children. Angie is a precocious 12-year-old sixth grader, and Todd is a 9-year-old who was diagnosed with classic autistic disorder at the age of 22 months. Todd has limited expressive language and relies on screaming and, when consistently prompted, an augmentative system to communicate his wants and needs. He displays numerous aberrant behaviors, (including self-injurious behavior when he becomes frustrated) a lack of social interest, and poor social interaction skills. Because he is believed to have severe mental retardation, Todd is a full-time student in a self-contained special education program for students with severe and multiple disabilities. In contrast, Todd's sister, Angie, is described by her teachers as bright, highly motivated to do well in school, and exceptionally socially mature.

Sheila and her husband separated and subsequently divorced after 11 years of marriage. Bill, the biological father of Angie and Todd, remained close to his children, and he and Sheila maintained a civil relationship following their divorce. Although the children lived with their mother, Bill Witherspoon attended his kids' school programs and other activities, assumed significant responsibility for Todd's outside-the-home therapies and care, and assumed responsibility for his children on most weekends. Tragically, Bill was killed in an auto accident approximately a year ago. Because he did not have a will and only minimal assets, his former wife assumed total financial and other responsibility for their children following his death. Even though she changed jobs to gain a higher salary, the family experienced lifestyle changes following Bill's death, particularly in the areas of financial and parental support.

Sheila's new job brought with it significantly more stress than her previous position, and she was required to work longer hours, including several evenings per month. As a result of this change, Angie has been asked to assume a significant amount of responsibility for her brother after school and on weekends. This newly assigned role has necessitated Angie's dropping out of several social and athletic programs in which she had regularly participated. This change has been upsetting to Angie, although she has not discussed these problems with her mother. In this connection, Angie has commented to her peers and one teacher that, "Mother has too much to worry about without needing to listen to me gripe about caring for Todd after school."

An Example of School-Based Sibling Support

Because Ms. Witherspoon had an ongoing relationship with her son's teacher, that individual took the initiative in addressing the issue of Angie's role in caring for Todd. This topic was presented as an element of Todd's regularly scheduled progress-report conference. Todd's teacher initiated the discussion by observing that related to living and caring for children with disabilities, siblings may require support services and accommodations. While initially defensive about this matter, Ms. Witherspoon volunteered to discuss this issue with her daughter. Following the discussion, wherein Angie shared her concerns about caring for Todd, Ms. Witherspoon subsequently initiated an appointment with school personnel to discuss how she might better support and accommodate the needs of both of her children.

At the follow-up meeting related to assisting Angie, it was recommended that the school's counselor coordinate several activities designed to help Angie better understand her brother and his special needs. This process involved recommending to Angie that she read two books about children with autism. Although this recommendation was presented as a voluntary assignment, Angie's teacher supported the recommendation by allowing her to read the recommended books as a part of her regular classroom requirements. Both Angie's teacher and the school counselor also suggested that she meet with them to discuss the books after she had finished reading them. Although Angie read both recommended books and made an oral presentation in her class on one of the books, she declined the school personnel's offer to discuss the readings.

Angie was also invited to visit her brother's classroom to observe and interact with his teacher and staff. Again, Angie's teacher supported the observation recommendation by allowing Angie to use the opportunity to fulfill a health-related class project. Angie chose to observe on one occasion. She did not ask questions or make comments while observing, and she declined the opportunity to visit with the school counselor or another school person about what she saw. However, Ms. Witherspoon reported that Angie initiated conversations with her related to her observations on several occasions. Ms. Witherspoon suggested to Angie that Angie might want to visit with a community mental health professional about matters connected to Todd and her father's death. Angie declined her mother's recommendation that she see a counselor, saying, "I'm OK with where I'm at with Todd and Dad." She also suggested that her mother might want to see a professional about "some of her issues." Angie later apologized to her mother about her comment, explaining, "all of a sudden everybody's worried about me for no reason," a situation that she reported finding somewhat disconcerting.

Finally, Angie and her mother were able to discuss and agree on Angie's role and commitment to helping Todd after school and on weekends. This negotiation process involved school personnel assisting the family in obtaining respite care services and after-school care several days per week, thereby releasing Angie from some of the child care duties that she had previously been assigned.

COPING AND PROBLEM-SOLVING SUPPORTS FOR A SINGLE MOTHER WITH MULTIPLE CHALLENGES

A Family's Need for Support

Wanda Blanchard is a 35-year-old single mother with a 12-year-old son named Nicholas. Wanda has never been married. During her adolescence and continuing into her mid-20s, Wanda had an alcohol-abuse problem. Wanda continued to abuse alcohol during her pregnancy, and consequently, Nicholas was born with fetal alcohol syndrome (FAS). The biological father has never admitted paternity, and Wanda, thankful to be rid of him, never sought any court action declaring his paternity. Although Wanda has turned her life around in the past 8 years and has maintained her sobriety for that length of time, Nicholas experiences many of the typical characteristics of children with FAS.

In addition to the characteristic facial features associated with FAS (e.g., small face, narrow eye openings, a larger than average nose), Nicholas has significant developmental delays. He has symptoms associated with ADHD, including inattention and impulsiveness. He suffers from extreme mood changes with aggressive behaviors and temper tantrums. He has problems forming positive peer relations due to his inability to control his impulses, to consider the consequences of his behavior, and to correctly interpret the actions of other people. His abstract thinking skills are limited, and he has great difficulty with math.

Although Nicholas is making consistent progress in his special education program at a local middle school, including his inclusion into two general education classes, Wanda is experiencing a lot of caregiving stress in parenting Nicholas. She has no extended-family members in the area to alleviate some of the caregiving demands placed on her by Nicholas's disability. Four years ago, Wanda went back to school and earned an associate degree as a licensed practical nurse. She is currently working the day shift at a nursing home. Wanda's support system is nonexistent, and she is perilously close to a nervous breakdown or, worse yet, a recurrence of her alcoholism.

An Example of School-Based Family Support

Nicholas's special education teacher and the school psychologist have established a trusting relationship with Wanda. Since they are in regular contact with her, both school professionals recognize that Wanda is in dire need of support. Wanda and the special education teacher decide that the first order of support is to help Wanda better manage Nicholas's negative behaviors at home. Over the past several years, Nicholas learned to get his way by engaging in temper tantrums whenever his mother tried to impose a demand on him that he does not want to do. Wanda backed off of making demands and enforcing rules because she did not have the energy to deal with Nicholas's behavioral outbursts. Knowing that most children with FAS respond best to environments that are highly structured with consistent routines, the special education teacher worked with Wanda to establish an after-school schedule for Nicholas. This schedule alternated 15-minute time periods when Nicholas was expected to be doing schoolwork or some household chore with 15 minutes of free time. A positive behavioral management program was established wherein Nicholas would earn "check book points" for appropriate behaviors (e.g., staying on task, complying with his mother's requests, completing household chores). Nicholas could spend these check book points to earn special privileges at school (e.g., free computer time) or on the weekends with his mother (e.g., going to a movie). The special education teacher checked weekly with Wanda to determine how the increased home structure and behavioral management program were going and to make necessary modifications. The home behavioral management program was a nice complement to the social skills instruction Nicholas was receiving at school.

The school psychologist was very helpful in teaching Wanda some specific coping skills. For example, Wanda was taught how to use the technique of passive appraisal. First, Wanda would exacerbate her stressors by believing every perceived problem involving Nicholas had to be addressed immediately. This perspective, quite naturally, served only to increase her stress levels. Wanda was coached to recognize that it is permissible to actively avoid some problems, to prioritize what problems need some immediate attention and what problems can be placed on the proverbial back burner. Second, the school psychologist worked with Wanda and taught her some simple relaxation skills. With encouragement from the school psychologist, Wanda set aside 15 minutes every evening for herself. She would listen to her favorite soft music, engage in guided imagery (i.e., think about a favorite vacation spot), and practice a muscle relaxation activity such as slowly rotating her head. The school psychologist also counseled Wanda to spend more conscious time reflecting on the positive aspects Nicholas has brought to her life, instead of constantly dwelling on the negatives. When Wanda engaged in this cognitive strategy, she began to recognize that Nicholas provided her with immense pleasure as she followed his consistent progress in school. Further, Nicholas served as the primary motivation for Wanda's becoming a responsible individual and a recovering alcoholic.

School professionals also provided coping supports to Wanda by referring her to a local respite care agency, which provided Wanda with one weekend every month of in-home respite care. During these weekends, Wanda was able to complete a number of regular errands and enjoy some free time. In addition, the school provided Wanda with information on support groups for families of children with FAS. Wanda found two groups to be especially informative: The National Organization on Fetal Alcohol Syndrome (NOFAS; www.nofas.org) and the FAS Family Resource Institute (www.fetalalcoholsyndrome.org). With the aforementioned school-based support services, Wanda Blanchard was able to successfully cope with the single-parenting demands of raising a child with significant disabilities.

SCHOOL SUPPORT SERVICES AND A PARTNERSHIP-SEEKING PARENT

A Family's Need for Support and Involvement

Sherrie and Dave Appleton were married for 12 years before deciding to start a family. Their only son, David Jr., was diagnosed with mild learning and behavior problems while in preschool. Currently in the fifth grade, David attends a general education classroom while receiving special education learning-center support services 2 hours daily.

Mr. and Mrs. Appleton both enjoyed careers as successful attorneys in private-practice corporate firms prior to David's birth. Following the birth of their son, Mrs. Appleton decided to leave her professional work to be with her son. While she had planned to resume her law practice after David began preschool, she did not return to work, in order to support her son. She and her husband jointly decided such support was needed because of their son's behavior and learning problems in preschool and continuing throughout his elementary years.

School personnel associated with David describe Mrs. Appleton as "high maintenance," "demanding," and "difficult to get along with." Mrs. Appleton acknowledges that she has made a commitment to learn as much about children with learning and behavior disorders as she can and to advocate for her son's interests. She is an active participant in IEP meetings and other conferences involving David's educational program and progress and openly states that she expects to be treated as a "full partner" in decisions and discussions related to her son. She has also been openly critical of school personnel when, in her opinion, they fail to follow though with agreed-on assignments or when they fail to "do their jobs." Although she and her husband have considered filing for due process hearings connected to two disciplinary incidents, they have not yet done so. However, the Appletons have been involved in two mediation hearings. In both cases, the mediation officer found in favor of the school. Mrs. Appleton has openly indicated that there would be no problems if school personnel did their job correctly and if she were permitted to be a legitimate partner in her child's education.

An Example of School Support Services

The director of special education for the district in which David attends school describes himself as "old school." In this context, this near-retirement-age administrator has privately shared that parents should be involved in their children's education, but if they are not professional educators, their role should not be that of equal partner. Following several years of "battling" with Mrs. Appleton, however, he privately met with special and general education personnel and indicated that he had made numerous errors in dealing with the Appleton family, especially Mrs. Appleton. He also noted that he was scheduling a meeting with Mrs. Appleton to invite her to be a "real partner" in her son's educational program. He also opined that the staff had been doing a good job in educating David but that they had restricted parental involvement. Consequently, he directed his special education staff to take steps to immediately offer Mr. and Mrs. Appleton an opportunity for partnership-level involvement. Furthermore, he recommended that general education personnel take similar actions. The director also noted that it was his intention to offer the same level of involvement and decision-making authority to other parents in the district.

The amended participation plan involved the director of special education holding the aforementioned meeting with the Appleton family. Both parents participated in the meeting. Subsequently, Mrs. Appleton and David's learning center teacher and general education teacher met to discuss perceived parent and family needs and wants along with parent/family-related program elements that school personnel desired. Subsequent to this discussion, the parents and teachers agreed to design a revised daily communication system. The system that was developed used both daily e-mail reports and a brief hour-by-hour summary sheet that David was required to have his teachers use to rate his behavior and academic work. Mrs. Appleton wrote a daily e-mail message describing David's home behavior and other information that she and her husband deemed important for school personnel to have.

Mrs. Appleton was invited to participate as a trainer along with school district personnel in a three-part in-service program on parent involvement and participation. Mrs. Appleton not only eagerly accepted this role but also volunteered to offer an evening seminar for parents of special needs students in the district. Although the seminar was sparsely attended, the parents who participated judged the program to be highly successful. The director of special education also received public recognition from the district's superintendent and school board for arranging this program.

District personnel and Mr. and Mrs. Appleton agree that there remain issues of disagreement between the family and school district. Nevertheless, both school district personnel and Mr. and Mrs. Appleton have noted that there has been significant improvement in comparison to previous problems. Mrs. Appleton in particular considers her role in her son's education to be more in keeping with her desire to be an active participant and decision maker and to have the same degree of authority as other members of David's IEP team.

COMMUNITY SUPPORT SERVICES FOR A FAMILY OF A YOUNG ADULT WITH SEVERE AND MULTIPLE DISABILITIES

A Family's Need for Support

Chuck and Sheila Fields have been married for 19 years. Chuck is an insurance agent, and Sheila is a real estate appraiser. The Fieldses have two children: Jennifer, who just turned 18, and Lindsay, age 11. Lindsay is a typically developing fifth-grade student. Jennifer has a severe cognitive disability. In addition, she has a seizure disorder and visual and hearing impairments. Jennifer requires extensive daily care assistance because she is not toilet trained, she cannot feed or dress herself, she has no verbal communication skills, and she does not walk. Despite the challenges created by Jennifer's severe and multiple disabilities, the Fieldses have managed to maintain a positive perspective and home life for both of their children.

Chuck and Sheila decided several years ago that they wanted Jennifer to transition from the family home at the same time that most children leave the family nest, at around 18 years of age. They realized that because of Jennifer's intensive daily need for care and support services, her transition from their home would be challenging and require long-range planning. As the Fieldses articulated this transitional plan for Jennifer, it became readily apparent that vocational and residential services would be two key supports. In terms of residential support services, they quickly discovered that the county agency for individuals with developmental disabilities could not provide any housing options. The county's group homes were full, as were supportive services for any kind of assisted living arrangements. Indeed, there was a long waiting list for services, with some individuals and their families having been on a list for several years. Chuck and Sheila were equally discouraged when they considered vocational options for Jennifer after she completed her public school education. Although the high school special education teacher had developed several supportive job placements for Jennifer in the past 2 years, the Fieldses had several questions about the appropriateness of the placement sites and whether Jennifer was receiving the kind of vocational training she needed to be able to perform a job as independently as possible in an integrated work environment.

An Example of School-Based Family Support

After an initial sense of panic about the lack of county housing services and a rather bleak employment outlook for Jennifer, Chuck and Sheila turned to the school for assistance in helping them realize this dream of community inclusion and maximum independence for their daughter. The initial planning for Jennifer's transition from school to the adult world began when she was 14 years old. The Fieldses and Jennifer's special education teacher, Jane Jacobs, worked on a transition plan that contained a key goal of finding community housing for Jennifer when she turned 18. In addition, Ms. Jacobs admitted that she had exhausted her ideas on job placements and vocational training activities for Jennifer. Chuck and Sheila and Ms. Jacobs agreed that the transition plan needed the involvement of the local VR agency. Beginning this transitional planning process energized the Fieldses, as they felt that school professionals understood and were very supportive of their family-determined goals for Jennifer. The school served as the catalyst, through the transition plan, by connecting Chuck and Sheila with VR agencies, residential service providers, and financial institutions.

Through the school referrals, the Fieldses were able to access supports that allowed Jennifer to finance the purchase of her own home. They secured funds from a county low-income home ownership program, which provided assistance for a down payment on the home. In addition, Chuck and Sheila were able to secure an interest-free rehabilitation loan to assist in some needed renovations, including a new furnace, a remodeled kitchen, and construction of a wheelchair ramp entrance and deck. Jennifer moved into her own home 6 months after her 18th birthday. She has a live-in home care assistant and a roommate. Actually, as noted by the Fieldses, their original plan to find a group home living arrangement for Jennifer could never have been as beneficial as the living arrangement Jennifer has now in her own home. As one of her home health aides commented, "You go into group homes, and all of people's things are labeled and it's often very institutional. This is a whole lot better. Because this is Jennifer's home, you feel more at ease and you come in with a much higher level of respect."

The school referral to a local VR agency also produced beneficial results for Jennifer. A VR counselor observed Jennifer in her three different job settings. The counselor was able to offer specific recommendations for modifying the work environment to assist Jennifer in being more task focused and increasing her interactions with fellow workers. In addition, the counselor served as a role model for the job coach in demonstrating how to provide the right amount of assistance to Jennifer and how to gradually fade the assistance and enhance independent work skills.

The transitional goals that the Fieldses had for their daughter, Jennifer, were realized because (a) school professionals respected the family's self-determined goals and future vision, (b) school professionals recognized specific family strengths and encouraged the parents to rely on their own skills and insights, and (c) the school was a supportive partner and referral agent linking the family to necessary community support services.

PARENT AND FAMILY ADVOCACY SUPPORT SERVICES AND A NONRESPONSIVE SCHOOL ADMINISTRATOR

A Family's Need for Support

Miguel Rodriquez and his wife, Estella, have three children: Sonia (14 years old), Carlos (12 years old), and Maria (8 years old). Mr. Rodriquez is employed at a local paper mill, and Mrs. Rodriquez works part-time as a receptionist and accounts manager for a dentist. Sonia and Carlos are typically developing children who perform quite well in school and are fully involved with their peer groups. Maria, on the other hand, has struggled since she entered the public school system. She is now a third grader and, according to her parents, is falling further and further behind in her schoolwork. In particular, Maria struggles with reading and math. Suspecting a learning disability, Mr. and Mrs. Rodriquez referred Maria to the school principal, indicating they wanted their daughter to be assessed by a special education evaluation team. The parents waited 6 weeks without hearing anything from the principal. Finally, Mrs. Rodriquez called the principal and was informed that the referral for special education evaluation would not be processed because the school feels that Maria will eventually catch up with her classmates and, thus, does not require special education services.

Although Mr. and Mrs. Rodriquez are upset by the principal's refusal to take seriously their concerns about Maria, they have never been ones to question authority figures or to "make waves." Mrs. Rodriquez stated to a friend, "I guess the school must know what they are doing. In any event, even if I disagree with the principal's actions, what can I do about it?" Her friend, who works for a United Way–funded social services agency, happened to know about a local parent support organization and encouraged Estella to contact the group. In addition, Estella's friend gave her the name of a special education teacher in the school district who is involved with the parent support group.

An Example of School-Based Family Support

Estella called the special education teacher, Nancy Wilson, the next day. Mrs. Wilson teaches in a different elementary school than the one Maria attends. The teacher suggested a meeting after school later in the week. Mr. and Mrs. Rodriquez came to school 2 days later to discuss their concerns about Maria with Mrs. Wilson. After listening to the parents, Nancy Wilson replied, "I believe your concerns are valid and you do not simply have to accept what the principal has told you." Mrs. Wilson laid out several initial steps for the parents. First, she helped Mr. and Mrs. Rodriquez write a letter to the principal reiterating their request for a special education evaluation for Maria. In this letter, the parents stated that they were prepared to take formal actions if the school refused to act on their daughter's referral for special education. Specifically, Mr. and

Mrs. Rodriquez stated they would request mediation from the state special education mediation system or, if the school district refused to participate in mediation, they would file a request for a due process hearing.

Mrs. Wilson also referred Mr. and Mrs. Rodriquez to the Parent Training and Information (PTI) Center for the state. The center enlisted the assistance of a local parent who had recently completed parent advocacy training sponsored by the PTI Center. The parent advocate met with Mr. and Mrs. Rodriquez and they mapped out a plan of action. First, the advocate helped the parents organize a file to document their concerns regarding Maria's school performance and to collect information about special education laws and procedures. Second, the advocate recommended that the parents contact an educational diagnostic center at a local clinic. The advocate explained the importance of having professional documentation concerning Maria's suspected learning disability. Further, as explained by the advocate, parents are entitled to submit results from an independent educational evaluation, and the schools are legally obligated to consider that information. Finally, the advocate urged the parents to call the principal and request a meeting to discuss the school's failure to proceed with a special education evaluation of Maria.

The next week, Mr. and Mrs. Rodriquez and their advocate attended a meeting with the principal. At the beginning of the meeting, the principal was still reluctant to schedule a special education evaluation for Maria. The principal's reluctance soon gave way when she realized the resolve of Mr. and Mrs. Rodriquez and that they were willing to pursue formal dispute resolution mechanisms to protest the school's decision. A special education evaluation team was assembled, and 6 weeks later, the multidisciplinary evaluation team meeting was held. By that time, Mr. and Mrs. Rodriquez had submitted an independent educational evaluation report concluding that Maria was learning disabled and that she should receive support in language arts and mathematics. The school's evaluation team, consisting of Maria's third-grade teacher, a school psychologist, the learning disabilities teacher, and a school social worker, reached a similar conclusion. Maria qualified for special education services, and an IEP was developed with both resource room support and in-class modifications. Perhaps just as important as the additional assistance Maria received was the empowering experiences her parents had as they learned that knowledge and support can lead to effective advocacy. In a very real sense, the school had educated both Maria and her parents.

SUPPORT FOR A FAMILY WITH CHILDREN EXPERIENCING EMOTIONAL AND BEHAVIORAL PROBLEMS

A Family's Need for Support

Jodi is a loving single mother of two boys: Mark, 12, and Jeffrey, 8. Their dad was killed in the conflict in Iraq. Jodi is still grieving his death. The loss of their father has greatly impacted both boys. Jeffrey has been quiet and introverted, but Mark started acting out a few months after they heard about his death. Watching the bombings and listening to CNN brought on nightmares and sleepless nights for the whole family. Mark was arrested for setting fires on school property 18 months ago. He has had multiple fights with boys on the bus and has started falling behind in his studies. Although Mark had been previously diagnosed with ADHD and dyslexia, he had been able to maintain good grades in school with minor classroom accommodations until his father's death. Mark's sixth-grade teacher, Ms. Chu, was aware of his father's death and tried to make accommodations for Mark during this difficult time, but his behavior in class was too disruptive to maintain a positive learning environment. Ms. Chu talked with Jodi and referred Mark to the student support team. The student support team consisted of the school social worker, the nurse, one special education teacher, one general education teacher, a representative from social services, the community liaison from the police department, a parent representative, and a local pediatrician. The student support team reviewed Ms. Chu's referral and invited Jodi into the conversation about support for herself and both boys.

An Example of Family and Child Support

Jodi was nervous when she received the letter inviting her to meet with the school support team. She was thankful that Ms. Chu was trying to help, but she was worried that this just meant Mark was in more trouble and beginning to get a local reputation as a problem kid. The letter explained that she should call the social worker at her convenience to set up the appointment. After work that day, Jodi called the social worker, who offered several possible meeting times. Jodi, the parent representative, and the social worker would meet in the community lounge at the school for coffee 30 minutes before the rest of the team would join them.

When Jodi met with the parent representative and the social worker, she was surprisingly comfortable. Talking about Steve's death and the boys was such a relief. The conversation between the three of them built Jodi's confidence so she was comfortable transitioning into the meeting with the entire support team.

The support team started the meeting with introductions. Ms. Chu described her reasons for referring Mark to the team. Although the team had invited Mark, Jodi was glad she had decided to have him stay in class. She believed reliving all of the difficult events of the past 2 years would be more painful than healing. The team made a large chart of Mark's interests, strengths, and needs. Then the group started to brainstorm a support plan for Mark. The support plan centered on Mark's needs but also included Jeffrey and Jodi. The meeting ended with an action plan and set a date to meet in 6 weeks.

The day after the meeting, the social worker came in and talked with Mark. They walked down to the community liaison police officer's room and then they went across the street to the psychiatrist's office. Mark and Jeffrey would go to the psychiatrist's office once each week to discuss their feelings about their dad's death. Afterward, they would walk back across the street to the after-school program while their mom attended the support group for grieving partners. The social worker set Mark and Jeffrey up with the Big Brothers program. The community liaison from the police department accompanied Mark on Wednesday afternoons to the karate class sponsored by the police department.

The support team met with Jodi 6 weeks later. During this meeting, Jodi was accompanied by Mark and Jeffrey. The boys and Jodi felt they had become closer in the last few weeks. Mark still was not very interested in school, but he enjoyed the after-school program and karate class and was glad that his probation from the incident with the fire was almost over. Jodi felt relieved at Mark's ability to talk about his life and was beginning to sleep better at night. With the ongoing support of the community connections that originated with the school support team, Jodi and her sons were beginning the process of healing and reimagining their futures.

This program worked because the school professionals had a process in place to welcome parents into the support system when their child was struggling, rather than being accusatory or demanding. The presence of local services within and adjacent to the school also allows for better use of supports. A program that is built on the strengths and needs of the child and the family will be most effective in supporting students with behavioral issues.

ACADEMIC SUPPORT FOR A FAMILY OF A YOUTH WITH A READING PROBLEM

A Family's Need for Support

Tory was a humorous and charming young man. At 14 he was the president of student council and had been voted Class Charmer in the most recent Sandstone Middle School Yearbook. He loved sports and music. Tory didn't seem to belong to one certain clique but was well known and liked by most students in his class. He had many friends from diverse backgrounds. Behind Tory's charm and humor, however, there was an overwhelming concern that he had not shared with anyone. Tory could not read his class assignments. He couldn't read the newspaper, and actually, he couldn't even read the cartoons in his comic book collection. In the fall, he would be starting ninth grade, as a high school freshman. He had scraped by with Cs and Ds on his report card by studying with friends, aided by his strong oral comprehension. However, he knew his reading problem was catching up with him. He was afraid of what would happen when he started high school.

Tory was going to stay with his grandparents in July at their summer home up north. He was excited to get away from all of his anxieties about starting high school and just enjoy swimming and fishing with his grandpa. A week into his trip, his grandma brought Tory to the public library so she could pick up some books to read in the evenings and on rainy days. She thought it would be nice for Tory to have a library card in town as well. Fear struck Tory. He almost couldn't get out of the car. That evening, his grandparents were sharing funny anecdotes from the books they were reading. His grandpa asked him to read to them from The Babe Ruth Story, the section about when Babe was a young boy. Tory began to cry. He told his grandparents about his reading problem. The next day, they talked with Tory's mother and then the school psychologist. His grandparents drove Tory down to the school for testing 2 weeks later. Tory was relieved and ashamed simultaneously.

An Example of Family Support and Involvement in Academics

The special education teacher and the school psychologist met with Tory and his family. They described his learning disability and recommended special education services. Tory was devastated. He didn't want anyone to know about his disability. Now the whole school would find out. Knowing that Tory could be helped only if he would accept the services, the special education teacher devised a plan. The special education teacher, Tory's baseball coach, his grandpa, and his mom would all work with Tory on his reading. His special education teacher would work with him individually during his study hall so he wouldn't have to deal with his social concerns about his learning disability until he became more comfortable.

The teacher wrote out a plan and provided training, modeling, and support to Tory's coach and his family members. The literacy program used to tutor Tory worked on his areas of greatest need but concentrated on one of his main interests, the lives of sports stars. He and his grandpa worked on comprehension as they read through several biographies that summer. When he returned in August from the cabin up north, Tory received a subscription to *Sports Illustrated for Kids* from his parents. As each monthly issue arrived, his mom would read the articles with Tory, and he would practice reading those same articles the rest of the month with his coach. Tory also began to manage his teammates' performance data, tracking their progress during practice and games. This provided Tory with reading opportunities that were functional for him, increased his appreciation for reading, and motivated him to work more at a skill that was so difficult for him.

In a few months, Tory began to spend time at the after-school day care in his neighborhood. He would read one of his favorite *Sports Illustrated for Kids* articles to a small group of elementary school–aged boys, and after reading together, they would play a game of kickball. This volunteer experience helped Tory's confidence. He was soon able to talk to others about his reading problems. Due to his personality and popularity, this self-disclosure helped to ease the stigma felt by other students in his high school who received special education support services.

With the instruction from the special education teacher and those closest to him, Tory made great progress. His reading scores improved several grade levels that year as the supports he needed were finally in place. Reading continued to be a challenge for Tory and he needed ongoing support, but he was proud of his progress. He began to understand and recognize his learning disability as one aspect of himself, rather than a life-encompassing deficiency. When family members and those closely involved with students can work together as a tutoring/teaching team, children can achieve both academically and emotionally.

PERSON-CENTERED PLANNING TRANSITION SUPPORT FOR A FAMILY

A Family's Need for Support

Carla and her son Robert had different concerns about his future. Robert hated school. He was so glad he was turning 18 and it would be over. He knew he had no chance of graduating; he was getting out with an attendance certificate unless he made up 40 credits. He thought he'd be 30 before that would happen, and he couldn't even imagine living that long. Robert wanted to get out of school, away from this town, and be an artist. After all, he didn't need a high school diploma for his plan. He hated the long North Dakota winters and the miles of nothingness. He was going to California to sell his drawings on the beach. He'd be warm and free, and his time would be his own.

Robert didn't know how he would get to California; maybe he'd hitchhike. He wondered how he would get all his art supplies out to California while hitchhiking. His mom, his family, they were another issue. Who was going to help his mom? If he went to California, who would watch his little brother and sister, make dinner for all of them, and hold the family together while his mom was always out working? It made him so mad. He didn't want to care, but he did. He just wanted to run away.

Carla was scared. Robert, her oldest son, was going to leave school when he turned 18 next month. What would happen to him then? Robert had always had difficulty in school—having emotional problems and learning disabilities had really made him turn away from both the academic and social aspects of school—but she always knew he was safe when he was there. Carla knew Robert needed the structure of school. He was good with his art, but if he didn't have structure, he just got himself into too much trouble. Carla was anxious about Robert's life. How would he get a job without a high school diploma? She knew she couldn't afford to send Robert to college, and he wouldn't be accepted even if it were affordable. Carla didn't know any other options. Robert's birthday was coming up so fast. She hated to ask for help, but Carla knew there had to be someone who had a better solution than just waiting to see what happened next month.

An Example of Support During Transition

Carla called Mr. Sanchez, the guidance counselor at Robert's high school. Mr. Sanchez knew Robert well. He had tried for years to work with Robert and Carla to set up a transition IEP, but to no avail. He felt that they were finally ready to begin this conversation. He was glad Carla called. He didn't want Robert walking out of school into a future that was so uncertain.

Mr. Sanchez talked to Mrs. Johns, Robert's special education teacher, and Mr. Watkins, Robert's art teacher. Mr. Sanchez remembered Robert had done really well in art class—he even won a prize in the Chamber of Commerce Young Artists Fair last year. The three of them weren't sure how to get Robert to be serious about a plan for his future. Robert was always telling them that there was no future, only today. He was quite a young philosopher, but not very helpful in developing a transition plan. Mr. Sanchez then called Ms. Ripon, the special education district coordinator.

Ms. Ripon had just returned from a training session on personal futures planning. She had learned about MAPS and PATH, two tools to help young adults plan their transition and achieve a better future. She had seen too many students like Robert, who didn't have any plan, quit school, and fell into the criminal justice system or social services. Maybe Robert could be the first student in their district to try out one of these planning programs.

The team wanted Robert to take as much responsibility for this planning process as he would accept, to improve his self-advocacy skills. To assist Robert in feeling as comfortable as possible, Ms. Ripon suggested that Robert host a party. The party would serve as the person-centered planning event. Robert liked the idea of a party. It wasn't a real party, but the idea of getting all his friends together to plan his going away sounded like fun. Ms. Ripon worked with Mrs. Johns and Robert to decide who to invite to the big event. Robert invited his friends, his old art teachers, his mom and his siblings, even some of the people from the Chamber of Commerce who gave him that money for his picture last year. Mrs. Johns had suggested some other people Robert didn't know, some counselors or teachers or something, but since she was helping to plan it, he figured she could invite whomever she wanted, as long as he could too.

Carla thought this planning process sounded like a good idea. She was glad she had called the school. Each night, she had been writing down responses to the questions that Ms. Ripon had sent to her. They were good questions that made her think all about Robert and what she knew he could do when he became an adult. Robert thought the questions Mrs. Johns told him to think about before his party were strange. He didn't think anyone would want to spend the whole party talking about his life, even if it was his party. He didn't know any of the answers; maybe he'd think about the questions later.

The day of the person-centered planning event, Carla baked a cake and brought M&M's, Robert's favorite candy, to school. Robert and his friends drove in together and met the team in the school cafeteria after the students cleared out from the breakfast program. Robert was amazed at all the people who showed up—there were over 30 people who had come to his party! He thought it was a drag that Ms. Ripon showed up and made everybody sit down like it was a class, but he was again surprised when everyone started talking about Robert and what a bright future he could have.

By the end of the party, there was a new plan, and Robert had decided not to move to California right now. Instead, he was going to take the High School Equivalency Preparation Course through the community college. This would get him a few college credits and get him a piece of paper much better than just an attendance certificate. While taking the preparation course, he would also be able to take two art classes. That was exciting. If he worked hard in the art classes in college, he wouldn't even have to take other areas like English and history, which he hated so much. Soon he would be on his way to a career making good money in graphic design.

Robert and Carla were amazed at what a significant difference a few hours' planning together could make. Ideally, transition should begin when a student is 12 to 14 years old. The most common reason students with learning and behavioral issues do not achieve satisfying careers and relationships after school is because they lack a vision for their future. Working together to develop a long-range plan and involving all service providers can make a big difference in the future of many students.

CONCLUDING THOUGHTS

Several recurring basic principles are the foundation for the 10 stories of school-based support for families in this chapter. These elements are also the guiding principles for this book. Related to their significance and enormity as success determinants, we felt it appropriate to conclude with a discussion of these basic principles.

First, and most fundamentally, we consider it imperative that professionals and policy makers recognize the importance of understanding and appropriately responding to the needs of families of children and youth with disabilities. Indeed, we consider it imperative that professionals respond to these needs with the same resolve they use to address the needs of students with disabilities. Accordingly, use of scientifically based, collaborative, and comprehensive programs and services for parents and families of students with disabilities is essential. Of course, the highly individualized and heterogeneous needs of diverse families cannot be addressed by application of routine and universal formulas. Yet, as we have outlined in this book, there are effective-practice strategies and utilitarian courses of action that bode well for service delivery success. The initial step in wide-scale adoption of these underpinning measures is for professionals, families, and policy makers to recognize the importance of supporting families, and to mandate courses of action that will lead to availability of resources, trained professionals, and well-informed parents and families, ensuring that the needs of families of children and youth with disabilities are adequately addressed.

A second premise on which this book and the above successful stories of school-based family support stand is that professionals must possess and apply suitable knowledge, skills, attitudes, and motivation to be effective parent and family support agents. Formation and maintenance of successful family and professional partnerships also require supportive and structured organizations. That is, even highly motivated and talented individuals will fail to be maximally effective without the backing of supportive and family-friendly policies, systems, and colleagues. These orchestrated systems support, sustain and structure effective family-related actions with forethought, careful planning, and a systematic allocation of resources and professional development. Sadly, there is evidence that many educators and other professionals lack the training and experience to be effective in their respective family-related roles, and those systems in which these individuals operate are often not designed for success. The reasons for this problem are complex and varied. However, this wanting is not a function of a lack of information. Strategies for, and the benefits of, establishing and maintaining effective relationships with parents and families of children and youth with disabilities and delivering school-based support services required by parents and families are indeed available. As a result, professionals who receive suitable training and experience and who work in supportive settings are able to put into operation strategies that facilitate cooperative professional–family relationships, implement procedures that lead to cooperative partnerships, and apply a variety of effective methods for addressing individual families' needs. A salient factor that drives success in this arena is the availability of supportive systems wherein professionals who have suitable knowledge and skills and who engage in scientifically based practices designed to develop and maintain strong and collaborative relationships with parents and families are able to not only support families but to maximally benefit students with disabilities. Clearly, when teachers, related service educators, and other professionals build on strong educational programs, and when they possess and use suitable knowledge, skills, dispositions, and experiences, the outcomes are effective parent and family support services.

A third and equally significant guiding principle of this book is the need to form and maintain cooperative and collaborative relationships. Such relationships unite parents and families and connect them to professionals, they bond professionals of different types and from different settings with a common purpose, and they tie these entities to common objectives and goals.

We are of the opinion that full-service community schools are the most efficient and effective mechanism for creating and maintaining cooperative and collaborative relationships and thereby most successfully support parents and families. The rationale for using schools as a full-service foundation is obvious. Schools are the common link to children and youth with disabilities, and thus to their parents and families. That is, schools are the common point of contact for the vast majority of families of school-age children and youth with disabilities. Furthermore, when teachers and related service professionals team together, they represent a relatively economical, available, and efficient resource for parents, families, schools, and communities. Finally, because educators are in an excellent position to communicate and gain the trust of parents and families, they are an efficient conduit and medium for referring parents and families to school-based community professionals; for communicating with, about, and between home, school, and community elements; and for maximally benefiting from collaborative interactions among families, school personnel, and community professionals. As we have suggested in this book, development and maintenance of full-service school programs are neither inexpensive nor easy to design and operate. Yet, they are certainly possible to develop and operate. Clearly, full-service schools have myriad advantages and the potential to most effectively, economically, and efficiently support parents and families of individuals with disabilities.

As previously opined, cookbook approaches are deficient and inadequate in supporting the unique and ever-changing characteristics, values, needs, and diversity of families. Instead, pragmatic, practical, and individualized strategies applied within supportive and collaboratively designed settings bode best for supporting parents and families. Such designs are best able to lead to genuine partnerships among families and professionals and programs that efficiently and effectively address the needs of students with disabilities and their families. While there is much room for improvement in supporting parents and families, there is also space for optimism. To be sure, such optimism is fueled by our knowledge and experience that effectual parent and family support programs lead to positive student and family outcomes that far exceed their initial design and operation effort.

QUESTIONS FOR DISCUSSION

1. Discuss the strategies and processes that were used by school professionals in the 10 stories of school-based support to address the needs of parents and family members. Identify the generic strategies and procedures that were common to the 10 stories and the unique procedural elements that are specific to particular disabilities, challenges, and situations.
2. Discuss the knowledge, skills, and attitudes of the professionals in the 10 stories of school-based support that were connected to the achievement of successful outcomes. Identify generic knowledge, skills, and attitudes that were common to the 10 stories as well as the unique knowledge, skills, and other elements that are specific to particular disabilities, challenges, and situations.

REFLECTION ACTIVITIES

1. Based on the 10 stories of school-based support, other information presented in this book, and your experiences, discuss the resources, infrastructure, and other factors that were required to achieve positive outcomes in each case.

2. Relative to each of the 10 stories of school-based support, identify and discuss the role that community professionals, including those associated with full-service community school programs, might play in achieving positive outcomes.

3. Cooperative and collaborative relationships are clearly important components of school-based support for parents and family members of a child or youth with a disability. Discuss strategies and procedures for achieving these relationships, including among (a) professionals and parents and family members of individuals with a disability, (b) school professionals, and (c) school and community professionals. Discuss markers that indicate how professionals may reliably gauge the degree to which cooperative and collaborative relationships are functioning and effective.

REFERENCES

Giangreco, M. F., Cloninger, C. J., & Iverson, V. S. (1998). *Choosing outcomes and accommodations for children* (COACH): A guide to educational planning for students with disabilities (2nd ed.). Baltimore: Brookes.

Name Index

Subject Index

●●●●●●●●●●●●●●●●●●●●●●●●●●●